MW00559426

"Hang Them All"

"Hang Them All"

George Wright and the Plateau Indian War

Donald L. Cutler

Foreword by Laurie Arnold

University of Oklahoma Press : Norman

Publication of this book is made possible through the generosity of Edith Kinney Gaylord.

Library of Congress Cataloging-in-Publication Data

Names: Cutler, Donald L., 1954– author.
Title: "Hang them all" : George Wright and the Plateau Indian War / Donald Cutler.
Other titles: George Wright and the Plateau Indian War
Description: Norman, OK : University of Oklahoma Press, [2016] | Includes bibliographical references and index.
Identifiers: LCCN 2015047754 | ISBN 978-0-8061-5337-7 (hardcover : alk. paper)
Subjects: LCSH: Yakama Indians—Wars, 1855–1859. | Indians of North America—Columbia Plateau—Wars. | Wright, George, 1803–1865. | Coeur d'Alene Indians—Wars. | Spokane Indians—Wars. | Paloos Indians—Wars. | Steptoe, Edward Jenner, 1816–1865. | Indians, Treatment of—Northwest, Pacific—History. | Indians of North America—Northwest, Pacific—Government relations.
Classification: LCC E83.84 .C87 2016 | DDC 979.7004/974127—dc23
LC record available at http://lccn.loc.gov/2015047754

The paper in this book meets the guidelines for permanence and durability of the Committee on Production Guidelines for Book Longevity of the Council on Library Resources, Inc. ∞

1 2 3 4 5 6 7 8 9 10

I want to express my appreciation for my wife,
Cynthia Maclyn Cutler.
She is wise, patient, and kind.
Her love is gentle, affirming, and eternal.
I dedicate this effort to her.

Contents

Illustrations

FIGURES

MAPS

Cartography by Gerry Krieg

Foreword

George Wright personifies an era in Pacific Northwest history. He led unnecessarily violent military actions against tribes and Native peoples of the Columbia Plateau, and these attacks were heralded across the United States as both just and deserved. To Plateau tribes, Wright and his behavior were anathema, and Wright's legacy of greatness on the Columbia Plateau has slowly been degrading under the weight of time and as a result of deeper historical inquiry.

"Hang Them All" illustrates the shocking inhumanity Wright displayed when he oversaw the slaughter of eight hundred horses. At the same time, it depicts a man whose experiences humanize him: family tragedy, career disappointment, unfulfilled hopes. This narrative illuminates how Wright came to be the man he was on the Columbia Plateau during those two fateful months in 1858, but it does not seek to justify his actions. Wright described himself as an ardent patriot who believed in Manifest Destiny; these twin principles informed Wright's belief that his actions against Plateau peoples were not only correct but also necessary. Wright brought terror and brutality to the region, and he did so intentionally and without apology.

Upon encountering the story of George Wright and the Plateau Indian Wars, Donald Cutler sought to make sense of it and to question why Spokane continues to honor Wright with street names and commemorative sites. In *"Hang Them All,"* Cutler asks us to no longer excuse historical actors for being products of their time, because acts of cruelty and terror create legacies that must be remembered and confronted. His book demonstrates that we can demand more from historical interpretation, and it illustrates how understanding region is integral to writing good history. Cutler represents the Columbia Plateau as tribal homelands because this narrative centers on ancestral places. Deep scholarly research augmented by interviews of local academics and tribal historians reveals Cutler as a thoughtful steward of the Indigenous and American stories that have become inextricably linked.

"Hang Them All" is an accomplished history. It provides a substantial contribution to studies of the Columbia Plateau and, consequently, the American West. It updates existing histories of Wright and the Plateau Indian Wars, and it connects academic scholarship to tribal scholarship. Following Larry Cebula's *Plateau Indians and the Quest for Spiritual Power* and Richard Scheuerman and Michael Finley's *Finding Chief Kamiakin: The Life and Legacy of a Northwest Patriot, "Hang Them All"* is the next important work in what I hope is a renaissance in historical inquiry into the nineteenth-century Columbia Plateau.

As our Plateau tribal communities continue to recover from the cultural and political interruptions of the nineteenth century, and as we remind ourselves that Native American history *is* American history, we need more scholarship that presents truths we may not want to acknowledge. We need more work like *"Hang Them All."*

Laurie Arnold
Spokane, Washington

Preface

A few miles southwest of Spokane, Washington, a hill rises five hundred feet above the plain. Wheat grows on the tilled lower slopes, while pines spread from the crest down one side. At the base of the pine forest sits the community of Four Lakes, which consists of a gas station and several square blocks spotted with small businesses and modest homes. A ten-foot-tall granite pyramid stands in town, placed in 1935 by the Spokane County Pioneer Society.

Battle of Four Lakes
On this historic ground,
Sept 1, 1858,
700 soldiers under Col. Geo. Wright, U.S.A., routed
5,000 allied Indians. Four days later the rallied hostiles were
decisively defeated in a running battle. They sued for mercy
and have ever since maintained lasting peace.

The monument stands in a vacant lot at the end of a lane covered with crumbling asphalt. The land around it is pockmarked with gopher holes. Windblown litter hangs in the weeds, and the ground is scattered with broken glass.

It was not always untended; a news photo taken in 1935 at the dedication of the monument shows it veiled in an American flag and surrounded by bouquets of flowers. A gaily dressed crowd looks on, everyone smiling. Referring to the monument's claim that Wright's victory "maintained lasting peace," the photo caption called the pyramid a "peace memorial."[1] On my first visit a decade ago, I wondered, who was George Wright? Furthermore, did the Indians think of the monument as a peace memorial?

I wondered how Colonel Wright's force could have defeated such a large confederation of warriors. Clearly, in 1935 the Pioneer Society believed him to be a hero for leading such an impressive victory. What else might have contributed to the narrative of a heroic George Wright? I set out to investigate George Wright and his actions and, in particular, for information about his words and actions from 1856, when he arrived in the Pacific Northwest, until his death in 1865, when he had just completed a five-year assignment in California. Over time, I became increasingly interested in him—not just for the recorded historical details, but also for the *lack* of them. In 1865, when he and his wife died in the wreck of the steamship *Brother Jonathan,* apparently his personal letters, journals, and other possessions were claimed by the Pacific Ocean. The tragedy did not just destroy details of his life—it also boosted Wright's heroic legacy. In the absence of Wright's personal papers, I began to believe that some observers of history filled in the blanks according to what they thought to have been true, or *wanted* to have been true, about George Wright and his actions during the Plateau Indian War.

During my research I was impressed by the depth of feeling triggered by his name. From 1858 onward, during his life and after his death, countless mentions of Wright include adjectives like "venerable," "noble," and "masterly." On one social occasion in San Francisco during 1864, an observer reported that "Every man in the vast assemblage showed the highest respect to the true old soldier."[2] Some held him in reverence; one man described him as having "soft features and a kindly face [resembling] an aging minister of the gospel."[3]

One of the most impressive tributes to Wright was written by Gen. Erasmus Darwin Keyes, who served as a captain under Wright and who, during the Civil War, would rise to the rank of major general of U.S. volunteers. In praising Wright, Keyes said, "If I were to give expression to my admiration and respect for that gallant soldier and gentleman, I fear my style would appear more flowery than the rules prescribe for the narrative of facts."[4]

In the late summer of 1858, Wright, the "gallant soldier and gentleman," led a military force into the interior Pacific Northwest. They trudged across rugged basalt scabland, over grass-covered hills, along the broad Spokane Valley, and through nearly impenetrable forest. Colonel Wright took hostages, burned food supplies, hanged prisoners, slaughtered animals, and conducted councils that combined lectures, threats, and executions. At each council he promised to treat the tribes fairly; in some cases his promises were punctuated with at least one execution. For his efforts, Wright was labeled an American hero.

In the years since the Plateau War, dissenting voices have sounded in both the American Indian community and the Anglo-American population. Even during the 1858 expedition, some of Wright's men quietly expressed reservations about the way he conducted "trials," which consisted of accusations, a few cursory questions, and a swift and cruel execution. Some historians have been blunt in their criticism. In 1917 Spokane historian and attorney William S. Lewis said, "The summary execution was contrary to the spirit of justice and fair play and was wholly unjustified."[5] In 1966 the scholar Robert Burns dismissed suggestions of Wright's heroism, referring to Wright's campaign as "one of the most expensive and futile parades in American military history."[6] In a 1970 statement that sums up how many Native Americans feel, Oswald C. George, vice chairman of the Coeur d'Alene tribe, said, "The hangings were strictly murder and the man who perpetrated them has been made a hero by the white community. Wright had no reason for hanging these people other than to intimidate the Northwest tribes."[7]

Since the mid-nineteenth century, Wright's supporters and detractors have expressed little patience with each other. In 1864, a year before Wright's death, a Los Angeles newspaper described his critics as "vile wretches, whose slime merely indicates the torturous path they have crawled over."[8] Even in more recent years, criticism of Wright has been met with strong reactions, and at times it has been answered with highly questionable claims, such as this one, written by a historian in 1992: "Some contemporary readers may consider Colonel Wright's methods harsh, but the Indians themselves considered them just."[9]

That statement is true only if one believes appreciation expressed at the end of a rifle barrel is genuine.

In the 1850s many officers in the regular army expressed some sympathy toward the tribes in the Pacific Northwest, including George Wright. In addition to Wright, Philip Sheridan and William T. Sherman were among the officers who believed white settlers were the primary cause of trouble in the region. After the Civil War, due in part to increasing political pressure and the urgency created by the accelerating pace of western expansion, the same officers became more belligerent, speaking in harsh terms and conducting violent campaigns against the tribes.[10]

During the last seven years of his life, while General Wright still blamed whites for causing a good deal of conflict, he also started to sound increasingly cynical about Indians. In written orders to a subordinate officer in 1862, he said, "I have generally found that by hanging a few of the worst Indians peace and quiet is soon restored."[11]

Despite his cavalier attitude, he knew what it felt like to experience deep emotional pain. Existing historical accounts note that he and his wife, Margaret, had three children, but during my research I discovered there had been two more. One died just short of his second birthday, the other at age five. I can only speculate what impact Wright's personal tragedies may have had on his character and actions, but at the least he understood what sort of pain his tactics caused others.

As recently as 1992 a historian claimed that George Wright "numbers among the heroes of Washington State to both the white and Indian cultures."[12] This claim is more optimistic than accurate, as it would be extremely difficult, if not impossible, to find a Native American for whom Wright is a hero, as I show in the following chapters. In recent years Wright's actions and legacy have been the subjects of paintings and books, as well as being connected to arguments over place names like Hangman Creek, Hangman Valley Golf Course, Fort George Wright, and the Creek at Qualchan Golf Course—named for his most notable hanging victim.

The narrative of George Wright's legacy is slowly losing the unqualified luster imparted by past generations of white historians. The stone monument at the site of the Battle of Four Lakes bears an incorrect claim: there were nowhere near five thousand warriors in the fight, and on visits to the monument while I was working on this book, I noticed that someone has been gradually scratching off the extra zero. Wright's army fought against perhaps five hundred to a thousand warriors—a number that casts Wright's victory at the Battle of Four Lakes in less impressive terms.

I wanted to find out why Wright's name and his actions have created such conflicting passions over the years. What influences changed him from a relatively sympathetic man to one who engaged in cruel violence? This book is a result of my curiosity. It is a look at his actions on the Columbia Plateau and an exploration of how those actions contributed to a legacy that still today sometimes portrays him as a hero. I take a particularly close look at Wright's fateful 1858 expedition—the one that nearly a half-century later the *New York Times* would call "one of the most brilliant campaigns in the history of Indian warfare."[13] I don't believe Wright was a hero, but I hesitate to condemn him, for to do that would make it easy to separate him from me—from all of us. For, as Steven Pinker writes, "Most of us—including you, dear reader—are wired for violence, even if in all likelihood we never have an occasion to use it."[14]

When I began my research, I spoke with Robert McDonald, the communications director for the Confederated Salish and Kootenai Tribes, located in the Mission Valley of Montana. McDonald, a former newspaper reporter for the *Spokane Spokesman-Review,* is skilled at getting to the heart of issues. His view of historical trauma summed up a message I was to hear from many Native Americans: "History must be acknowledged in order to move forward."[15]

Dr. Laurie Arnold, director of the Native American Studies program at Gonzaga University, told me that she views Wright's actions on the Columbia Plateau as part of one continuing narrative, each portion of which is important to understanding what Dr. Arnold calls "an interruption of the lifeways and lifestyles of Plateau peoples." Despite the tragedies that befell native peoples, their cultures adapted and survived. Dr. Arnold teaches her students to focus on "what comes next," but in order to do so, it is necessary to step back in time and understand what happened.[16]

I hope this book helps in that process.

A NOTE ABOUT THE NATIVE AMERICAN VIEW

The events of the 1850s still resonate for some Native Americans in deeply personal ways. A true telling of the generational trauma is beyond the scope of this book, and while I have addressed a few aspects of the present-day emotional impact of those events, this one volume cannot do those aspects justice. I have included accounts of the events from Native Americans who witnessed the conflict, among them Coeur d'Alene chief Seltice, Yakama chief Owhi, Spokane chief Garry, Palouse chief Hoosis-moxmox, Mary Moses, and Lo-kout.

For recent interpretations of the events and their aftermath I had help from many educators and historians. They are acknowledged following the bibliography. Their views and opinions vary, but two common themes emerge. First, look to the future, but do not forget the past; it must be illuminated and understood and its victims honored. Second, it is not constructive to place blame.

In this book, that is what I have tried to do. The parts that succeed are a collaborative effort; those that fall short are mine alone.

NOTE ABOUT TERMINOLOGY

In most cases in the text I use the term "Indian" to refer to Native people instead of "Native American." I realize that preferences vary between individuals and tribes, but I have chosen the former because it was commonly used during the nineteenth century. In discussions about current times, I use "Native Americans," "American Indians," or "Native people," which, in one form or another, are in common use today.

To refer to non-Native participants, I sometimes use the terms "whites," "Euro-Americans," or "Anglos." None of the terms is entirely adequate, but they have been in common use at one time or another since the Plateau War. In fact, color and cultural lines often were not clear, as peoples mixed and alliances shifted. Thus, the term "white" is used to reference Euro-American cultural viewpoints, rather than a strict racial definition.

Since words in the Salish and Sahaptin languages were transcribed by various people, spellings in historical records vary. For example, "Qualchan" is also spelled "Qualchien" and "Qualchin." "Spokane" is the modern spelling of the city and tribe, but in the nineteenth century the tribe was sometimes referred to by whites as "Spokan." The tribe of Indians who lived in the region known today as the Yakima Valley are referred to as Yakamas, which was the spelling in most official records of the day (and is the tribal preference today). More than twenty names, or alternate spellings of names, have been recorded for what is now known as "Hangman Creek." In the nineteenth century it was frequently referred to by variations of Indian names, such as "Ned-wauld," "Sin-sin-too-aley," or variations of "Latah," such as "Lartoo."[17]

Details of certain events vary in historical records. For example, some records list 158 officers and soldiers with Col. Edward Steptoe's army, others give the number as 159, and yet another states 163. His force also included scouts and packers, which would have added to the count. The number of horses killed at Horse Slaughter Camp varies from six hundred to over twelve hundred. Nailing down these figures can be difficult; even official reports are sometimes inconsistent. I have done my best to sift through information to arrive at what I feel are accurate representations of events.

“Hang Them All”

Prologue

Brother Jonathan

SAN FRANCISCO BAY, FRIDAY, JULY 28, 1865.

The Broadway wharf was cluttered with people and cargo waiting to board the *Brother Jonathan,* a steam-powered paddle ship about to sail for Portland, Oregon, and Victoria, British Columbia. The wharf was one of the busiest in the harbor, its pilings and planks jammed with warehouses, sheds, and stacks of barrels and crates waiting to be loaded onto steamships and sailing vessels. Fashionably dressed passengers wove through the clutter, braving the stench of fish, animal waste, and stale seawater. With as much dignity as circumstances allowed, the passengers were assisted into tenders used to ferry passengers into the forest of ships anchored in the harbor.

Among the embarking passengers making their way through the clutter of boxes and nets was Anson G. Henry, once Abraham Lincoln's personal physician and close friend. Just a few months earlier, shortly before his assassination, President Lincoln had appointed Henry governor of Washington Territory; the new governor was on his way to assume his responsibilities in Olympia, at the southern end of Puget Sound.[1] Another figure easily recognizable to the citizens of San Francisco was James Nisbet, the highly respected editor of the *San Francisco Bulletin.* And the stylishly dressed Roseanna Hughes Keenan created a stir as she escorted seven young ladies onto the ship. They were on their way to Vancouver Island, where the ambitious Miss Keenan planned to open a brothel in Victoria.

The most striking party boarding the ship consisted of people also well known in northern California: Gen. George Wright, heading up a small entourage consisting of his wife, Margaret; his adjutant, Lieutenant E. D. Waite; and Major E. W. Eddy, an army paymaster carrying $200,000 in currency for soldiers' payroll at Fort Vancouver. General Wright's two horses were led on board and stabled below deck next to two camels belonging to a traveling circus.[2] The animals were in good company, as they were also stabled next to a large supply of gold coins under the care of William Logan, the Indian agent for the Pacific Northwest. Logan was escorting the gold to Northwest tribes as payment to meet treaty obligations. In addition, the hold was packed with crates of supplies for the rapidly growing settlements in the Pacific Northwest and on southern Vancouver Island.

General Wright was heading to his new posting at Fort Vancouver, a position about which he had mixed feelings. At his age—nearly sixty-two—he realized he was being pushed aside; no longer would he be in charge of army operations along the Pacific coast. During the Civil War he had held the lofty position of commander of the Department of the Pacific, but had not been satisfied. Several times he had pleaded for a war posting in the East, but his requests were always denied. Some of his peers said his age was to blame, but when the Civil War broke out, Wright's former commander Gen. John Wool was given a command at the age of seventy-seven.[3] However, George Wright, though a West Point graduate and an experienced soldier and officer, had always lacked the political savvy of his old commander. He believed his long and loyal service was unappreciated by the army and his reputation sullied by a few officers with whom he had disagreed. Nonetheless, General Wright would rather take the position in Washington Territory than retire. For a short time at least, he and Margaret would be living near their daughter, Eliza, and her husband, Brig. Gen. Benjamin Alvord, who was awaiting orders for a new posting. Besides, George Wright always performed his duty. To refuse a new posting would be unthinkable.

The *Brother Jonathan* was a sturdy, powerful ship with a steel hull, driven by giant paddlewheels affixed midship on either side and outfitted with three masts that held more than a dozen sails for use when the engines failed or coal was in short supply. Since its construction in 1851, the ship had sailed both the Atlantic and the Pacific, carrying passengers, cargo, and, frequently, large amounts of gold mined during the California gold rush. An article in the *San Francisco Daily Alta California* published when the *Jonathan* was launched described it as "one of the finest steamers ever built . . . equal to any other in point of speed." The vessel was 220 feet long with sides reinforced with iron braces "as strong as wood, iron, and copper can make her. Her cabins are well ventilated for warm climates, and the saloons finished with white enamel gold."[4] For the previous several years the *Jonathan* had sailed the northern Pacific coast, braving the strong winds out of the west and south, its hull accustomed to the hammering swells driven by Pacific storms. While tough on the outside, below deck the ship was comfortable, even luxurious, with cabins and suites, and a dining area built of redwood and furnished with fine linen and crystal.

Friday evening, after departing San Francisco Bay, the *Jonathan* headed north along the California coast. During the night the wind picked up, increasing in intensity throughout the day on Saturday. The swells were larger than normal, rising ten, then twenty feet. Lying in their cabins, holding on to their berths to keep from being flung to the floor, many of the passengers fell ill. Even those not affected by seasickness could do little more than find a secure place to sit and hold on to a railing. Normally the heavy seas and wind would not have worried Capt. Samuel DeWolf, but the ship's owner had ordered the captain to take on board an ore crusher weighing several tons. As a result, the *Jonathan* was top-heavy, and as the swells became more powerful, the ship began to lurch from side to side, knocking around people, furnishings, and freight. Near midday Saturday, Captain DeWolf decided to turn around and head toward Crescent Bay, twenty miles south of the Oregon border, where he intended to wait out the storm.

Just before two o'clock in the afternoon, fewer than ten miles from safety, the *Jonathan* rose on the crest of a huge swell, then slammed down bow-first, crashing onto a submerged rock that tore through the hull. With the ship impaled on the sharp pinnacle, savage swells wrenched the hull, and the heavy ore crusher on deck applied downward force, ripping steel like paper. The next forty-five minutes were pandemonium, as wind and sea overwhelmed the passengers' efforts to save themselves.

As the *Brother Jonathan* slid beneath the waves, witnesses reported seeing General Wright standing arm-in-arm with his wife on deck, Captain DeWolf at their side. The scene made an impression that lasted for generations. Decades later, in 1900, a retrospective article in a Spokane newspaper summed up statements from survivors who witnessed the Wright couple, stalwart against the storm: "The brave and gallant General Wright was seen to take off his long military cloak and [wrap] it around the delicate form of his wife. It was so large as to completely cover her body in its ample folds. He then gently and lovingly folded his arms around his wife's waist, and both stood still until the last lurch of the doomed vessel was given, and all was ended. Thus, with unfaltering courage, George and Margaret Wright descended into darkness and death."[5]

Two-hundred-twenty-five people died in the catastrophe; only nineteen survived, all passengers in the single lifeboat that survived the battering wind and waves.[6] Over the next three days rescue parties, including members of local Indian tribes, took boats to the site of the wreck and to nearby rocky protuberances, to no avail. Soldiers from a nearby army post joined civilians in the search for survivors. Col. Thomas Wright, the Wrights' son, organized a search party and offered a reward for the return of his parents' bodies, but the searchers found nothing. By August 20 it seemed that many of the bodies would never be recovered. The passenger remains not swallowed by the sea would, over the next two months, end up on beaches, some a hundred miles or more away.

Postmortem praise for George Wright began immediately. An August 4 editorial in the *San Francisco Daily Alta California* read, "One of the truest and best of men has been taken from us. As a military chieftain, his record stands among the most distinguished of American Generals. Not alone was he great in the field—where masterly ability characterized his every action—but his diplomatic tact, as evinced during the trying period of the past four years, enabled our people to enjoy the blessings of peace."[7] In San Francisco, the army fired a thirteen-gun salute in honor of General and Mrs. Wright, and American flags were lowered all over the city. In Sacramento, flags were lowered and church bells tolled.

Finally, on August 23, Margaret Wright's body floated ashore. George Wright's body was not discovered until September 27; it had drifted 150 miles from the site of the wreck. The men who found the general's remains attested that "the body appeared to be that of a large man, and advanced in years." The pants were blue broadcloth, military issue, and the suspenders were still attached. He wore "fine white flannel drawers, a pair of fashionable boots, size 9, and nailed. The boots were partially covered in barnacles, as were the pants." Both arms were missing, and the rest of the body was badly decomposed, with identification confirmed by a tag on the clothing bearing the name "G. Wright."[8] The body was temporarily buried nearby and retrieved later.

Two funerals were held for the Wrights, the first on Saturday, October 21, at Calvary Church in San Francisco. After the service, an honor guard escorted two hearses bearing the caskets along streets that had been cleared by soldiers. Bands from the Ninth Infantry and Second U.S. Artillery played the dead march. Platoons of Wright's old command, the Ninth Infantry, led the procession, followed by the hearses; then came Generals Halleck and McDowell, walking next to the hearses. Ranks of infantry, horse-mounted troops, and artillery followed, along with scores of civilians. The sidewalks were crowded with onlookers, all "standing in reverential silence to testify their respect for the memory of the honored dead."[9]

From San Francisco the caskets were taken by steamboat to Sacramento, where early the next morning, October 22, a committee of reception took charge and escorted the remains to the state senate chamber. Church bells and fire bells rang, flags hung at half-staff, and businesses and homes bore black banners. At the senate chamber, the committee on decorations placed the Wrights' caskets amidst mourning banners, tree boughs, flags, and feathers. Silver plates with inscriptions were placed on each coffin, and each was attended by an honor guard. For several hours visitors streamed past paying their respects, and at two o'clock, the bodies were taken to the Congregational church on 6th Street. The church was packed, and hundreds of people had to wait outside, having to be satisfied with joining the procession once the service was over.

The day prior, the *Sacramento Daily Union* had published a detailed schedule and order of procession. The parade started with the Fourth Regiment of Infantry, followed by a company of light artillery, a company of cavalry, then the hearse drawn by six horses and escorted by twelve pallbearers. Following that were carriages with friends and chaplains; on foot, there were hussars, members of the Pioneer Association, Knights Templar, Masons, Odd Fellows, Typographical Association, Turn-Verein Association, Draymen's Association, Teamsters' Association, and at least a half-dozen fire companies. Finally, the citizenry brought up the rear, on foot, in carriages, and on horseback. There were a band, an artillery salute, and small arms salutes. The *Daily Union* reported that the funeral cortege—which was over a mile in length—was one of the largest ever witnessed on the Pacific coast. The procession required nearly an hour to pass any given point.

News of the disaster took nearly a month to reach the East Coast, since telegraph lines had been down. The *New York Times* finally reported the news on August 26, under a banner headline: "GREAT DISASTER." On September 7, the *Times* followed up with a laudatory biography of General Wright:

> He was a gallant and distinguished soldier, and an accomplished officer; frank, genial and dignified in his manners. . . . He possessed fair abilities and great personal influence, and his long contact—since 1852—with the people on the Pacific Coast, enabled him to exercise much prestige in favor of the Union party. He was an ardent admirer of the immortal WASHINGTON, whose counsels would,

> if followed, have saved our country from the recent civil war. It is hard for the friends of GEORGE WRIGHT to see him thus make his exit, by the sinking of a steamship on a sunken rock. He would have gladly closed his career on the battle-field, in the recent war, fighting for the preservation of our unity and our liberties.[10]

The great display of lament and respect honoring Wright at his death gradually faded. His personal character and military successes were enough to win him respect among those who served with him, but they were not great enough to secure his place in American memory like McClellan, Sheridan, Sherman, Grant, Pickett, and other military leaders who served in the Pacific Northwest, some as Wright's subordinates. Due in great part to their Civil War experiences, they found fame and an enduring legacy. In some ways, General Wright's funeral was the highlight of his career. It would be up to the white population of the West Coast to create his heroic legacy.

His death took on a mystic quality to some. Years later, Lo-kout of the Yakama tribe spoke of the events of 1858, of how Wright had executed Qualchan, Lo-kout's brother. Lo-kout believed there was justice in Wright's death and described a vision he had experienced: "I saw a soldier sitting by a tree with a paper," he said, "and I saw my brother lying there dead. . . . After a while we learned that Colonel Wright drowned in the ocean, and we were glad."[11]

Judge William Compton Brown, who in the early twentieth century spent more than three decades among the upper Columbia Plateau tribes and interviewed survivors and their descendants, wrote about how some Indians felt about Wright: "The old folks tell us under their breaths in whispered tones and low, accompanied by many a mysterious nod and many a knowing gesture, that Heaven heard the imprecations of their medicine men—heard the mournings of the women—heard the accusing spirits of the dead, and that Wright's life was not choked out by waters of the Pacific Ocean but by the strangling fingers of a *solux tomahnowis* (angry god or destroying angel) sent down to avenge the wrongs the Indians had suffered at Wright's hands."[12]

ROCK LAKE, WASHINGTON TERRITORY, APRIL 1877

Twelve years after General Wright was interred, another funeral took place, this one eight hundred miles northeast of San Francisco Bay in the basalt scablands of eastern Washington Territory. George Wright's old enemy, Chief Kamiakin of the Yakamas, in his upper seventies, passed away quietly, surrounded by family and attended by a Catholic priest, who baptized the chief. Two of the chief's friends, white ranchers, built a coffin in which his body was placed, and he was buried on a bluff above Rock Lake, coincidentally located along the route taken nearly twenty years earlier by George Wright. Chief Kamiakin's passing received little notice in the non-Indian community, but among the tribes, his passing was mourned and his life was celebrated. Several years after his death, his grave was found desecrated, his skull missing. A fossil hunter, infamous for his disrespectful attitude toward Indians, was identified as the thief, but the skull has never been found.[13]

SPOKANE, WASHINGTON, JANUARY 1892.

The *Spokane Spokesman-Review* noted that another of Wright's old adversaries was dying: "Old Chief Garry of the Spokanes has been lying at the point of death in his teepee on Hangman Creek, with not a friend to succor him in his old age. The doctor and the constable, learning of the chief's sickness, drove out there yesterday to learn the facts. Old Garry was found in a pitiable condition—sick and unable to help himself, and no medicine or food within his reach."[14] On January 14, Chief Garry, once the peace-seeking chief of his people, passed away, aged about eighty-one. Late in life, he had been cheated out of his farm and reduced to poverty, for a time living in a teepee at the base of a hill, from the top of which the town's boys liked to throw rocks at him. His burial was paid for out of a fund established by Spokane County for indigent people.[15]

The *Spokesman-Review* ran a lengthy obituary on January 17, in which it called Garry "the last conspicuous savage figure in a war that was a singular blending of the sublime and the absurd." Garry, the column pointed out, had frequently warned his tribesmen of the folly of warfare against the whites, and for his concern was often scorned by his people. The paper gave Garry credit for standing up to Wright after the Plateau War, noting that the chief was "the first to brave the anger of the conqueror and intercede for his people."[16]

The Spokane paper's editorial regarding Chief Garry carried a tone of regret. Although it referred to the tribes' losses at the hand of the "firm and gallant Wright," the balance of the piece was restrained and respectful of the Spokane people, at least compared with the prevalent sentiment toward Indians at the time. The paper lamented "their extinction by slow degrees in the miserable struggle for existence after conditions had changed and the hand of adversity had been linked with that of a cruel destiny."[17]

For thousands of years the tribes had prospered on the Columbia Plateau, thriving on the region's abundant fish, game, and plant life. To the optimistic and energetic newcomers in the Inland Northwest, Garry's passing was but a footnote in a changing narrative that would tell of economic opportunity, pride, and the achievement of destiny.

The story began with the land.

ONE

A Land of Great Forces

The land *is at the root of the war.*

George Gibbs

The Columbia Plateau overlaps the boundaries of what today is referred to as the inland Pacific Northwest, also frequently referred to as the inland Empire. It has long been a quiet, relatively unknown part of the United States, a region that is today crossed quickly by cars heading west on I-90 to Seattle or on I-84, toward Portland, Oregon.[1]

Until the 1850s the inland Pacific Northwest was literally off the beaten path. The Lewis and Clark expedition, explorers, pioneers, and settlers traveling west generally crossed the southern part of the plateau, following the Snake River to its confluence with the Columbia, then on to the Pacific. The land to the north lay like a quiet eddy, easily ignored. Maps made of the area in the mid-nineteenth century show some detail along waterways, but near Spokane the detail is replaced by cartographic notations like "Hilly country hidden from view."[2]

Syracuse University geographer Donald Meinig (who was born and raised in the town of Palouse, in the Palouse region of the plateau) wrote, "One can search in vain through the standard of America used in schools, colleges, and universities for any mention of the Palouse, Spokane, or Inland Empire. . . . By such accounts it seems hardly to have participated in history at all."[3] Yet one historian claimed that despite the isolation, "in no other part of the United States was the conflict between red man and white pursued with more persistence or more bitterness than along the lonely rivers, in the mountain defiles, and amid the dense forests of the Pacific Northwest."[4]

The boundaries of the plateau differ depending on one's professional and cultural perspective. The U.S. Environmental Protection Agency defines the area as an ecoregion encompassing approximately thirty-five thousand square miles that includes northeastern Oregon, most of interior Washington, and an adjoining section of northern Idaho. From a geologist's viewpoint—which encompasses the underlying lava flows—it is much larger: perhaps sixty-three thousand square miles, the size of England and Wales combined. It is a region of unique topography, consisting largely of farmland, grass-covered dunes, basalt scablands, and pine-forested hills. It is also a land of water. Five hundred miles of the Columbia River and its tributaries meander through the Columbia Plateau. These life-giving veins once brought fish to the Native peoples, provided a network of transportation, and enhanced trade and communication between tribes.

ANCIENT FORCES

The birth of the current landscape began more than five million years ago, when lava broke through the earth's crust, beginning a long process of altering the surface. For several million years, molten waves, some a hundred feet deep, suffocated the land, sometimes creeping, sometimes moving at thirty miles an hour. Over millennia, basalt dams blocked streams, creating lakes and rerouting rivers. Molten bubbles formed and broke, producing shallow caves that would one day be used as shelters for animals and people.

During the Pliocene Epoch—two to five million years ago—shifting earth plates combined with the pressure of molten lava below to form the Rocky Mountains to the east and the Cascade Mountains to the west, the ranges that define the boundaries of the Columbia Plateau. Between the mountain ranges, the weight of the basalt—up to three miles deep—slowly nudged the land downward, creating a gentle slope from east to west, falling a thousand feet over a distance of two hundred miles, or one inch for every nine horizontal feet.[5]

After the final waves of lava cooled and hardened, streams began carving paths through basalt. Two million years ago, persistent winds began sweeping loess from the west and south, depositing up to three hundred feet of fertile soil in the area known today as the Palouse, in southeastern Washington and northern Idaho. Periodic eruptions from Cascade volcanoes deposited ash, enriching the soil. Ancient winds sculpted silt and ash into great dunes, with smooth, upward-sloping south sides and steeper north faces that dropped off into sheltered nooks where pines took root and formed protected oases where Native people made shelters.[6]

As the winds calmed, a few ancient mountains remained exposed. One became known by the Nez Perces as Yamustus, or Holy Mountain.[7] Western settlers called it Pyramid Peak, and not much later its name would change again: it would become known as Steptoe Butte, named after Col. Edward Steptoe, the officer whose force was defeated in 1858 by a confederation of Indians, triggering George Wright's fateful expedition.[8]

The next great force was ice, which began accumulating one hundred thousand years ago and retreated ten thousand years ago. The Cordilleran ice sheet crept as far south as present-day northern Idaho, stopping approximately sixty miles northeast of the City of Spokane. As the ice melted, it pooled behind immense ice dams, creating glacial Lakes Missoula and Columbia; at one time the lakes contained more water than Lakes Ontario and Erie combined. Over thousands of years, the dams underwent a series of breaks and reformations, releasing the greatest floods the earth has ever known. Walls of water two hundred or more feet high thundered across the land at speeds up to fifty miles per hour, ripping apart basalt columns, gouging canyons and coulees, and depositing some debris as far away as the Pacific Ocean, nearly four hundred miles to the west. Each flood emptied the lakes in a matter of days; each created a flow up to fifteen times the total volume of all the rivers on earth; each breach released energy equivalent to 225 Hiroshima bombs. The waters left behind what geologist J Harlan Bretz called scabland: a wounded basalt landscape, cut with cracks and channels. In some places—especially close to present-day Spokane, where Colonel Wright conducted most of his campaign—the floods were particularly powerful, leaving behind plains broken by craggy basalt formations and lakes rimmed with basalt columns and great heaps of rocky debris. Later, pine forests and nutritious vegetation spread over the area, providing food for people and animals.[9]

Western science has known about the floods for fewer than one hundred years, but Native people have known much longer. One story, told by the Spokanes, speaks of a monster who, in a rage, had thrust his claw into a great lake in the east and ripped the land so fiercely that it created a river flowing toward the west. The lake is known today as Coeur d'Alene—a remnant of glacial Lake Missoula—and the drainage is the Spokane River, which passes through downtown Spokane, then flows westward to the Columbia.[10] Thus, the monster created the valley through which Colonel Wright would travel during the most destructive part of his march.

The tribes remember the great torrents that changed river courses, uprooted entire forests, and killed animals and people. The Yakama Indians know of an "evil monster, Wish-poosh," also called Big Beaver, who lived in a lake in present-day central Washington. Wish-poosh prevented people from fishing in his lake, and they were starving. Coyote (also called Speel-yi) speared Wish-poosh, who dove deep into the water, dragging behind Coyote, who was tethered to the spear. They thrashed and fought, tearing through mountains and forests, forming what would later be called Union Gap in the Yakima Valley, and as they thrashed south and west, they burst through the mountains, creating the Cascades Rapids of the Columbia River. By the time they reached the sea, Coyote was unconscious, and Wish-poosh was dead. Coyote returned home to the lake that had once been protected by Big Beaver. On his journey, "He saw the muddy river flowing through the tunnel he and the monster had made. All the waters from all sides were flowing into this great channel and making land visible everywhere. The lakes that had covered the valleys of the Yakima had disappeared, leaving the ground wet. Indians were wading in the mud to the new ground."[11] The tribes knew the great floods to be cleansing. The powerful waters destroyed some species of animals, which were called *anakwi kakyama* (thrown-down animals).[12]

In 1878 the missionary and educator Myron Eells wrote, "When the earliest missionaries came among the Spokanes, Nez Perces, and Cayuses, they found that those Indians had their traditions of a flood, and that one man and his wife were saved on a raft. Each of those three tribes, also, together with the Flathead tribes, had their separate Ararat in connection with the event. In several traditions the flood came because of the wickedness of the people."[13]

Sometimes, Indian and white traditions are supported by scientific research. Today, work by the Cultural Resources Program of the Confederated Tribes of the Umatilla Indian Reservation integrates oral history with geologic science: "This story of Beaver and Coyote relates how the Bretz Floods would have looked to those who witnessed them over 12,000 years ago. . . . How the trees and rocks were being destroyed along the river, can be interpreted as the roaring and rolling of the flood waters down the Columbia River Gorge."[14]

By the middle of the nineteenth century, natural changes in the land gave way to those caused by newcomers. In 1858 topographer Theodore Kolecki worked with John Mullan to map the Columbia Plateau region. From atop Pyramid Peak, at an elevation of thirty-six hundred feet (approximately one thousand feet above the surrounding terrain), Kolecki described the land that was home to the Plateau Indians, the land over which the army fought the tribes. He portrayed a view that looks much the same today:

> From the top we had a view of the whole country for eighty miles around us. The outlines of all objects were, for a very short time, very clearly defined by the last rays of the setting sun. The Blue Mountains, the high table-land stretching from new Fort Walla Walla to the Columbia, and beyond it the mountains around the Coeur d'Alene

> Mission and lake and the Bitter Root Mountains, were distinctly visible. The Palouse, as far as I could see, followed an east and west course. The spurs of the Bitter Root Mountains, from which it proceeds, were gently sloping and densely wooded. Pine timber, in scattered groves, reaches from them to within four or five miles of the foot of the Pyramid Peak. The whole country enclosed by the above-mentioned mountain systems is rolling prairie, very much resembling a stormy sea.[15]

LIVING LAND

Native and white cultures held different values regarding the land. The non-Native collective narrative began with the assumption that the land existed in *stasis*, and its natural resources belonged to those with the will to take them. In contrast, the tribes viewed the land as having a past and future, believing that it had grown and changed and thus deserved to be treated like a living entity. Indian oral traditions about the region's natural history were part of each generation's legacy; it was the elder generations' duty to pass along the stories of how the land changed over time. The differences between the two views greatly impacted the relationship between Euro-Americans and Indians.[16] One point of contention was the concept of land ownership. Ownership of the land involved establishing boundaries that were registered in official documents and often enclosed with fences, both legal actions that the tribes did not understand and abhorred. In order for logging, mining, and ranching to be economical, the land required boundaries. Yet when survival depended on following food sources, people had to be able to move with the fish and game and to harvest plants on nature's terms. Thus, land ownership and strict boundaries interfered with the flow of life.

While Indians did not believe land should be owned, they did have a strong sense of place. A specific location, such as a mountain or stream, might be sacred. One tribal elder recently said, "We have to know where we came from, who we are, and where

Paloose (Palouse) Falls along George Wright's route in 1858. Drawing by Gustavus Sohon. From Mullan, *Report on the Construction of a Military Road* (1863), in the author's collection.

we're going. When it is an Indian's time, he takes things that are important to him and places them in meaningful places. In the future, descendants will visit those places, and their ancestor's spirit may appear to [them]."[17]

Places were given names much as were people. One researcher has recorded over one thousand place names in the Sahaptin language family, one of the two most prominent languages spoken by Plateau tribes.[18] To native people, the land was a means of survival, but it was also a part of their being. The land is woven into the fabric of their identity, and their lives move in unison with the flow of the rivers. The tribes viewed the land as a gift from the creator, and they literally drew breath from it.[19] The Coeur d'Alene tribe, one of those forced into submission by Col. George Wright, call themselves the Schitsu'umsh, translated as "the ones who were found here." To members of the tribe, the name "reiterates and affirms an identity anchored in a specific landscape."[20] Like other people of the plateau, the Palouse bands occupying land along the Snake River and northward into the rolling hills believed the creator made the earth for all living creatures, and the land and all life were inseparable.

OUR GARDEN

For thousands of years, the Columbia Plateau had provided sustenance for the tribes. Perhaps ten to twelve thousand years ago, the Indians hunted mammoths, mastodons, bison, and numerous other large mammals. In more recent times, the forests yielded deer, bear, elk, and mountain caribou. The people harvested roots and berries and caught fish; and along the Snake, Columbia, Palouse, and other rivers, they cultivated wheat, corn, and vegetables.[21] The Spokanes, with villages along the Spokane River, held salmon to be a gift from the Great Spirit. In addition, they depended on camas fields to provide a winter staple for their diet. In spring, at the beginning of the camas season, they would hold a ceremony to give thanks for the harvest provided by the land.[22] One elder recently expressed his tribe's view of

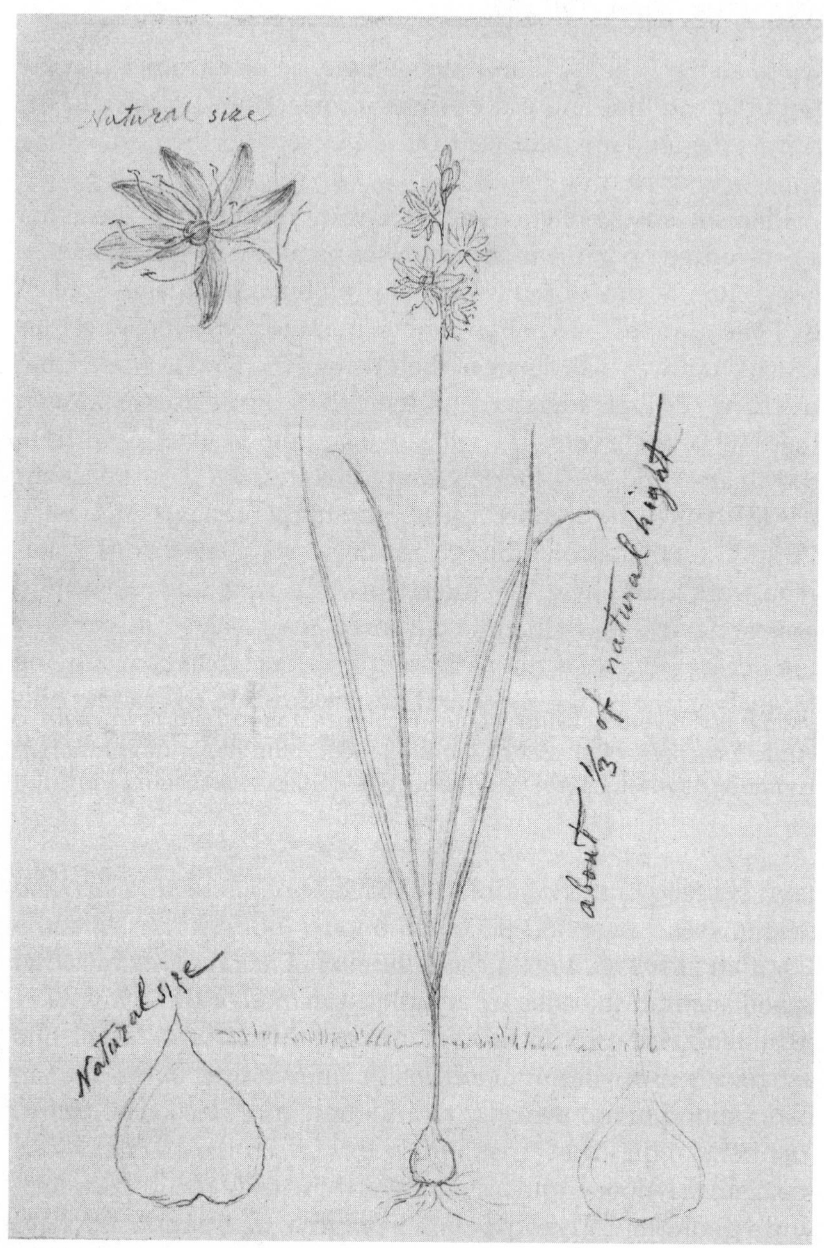

Cross-section of a growing Camas plant. Camas was a staple food for tribes across the Columbia Plateau. The bulbs were boiled or roasted, and flour made from the bulbs was used for bread. Drawing by Gustavus Sohon. National Anthropological Archives, Smithsonian Institution (MS 385680).

living in harmony with the land: "Take care of the land, and it will take care of you." Today, it is a way of living that both guides day-to-day use of natural resources and forms a philosophical base for long-term scientific projects to protect fish populations, land use, and other efforts aimed at restoring and protecting the environment.[23]

Several chiefs, including Garry of the Spokanes, met with Washington territorial governor Isaac Stevens at an 1855 council on the Spokane River. Catholic Missionary Joseph Joset was in attendance, and wrote, "All the chiefs were agreed in one point: they begged that the troops should not come across Lewis [Snake] River. . . . The territory between Lewis and Spokane Rivers is our garden, they said; it is there our women dig the roots on which we live; if the soldiers come into these parts, the women will not dare to go and there will be famine."[24] This warning foretold what would later happen on the upper plateau, causing great disruption and tragedy.

Today, the land continues to form and change. In May 1980 Mount St. Helens blasted out 520 million tons of ash that drifted east, darkening the skies over Spokane, causing streetlights to turn on in mid-afternoon. Ash settled across the Columbia Plateau, and even today, each time the wind blows, clouds of ash and dust drift across the plateau, settling over the Palouse and Spokane areas, continuing the eternal process of transforming the land.[25]

TWO

An American Birth

The question which has thus suddenly arisen is, what right had the first discovers of America to land, and take possession of a country, without asking the consent of its inhabitants, or yielding them an adequate compensation for their territory? . . . Until this mighty question is totally put to rest, the worthy people of America can by no means enjoy the soil they inhabit, with clear right and title, and quiet, unsullied consciences.

WASHINGTON IRVING, 1809

In 1803 the new nation was looking forward and westward. The Louisiana Purchase added 820,000 square miles for a land-hungry population to settle. Meriwether Lewis was making preparations to explore the West. On October 21, in the village of Norwich, Vermont, on the Connecticut River, George Wright was born to tough, adventurous farmers.[1] His early story laid a strong foundation to support the heroic narrative created by nineteenth-century white America: he was raised in New England, educated at West Point, became a decorated war hero, and, above all, he passionately supported God and country.

For centuries, the land on which Norwich was located had been part of the homeland of the Abenakis, an Algonquian-speaking people.[2] The Abenakis depended on the Connecticut River for fish and grew corn in the fertile land along the river. Two centuries before white settlement of the Pacific Northwest began, they suffered drastic change when their population was decimated by at least two epidemics. In 1617 plague swept from the New England coast inland, and in 1633 smallpox devastated more than 50 percent of the region's population. During the first half of the eighteenth century, periodic battles with settlers and British forces resulted in the Native peoples being pushed north into Canada. Hence, by the time of Norwich's founding, the Native population had been reduced to less than a quarter of its total a century earlier, and the colonists met little, if any, resistance when they established the town.

A thick volume recounting the history of Norwich mentions Indians fewer than a dozen times, most significantly in regard to education. While many educators no doubt had good intentions, education was also a means through which Indians might be made more acceptable to whites. For example, "Doctor [Eleazar] Wheelock, through his Indian pupil, Samson Occum, and other agents, had collected in England several thousand pounds to be expended in the establishment and support of a new college in the wilderness. . . . The conversion and education of Indians was the leading purpose that animated Doctor Wheelock in thus setting up his college on the very border of civilization."[3] The institution, opened in 1769, was called Dartmouth College, and was located in Hanover, New Hampshire, directly across the Connecticut River from Norwich. In the early years of Dartmouth there were at least two dozen Indian students.[4] George Wright's grandfather and great-grandfather each contributed a small amount to help the fledgling college. Before the first buildings were completed, students lived in shelters made from bark and tree boughs, a skill they learned from the Abenakis.[5] In 1816 George Wright, at the age of thirteen, began his formal education at Dartmouth Academy.[6]

THE NEW ENGLAND WAY

The people of Norwich followed the tenets of Congregationalism, which had evolved from Puritanism into a less centralized set of beliefs that became known as the "New England Way." Rather than a formal religion, it was a movement with no clearly defined doctrine or profession of faith, as was the case with Catholicism and Lutheranism.[7] Today, some scholars believe Puritanism to be a temperament and associate it with a "puritan character," which includes the intent to "lead an exemplary life."[8] The same idea was expressed by Erasmus Darwin Keyes, George Wright's second-in-command and confidant during the 1858 expedition. A fellow New Englander, Keyes believed that "a man might lose his religion and not cease, apparently, to be a Puritan." Keyes wrote that Puritanism made him "full of the vague apprehensions and the fearful sense of accountability that are infused in the minds of all Puritan children." He wrote that only when he attended West Point did he "commence the battle of life with youths from every State in the Union, the majority of whom were ignorant of the nature of Puritanism, which I had supposed was universal and infallible."[9]

Order and structure were key values for those living "exemplary lives." Townships provided a basis for such structure; the township documents for Norwich were drawn up nearly a year before the first settlers arrived, and detailed minutes were kept of every meeting, celebration, and dispute.[10] The New England sense of structure and discipline was not lost on young George Wright. Wright's reputation for discipline, preparation, and organization would be important factors during his career, and especially during his military expeditions.

One component of the New England Way was a belief in the importance of strictly punishing those who violated the community's values and mores. This belief was important not only on a local level, but also during military campaigns in the west. According to military historian William B. Skelton, "A punishment theme pervaded officers' thinking on Indian warfare." Thus, when Wright and other army officers headed west, first to police and then to suppress Indian tribes, they carried with them a tendency to view violent suppression as retribution for real or imagined transgressions by Indians. They justified their actions by claiming that Indians were "treacherous and savage"; therefore the usual rules of war did not apply.[11] Indeed, even many of Wright's official letters express his desire to "punish" or "chastise" Indians, and he seemed confident of his power. In 1856, during an expedition in the Yakima Valley, he wrote to Gen. John Wool: "I was determined to assume with these chiefs a tone of high authority and power. . . . They must be made to see and feel that they are completely in my power; they are, as I told them, 'Children in my hands.'"[12] Sometimes the threat of punishment was embedded in speeches that used phraseology that sounded as if it was from the Bible. During the 1858 campaign, for example, Wright told the tribes "You must put your faith in me and trust to my mercy."[13]

Although details of Wright's youth are scant, there is no reason to believe that his upbringing was anything but normal for a son of a hardworking, religious New England family. His character was reflected in a letter of recommendation written by Congregational Pastor James Woodward. In July 1817 Reverend Woodward wrote to admission officials at West Point, referring to Wright as "a youth of superior natural endowments and whose acquirements, especially in arithmetic and the English language, are far beyond his age."[14] In May 1818 Secretary of War John C. Calhoun wrote to young George notifying him of his appointment to the military academy. In September, one month before his fifteenth birthday, Wright entered the academy. By the time he graduated four years later, he had been immersed in a strict curriculum that emphasized ethics, military science, and discipline.

CREATING "NATION-BUILDERS"

Prior to Wright's acceptance to the academy, West Point had little of the reputation for discipline and scholarly excellence that it later achieved. In fact, in the early part of the nineteenth century it was disorganized and rife with dissension among students, administrators, and faculty. At times it resembled little more than a social club for young men from privileged families, with drinking and insubordination more prevalent than formal education. In 1817 Sylvanus Thayer was appointed superintendent, and the nature of the military academy quickly changed. The curriculum

42nd ANNUAL REUNION

Old Wasco County Pioneer Association

Saturday, May 2, 1964

THE DALLES, OREGON

Colonel George Wright was born in Vermont in 1803. He received an appointment to West Point and graduated in the class of 1822. He served at Fort Dalles in 1856 and 1858. He was promoted to Brigadier General in 1861 and assigned to command the Department of the Pacific. He died in the ship wreck of the steamer Brother Jonathan off the coast of Crescent City, Calif., July 9, 1865. At the time of his death he was on his way to Vancouver Barracks.

Made country safe from Indians

Yakima Indian War Com. 1855-56.

George Wright, early in his military career. The dates of Wright's command were actually 1856–58. Wasco County [Oregon] Pioneer Association and Columbia Gorge Discovery Center.

developed by Thayer was intended to produce "nation-builders firmly committed to republican ideology—ready and able to lead citizen-soldiers in the event of war but whose primary purpose would be to wage peace."[15] In 1818, the year after Wright began his West Point education, using Thayer's recommendations the Department of War issued a comprehensive set of regulations that included a curriculum, an academic schedule, inspection procedures, standards of conduct, and disciplinary procedures.[16]

Military scholar Lori Bogle asserts, "While now a relic of the past, the Thayer system was intrinsic to an understanding of Army and Navy officers." Bogle writes that Thayer created a "four-pronged program of ethics education" as the foundation of the curriculum at West Point: "First, he created a uniform military experience that was devoid of class distinction. Next, he instilled the officer corps with discipline, both mental and physical. Third, he capitalized on religious revivals as a means to undermine a cadet code of conduct that chafed at any restrictions of personal liberty. Finally, he supported a formal course in moral philosophy that taught practical as well as theoretical ethics to the army officer corps during the early nineteenth century."[17]

Beginning in 1820 seniors were required to take a course in "Christian ethics," which counted as 20 percent of their class ranking. By addressing moral philosophy, Thayer intended "to make better officers by increasing the cadet's obedience to authority and respect for the law." The curriculum and culture did not encourage individual thinking; rather, cadets memorized texts and recited them when asked. In fact, the text used in each class was read aloud twice during the term, word for word, and cadets had to be able to recite key passages from memory.[18]

The education George Wright received at West Point would underlie many of his words and actions during his career. One of the key texts used while Wright was at West Point was Swiss legal expert and philosopher Emer de Vattel's *The Law of Nations, or, the Principles of the Law of Nature Applied to the Conduct and Affairs of Nations and Sovereigns*, first published in 1758. Vattel's words and ideas formed the basis of the values held by the culture that created the narrative of George Wright as a hero. Vattel established philosophical guidelines for making ethical decisions in warfare, but his dictums left plenty of room for interpretation. Indeed, during his tenure in the Pacific Northwest, Wright believed his actions to be ethical, but to the people he fought, they were cruel.

One assertion made by Vattel concerned the preemptive destruction of property: "Whenever I am at war with a nation, both my safety and welfare prompt me to deprive her, as far as possible, of everything which may enable her to resist or injure me. In this instance, the law of necessity exerts its full force." During his march along the Spokane River in 1858, George Wright would use the same logic and nearly identical verbiage to justify the destruction of Indian horses and food stores and the harsh treatment of the local people. In the case of the horse slaughter, Wright said, "I deeply regretted killing these poor creatures but dire necessity drove me to it."[19] Several times during his campaign he used the terms "necessity," or "dire necessity," which had, and still have, a basis in law.[20] Under the doctrine of necessity the perpetrator of an illegal act might escape punishment if they could claim necessity. In nineteenth-century law, "necessity creates a genuine right . . . not a mere excuse."[21] However, the distinction between a "right" and an "excuse" was more of a concept than a clear line.

Vattel advocated protection for adversaries who surrendered in battle; they must not be harmed. This provision relates directly Wright's actions during his 1858 expedition. Vattel provided a rationale for harsh treatment of prisoners:

> There is however, one case in which we may refuse to spare the life of an enemy who surrenders. . . . It is, when that enemy has been guilty of some enormous breach of the law of nations, and particularly when he has violated the laws of war. . . . When we are at war with a savage nation, who observe no rules, and never give quarter, we may punish them in the persons of any of their people whom we take (these belonging to the guilty), and endeavor, by this rigorous proceeding, to force them to respect the laws of humanity.[22]

Vattel asserted that executing a prisoner was an acceptable action if he or she was a member of a "savage nation." The practice of killing a citizen as punishment for the perceived sins of his nation was one George Wright would undertake with fervor. The reverse was also true: he would punish a tribe for the transgressions, or perceived transgressions, of an individual. The situation was made worse by the fact that an act of resistance was viewed as an act of aggression, and therefore was subject to violent suppression. This circular reasoning meant that when fighting invaders, according to whites, Indians had little or no justification to answer violence with violence.

In a section that would later be exemplified by Wright, Vattel wrote, "This leads us to speak of a kind of retaliation sometimes practiced in war, under the name of reprisals. If the hostile general has, without any just reason, caused some prisoners to be hanged, we hang an equal number of his people, and of the same rank, notifying to him that we will continue thus to retaliate, for the purpose of obliging him to observe the laws of war."[23] In 1858, during his retaliatory expedition following the Steptoe battle, George Wright made this point clear to the tribes. He wrote, "I will make war on them; and if I come here again to war, I will hang them all, men, women, and children."[24] In addition, on September 30, 1858, he wrote that he had warned the tribes that if they remained hostile, he would "annihilate the whole nation."[25]

RELATIVE MORALITY

The West Point curriculum also included an ethics course based on William Paley's *Principles of Moral and Political Philosophy.* First published in 1784, Paley's text assumed a strong tone of moral and religious righteousness, along with a considerable amount of sympathetic verbiage for the oppressed and underclasses. It carried little of the cultural arrogance that would later be expressed in the doctrine of Manifest Destiny, but it offered a flexible and potentially destructive version of morality that was later embraced by Wright during his campaign against the Plateau tribes.[26] In Paley's text, and in Wright's actions, the concepts of morality and compassion were not necessarily linked.

A person might be seen as having a strong moral sense, but he or she might not act compassionately. In addition, Paley did not address the fact that what was "moral" to one culture might be immoral to another. Thus, Wright would view his own actions as "moral," based on a Euro-American context. The collective narrative about Wright's heroism likewise is based on a set of values that frequently ignored tribal values.

Paley's argument was, and sometimes still is, used by historians as justification for George Wright's actions against the tribes. Paley believed that "a nation at war is not only bound to mitigate its evils, by principles of humanity, but to bring it to a termination as soon, and with as little loss of blood and treasure, as may be possible."[27] The collective narrative has held that in Wright's case, while his violent means were perhaps cruel, his tactics were designed to force the tribes into submission without widespread bloodshed. However, this claim presupposes that minimizing casualties was the primary objective of his campaign. In fact, contrary to the view contained in the popular narrative, official letters show that the army's objective was not to limit bloodshed; it was to punish the tribes and subjugate them to the wishes of the army and the government by any means necessary.[28]

Paley also argued for a formal legal basis for European colonization of new lands, building on Vattel's earlier definition of the "Law of Nations." The "right of discovery" regarded newly discovered land as the property of, in Paley's words, "the prince or state whose subject makes the discovery; and, in pursuance of this rule, it is usual for a navigator, who falls upon an unknown shore, to take possession of it . . . by erecting his standard, or displaying his flag upon a desert coast." Ironically, in what might seem a prescient viewpoint, Paley admitted that such a rule lacked common sense, was "fanciful," and consisted of "pretension." Yet, he asserted that a rule of some kind was necessary to deal with such situations, since the alternative would have had "ruinous and fatal consequences."[29]

The society into which George Wright was born was not oblivious to the treatment of native people. Washington Irving took note of the pretension in Paley's work, taking aim at the legal arguments that established the right of Europeans to take land that they had "discovered." In 1809 he wrote that one argument in favor of taking land was the lack of human population. "This would at first appear to be a point of some difficulty," he wrote, "for it is well known, that this quarter of the world abounded with certain animals, that walked erect on two feet, had something of the human countenance, uttered certain unintelligible sounds, very much like language, in short, had a marvelous resemblance to human beings."[30] Irving's satirical writing, while popular reading in the Northeast, had no influence on national Indian policy. He was one of relatively few Americans willing to publicly express scorn for how their countrymen treated the native inhabitants.

Paley believed that violence was allowed if it was intended to achieve peace. He drew a line, however, by asserting that there was no place for "gratuitous barbarities" or the "slaughter of captives." Paley also explicitly stated that "the extension of territory or of trade; the misfortunes or accidental weakness of a neighboring or rival nation" are not just causes of war.[31] However, he wrote broadly, basing his arguments on European laws and traditions; thus, it is clear he did not intend to include Indian tribes as "nations."

Thus, within a few hundred pages of European-centered reason and logic, Vattel, Paley, and others created philosophical and moral justifications to conduct "just war," the kind George Wright studied at West Point and the kind he conducted against the Plateau tribes. Wright's education did not lead or force him to use harsh measures, but it contributed to a climate of excuses and permissiveness. In part because of his upbringing and education, Wright acted violently, knowing his actions would not be subject to the same consequences that would apply had he committed the same violence against Euro-Americans.

Washington Irving's biting commentary listed the rights invoked by Europeans to claim and occupy the land: discovery, cultivation, and civilization. He wrote that those three rights of the conquerors implied a fourth: "The right by EXTERMINATION, or in other words, the RIGHT BY GUNPOWDER."[32]

COMPELLING PEACE

Until well into the nineteenth century, warfare in North America had frequently consisted of quick attacks and skirmishes, with few sustained battles, let alone comprehensive battle plans. In fact, it more resembled Indian warfare, suited to small bands of fighters without a strong central commander. A military scholar recently wrote, "When the armies of the United States went to war in 1812, they did so without a uniform system of tactics or even a single vision of what war was or how it was fought."[33]

While that may have been true in a sense, there were military leaders who knew how to defeat Indian tribes. One of the first was George Washington, who used extirpative tactics with great effectiveness. Washington wrote that the goal of the fight against the Iroquois was "total destruction and devastation of their settlements and the capture of as many prisoners of every age and sex possible." He believed that if Indian crops were destroyed and their pleas for peace were ignored, "it is likely that their fear, if they are unable to oppose us, will compel them to offers of peace." He also advocated taking hostages, a tactic that Wright would use during his campaign.[34]

In the early nineteenth century, Gen. Winfield Scott became intrigued with the structure and strategies of the French army, and during the War of 1812 he began to instill in his men French-style discipline. In preparation for battle, his men drilled ten hours a day, seven days a week. Scott's force won an impressive victory at the Battle of Chippewa, and his superiors were impressed enough to have Scott lead an effort to create a new U.S. Army, using the French system as a model. The French battle tactics were fairly simple but potentially devastating: groups of skirmishers would engage the front line of the enemy, trying to create disorder. Lines of infantry would then charge with bayonets, with light artillery used only in support, rather than as a primary means of attack. French officers—most notably Napoleon—would select the place of battle, avoiding swamps, forests, towns, and any place that would make their aggressive tactics difficult to use.

In 1821, the year before George Wright graduated from West Point, Scott ordered the publication of a translation of the French army manual. The *General Regulations for the Army* was the U.S. army's first significant attempt to establish a professional military using formal rules of conduct.[35] During Wright's 1858 campaign, his preparation and tactics mirrored those of the French, and a great deal of his military success was a result of his devotion to long days of drilling to assure French-style discipline in battle.

The new curriculum at West Point quickly became successful. Historian William Skelton writes that at the time of Wright's graduation, the graduating cadets had "institutional loyalties and common modes of behavior."[36] By the time Wright graduated in 1822 at age eighteen, the academy's once-mediocre curriculum had been transformed into an exhaustive series of courses that turned undisciplined cadets into highly disciplined officers.[37]

WRIGHT'S EARLY CAREER

In 1822 George Wright graduated twenty-fourth out of a class of forty and received a commission as a second lieutenant in the Third Regiment of Infantry. He spent most of the next four years at Fort Howard, Wisconsin, a relatively peaceful posting. It was a busy crossroads for military forces, settlers, and Indians, most of who enjoyed quiet, sometimes respectful, relations. In late 1826 the Third Infantry was ordered to participate in the construction of Jefferson Barracks, a new post near St. Louis. Other than the hardships encountered in forging a new post out of the wilderness, it was not a particularly dangerous assignment, and the officers spent a good portion of their time listening to concerts put on by the regimental band and attending banquets.

Wright received his first promotion, to first lieutenant, in September 1827, five years after graduation. In early 1828 he moved to rustic Cantonment Leavenworth, near present-day Kansas City, and worked to improve and expand it.[38] When the Third Regiment arrived, the quarters consisted of tents and huts built of timber and bark. Only twelve officers and two hundred men were posted at Leavenworth, a small force to be responsible for keeping peace in a large region roamed by bands of Pawnees. In the late winter of 1828–29, Wright was ordered to take a command to Council Bluffs on the Missouri River to investigate the mood of the tribes in the area. From early March through April 1829, Wright traveled nearly five hundred miles in a loop from Cantonment Leavenworth, through Council Bluffs, and back to the post.

The trip provided him with invaluable experience in dealing with Indians and provided a first glimpse of how Wright, as a military leader, would view conflicts with the tribes. Along the Platte River, Wright's command was followed by a band of Grand Pawnees who, he reported, became "quite too familiar with ourselves, but much more so with our property." However, he did not report any violence. He visited villages, interviewed traders and Indians, and listened to the tribes' grievances, taking detailed notes. His report reflects tact and professionalism, and there are none of the slurs often found in reports written by others of the time: no remarks about "savages" or any comments about the people he encountered being anything but worthy of his concern. In fact, near the end of his trip his group was caught in a violent storm, and he wrote that they were "received and treated kindly at the village." Wright talked with the local chiefs, who told him that while many of the older members of the tribe felt friendly toward whites, the "young men were not all of the same disposition." Even with the knowledge that some of the men were not peaceably inclined, Wright did not feel uncomfortable visiting the tribes, writing, "I do not think that myself or [my] party will incur any great risk in visiting their villages."[39]

In April 1829, at the end of the trip, Wright concluded that the Pawnees had little intention of engaging in war with the United States, although certain members of the tribes would "continue to rob and murder whites as before." He reported that such scattered attacks would continue until "decisive measures are taken by the government."[40] At least at this stage in his career he did not specify what he meant by the term "decisive measures," but in later years he used the phrase several times when planning military operations against the tribes of the Columbia Plateau.

During Wright's absence, malaria had spread through Cantonment Leavenworth, and in an effort to control the spread, the Third Regiment withdrew to Jefferson Barracks. Malaria and cholera periodically spread through the barracks, and cholera was particularly devastating to nearby Pawnee villages.[41] For the next year, the regiment nursed the sick and continued construction on the cantonment. In 1831 Wright's diligence and competence in completing his duties at Cantonment Leavenworth resulted in promotion to regimental adjutant, a position he would maintain for the following five years.

LOVE AND TRAGEDY

George Wright married Margaret Wallace Forster in 1828 or 1829, and facts about their marriage are scarce.[42] His official letters rarely, if ever, mention Margaret, and even his few known surviving personal letters do not mention her. We know that she was born in Erie, Pennsylvania, into a prominent family, the daughter of Col. Thomas Forster, Sr., who served as a judge and a Pennsylvania state representative. Margaret was the youngest of eleven children, and her mother died two years after she was born. Existing histories tell of George and Margaret moving in late 1836 from a military posting at Fort Jesup, Louisiana, to Pennsylvania.[43] At least one account tells of Wright making the move for recruiting duty, but to a historian, it looks like an unusual move for a man so driven to gain field experience and advancement up the ranks. In fact, the Wrights spent at least several months in Norwich, Vermont, George's ancestral home.[44]

The timing coincides with personal tragedies that explain the interlude in his career. Published histories have reported that George and Margaret had three children, all of whom lived into adulthood. His first son, Thomas, was born in 1830 and in 1874 would be killed in the Modoc Indian War. John, the youngest, was born in 1839 and had an illustrious career, rising to the rank of brigadier general in the army and serving as chief marshal of the U.S. Supreme Court. Eliza, his only daughter, was born in May 1837 and lived to adulthood, but toward the end of her life she lived in poverty. However, the Wrights had two more children, neither of whom lived past early childhood. James Heron Wright was born in 1832, and Roswell Wright was born in 1834. An obituary in the *Army and Navy Chronicle* dated March 31, 1836, while Wright was posted at Fort Jesup, Louisiana, tells the fate of Roswell: "DEATHS: *At Fort Jesup, Lou., on the 4th ult. Roswell, son of Lieut. George Wright, adjutant 3d Infantry, U.S.A., aged one year and nine months.*"

The cause of Roswell's death is unclear, but yellow fever and malaria were common in the area. While posted at Fort Jesup in 1845, Ulysses Grant noted that mosquitoes "were of great multitudes and of great voracity."[45] Childhood deaths by disease were not unusual, but there must have been something about Roswell's death that struck the editors of the *Chronicle,* since in addition to the death notice, they devoted a half page to lyrics from a Thomas Moore hymn, noting that it was dedicated, "On the death of Roswell, son of Lieutenant Geo. Wright, Adjutant 3d Infantry U.S.A." Moore had written the words to honor a friend's young daughter, who had died of "fever."[46] Another tragedy befell Lieutenant Wright and his wife just over a year later, in June 1837, when five-year-old James Heron died of an unrecorded cause. James was buried in Norwich, near other members of the Wright family.[47] Margaret Wright's father died in June 1836; thus, in the space of barely more than a year, Margaret and George Wright lost two young children and Margaret's father—and delivered a baby girl, Eliza. One can only speculate on the effect the tragedies may have had on Wright and his wife, but certainly he was not immune to suffering. Later in his career, General Wright would belittle gold miners who would abandon their "little ones" in their search for riches.

WAR AND HONOR

Still a lieutenant after fourteen years of active service, Wright was promoted more slowly than he felt justified. For his West Point class of 1822, on average officers reached the rank of captain in thirteen years.[48] In early 1836 he wrote at least twice to army headquarters requesting a promotion to captain, which was finally granted in October 1836. In 1842, for his service in the Seminole War, Wright received a brevet, an honorary—and temporary—promotion to major.[49] In 1845 Captain Wright left his recruiting duty to join Brig. Gen. William J. Worth's command in the Mexican-American War.

During the war, Wright would become a hero in one of the bloodiest battles in the early history of the United States. On August 20, 1847, General Worth was ordered to take the village of Churubusco, where 1,300 Mexican soldiers had established a defense in a convent. At its entrance they had positioned seven cannons. Several thousand more Mexican soldiers had established positions outside the convent, to protect the flanks. For most of the day, the two sides blasted each other with bullets and cannon fire, assaults and counter-assaults. Each side attempted bayonet charges with limited success. One of the more successful charges was led by Wright, who guided his troops through a farm field in a frontal assault. The maneuver was both successful and catastrophic, with more than 1,000 of the 2,600 U.S. soldiers killed or wounded, while the Mexican forces suffered 2,000 casualties out of a force of 7,500.

Wright's bravery and tenacity earned him another dangerous mission. The next day, August 21, Maj. Gen. Winfield Scott ordered General Worth to take the town of Molino del Rey. Worth ordered Wright to take five hundred men and attack the center of the defender's lines, where most of their artillery was located. Again, Wright's men suffered heavy casualties, but those who managed to survive the grapeshot rallied and attacked with bayonets. During the battle Captain Wright was shot in the shoulder and was helped from the battlefield by Lt. Isaac Stevens, whose relationship with Wright would later sour while they both served in Washington Territory.[50]

For his gallantry, Brevet Major Wright received another brevet, this time to colonel. Shortly thereafter, he was promoted to the rank of major of the Fourth Infantry, and in 1848 assumed command of Fort Ontario, New York. Following that posting, in July 1852 Wright and the Fourth Infantry embarked on the forty-day trip by sea and land to Northern California, where he became the commander of the Northern California District of the Pacific Division, located at Fort Reading. In northern California, he experienced the complexities and frustrations of trying to balance Indian-white relations and generally received praise for his conduct and skill in his peace efforts. In March 1854 Wright reported that the tribes were peaceful and that because of white encroachment on tribal land, Indians resorted to thievery to survive. He wrote, "In retaliation, the whites fall upon the Indians and murder innocent and guilty indiscriminately. . . . I have no doubt most difficulties with Indians have been brought on by the wanton aggressions of the former."[51] For the next few years, Wright would usually blame whites for violence with Indians.

Fort Reading was a rustic post consisting of a collection of small buildings occupying ten acres chopped out of an oak forest. It was no place for an officer's family, and Wright fulfilled his duty without seeing Margaret or his children for more than two years.[52] Men posted at Fort Reading were at constant risk of diseases, particularly malaria. Inspector general reports from 1852 and 1854 stated that at least a quarter of the men were incapacitated by illness. The strongest of the group, according to one inspector, was Brevet Col. George Wright, who took quinine pills when he began to feel ill.[53]

In 1855 Wright was promoted to full colonel and was given command of the newly formed Ninth Infantry regiment, created to occupy the Pacific Northwest. His new assignment meant a trip back to the east coast, where he established regimental headquarters at Fort Monroe, Virginia, and began to train his recruits. On December 15, 1855, Wright's new command boarded two steamships for the trip west, crossed the Isthmus of Panama by train, and boarded two ships for the journey north along the Pacific Coast. They arrived at Fort Vancouver on the Columbia River, Washington Territory, on January 21 and 22, 1856.[54]

AN IDEAL AMERICAN

Thus, by 1856, when George Wright arrived in the Pacific Northwest, his character reflected New England sturdiness, a robust religious foundation, a strong education in the theory of war and Indian warfare, and a sense of duty that he not only tried to live up to, but also frequently referenced in his letters. He had led heroic charges into enemy fire, been wounded, experienced great personal suffering, and established himself as a tough, dependable officer.

Wright's character (as perceived by many whites) was summed up by Lt. (later general) George B. Dandy, who served in Wright's command and would later be decorated four times during the Civil War. Dandy considered Wright the best commanding officer under whom he had served. In his memoir, he wrote:

> Colonel George Wright had a fine social side. When not engaged in the strict performance of duty, he was genial, whole-souled, kind and hospitable, full of wit, and possessed of a keen sense of humor. One could not be in his presence long without feeling charmed by this personality, his refinement, and general attractiveness. One felt him to be a friend, as well as a just and impartial commander. In person, he was of medium size, manly appearance and of rather handsome features. He was a fine looking soldier and a thorough gentleman.[55]

Within two months of arriving in the Pacific Northwest, the "kind and hospitable" Wright would quickly show another side of himself.

THREE

People of the Plateau

Secretary of the Interior Jacob Thompson informed Congress in 1857 that there were three kinds of Indians in the United States: the first two types had either been "civilized" by American society or were making progress toward civilization. Then there was the third kind: those in Oregon and Washington Territories, who were

> wild, roving, fierce, retaining all the traditionary characteristics which marked the race before the advent of the white man. . . . To this class, comprising nearly three/fourths of the whole number, belong most of the bands whose hunting grounds lie in the interior of the continent, and in the Territories of Oregon and Washington.[1]

The secretary went on to assert that the tribes "are controllable only through their fears." He believed that by forcing the tribes onto reservations, they would have to stop what he called "their roving habits." Secretary Thompson was unintentionally acknowledging the connection between the people and the land, as their "roving habits" were their adaptation to the flow of life on the Columbia Plateau.

Long before Secretary Thompson made his remarks, the Plateau tribes were already in decline from disease. According to anthropologist Robert Boyd, the population of Pacific Northwest tribes in the late 1700s numbered between 35 and 40 thousand, down from more than 180 thousand before the first contact with European culture a hundred years earlier.[2] A census conducted by Isaac Stevens estimated a total Columbia Plateau population of between 12 and 15 thousand.[3] Tallies per tribe varied according to the census taker and depended upon how tribal boundaries were drawn and the degree of illness since the last census. In 1851 Oregon's superintendent of Indian affairs, Anson Dart, believed there were 1,093 members of the Yakama, Klickitat, and Walla Walla tribes; in 1854 ethnologist George Gibbs estimated the number at just over half that.[4]

In the mid-1850s the tribes that would most directly be impacted by Wright's 1858 march numbered about twelve thousand, including the Spokanes, Coeur d'Alenes, Palouses, Nez Perces, and Yakamas, as well as adjoining tribes.[5] Plateau tribes were typically grouped according to their linguistic foundations. Tribes in the northern section spoke Salish dialects, including the Spokanes, Coeur d'Alenes, Kalispels, and Flatheads. Around the intersection of present-day Washington, Oregon, and Idaho, the Nez Perces, Walla Wallas, Palouses, and Umatillas spoke Sahaptin, as did the Yakamas and Klickitats on the western plateau. The Cayuses spoke their own tongue, the Waiilatpuan language, although for trading and social purposes they often spoke Sahaptin. Many speakers of Salish dialects could also speak Sahaptin, and vice-versa, and in many ways tribal cultures were similar, regardless of language. Tribes in the Northwest, especially those living along the Columbia River, also spoke the Chinook jargon, a mix of European and Indian languages that developed to allow various cultures to communicate about trade, travel, and culture. It eventually spread along the west coast of the United States and Canada and extended southeast into the Rockies. It was a dynamic language, changing as people moved around the region.[6]

Before and after Europeans arrived in the Northwest, tribal cultures changed and evolved.[7] In the early twentieth century, at least one prominent anthropologist claimed the Plateau tribes represented a "transitional culture," the elements of which were taken from Pacific coast and Great Plains tribes.[8] Later in-depth research revealed that this interpretation had resulted from a cursory examination of the tribes, and when the people and their cultures were examined more closely, the results were much

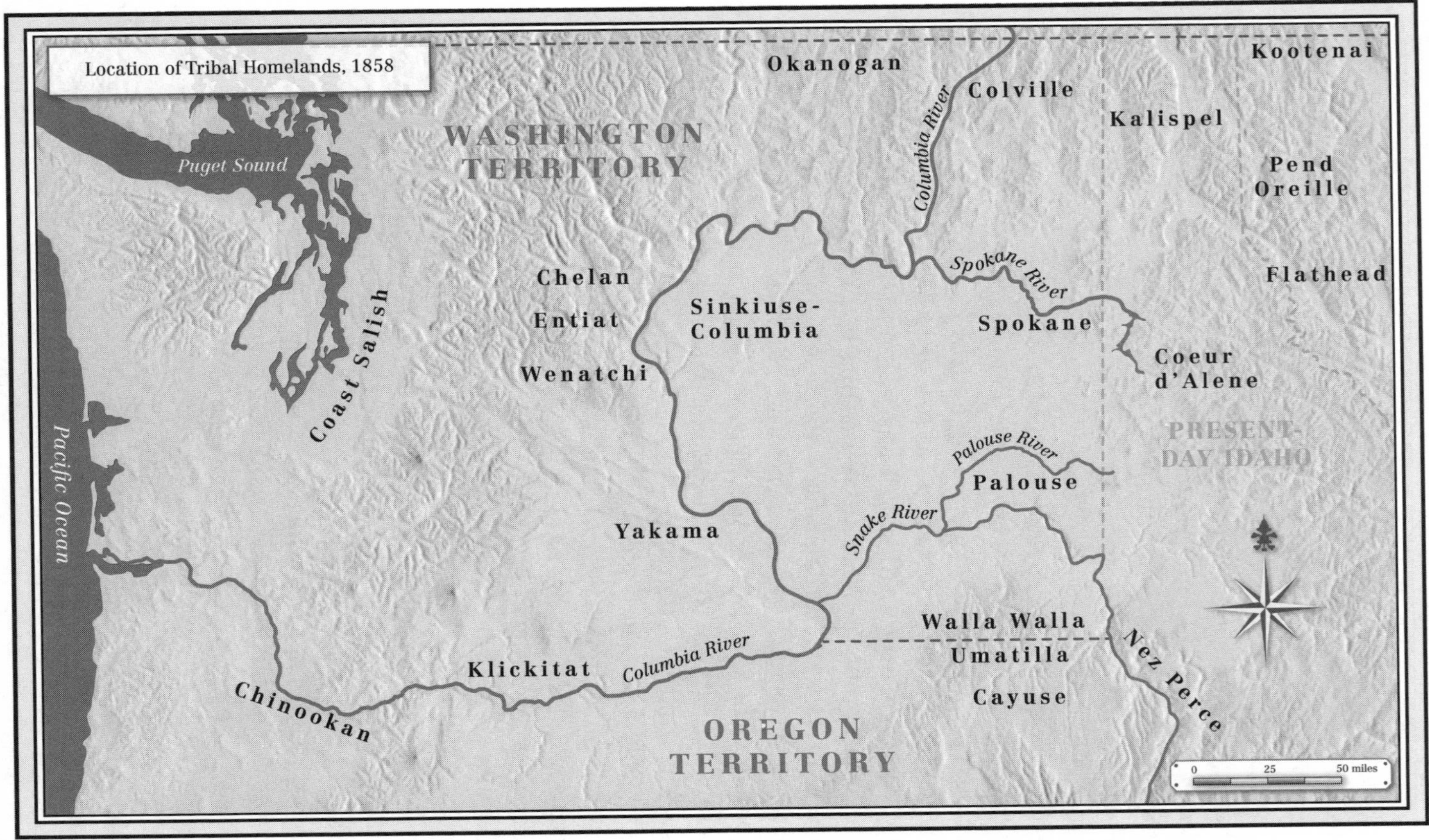
Location of Tribal Homelands, 1858
Okanogan
Colville
Kootenai
Kalispel
Pend Oreille
Flathead
WASHINGTON TERRITORY
Puget Sound
Columbia River
Spokane River
Chelan
Entiat
Wenatchi
Sinkiuse-Columbia
Spokane
Coeur d'Alene
Coast Salish
PRESENT-DAY IDAHO
Pacific Ocean
Palouse River
Palouse
Snake River
Yakama
Walla Walla
Umatilla
Cayuse
Nez Perce
Klickitat
Columbia River
Chinookan
OREGON TERRITORY
0
25
50 miles

different. Some of the Plateau tribes lived among a network of waterways that provided food and facilitated transportation. Life was a flow not only of water, but also of ideas and culture. Tribal members intermarried, worked together, and traded goods. Large-scale intertribal wars were rare, although at times the Plateau peoples banded together to fight common enemies, such as the Blackfeet east of the Rockies. They were not resistant to constructive change, and they readily traded for tools, clothing, and goods that might make life easier. For many Native people, their resistance to white settlement originated more from how it came about. The presence of respectful white settlers was often tolerated, and in some cases welcomed. After all, the Native people certainly understood the benefit of vaccines, weapons, and other inventions of European-American culture, and they understood the value in establishing economic ties with white trappers, traders, farmers, and others.

Differences between tribes could be as varied as differences in the personalities of their members. Calling Native people "Indians" without acknowledging differences led to the impression that tribes, and individuals within tribes, behaved alike, at least when it came to attitudes toward westward expansion and colonization. A member of the salmon-dependent Spokane tribe not only had a different method of earning sustenance than a buffalo-hunting Nez Perce, but he or she might also have different values. During George Wright's 1858 invasion of the plateau, some of the Nez Perces worked as scouts for the army, and some even fought with the army against the confederated tribes. Some of the Spokanes, Coeur d'Alenes, and other tribal members were friendly to white settlers and some were not. Some values held by Plateau tribes differed from those commonly found in coastal tribes, even though they might all speak Salish dialects. For example, some Pacific coast tribes were more warlike, with the northwestern coastal tribes particularly noted for their brutality in warfare. Ethnologist Verne Ray was struck by the differences in the tribes' attitudes toward war: "What a contrast is presented by the Plateau emphasis on pacifism!"[9]

In 1840 Father Pierre-Jean De Smet wrote that the Coeur d'Alenes, Kalispels, and other tribes treated him with "one continued act of kindness and of attention."[10] Politicians and settlers would often characterize the Plateau tribes as warlike, in part due to ignorance and in part to justify violence or land grabs. In fact, while the tribes would engage in skirmishes or temporary feuds, they rarely engaged in war against their neighbors. Raids and skirmishes between villages and tribes were not uncommon, but they were typically of short duration and caused limited damage. In particular, the Sanpoil people, situated in the north-central part of the plateau, valued peace; Ray said they "emphasize no other value in life more than pacifism, unless it be the fundamental equality of all men."[11] Even when violence appeared to be inevitable, some Indians tried their best to prevent it. When the army was at war with the plateau tribes, a Spokane chief tried to talk Chief Kolaskin of the Sanpoils into joining them but was rebuffed.[12]

Horses and canoes provided efficient transportation among tribes all across the Columbia Plateau, and tribal boundaries were generally vague or flexible. The Nez Perces lived in a large area of what is now northeastern Oregon, north-central Idaho, and southeastern Washington. The Palouses lived along the Snake River and north along the Palouse River into the rolling hills of the southern Palouse region. The Upper Spokanes lived in the region of the present-day Washington-Idaho border, the Middle Spokanes in the area of the City of Spokane, and the Lower Spokanes near the confluence of the Spokane and Columbia Rivers. A joint village near the present-day town of Leavenworth, on the eastern slope of the Cascade Mountains, consisted of both Wenatchi people and Kittitas (a northern branch of the Yakamas), most of whom were bilingual.[13] Hence, the Kittitas people had more in common with the Salish-speaking Wenatchi than they did with the Sahaptin-speaking members of the main body of their own tribe.[14]

Tribal names were, in most cases, given by Europeans and Americans to a group of people based on their geographical location (Sanpoils), a physical attribute (Nez Perces), or a tribal characteristic (Coeur d'Alenes). The political and social structures of the tribes could differ significantly. For example, while the Spokanes and Coeur d'Alenes had much in common culturally, the Spokanes leaned toward centralization of tribal power, at least in comparison to the Coeur d'Alenes, who had a weak tribal orientation, but a strong village orientation.[15]

Most Plateau tribes ate a fish-based diet, since in those days the rivers were at times nearly choked with salmon. This diet was supplemented with deer, bear, and other big and small game; this was true particularly of the tribes on the eastern side of the plateau, such as the Coeur d'Alenes and Nez Perces. Members of any tribe might ride east of the Rockies to hunt buffalo, but again, this was more usual with the eastern Plateau tribes. Any of the Plateau people were likely to travel south to California to trade horses, buy cattle, or engage in other commerce.[16] Trips westward along the Columbia River or across the Cascade Mountains were common, especially during summer and fall fishing runs, when people from tribes all over the Northwest would gather on the Columbia at The Dalles, Celilo Falls, and Cascades Rapids. Tribes would also gather on the southern plateau in the Grande Ronde Valley of northeastern Oregon to hunt, gather roots, and often most important, to settle disputes without violence.[17] Myra Eells, who moved to the region in 1839 to open a mission with her husband, Cushing, wrote about the life of the Indians:

> They live upon fish and roots, which are found in many different places. They live in lodges set in a circle on the ground, and drawn together at the top and fastened with a string leaving a place at the top for the smoke to pass out. Over this frame they throw skins, grass, willows and the like. They build their fire upon the ground in the center, around which they live and sleep. They generally have a kettle in which they boil their fish, meat, corn and potatoes, if they have any. They eat standing with the kettle in the middle, their hands supply the place of all dishes.[18]

Horses appeared on the plateau in the early to mid-1700s, possibly introduced by the Shoshone people of present-day southern

Idaho.[19] The addition of horses to the culture meant the tribes could ride to buffalo, and by at least the late eighteenth century, Plateau tribes would unite for hunting trips, gathering up to one thousand people for the trek. Salish and Sahaptin tribes would band together as a defense against their common enemies, the Blackfeet to the east and the Shoshones to the south. Thus, it was not unusual for the Spokanes to travel with the Nez Perces to buffalo country, in part for self-defense.[20]

Although slavery was fairly common among some tribes along the Columbia, farther north one was less likely to encounter tribes holding slaves. Yakama chief Kamiakin kept slaves, but a short distance to the northeast, the Kalispels, Spokanes, and Coeur d'Alenes generally avoided taking slaves. Treatment of slaves differed by tribe and region. The Klamath, in present-day southern Oregon, were active slave traders and were often participants in a slave market located at The Dalles, a popular gathering place for tribes from all over the Northwest. At The Dalles, most tribes engaged in fishing, horse racing, and games, and enjoyed a cooperative, rather than oppressive, environment. Verne Ray, in his ethnology of the Plateau tribes, wrote, "The outside origin of Plateau slaves is directly correlated with friendliness within the area. Throughout the central region relations are so thoroughly harmonious that the taking of slaves is unthinkable."[21] As with his remark about the tribes' pacifism, Ray's conclusions were perhaps sweeping, but his general observation seemed to hold true: the Plateau tribes would not shy from a fight, but their identity was more closely associated with their natural environment and not with a culture of conflict suppression.[22]

HUMANE AND JUST TREATMENT

Relationships between Indians and settlers varied. From about 1800 through the 1840s, during the period of exploration, relations were usually peaceful and often respectful. In 1812 Ross Cox, while traveling in the Spokane Valley, became lost. He came upon two Indian men, "who came running to me in the most

Chief Garry, 1855. Drawing by Gustavus Sohon. Washington State Historical Society.

friendly manner. On seeing the lacerated state of my feet they carried me in their arms to a comfortable dwelling covered with deerskins." Cox told of how a woman cleaned his wounds and fed him roasted roots and salmon, treating him with "affectionate solicitude."[23] Twenty-five years later, the Rev. Samuel Parker traveled through the upper Columbia Plateau and spoke of

Chief Kamiakin, leader of the fight to defend the Plateau tribes' homeland. Drawing by Gustavus Sohon, 1855. Washington State Historical Society.

the intelligence and integrity of the people, saying of some, "I never heard voices more expressive of kindness."[24] Across the Pacific Northwest employees of the Hudson's Bay Company also enjoyed peaceful relations with the tribes, although some would later contribute to the region's problems by selling unlimited quantities of arms and liquor to Indians.

Chief Owhi of the Yakamas, 1855, tribal leader, father of Qualchan, and hostage of George Wright. Drawing by Gustavus Sohon. Washington State Historical Society.

According to historian John Unruh in his classic *The Plains Across,* as emigrants reached the Columbia Plateau, "many overlanders willingly entrusted their stock, wagons, belongings, and even their families to Indian swimmers and boatmen at dangerous river crossings all along the trail. Many pioneers spoke warmly of the Indians, particularly along the Columbia

River, noting their generosity and concern for the travelers' well-being." Along the route from the Mississippi to the Pacific Northwest, the danger of death at the hands of Indians was greatly exaggerated. Unruh concludes that for the period 1840–1860, total white emigrant fatalities on the Oregon Trail attributable to Indians numbered 362, an average of 17 per year. Using the same research methods, he concluded that 426 Indians died along the trail at the hands of settlers. In contrast, estimates of total emigrant deaths along the Oregon Trail range from 10,000 to 30,000 for the period 1842–1859. Therefore, deaths at the hands of Indians amounted to less than 4 percent of total fatalities, with the balance coming from disease and accidents. Among the most devastating diseases were cholera, scurvy, smallpox, mumps, and "mountain fever," all of which claimed tens of thousands of Indian lives as well. Unruh's counts do not include deaths caused by armed confrontations between Indian tribes and army or militia forces. Unruh wrote, "Influenced by the exaggerated reminiscent accounts, most writers have fostered the impression that the Indians were implacable foes throughout the immigration period. Unfortunately, few have endeavored to lend substance to such generalizations with precise statistical evidence."[25]

Newspaper editors and politicians stoked fears about Indians for political and personal gain. What might have been a skirmish in Oregon could end up being described as a massacre by the time the story reached New York papers. In 1855 a newspaper in Illinois claimed that "many, if not all" of the emigrants who headed for Oregon and California in the spring of that year were killed by Indians, when in fact none were. Another so-called massacre was trumpeted by at least five newspapers, who claimed that nearly three hundred pioneers were massacred by two thousand Sioux and Cheyenne Indians. That story started with an Oregon newspaper, spread around the country, and was accepted as fact until finally someone figured out that the entire story was fraudulent and that there had been no unfriendly Indians within miles of the alleged massacre site for at least a year. In fact, by 1850 many Indians were staying away from heavily traveled trails for fear of catching diseases from the settlers. Most had little interest in engaging with settlers, let alone trying to kill them or steal their goods.[26]

In December 1853 Secretary of the Interior Robert McClellan reported to Congress that problems with Indians along the Oregon Trail were "comparatively small." He added, "By kind, humane, and just treatment, their condition may be improved, and the hostile feelings so often manifested by them, and so frequently engendered by a mischievous course of conduct on the part of the whites, and the dereliction of duty of public officers, may be subdued." McClellan goes on to say that it is useless to attempt conciliation with the tribes by "coercion, oppression, and injustice."[27]

Attitudes toward Indians were not uniform among white officers and settlers, and the tribes did have some friends among the newcomers to the Pacific Northwest. Many army officers and soldiers were sympathetic to their situation and abhorred the treatment dished out by white settlers and members of volunteer militias. One such soldier was August Kautz, a German American who spoke out against the tragic and illegal treatment of Chief Leschi in western Washington Territory. For a brief time in 1858 he published a newspaper, the *Truth Teller,* in which he countered the belligerent tone of Washington Territory's newspaper of record, the *Pioneer and Democrat*, published in Olympia.[28] At midcentury, before George Wright's 1858 expedition, military leaders such as Generals Ethan Allen Hitchcock and John Wool frequently voiced objection to U.S. Indian policy in the Northwest. Hitchcock, a son of Vermont like Wright, was a strong critic of fraud and corruption in U.S. dealings with Indian tribes. He spent a good deal of time with tribes across the country and later wrote extensively about Indian culture.[29] In 1844 William T. Sherman suggested that the white race deserved to be cursed for "not protecting the Cherokees."[30] In 1853, while serving in Oregon Territory, Capt. Ulysses S. Grant wrote a letter to his wife in which he expressed a sentiment common with many military men in the Pacific Northwest: "It is really my opinion that the whole race would be harmless and peaceable if they were not put upon by the whites."[31]

A CHANGE IN PERSPECTIVE

In 1847 the Whitman massacre brought national attention to the region and served to fuel anti-Indian sentiments. Measles had been decimating the tribes along the Columbia, and Cayuse and Umatilla warriors, believing Dr. Marcus Whitman was spreading the disease, attacked the mission, killing Whitman, his wife, and eleven others.[32] In June 1850, in Oregon City, Oregon Territory, five Cayuse Indians were sentenced to be executed for their alleged role in the attack. One witness later said that the captives asked to be shot rather than hanged, since "to die by the rope was to die as a dog and not as a man." Joseph Meek was the territorial marshal directed to carry out the executions, which he did with enthusiasm, since his daughter had been taken captive by the Cayuse during the attack on the mission. While an Indian captive, she died of the measles and forever after Meek blamed the Cayuses. Later, Meek asserted that the chief, Ki-am-i-sumpkin, "begged me to kill him with my knife, for an Indian fears to be hanged—but I soon put an end to his entreaties by cutting the rope which held the drop, with my tomahawk." Meek gained some satisfaction in the executions:

> As I said, "The Lord have mercy on your souls," the trap fell, and the five Cayuses hung in the air. Three of them died instantly. The other two struggled for several minutes; the little chief, *Tam-a-has,* the longest. It was he who was cruel to my little girl at the time of the massacre; so I just put my foot on the knot to tighten it, and he got quiet. The victims dangled in their nooses for thirty-five minutes, then [were] taken down and buried.[33]

In 1848 Oregon Territory was established, in part to provide a more formal political structure with which to defend settlements from further Indian attacks like the one at the Whitman Mission. In 1850 the Donation Land Claim Act was passed by Congress. It authorized land grants in Oregon Territory, consisting of 320 acres for single white male citizens and 640 acres for married couples. Claims filed after December 1, 1850, were allowed half the previous acreage, and mixed-race people were allowed to file a claim as long as they were no more than half Indian. For married couples, the husband and wife each held half the land in their own names. The segregation and allotment of land was done by the territorial government, and the tribes received no remuneration for land taken from them and given to settlers. The new law attracted more than seven thousand claims.

In early 1851 Secretary of War Winfield Scott ordered Brig. Gen. Ethan Allen Hitchcock to assume command of the army's Pacific Division. Not only was Hitchcock ordered to maintain peace between white settlers and Indians, he was also directed to investigate corruption among federal agents appointed to oversee the welfare of California's tribes. Scott warned Hitchcock that the California legislature viewed the army as useless, either unwilling or unable to suppress the tribes, and that the lawmakers would resist what they would see as Hitchcock's interference in white-Indian affairs. Hitchcock sailed from New York in May 1851, and on July 8 he arrived in Benicia, California, to assume command of military forces in California and Oregon.[34]

General Hitchcock possessed a high intellect and an unceasing sense of curiosity that led him to lengthy ruminations in his journal about life, death, ethics, the nature of the human soul, and numerous other philosophical issues. He often turned to Spinoza for intellectual stimulation but found Plato "tedious." His personal library consisted of over two thousand books, and he paid to have them shipped around Cape Horn to California.[35] Hitchcock was fascinated by the philosophical questions and problems raised by the study of ethics, and he frequently lamented the ill-treatment of Indians by whites. Unfortunately for the tribes of the west, Hitchcock's tenure there was short. The presidential election of 1852 pitted Winfield Scott against Franklin Pierce, who had once been Scott's subordinate. Pierce was politically aligned with Jefferson Davis, and when Pierce won the election, he installed Davis in Scott's position as secretary of war. Davis in turn replaced Hitchcock in early 1854 with Gen. John Wool.

Those hoping for a more aggressive stance toward Indians were disappointed with General Wool, since his attitude toward the tribes was much like his predecessor's. Thus, at least along the Pacific Coast, the army's blame for white-Indian violence continued to fall primarily on settlers, miners, and ranchers, rather than on Indians. In February 1854 Wool directed Wright, who was still the commander at Fort Reading, to "cultivate a good understanding with Indian tribes . . . but promptly to chastise those who commit depredations or hostilities."[36]

John Wool was born in 1784, and by the time of his death in 1869 he had earned a reputation as a remarkable officer and, like Hitchcock, a man of great intellect. One soldier who served under him described him as a "small, neat man with violet-colored eyes. These I noticed above all the glitter of his uniform or that of his staff."[37] Indeed, Wool had considerable "glitter," as he was a veteran of the War of 1812 and the Mexican-American War. He would serve in the army for fifty-one years, retiring at the age of seventy-nine. He could, at times, display a quick temper that matched that of his political rival in the Northwest, Washington territorial governor Isaac Stevens. During the 1850s they exchanged venomous letters, and neither would hesitate to sharply criticize the other in official correspondence. While Isaac Stevens focused on expansion of U.S. interests into the Pacific Northwest—and many would say, his own career—Wool had a considerably broader perspective and much more experience.[38] Decades earlier, in 1816, he had been appointed inspector general of the army, a position that included responsibility for assessing readiness at military posts. In 1819 he objected to the emphasis on engineering at West Point, writing that great military victories "were not achieved by the 'rule and compass' or the 'measurement of angles.' They were the product of enlarged minds, highly cultivated and improved by a constant and accurate survey of human events."[39] Wool's advocacy of "enlarged minds, highly cultivated" was exemplified in his attitude toward Indians, which was much more sympathetic than that of any other prominent figure in the Pacific Northwest, especially Isaac Stevens. Although Wool was besieged by criticism from Stevens and newspapers in the Northwest, he had more than his share of admirers elsewhere. In 1854 Congress passed a resolution requesting that President Pierce "cause a sword with suitable devices to be presented to General Wool" as a representation of the high regard in which Congress held him.[40]

"MOST TRYING CIRCUMSTANCES"

In 1849 oversight of the Bureau of Indian Affairs was shifted from the Department of War to the Department of the Interior. For seven years after the change, Commissioners of Indian Affairs Luke Lea and George Manypenny sought to separate Indians from whites using a system of reservations. In November 1851 Commissioner Lea presented his annual report to Congress in which he said that the Indian possessed "all the powers, instincts, and sympathies which appertain to his white brother."[41] Lea's remarks a year later to Congress provide an example of shifting attitudes often exhibited by politicians and military personnel. In this case, it was a change for the worse. In his 1852 report, he said, "When civilization and barbarism are brought in such relation that they cannot coexist together, it is right that the superiority of the former should be asserted and the latter compelled to give way."[42]

George Manypenny, the next commissioner of Indian affairs, addressed Congress in November 1856. Tension had been increasing between whites and Indians in the Pacific Northwest, and Isaac Stevens, among others, was vociferous in his attacks on those whites who he believed were protecting Indians at the settlers' expense. While Stevens was concerned about the welfare of whites, Manypenny pointed out something that was obvious to the tribes: laws intended to protect the Indians and their property were "sadly defective." Speculators disregarded Indians' rights and in many cases cheated them out of property. Manypenny went further, saying,

> Trespasses and depredations of every conceivable kind have been committed on the Indians. They have been personally maltreated, their property stolen, their timber destroyed, their possession encroached upon, and divers other wrongs and injuries done them. Notwithstanding all which they have afforded a praiseworthy example of good conduct, under the most trying circumstances.[43]

Washington territorial governor Isaac Stevens seized the opportunity to try to consummate treaties with Northwest tribes. He had long complained that the army was not aggressive enough in dealing with the Indian problem, and he overlooked or sometimes even praised actions by the volunteer militias, no matter how brutal.[44] The treaty system gave him a chance to remove Indians from land desired by whites, and it gave him an opportunity to promote himself in the Northwest and Washington, D.C.

Stories relating positive relations between Indians and settlers were often buried in newspaper rhetoric, which regularly endorsed and amplified the views of politicians espousing quick relocation of the tribes. For example, during the early years of Euro-American westward migration, the Walla Walla Indians were both wary and welcoming of newcomers. In 1843 a young woman and her parents on their way west rested four miles from the Whitman Mission, then moved a few miles away to Old Fort Walla Walla, at Wallula. When they were ready to continue their journey westward, a representative of the Hudson's Bay Company "suggested that they leave their cattle and horses for the winter in the care of the Walla Walla Indians. This they did and all were returned to them the following spring in good condition."[45]

General Wool was responsible for policing an area nearly twice the size of Great Britain, at times with fewer than a thousand troops, but never with more than eighteen hundred. His men had to deal with mountain ranges, wild rivers, deserts, incessant rain and windstorms, bad communication, and high expenses. Living quarters were inadequate and in many cases provided little protection against bitter cold and blazing heat. Perhaps most challenging of all, politicians and newspaper editors seemed determined to create as much conflict as possible not only between white settlers and the tribes, but also between the army and the local white population. The region's newspapers sparked and inflamed the collective narrative that trumpeted the inferiority of Indians. The theme was clear and direct: Indians were subhuman. In October 1855 the *Portland Weekly Oregonian* asserted that "these inhuman butchers and bloody fiends must be met and conquered, vanquished—yes, EXTERMINATED; or we can never hope for, or expect peace, prosperity, or safety."[46] The result, as noted by historian Robert Utley, was that "in California and Oregon rationalizations were rarely contrived; the Indians were simply annihilated."[47] Despite the intentions of officers like Wool, other people in high places—like Washington's Governor Stevens—were able to gain public support for positions that involved little consideration for the tribes.

By the mid-1850s the tribes felt they had been deceived, and they had suffered bloodshed at the hands of the militia and army. With a few exceptions, they had shown restraint and patience. Their patience would receive one of its greatest tests at the Walla Walla Treaty Council of 1855.

FOUR

"The Grand Blunder"

Mr. Stevens has them right under his thumb—they are afraid as death of him and do just as he tells them.

MARGARET STEVENS, WIFE OF ISAAC STEVENS

The Walla Walla Treaty Council of 1855 was one in a series of incidents that sent tremors across the Columbia Plateau, and for many people in the Northwest tragedy quickly followed. George Gibbs had lived and worked with the tribes since his arrival in Washington Territory in 1853 and frequently acted as an interpreter. A few years after the Plateau War he recalled the events of 1855: "All that summer, rumors came in of the intention of the Indians to break out. . . . Indian women living with white settlers warned their husbands to take care of themselves; but these reports were disregarded, because we had so long slept on the volcano that we did not believe it could burn."[1] The embers of conflict detected by Gibbs were inflamed by Isaac Stevens's 1855 Walla Walla Treaty Council, which set the stage for George Wright's fateful 1858 expedition.

Rumors of uprisings triggered an increase in the army's forces in the Pacific Northwest. At the end of 1854 there were fewer than 400 troops stationed in the region. The following year, Col. Edward Steptoe arrived with two companies of the Third Artillery, joining the Fourth Artillery at Fort Vancouver. By the end of 1855 there were 750 troops in the Northwest located among five posts. Department of the Pacific commander General Wool, concerned about the heated rhetoric coming from newspapers in Portland and Olympia, asked Jefferson Davis for at least six additional companies and the money to place them at various posts. Davis refused, concerned about the expense.

During the 1850s observers began to suggest reservations as a way to "protect" Indians from the spread of white civilization, and humanitarian arguments in favor of reservations appeared with increasing frequency. Government officials began to use the treaty system as a "legal" way to move Indians onto reservations. The success of the treaty system depended in part on the tribes' ignorance of how colonial finance worked. They knew they could sell a horse for seventy-five or a hundred dollars, but what was land worth? To Indians land had never been a commodity or prize that could be sold, and the concept was disconcerting. Making a bad land deal would not cost just a horse or a musket; the Indians' lifeways and culture were at stake. Isaac Stevens saw an opportunity to take political and financial advantage of their inexperience with white culture.

AN AMERICAN NAPOLEON

Isaac Stevens was born in 1818 in Massachusetts, and like George Wright, he was from a New England farming family. When he was born, his head was too big and his legs too small, perhaps from a defect in his pituitary gland. His size would be an issue his entire life, and he was sometimes compared to Napoleon. To Stevens the comparison, often intended as an insult, was a compliment. Although he graduated first in the West Point class of 1839, he did not consider himself particularly intelligent. He once told a friend, "Men like Milton and Napoleon achieved success as a result of hard work and study, not from inherited genius."[2]

Stevens rarely shrank from an argument; in fact, he would be the first into a scrap and the last one out. Stevens worked hard at everything he did, whether languages, engineering, military science, or politics. During the Mexican-American War he, like George Wright, had been decorated for bravery.[3] Stevens and Wright had more in common than New England, West Point, and the Mexican war. Wright's courage matched that of Stevens, as

Isaac Stevens, the first governor of Washington Territory (1853–57) and congressional representative (1857–61). Stevens was killed at the Battle of Chantilly, September 1, 1862. Washington State Historical Society.

did his drive to succeed. However, while Wright strove to be recognized for his sense of duty to God and country, Stevens often seemed more interested in accumulating and using power.

Stevens had been a strong supporter of Franklin Pierce's presidential candidacy, and in 1853 the newly elected president appointed him Washington Territory's first governor. He concurrently held the position of superintendent of Indian affairs for the territory, a job intended to provide protection for the tribes. His political acumen had also led to his appointment as surveyor

Fort Walla Walla, which served as the base for both Steptoe's and Wright's expeditions. Drawing by Gustavus Sohon. From Mullan, *Report on the Construction of a Military Road* (1863), in the author's collection.

to map a northern route for a proposed Pacific railway. Stevens took an overland route to the territory in order to survey the future railroad line, finally assuming his duties as governor in November 1853. Few people questioned the obvious conflict inherent in his mandate to look out for the Indians' best interests while also serving the interests of the railroad. The railroad wanted the land occupied by the tribes, and Stevens set out to move aside and consolidate on reservations any Indian tribes that might hinder his efforts. In addition, some observers saw his position as governor as rife with possible conflicts with his other duties. To Stevens, it just made sense that such important duties be concentrated in the most capable hands.

After spending a few months at his new post in Olympia, Isaac Stevens went back east, where he passed the next eight months gathering political support for his ambitious plans for Washington Territory. Shortly after his return to the Pacific Northwest, he began what would be a blitz lasting just over a year, during which time he consummated fifteen treaties through ten councils, many with the assistance of Joel Palmer, superintendent of Indian affairs for Oregon Territory. By early 1856 they had consummated treaties that called for many of the region's tribes to surrender much of their land in return for annuity payments and other considerations. Notable omissions to the treaties included the Spokane, Palouse, and Coeur d'Alene tribes; their turn would come later, with Colonel Wright. One of the most controversial councils was held in present-day southeastern Washington.[4]

In May 1855 Stevens and Palmer requested that chiefs of the inland tribes meet with them for a treaty council in the Walla Walla Valley, a broad, fertile valley that could be blistering hot. The ultimate objective was to extinguish the tribes' title to the land and move Indians aside in order to make way for the railroads and settlers. From the standpoint of the territorial and federal governments, the decision had already been made; the treaties were necessary to justify the inevitable transfer of land from Indians to whites.

The *New York Times* ran an editorial in 1855 addressing the violence between Indians and whites across the West, making note of events in the Pacific Northwest and of General Wool's frustration with the actions of the thuggish militias. It asks questions that the treaty process aimed to answer:

> It is for the good and the wise to consider whether the system from which these results flow is the best one for managing the poor remnants of the Aborigines. Extermination may be an effectual mode of preventing all 'agitation' of perplexing Indian questions, and so may be pronounced constitutional and conservative, but is it just, humane, or right? Is there no way of adjusting and concluding this conflict of races except by extirpation of the weaker?[5]

That same year nineteen-year-old Lt. Lawrence Kip wrote that while he was stationed at Fort Dalles, Governor Stevens passed through on his way to Walla Walla for the treaty council. Stevens knew the Indians would be unhappy about his proposals, so he requested an armed guard to meet his party at the council grounds. Kip was one of forty men assigned to the command of

Lt. Archibald Gracie. Their guide was a Cayuse known as Cutmouth John, due to a wound received in a battle with the "Snake Indians," which had left him with "a dreadful distortion of visage."[6] Cutmouth John would prove to be a reliable ally and colorful companion to the soldiers in the coming years, including those on Wright's 1858 expedition.

One of the stops during the five-day journey to Walla Walla was at a Cayuse village. Kip noted that the location was "a beautiful, well-watered valley, which I am not surprised they are unwilling to give up." Kip seems to be acknowledging that the upcoming treaty session would not likely end in the tribes' favor. In fact, all of the tribes on the Columbia Plateau had been on edge since at least 1853, when Capt. George B. McClellan, as part of Stevens's surveying expedition, passed through Yakama territory. Kamiakin's younger brother, Skloom, had met McClellan and learned from him that "a Great Chief from the East (Stevens) would come to buy the Yakima's land and open it to white settlers."[7]

On the evening of May 21 Governor Stevens's party arrived at the treaty grounds, drenched after riding in heavy rain all day. The treaty council was a large undertaking with complex logistics and carefully considered decorum. Stevens had a private tent with a separate "dining room." A wooden arbor had been built nearby, under which stretched a long pine table for guests. While Lieutenants Gracie and Kip had a tent, the soldiers had to construct shelters of pine boughs and try to weatherproof them with pack covers.[8]

On the morning of the 24th, the Nez Perces arrived, making a dramatic impression. They and their mounts were painted and decorated with skins, feathers, beads, and trinkets, making what Kip called a "wild and fantastic appearance." After a ceremonial greeting by a group of chiefs, the rest of the band rode into the council ground, twenty-five hundred of what Kip called "wild warriors of the plains," along with perhaps a hundred women singing, beating drums, and circling Governor Stevens, Superintendent of Indian Affairs Palmer of Oregon, and the humbled army force from Fort Dalles, who stood at "the center of their wild evolutions," according to Lieutenant Kip. "They would gallop up

Arrival of the Nez Perces at the Walla Walla Treaty Council of 1855. Drawing by Gustavus Sohon. Washington State Historical Society.

as if about to make a charge, then wheel round and round, sounding their loud war whoops until they had apparently worked themselves up into an intense excitement."[9]

The next few rain-plagued days were spent resting and waiting for more representatives to appear. On the evening of the 26th, three hundred Cayuses arrived and made camp near the Nez Perces, along with a contingent of Walla Wallas and Umatillas. These tribes were decidedly less friendly than the Nez Perces; their chiefs refused to smoke with Stevens and Palmer.[10] The following morning, the Nez Perces hosted a large church service, with the speaker using the Ten Commandments as a basis for his talk. Kip wrote that their singing "had an exceedingly musical effect." That night, Governor Stevens hosted a dinner for the officers, although he was the only one to have the advantage of a table; the others lounged on the ground around a buffalo hide. The menu was simple, but hearty: beefsteak, potatoes, dense

Chiefs at dinner, Walla Walla Treaty Council. Drawing by Gustavus Sohon, 1855. Washington State Historical Society.

bread, and coffee. Kip noted that because they were so hungry, the plain fare "required no French sauces."[11]

The council was to have lasted less than a week, but as some of the participants were late, the soldiers passed the time socializing with each other and with Indians and exploring the countryside. Some spent a good deal of time at the Nez Perce camp, fascinated by the singing, dancing, and speeches. In total, five thousand Indians attended the Walla Walla conference, including many families, representing primarily Sahaptin-speaking tribes from present-day southeastern Washington and the lower Snake River region: Yakamas, Nez Perces, Walla Wallas, Palouses, and Cayuses, among others, were present. Salish tribes sent observers, including the Spokanes and Kootenais.

On Tuesday, May 29, the council finally began, but it ended in a rainstorm two hours later. James Doty wrote, "Nearly all the

Indians departed immediately but the Chiefs Peopeo-moxmox and Kamiakin remained a short time smoking their own tobacco."[12] The next afternoon, May 30, it began in earnest. Kip described the scene: "Directly in front of Governor Stevens' tent a small arbor had been erected, in which, at a table, sat several of his party taking notes of everything he said. In front of the arbor on a bench sat Governor Stevens and Commissioner Palmer, and before them, in the open air, in concentric semicircles, were ranged the Indians, the chiefs in the front ranks, in the order of their dignity, while the far back ground was filled with women and children. The Indians sat on the ground (in their own words), 'reposing on the bosom of their Great Mother.'"[13] For the balance of that day and most of the next, Stevens and Palmer made speeches focusing on the treaty proposals and the benefits to the tribes. Stevens gave a review of the history of white/Indian relations, starting with the early colonization period, when "the red man received the white man gladly; but after a while difficulties arose; the blood of the red man was spilled and the blood of the white man; there was cold, there was hunger, there was death. . . . It was found that when the white man and the red man lived together on the same ground, the white man got the advantages and the red man passed away."[14]

Over the days of the council, Stevens and Palmer made repeated claims about new homes, farmland, schools, clothing, tools, and so on, all of which would be given to the tribes. They would still be able to hunt buffalo, dig roots, and continue their customs; the treaties would not interfere with their way of life. In fact, when the Blackfeet, the traditional enemy of the Plateau tribes, saw the benefits the treaties created, they would want the same for themselves, thereby leaving the Plateau tribes in peace. For each concern or objection made by a chief, Stevens or Palmer had an answer or rejoinder, assuring the speaker that the government had only their best interests at heart.

It is unclear why Stevens spun a version of events that few chiefs were likely to believe. He may have been so blinded by haste and ambition that he heard what he wanted to hear at the council. Stevens was a highly intelligent man who had spent a good deal of time traveling among the tribes, and he must have understood the effectiveness of their communication network. Not only were northwest tribes in frequent contact with each other, communication with eastern tribes was not unusual. There had been eastern Indians in the region for years, including several at the Walla Walla conference. The Iroquois had been traveling in the area for decades, Plains tribes were frequent visitors, and one of the interpreters at the Walla Walla conference was a Delaware man. Certainly the chiefs knew that in December 1854 Stevens had completed the Medicine Creek treaty council, followed by a six-week stretch of more councils that had not pleased many of the participants. Councils in the western part of Washington Territory had created nine reservations with a total area of just 93 square miles. In contrast, the tribes around Puget Sound gave up 20,000 square miles of land, as well giving up as any recourse should the government fail to live up to its promises.[15] Within a few days of the Medicine Creek treaty many people, white and Indian, felt as if the treaties were unfair and likely to lead to conflict if not amended in the tribes' favor. Word spread over the Cascade Mountains to the Plateau tribes, and by the time the Walla Walla council began, the chiefs were skeptical about Stevens's intentions. Even a young soldier like the observant Lieutenant Kip understood what Stevens's ultimate intent was before the talks started: to take as much of the tribes' land as possible without causing a war. Perhaps the governor hoped that if he persuaded a few key chiefs to agree to the treaty provisions, they would sway the others.[16]

Thursday, May 31, Stevens spoke for two and a half hours, and Palmer spoke for an hour. Apparently they said little of interest to the chiefs, for Doty wrote that they "dispersed quite wearied with the length of the council."[17] That evening the tribes held horse races, which the soldiers found fascinating. "They will ride for miles, often having heavy bets depending on the result. On this occasion we saw nearly thirty Indians start at once and dash over the plain like the winds, sweeping round in a circle of several miles." Some of the horses, Kip noted, were branded with marks that indicated they had been "stolen from the Spaniards in Upper Mexico."[18] It was not unusual for tribes to travel hundreds of miles south in order to trade for horses. The Spanish horses had likely been purchased from tribes in California. In Kip's accounts of the Walla Walla council of 1855 and George Wright's campaign of 1858, he sometimes made side comments that indicated he spent at least a few moments considering the position of the tribes and the irony imbedded in the interactions between white leaders and Indians. At the council, he noted that Palmer gave a long speech that included "an account of the Railroad and Telegraph. It was sufficiently amusing to listen to this scientific lecture . . . but it would have been much more diverting, could we have known the precise impressions left upon the minds of his audience, or have heard them talk it over afterwards in their lodges."[19]

No matter how inept Palmer might have been at communicating with the tribes, it might be that he was trying to connect with them in a way that Stevens did not. By describing the wonders of Euro-American culture, he may have been trying to emphasize the real-world benefits to the tribes. Palmer's attitude toward the tribes varied from sympathetic to scolding, but unlike Stevens he rarely tried to put a positive spin on news that was clearly detrimental to the tribes. Several years earlier, expressing anger toward a white man who had led an attack on an Indian village in Illinois, Palmer said, "Arrests are evidently useless, as no act of a white man against an Indian, however atrocious, can be followed by a conviction."[20]

On Saturday, June 2, the first clear signs of conflict arose when a Cayuse chief made a speech in which his tone was "unfavorable to the reception of the treaty." Sunday was spent resting, and for some, attending religious services. The next day, Monday, June 4, Stevens's and Palmer's patience began to wear thin. The tribal leaders seemed to be in no hurry to agree to the proposed conditions. On June 5, tension increased when Lieutenants Gracie and Kip visited the Cayuse camp. The next evening Kip and Gracie again visited the camp to gauge their mood. "There was no attempt to exclude us," Kip wrote, "though if savage and scowling looks could have killed, we should both have ended our mortal career this evening in this Valley of Walla Walla."[21]

On June 7 Kip took a turn as a scribe during the session, and his journal quotes from the transcript. When Stevens asked to hear from the tribes, Chief Lawyer of the Nez Perce was the first to speak. He spoke of the history of European settlement, beginning with Columbus, having heard the story from missionaries. At the end, he "expressed his approval of the treaty, only urging that the whites should act towards them in good faith." Young Chief, a Cayuse, spoke next, expressing skepticism of the treaty. One of his objections stemmed from his uncertainty about what Stevens's offer really meant: "I walk as it were in the dark," he said, "and cannot therefore take hold of what I do not see." Peopeo-moxmox of the Walla Wallas spoke next. He was a widely respected chief among Indians and some whites, noted for his wisdom and patience. He wanted time to consider the commissioners' words and to meet with Chief Lawyer to discuss the proposal. "I do not know what is straight," he said. "My heart cried when you first spoke to me. I felt as if I was blown away like a feather." He said he wanted to again meet with Stevens, but he suspected what lay ahead: "Stop the whites from coming up here until we have this talk. Let them not bring their axes with them." As all the Indians would soon find out, the chief's words would fall on deaf ears.[22]

UNEASY AGREEMENT

In turn, each chief spoke in a similar vein: they all were deeply unsettled by the thought of giving up or selling parts of their homeland, and they needed time to consider the commissioners' words. Kamiakin of the Yakamas refused to say more than a few curt words expressing his disgust with the proceedings. Palmer and Stevens, beginning to lose patience, gave talks in which they told the chiefs they did not need more time to consider the treaties, insisting that the treaties were more than fair. Both the governor and the superintendent no doubt insulted the chiefs

Chief Lawyer of the Nez Perces, 1855. Drawing by Gustavus Sohon. Washington State Historical Society.

in any number of ways. When the relatively positive approach failed to win supporters, Palmer tried turning attention to the wrongs committed by the tribes. He told the chiefs that Indians had "sometime done wrong," and that as a result, "Our hearts have cried. Our hearts still cry. But if you will try to do right, we will try to forget it."[23]

In another of his asides, Kip noted what was obvious to the chiefs but apparently not to Stevens and Palmer: "These extracts will give a specimen of the kind of 'talk' which went on day after day. All but the Nez Perces were evidently disinclined to the treaty, and it was melancholy to see their reluctance to abandon the old hunting grounds of their fathers and their impotent struggles against the overpowering influence of the whites." At the end of the day's session, Stevens invoked God in order to put pressure on the chiefs: "I do not think God will be angry if you do your best for yourself and your children. Ask yourself this question tonight. Will not God be angry with me if I neglect this opportunity to do them good?"[24]

The next afternoon, Friday, June 8, Kip reported, "It seemed we were getting on charmingly and the end of all difficulties was at hand, when suddenly a new explosive element dropped down into this little political caldron." Nez Perce war chief Looking Glass and twenty warriors rode into camp. Looking Glass "made a short and very violent speech" in which he expressed his anger and disgust at the thought of selling their homeland. On Saturday, June 9, treaty papers were presented for signatures. Looking Glass again "made such a strong speech against the treaty, which had such an effect, that not only the Nez Perce but all the other tribes refused to sign it."[25]

Matters simmered until Monday, June 11, when the chiefs finally signed the documents. For some reason Looking Glass dropped his objection to the treaty. Kip noted that some kind of deal must have been made between Lawyer and Looking Glass, since "we suppose savage nature in the wilderness is the same as civilized nature was in England in Walpole's day, and 'every man has his price.'"[26] While some speculated that a backroom deal must have been made, the coming months would reveal the actual reasons the chiefs suddenly agreed to sign the treaty: few of them believed Stevens's promises, they had no intention of giving up their homeland, and they viewed the treaties as sham transactions. The chiefs turned the table on Stevens; just as he was telling them what he believed they wanted to hear, they ended up doing the same thing. In truth, many of them were willing to buy time and prepare for war. Later, Yakama chiefs Owhi and Teias would tell Colonel Wright that the Walla Walla treaty was forced on them by Stevens, and was a direct cause of hostilities.[27]

In Stevens's mind, all was well—at least for the time being. However, Kip reported that the entire episode was very nearly a disaster for Stevens and the soldiers, since it was learned that the Cayuses had intended to attack and eliminate the armed escort, then attack the undermanned Fort Dalles. According to Kip, the Nez Perces refused to participate, and without their considerable numbers, the plan was unlikely to succeed.[28]

BETRAYAL

On June 29, 1855, the *Olympia Pioneer and Democrat* inaccurately announced the "ratification of treaties" at the Walla Walla council. In the same issue a public statement signed by Isaac Stevens and Joel Palmer asserted, "By an express provision in the treaty, the country embraced in the cessions and not included in the reservations, is open to settlement, excepting that the Indians are secured in the possession of their buildings and improvements till removed to the reservation." The newspaper announcement, which appeared numerous times during 1855, was in direct contradiction to Article 11 of the treaty: "This treaty shall be obligatory on the contracting parties as soon as the same shall be ratified by the President and Senate of the United States."[29] The deadline for ratification was unclear, and at the time Stevens and Palmer had no reason to believe it would happen anytime soon. In fact, the treaties would not be ratified until 1859, by which time the protections they afforded had been eroded by illegal settlement and incursions by military forces.[30]

Concurrent with the Indian homelands being opened for settlement, Stevens ran another announcement, entitled "Claims for Damages by Indians."[31] It set forth a procedure for white citizens to file claims for reimbursement for damages caused by Indians. The document set forth not only the steps to file a claim, but also outlined the consequences for the alleged perpetrator:

"Whenever directed by him, a demand will be made by the superintendent, agent, or sub-agent, upon the nation or tribe to which the Indian or Indians committing the injury belonged for satisfaction." If the tribe or nation did not respond in a "reasonable time, not exceeding twelve months . . . further steps may be taken as shall be proper, in the opinion of the President, to obtain satisfaction for the injury."[32]

Several aspects of this process stand out, and in 1858 the incongruities would be played out by George Wright. The first is the assertion that a "nation or tribe" is responsible for the actions of a member. The same did not apply to non-Native groups. Second, no process was set forth for the assessment of guilt or innocence of the targeted party. The sworn statement of the victim was enough to establish guilt, unless the accused could produce proof of innocence. In other words, when it came to alleged property damage or theft, Indians were assumed to be guilty unless proven otherwise. Third, no laws were established to allow Indians due process, and the concept of what was "proper" for a transgression was typically left up to the army, or worse, the territorial militias. Thus, George Wright, or any other commander, could draw from a wide range of punishments based on opinion, rather than law.

In 1858, three years after the Walla Walla council, General Wool asked Capt. T. J. Cram to complete a topographical memoir of the Department of the Pacific. Cram's observations and conclusions strayed beyond what was typical of topographical memoirs, which may well be because Wool wanted to advance his criticism of Stevens.[33] Cram believed that the treaty council was doomed from the start. When the Indians made their ceremonial entrance, they were greeted by Stevens and other men who were road weary and, according to Cram, "shabby, diminutive, and mean in appointments generally, and deficient in all those points of show, in particular, that are so well calculated to strike the fancy or command the respect of an Indian." The small escort of soldiers were mounted on "lame, gaunt horses and mules." The assembled Indians saw Stevens and his cohort as weak and disrespectful. Cram observed, "No disinterested witness to the proceedings believed that a single chief signed that treaty with the slightest possible intention of abiding it."[34]

In July 1855, fresh after what he viewed as the successful Walla Walla Treaty Council, Stevens traveled east into present-day western Montana and completed a treaty with the Flathead (Bitterroot Salish), Pend Oreille, and Kootenai tribes. For purposes of the treaty, Stevens consolidated the tribes' interests into one, appointing Chief Victor of the Flathead tribe as head of all three tribes. As with the other treaties, none of the tribes was happy with the outcome, and the Kootenais later claimed their representative's signature on the treaty was forged.[35] As in other treaty sessions, Stevens grouped the tribes together by geographical proximity, ignoring cultural differences. For example, while the Flatheads and Pend Oreilles spoke Salish dialects, the Kootenais spoke their own language.[36]

In October, east of Fort Benton, Montana Territory, Stevens conducted a council with the Blackfeet. Also in attendance were chiefs of the Nez Perce, Cree, Kootenai, Pend Oreille, and Flathead tribes.[37] When he returned to Olympia in January 1856, he was greeted with thirty-eight cannon shots, one for each state and territory in the Union. A local newspaper reported, "All was joy and gladness on the occasion, and our citizens seemed to look upon him as their deliverer—their hope—in speedily freeing them from Indian hostilities, which for months past has cast such a thick gloom over this portion of our devoted territory." On January 18 Stevens told the Washington legislature that the "war shall be prosecuted until the last hostile Indian is exterminated."[38] His definition of "hostile Indian" was, of course, intended to target any who defied white occupation of their homeland.

In years to come, some of Stevens's correspondence carried tones of both defensiveness and self-congratulation. Three years after the Walla Walla treaties, he wrote to his old friend Col. J. W. Nesmith of Oregon, who was then superintendent of Indian affairs for Washington and Oregon Territories:

> I feel well acquainted with the Interior Tribes of Washington including the Nez Perces, Cayuses and Walla Wallas, common to Oregon

> & Washington, and I am satisfied that they will be gratified with the Treaties. I still believe, after all the opportunities I have had to study the question, that they are well adapted to the Indians and do justice both to the Indians and to the Government. In making the Treaties, I did not endeavor to drive a bargain, but proposed to do what was just, as between the two races.[39]

Less than a month earlier, in May 1858, he had given the same message to the U.S. House of Representatives. By then an elected representative of Washington Territory, Stevens reported that the 1855 treaty council had ended with "a cordial farewell on all sides." He claimed that Kamiakin "parted from me in the most cordial manner, expressing the utmost satisfaction at the results of the treaty."[40] There are no records that indicate that other officials, Indian or white, agreed with him.

"SUMMARY JUSTICE"

While Stevens was east of the Rockies, violent incidents on the Columbia Plateau increased tension and bitterness between Indians and settlers. In 1855 gold had been discovered in Yakama territory and in the Colville region of present-day Washington state, and miners from the Puget Sound area were heading eastward. After the Walla Walla Treaty Council, the tribes were upset by the talk of their land being opened for settlement. They warned miners to avoid passing through Yakama territory, as their lives would be in danger. Nonetheless, several parties of miners made the attempt, and in separate incidents some were killed by bands of Isle de Pierres and Yakamas.[41]

In September 1855 Indian agent Andrew Bolon heard the news of the miners' deaths from Chief Garry of the Spokanes and immediately headed into the Yakima Valley to investigate. Bolon traveled alone, indicating he felt comfortable with the Yakamas. Although some Indians did not like the agent's strong personality, he had friends among the tribe, including Showaway, Chief Kamiakin's younger brother. Bolon hoped to meet with Kamiakin, but Showaway warned him to turn back or risk his life. Heeding Showaway's advice, Bolon headed south toward what he hoped would be safety, but he was met along the way by a small party of Yakama men, including Mosheel, Showaway's son. Bolon was overpowered and his throat was slit. For years afterward, many whites, including George Wright, incorrectly believed that the Yakama warrior Qualchan had murdered Bolon.

Word of Bolon's murder spread quickly around the Northwest. Since Governor Stevens was on the treaty circuit, acting governor Charles Mason called for volunteers to mount a response. The *Olympia Pioneer and Democrat* called for "summary justice" for the tribes, "instead of going to the trouble to ferret out individual guilty members thereof." The paper demanded that the force sent against the Indians would "teach them such a lesson as will be remembered by them for all time to come."[42] Public sentiment seemed to be firmly on the side of the newspaper when it published an editorial emphasizing the hope that the Yakama tribe should be *"rubbed out—blotted from existence."*[43]

In response to Bolon's murder, Maj. Granville Haller took 105 men and marched north from Fort Dalles toward the Yakima Valley. Sixty miles north of the Columbia River, they met a large force of warriors at Toppenish Creek and fought for three days. Overwhelmed, the expedition struggled back to Fort Dalles. Five of Haller's men had been killed, seventeen wounded, and most of his supplies abandoned. The Indian force included perhaps as many as one thousand men, and the outcome could have been much worse, but the warriors had intended only to repel Haller's force, not to destroy it. Indian tribes tended to engage in occasional skirmishes meant to acquire horses or other property, to retaliate for a perceived wrongs, or to prove a point. They were not used to the scorched-earth tactics used by the army.[44]

Captain Cram's report also took aim at the much-lamented murder of Indian agent Bolon in the Yakima Valley. Although Indians had been accused of murdering miners on their way to the Colville gold fields, Cram found that some of the murdered whites had committed "excesses and outrages of the grossest kinds on the very tribes the proceedings of the [Walla

Walla council] had so much and so recently disturbed." After two investigations, Cram concluded that the Indians' claims that the miners had raped women and girls were true. Bolon had not only dismissed the Indian claims, he had also threatened the tribes with the might of the U.S. government.[45]

PEOPEO-MOXMOX

In October 1855 Indian agent Nathan Olney set out from The Dalles with five hundred dollars in silver as the first payment stipulated by the June treaty. He arrived at Old Fort Walla Walla in mid-October and sent for Chief Peopeo-moxmox.[46] The Walla Walla chief sent an angry reply, saying he had repudiated the treaty and wanted neither money nor gifts from the government. (Peopeo-moxmox's son had been murdered by whites while in California, which had hardened the chief's feelings toward all whites.) Fearing an attack, the Indian agents, the resident Hudson's Bay Company personnel, and a few settlers decided to abandon the fort. They dumped stockpiled arms and ammunition in the Columbia River and headed to Fort Dalles. The retreat of Agent Olney and his party encouraged the Indians to take cattle belonging to settlers. They also plundered and burned several houses and the old fort. Joining the Walla Wallas in the raids were Yakamas, Palouses, Cayuses, and Umatillas.

The governor of Oregon Territory, George Curry, mounted a swift response. In early November 1855 he ordered Col. J. W. Nesmith and his militia to leave the Yakima Valley and head to Fort Walla Walla, where two more companies of volunteers would meet him. In the meantime, Maj. Mark Chinn took a force to the Umatilla Mission to wait for reinforcements. Three companies were sent from Fort Dalles to support him, accompanied by Lt. Col. James K. Kelly, who would command the combined forces. Colonel Nesmith sent a request for two howitzers to district commander Maj. Gabriel Rains and General Wool, but was denied. Wool was convinced that the militia campaign was unnecessary, inflammatory, and would only result in numerous deaths and wasteful government expenditures. At the time, regular army troops were stationed at Puget Sound, Fort Vancouver, and Fort Dalles, with a modest force at the Cascades Rapids on the Columbia River, and Wool believed there was little chance of an Indian attack until spring. Even then, he believed the odds of an attack were slim, since there had been few incidents to incite violence on the part of the tribes.

Wool believed that Governor Curry should call off the militia, and he refused to supply the desired howitzers or any other support. George Wright and the Ninth Infantry were en route to Fort Vancouver and would arrive in a few months. If a military operation was necessary, Wool wanted Wright to lead it, so there was no need for a volunteer militia to complicate and inflame the situation. Regardless of Wool's preference, while the regular army remained at Forts Vancouver and Dalles, the militia soldiered on, disregarding the dangers of a winter campaign. The November weather had turned colder, and Colonel Nesmith reported, "Many of the men were frost-bitten on the late expedition, and can hardly be said to be fit for duty."[47] Only a quarter of their horses were healthy, and half the command wanted to go home. Nesmith reported great suffering due to the weather, since they were short of tents and warm clothing. By the end of November more than 500 volunteer soldiers and officers had gathered at Fort Henrietta, fifteen miles south of the Columbia River in northern Oregon, and Kelly decided to move quickly. Major Chinn took 150 men to the mouth of the Touchet River across the border in Washington Territory, and Colonel Kelly took a force of 200 and moved up the Touchet. As he approached a hill, Indians appeared. Chief Peopeo-moxmox left the group and rode toward Kelly, waving a white flag. A large force of Indians appeared over the hill behind Peopeo-moxmox and stopped. Agent Olney was called forward to meet with the Walla Walla chief. A conference was held, after which it was agreed the parties would retire to a nearby Walla Walla village. Some of the officers wanted to proceed immediately to the village while feelings were calm, thinking they would have the entire local population at their mercy if anyone started a fight. Olney and Kelly decided the army would

Chief Peopeo-moxmox, 1855. Drawing by Gustavus Sohon. Washington State Historical Society.

wait until morning to continue the parley, and they set up camp, holding Peopeo-moxmox and a few other Indians as hostages.

As was the case with many militia operations, discipline was poor and behavior sometimes violent. Most of the volunteers were ordinary farmers, ranchers, and miners who had banded together to eliminate the Indians. They were tired of the cold and snow. What little food they had was of poor quality, and many of the men wanted to shoot the hostages and go home. Peopeo-moxmox and the other hostages, hearing the angry cries to kill them, began to shout to Indians who had approached within earshot. An uneasy night passed. Sunrise revealed a large number of Indians encircling the camp, concerned for the safety of their chief and other hostages. Hoping to buy time for his people to pack and flee, Peopeo-moxmox told Kelly he would instruct his force of warriors to withdraw. Shots were exchanged, and hope for a peaceful resolution evaporated.

Over the next several days, the militia fought the Palouse and Walla Walla Indians with hit-and-run attacks ranging over ten miles of terrain. After the fighting, Peopeo-moxmox allegedly tried to grab one of the soldier's guns, and he was struck hard enough to knock him unconscious. A number of soldiers then shot him from close range. The soldiers then cut off his hands, gouged out his eyes, cut off his ears, and flayed his skin. Some militia members were appalled, one of whom noted that the killing of Peopeo-moxmox was "nothing short of murder."[48] The fate of Peopeo-moxmox was remembered as a troubling event not only by Indians, but also by some whites. In 1917 one pioneer woman, Elizabeth Ann Coone, recalled hearing of the murder as a child: "Some of the volunteer soldiers from our neighborhood had brought back razor straps made out of his hide. His ears were cut off and pickled and brought back as trophies by one of the neighbors."[49] One report claimed that some of the chief's body parts were later displayed in settlers' homes in Oregon.[50]

Details of the gruesome debacle with the Walla Wallas spread quickly around the region, with the tribes along the lower Columbia and up the Yakima Valley hearing the news within a few days. As the news traveled, anger and fear continued to build, and some members of the generally peaceful tribes began to talk of taking action. The missionary Father Eugene Casimir Chirouse wrote to General Wool complaining of the volunteers' actions and warning of further trouble: "The volunteers are without discipline, without order, and like madmen. . . . Everyday they run off horses and cattle of the friendly Indians. I will soon be no longer able to restrain them." The volunteers did not stop, and Father Chirouse's words proved to be prophetic.[51]

ECHOES

The Walla Walla Treaty Council of 1855 resulted in many of the Walla Walla, Umatilla, Cayuse, Yakama, and Nez Perce people being forced onto reservations that, to one degree or another, still exist today. The Umatilla, Walla Walla, and Cayuse tribes gave up more than 6 million acres in exchange for 250 thousand acres located in northeastern Oregon. Later legislation reduced the total reservation to 172 thousand. Today, they are known as the Confederated Tribes of the Umatilla Indian Reservation.[52]

In south-central Washington, a total of fourteen tribes and bands of native people ceded more than 11 million acres and were consolidated on the Yakama reservation, consisting of 1.2 million acres. They include the Yakamas, Klickitats, Wenatchis, Wishrams, and others.[53]

In 1877 the Nez Perce people were ordered to move onto the reservation created for them. While some did, Chief Joseph's Wallowa band fled and were pursued nearly twelve hundred miles by Gen. Oliver O. Howard and more than two thousand soldiers. When Joseph and his surviving people surrendered, they were exiled to Oklahoma for eight years, then removed to the Colville reservation in north-central Washington, where some descendants still live. Today the Nez Perce reservation consist of 750 thousand acres in north central Idaho. There are approximately 3,500 enrolled members.[54]

In 1879, two years after the defeat of Chief Joseph's Nez Perces, the chief appeared before a full house of Congress and explained why he and his people had decided to fight against the army. He spoke of his father, Joseph, who had attended the Walla Walla Treaty Council in 1855. The younger Joseph told Congress that Governor Stevens said that "the Indians should have a country set apart for them, and in that country they must stay." He added, "My father, who represented his band, refused to have anything to do with the council, because he wished to be a free man. He claimed that no man owned any part of the earth, and a man could not sell what he did not own." As the elder Joseph lay dying, he said to his son, "You must stop your ears whenever you are asked to sign a treaty selling your home. . . . Never sell the bones of your father and your mother." The younger Joseph said that he "pressed [his] father's hand and told him I would protect his grave with my life."[55]

The Nez Perce Trail Foundation is working to post interpretive information along the route of the army's 1877 fight with the Nez Perce. Paul Wapato, former chairman (and current board member) of the foundation, notes that in part, the Nez Perce War was one result of the promises and lies of the 1855 Walla Walla Treaty Council: "The army, with George Wright's march, and later, the Nez Perce War, was trying to control the 'savages.' They just didn't think we were human, like they were."[56]

In 1867 President Andrew Johnson signed an executive order establishing a reservation for the Coeur d'Alene tribe, covering some of their ancestral land in the Idaho Panhandle. The tribe was unaware of the order until 1871, at which time they protested the boundaries. In 1873 President Ulysses S. Grant signed an executive order establishing a reservation of 600,000 acres; in turn, the tribe relinquished 2.4 million acres. More land was relinquished in 1887, and agreements reached in 1887 and 1889 resulted in further changes to the boundaries. A series of lawsuits over the following decades resulted in yet more boundary adjustments, as well as compensatory payments to the tribe. As of 2014 the Coeur d'Alene reservation covers 345 thousand acres, with 2,200 enrolled members.[57]

The Colville reservation, northwest of Spokane, is home to a confederation of twelve tribes, including people with Palouse and Nez Perce heritage. The reservation was first established on April 19, 1872, by the executive order of President Grant. As with many other tribes, there have been boundary adjustments and lawsuits related to U.S. Indian policy mismanagement and disputes over treaty issues and natural resource management.

There are nearly ten thousand enrolled members of the Confederated Tribes of the Colville Reservation.[58]

The Spokane Indian Reservation, between Spokane and the Colville reservation, was created by executive order on January 18, 1881. In March 1887 the Spokanes deeded "all right, title and claim which they had, or ever would have, to any and all lands lying outside the reservation." Despite devastation by disease and violence more than a century ago, today there are more than 2,600 enrolled tribal members, roughly triple their number in the mid-nineteenth century.[59]

FIVE

The Cascades Massacres

The Columbia River is the artery that salmon swim up to reach inland rivers like the Snake, Spokane, and Clearwater, among hundreds of other waterways. In the nineteenth century, adventurers could, with enough time and stamina (and help from a guide), follow the salmon, traveling three hundred miles from the Pacific Ocean to the Snake River, then trekking two hundred more through Walla Walla and Nez Perce country; or they could go north to the Spokane River, then eastward through Spokane country into the heart of the Coeur d'Alene homeland in present-day northern Idaho. Smaller waterways weave across the Columbia Plateau, including the Palouse River, the lifeline for the people of the same name. Before the advent of roads and railways, traveling from the coastal lowlands into the plateau region required a journey up the Columbia River, and that meant braving the Cascades Rapids, the site of tragedy in March 1856.

As voiced in many published histories, the collective narrative calls the violence at the Cascades Rapids the Cascades Massacre. That narrative tells of a band of warriors that attacked a white settlement and killed men, women, and children, in the process engaging in barbaric acts. Certainly, parts of the narrative are true, but it is also true that there was another massacre at the scene, one frequently overlooked.

The Cascades violence against whites presented George Wright the opportunity to conduct the first of his "military tribunals" in the Pacific Northwest, hearings that normally consisted of a few questions followed by a scolding or hanging, or sometimes both. The narrative typically excludes the darker side of

Wright's actions at the Cascades Rapids: that he refused to pursue the white men who had viciously murdered the family of Spencer, an Indian who had accompanied Wright on his journey along the Columbia and was considered a friend of whites.

Something else resulted from the violence at the Cascades: according to Catholic missionary Father Pierre-Jean De Smet, the incident was a contributing factor in the Indians' hostility toward Colonel Steptoe's force two years later in May 1858—the debacle that was the final trigger for Wright's devastating march across the upper plateau.[1]

THE RIVER

Over its 1,200-mile length, the Columbia collects water from a region larger than France.[2] Near the end of its path to the ocean, 180 miles from the Pacific, the flow channels into a gorge four miles long and in places just a few hundred yards wide, churning with what Father De Smet called "irresistible impetuosity over rocky reefs and prostrate ruins," and forming what became known as the Cascades of the Columbia.[3] With imposing cliffs seeming to press down on the rapids, a dearth of sun, and the presence of numerous Indian mausoleums, the Cascades could be a gloomy, frightening place.

The Cascades Rapids were located at the midpoint of the eighty-mile stretch between The Dalles, in northeastern Oregon, and Fort Vancouver, in southwestern Washington Territory. Hills and bluffs rise above The Dalles, and the area experiences blistering summers and winters that can bring high winds, ice, rain, and snow. As one journeys downstream from The Dalles, the climate becomes more temperate and the landscape more lush, first with stands of pine and sagebrush, then, approaching the Cascades Rapids, mountainsides thick with fir and cedar standing over thickets of berry bushes and ferns. Closer to Fort Vancouver, across the Columbia from Portland, the cliffs recede from the river, allowing it to broaden and flow more gently along meadow-topped banks and around sandy islands. The river pushes westward until the current surges against the Pacific, creating sometimes mountainous, ship-swamping swells.

Viewed from far above, the Cascades Rapids appear to be a great wound in the Cascade Mountains, as if they had been slashed with a knife. The turbulent stretch was a reminder of the great glacial floods, when waves from the east came pounding over boulders and thundering through narrow passages, creating and destroying islands, sandbanks, and side channels. Like the river, the shore was frequently in motion, the movement sometimes barely noticeable—erosion by rain and wind—but sometimes change occurred with great force. In springtime, it was not unusual for floods to rip away chunks of shoreline and anything on them including, in the early years of settlement, buildings. Massive landslides sometimes changed the river's current and created new rapids.[4]

The rapids were home to a tribe Lewis and Clark called the Shahalas.[5] Culturally, they were part of the Chinookan peoples that ranged from the mouth of the Columbia to the Cascades and included tribes living along tributaries of the Columbia, such as the Klickitats. The tribes from the Pacific to the Cascades spoke Chinook dialects, while the Klickitats spoke a Sahaptin-based dialect related to that spoken by the Yakamas and Nez Perces. Lewis wrote of some subgroups of the Shahalas, including the Yhehuhs (upper rapids), the Clahclellahs (along or at the bottom end of the rapids), and the Watlalas (just below the rapids). These tribes, together with several other subgroups, became known generally as the Cascade Indians.[6]

Lewis's journal entries for late October and early November 1805 contain numerous comments about visits to villages along the river just above the rapids. Men in the expedition shared meals with local families; traded for roots, fish, dogs, and other goods; and in most cases, were well received.[7] Arriving at the home of the principal of the Chillickittequaw (Hood River) people, located a few miles above the rapids, Lewis wrote, "He received us very kindly, and set before us pounded fish, filbert nuts, the berries of the Sacacommis, and white bread made of roots."[8] During their return trip, Lewis reported trouble with an

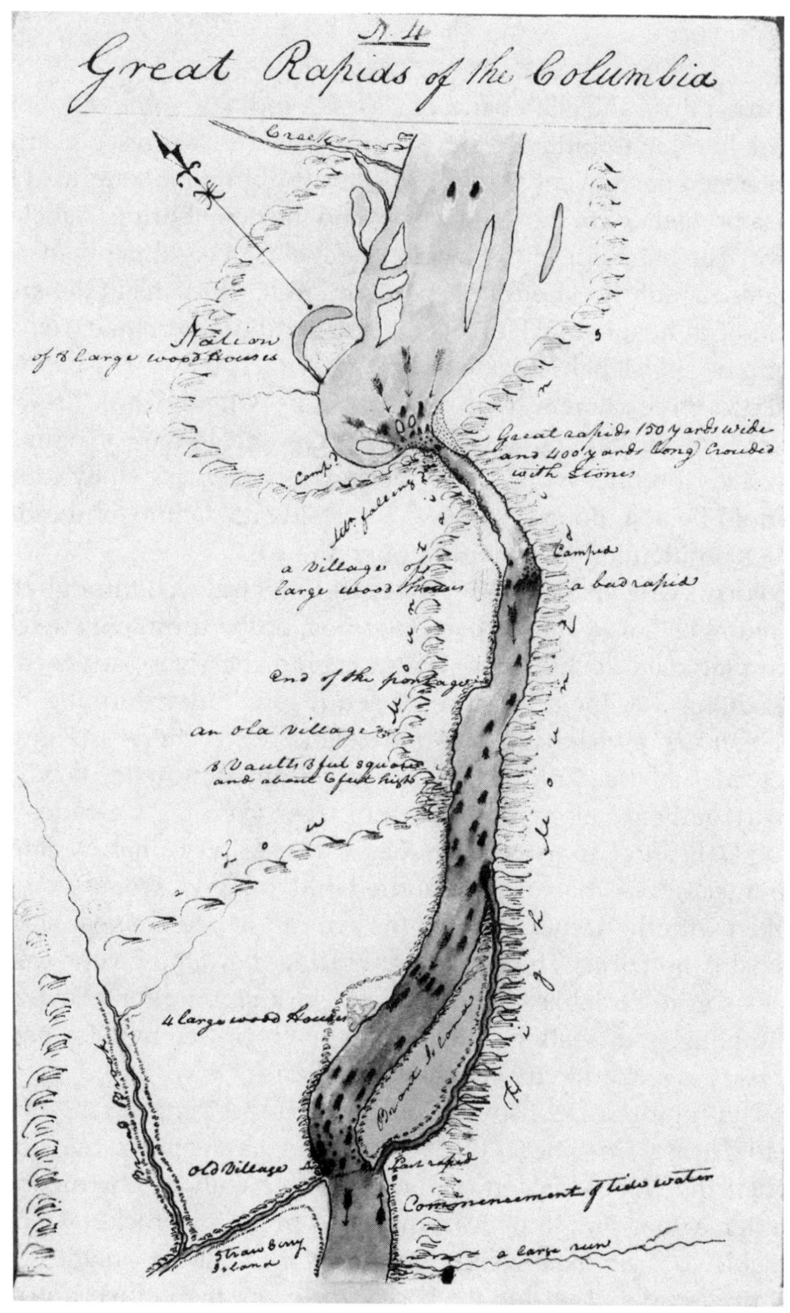

William Clark's map of the Cascade Rapids showing the location of Indian settlements. (The island shown as Brant Island on Clark's map is Bradford's Island on Rosebush's *Frontier Steel* map, p. 98). Today Bradford's Island is part of the Bonneville Dam complex. Courtesy of the Missouri History Museum, St. Louis. Voorhis journal 4, Capt. W. Clark's ms., notes, tables, etc., Lewis and Clark's Journey, p. 4. NS 26834.

unfriendly Wahclellah band of Cascade Indians, some of whom took his Newfoundland dog, Seaman. The dog was rescued after an armed party went after the miscreants, but theft continued to be a problem with the Wahclellahs and the neighboring Clahclellahs. The behavior of the tribal bands who lived along the Cascades Rapids stood out to Lewis, since other Indians in the area had been hospitable. However, the expedition did make friends with a Clahclellah chief who, along with some of his people, helped the explorers bypass the rapids.[9] William Clark drew a sketch of the rapids, noting the villages and lodges of Indians on the shoreline. Within a few years the homes drawn by Clark would be abandoned, many of the residents victims of the frequent epidemics that swept through the area.

Forty years later, in 1846, Father De Smet traveled through the Columbia Gorge, taking particular note of the turbulent stretch. He marveled at the scene, writing about the river "advancing headlong . . . for a distance of about four miles; forming the dangerous, and indeed last remarkable obstruction—the great cascades of the Columbia."[10] People from hundreds of miles away gathered along the stretch of river from the Cascades to The Dalles to harvest salmon. On one occasion Father De Smet counted more than eight hundred Indians and seemed quite taken with the scene. "All that the eye can see, or the nose smell is fish," he wrote. The gatherings during the salmon runs were a reason to socialize: "This is their glorious time for rejoicing, gambling, and feasting. . . . The long lent is passed by; they have at last assembled in the midst of abundance."[11]

The rapids were a special place for native people. One man told Father De Smet, "Our grandfathers remember the time when the waters passed here quietly and without obstruction, under a long range of towering and projecting rocks, which, unable to bear their weight any longer, crumbled down, thus stopping up and raising the bed of the river; then it overflowed the great forests of cedar and pine, which are still to be seen above the cascades." De Smet noted the presence of trees standing in deep water and wrote, "No person, in my opinion, can form a just idea of the cause that produced these remarkable changes without admitting the Indian narrative." Later work by geologists confirmed that, indeed, there have been several major landslides, with the most recent occurring in about 1450. In addition, that part of the river was sacred, and several small islands served as homes for the dead. Father De Smet reported that bodies were placed on scaffolds or in huts made of cedar as protection from the elements. "Great care is taken to hinder birds of prey, or the rapacious wolves, with their hyena stomachs and plundering propensities, from breaking in upon the abode of the dead," he wrote.[12] Later emigrants would visit the largest of the burial places, a cemetery on the north bank of the river. In 1843 one reported that "the bones of hundreds were heaped together in pens," and in 1851, "skulls and other bones of all sizes and ages [lay] scattered about, the wagon crushing them as it passed along."[13] In 1852 one pioneer wrote,

> On our way down we passed a pile of human bones that had been thrown out of a shanty that, I suppose, had been built for a vault. Perhaps they were the remains of Indians who had died in the contagious fever of 1839. The bones were scattered all around—skulls, backbones, thighbones, and pelvis in high profusion. Alas, the poor Indian! Not even his bones are allowed the rest of the grave, but are knocked about with the utmost contempt, and of the once powerful tribe of the Cascades but few now remain, the remnant of a mighty race.[14]

SETTLEMENT

The Cascades were a busy place. During the years 1843–55, approximately twenty-two thousand emigrants passed through the Columbia Gorge. According to historian John Unruh, "For all practical purposes the Oregon trail ended at The Dalles of the Columbia River. From that point it was necessary to travel by water down the treacherous Columbia, portaging around the Cascades, to Fort Vancouver, Portland, or Oregon City."[15] The trip involved hiring Indian guides and boatmen or using one

Desecrated burial lodge on the Columbia River near Cascade Rapids. The destruction of burial lodges by emigrant parties usually occurred by accident but, at times, intentionally. The desecration of these sacred places angered the tribes and increased tension along the Columbia. From "A Curious Indian Burial Place," the *Cosmopolitan* (January 1899), in the author's collection.

of the commercial services running from The Dalles to the Cascades. High winds funneling through the gorge frequently made boat travel treacherous even over the most benign stretches, and travelers would have to encamp on the bank and wait for better conditions, sometimes traveling at night when the winds died down. The forty-mile trip from The Dalles to the Cascades portage could take two weeks, depending on conditions and the availability of guides. The trip required immense fortitude, courage, and luck. In 1847, before the construction of a wooden railroad, one woman made the following diary entries:

> November 18: My husband is sick. It rains and snows. We start this morning around the falls with our wagon. We have 5 miles to go. I carry my babe and lead, or rather carry another through the snow,

> mud, and water almost to my knees. . . . When I got here [lower Cascades] I found my husband lying in Welch's wagon, very sick. . . . I have not told half we suffered. I am not adequate to the task. Here was some hundreds camped, waiting for boats to come and take them down the Columbia to Vancouver or Portland or Oregon City.[16]

During high water the journey required a portage of two-and-a-half miles, and in late summer, the dry season when more rocks were exposed, the detour became five miles. In 1851 a crude railway was constructed to bypass the rapids. At the upper landing, cargo would be offloaded from steamboats and put into wood carts, then pulled over wood rails to the lower landing, where another steamboat would pack travelers and cargo for the trip downriver to Fort Vancouver, Portland, or Oregon City. For journeys upstream, after enduring the portage, passengers would board a steamboat—the *Mary* or *Wasco*—and travel another forty miles eastward to Fort Dalles.

In late 1855 brothers Daniel and Putnam Bradford began rebuilding the tram, requiring more workers to live along the Cascades, thus drawing more attention from the tribes in the area. By early 1856 the upper landing had a store, boarding house, blacksmith forge, and livestock corrals.[17] In addition to perhaps ten families of white settlers, about sixty Indians lived in close proximity, remnants of the disease-decimated Cascade tribe.

THE ARRIVAL OF COLONEL WRIGHT

Col. George Wright and ten companies of the Ninth Infantry reached Fort Vancouver in January 1856, and General Wool's orders were waiting for him. Colonel Wright was to promptly assess the military readiness of Forts Vancouver and Dalles and request provisions, horses, and arms as needed; and, as soon as practical, he was to march eastward to establish military posts in the Walla Walla and Yakima Valleys. Wool's instructions were precise and detailed and included maps that noted distances

Settlement at the upper Cascades, near present-day Stevenson, Washington. Photo taken after 1856, possibly in late 1850s. Wasco County [Oregon] Pioneer Association and Columbia Gorge Discovery Center.

between points, suggestions for post locations, and possible river crossings. In addition, Wool ordered Lt. Col. Silas Casey to take two companies north to Fort Steilacoom, on Puget Sound.[18]

Wright's new command reflected his sense of military honor and discipline. Shortly after he arrived at Fort Vancouver, his men began to drill accompanied by bugle calls rather than the usual drums, and they were "smartly turned out in pomponned kepis, full-skirted coats, and epaulettes."[19] Lt. Philip Sheridan, who was already posted at the fort, was impressed with the colonel, later noting that Wright's battle experience and long army tenure had lent him "excellent soldierly qualities" which were to prove "of much benefit in the active campaigns in which, during the following years, he was to participate."[20]

No matter how skilled he might have been in military matters, Colonel Wright was to learn that fighting Indians in the Pacific

Northwest required an ability to maneuver in a volatile political environment—in particular, trying to please General Wool while not alienating Washington territorial governor Stevens. Governor Stevens was vociferous in his demands that volunteer militias take the lead in military actions in Washington, since he believed the army, and in particular General Wool, was incompetent. In a letter to Secretary of War Jefferson Davis dated February 19, 1856, Stevens accused Wool of "signal incapacity," and compared him to "the dog in the manger—[wanting] neither to act himself, nor to let others act."[21] In contrast, Wool was convinced that if Stevens had his way, the governor's undisciplined and frequently barbaric militias would undermine the peace that the army was trying to enforce, as they had in December 1855 when the Oregon Militia undertook their unnecessary and vicious campaign against Peopeo-moxmox and his Walla Walla people.

Governor Stevens and Governor George Curry of Oregon Territory visited Colonel Wright at Fort Vancouver and tried to convince him that the Walla Wallas were again stirring up trouble. Therefore, they wanted him to take a force and head directly into the Walla Walla Valley, rather than split his force, as General Wool had ordered. In March 1856 Wright, likely influenced by the governors' pressure, decided to head toward Walla Walla with the main part of his force, an act that would have fatal consequences and would later draw criticism from Wool. Wright's rationale for disobeying Wool's orders is unclear. The colonel's actions seem particularly curious since there had been no incidents or credible reports that could have justified actions contrary to his commander's orders.

The white settlement at the Cascades consisted of three primary sections spread out over four miles: the lower landing, at which steamboats from Portland and Fort Vancouver would land; the middle Cascades, where a blockhouse was located; and the upper landing, with moorage for steamboats heading upriver to The Dalles. The upper landing was the site of the largest settlement, with its most significant structure being the Bradford brothers' store, a two-story building also used as a residence and boarding house.

The blockhouse at the middle Cascades, known as Fort Rains, was built in the fall of 1855. It had been named after Maj. Gabriel Rains, the officer General Wool had placed in charge of its construction. Unfortunately for the army, it was positioned where it could provide little protection to either landing, and it also made an easy target. To make matters worse, by the time George Wright passed though in March 1856, it was guarded by only nine soldiers, commanded by Sgt. Matthew Kelly of the Fourth Infantry. Another blockhouse, called Fort Cascades, was built at the lower end of the rapids, but it was normally unattended.

For the army to function, everything had to pass through the Cascades: men, armaments, food, all that was needed to conquer the Columbia Plateau. Without control of the Cascades, the army would have to traverse mountains to the north or south, ensuring a much longer and more arduous journey. The importance of the location to the tribes was apparently lost on General Wool and Colonel Wright, since they left it poorly defended. Given the strategic importance of the settlement, it attracted the attention of Chief Kamiakin of the Yakamas, who organized a force of perhaps one hundred Yakamas, Klickitats, and Cascades to stage an attack.

THE ATTACK

The morning of March 26, 1856, was clear, with a strong wind blowing through the Columbia gorge from the east, as it often does in springtime. A group of men pulling ropes staggered along the shoreline at the lower landing, struggling to draw a fully loaded bateau against the current.[22] Their task was interrupted by a frantic visit from Indian Jack, a man who often worked with the settlers. All morning the men had heard the sound of blasting from upriver, where another work team was carving out a new roadbed along the shoreline. However, Jack told them, the sound they had been hearing was not dynamite; it was the howitzer at Fort Rains at the middle Cascades, which was under attack by Indians, as was the settlement at the upper landing four miles upriver.

The first attack, on a party working on the wooden railway at the upper landing, killed one settler and wounded several others. The survivors split into two groups, some heading for the store, others for the mules, intending to escape downriver to the blockhouse. A fifteen-year-old boy, Jacob Kyle, was shot and killed, but the others made it safely. Many of the settlers quickly gathered at the store, as it was the most defensible structure. Punching out shingles and opening chinks between logs, they began firing back, with little apparent effect.[23]

A mile away, five men working at the sawmill were attacked. B. W. Brown, his eighteen-year-old wife, and her younger brother were killed, scalped, and their bodies thrown in a stream. A warrior in possession of Mrs. Brown's scalp was later captured and hanged. At the upper landing, several men and an eleven-year-old boy made a break for the steamship *Mary,* which was tied to the bank a short distance upstream. They conducted a running battle along the way, with the boy shooting a warrior, wounding himself in the process. The *Wasco,* moored on the Oregon side of the river out of danger, loaded up the settlers on that side of the Columbia, and both ships headed upriver towards Fort Dalles.

Other families around the upper landing fled to the Bradfords' store, bringing the number inside to forty. In the initial chaos, one man, James Sinclair, peeked out the front door and was promptly shot and killed. The settlers secured the two floors and the small attic and began their defense. According to one of the besieged, Lawrence Coe,

> After a while Finley came creeping around the lower point of the island toward our house. We shouted to him to lie down behind a rock and he did so. He called that he could not get to the shore, as the bank above was covered with Indians. He saw, while there, Watkins' house burn. . . . We then saw Watkins and Bailey running around the river side toward the place where Finley was, and the Indians in full chase after them. As our men came around the point in full

> view, Bailey was shot through the arm and leg. He continued on, and plunging into the river, swam to the front of our store and came in safely, except for his wounds. Finley also swam across and got in unharmed, which was wonderful, as there was a shower of bullets around them.[24]

Watkins was shot in the arm and pinned behind a rock for the next two days and nights. During that time he positioned himself so that if he passed out, he would roll into the cold water and startle himself awake.

On the second day, of the forty people inside the store, four women and eighteen men were still well enough to fight, while eighteen men and children were wounded or dead. The small store was cramped, the stench only bearable in comparison to what waited outside; they ran out of water, and the supply of ale and whiskey did not last long. Lawrence Coe wrote that a Spokane Indian, who had been traveling through the area and had become trapped, volunteered to go for water. He made repeated trips to the river, going "to and fro like lightning." During the second night, the body of James Sinclair was rolled out the door, "as the corpse was quite offensive."[25] The body of Sinclair's wife was later found in a stream.

At Fort Rains, a mile downstream, the soldiers, a few workers, and a family were fending off an attack from the relative safety of the blockhouse. Private Lawrence Rooney was away from the blockhouse chopping wood and was taken prisoner. He was moved within earshot of the blockhouse, where he was tortured and eventually strangled with a willow branch. Casualties at Fort Rains would most certainly have been higher if not for their howitzer, which not only fired lethal grapeshot, but also was loud and served to warn away attackers. The noise alerted the settlers at the lower landing, who quickly boarded the steamships *Belle* and *Fashion* and headed downriver toward Fort Vancouver, leaving their settlement in flames behind them.

Later estimates put the Indian force at from fifty to three hundred warriors; in the craggy and densely forested terrain, it was

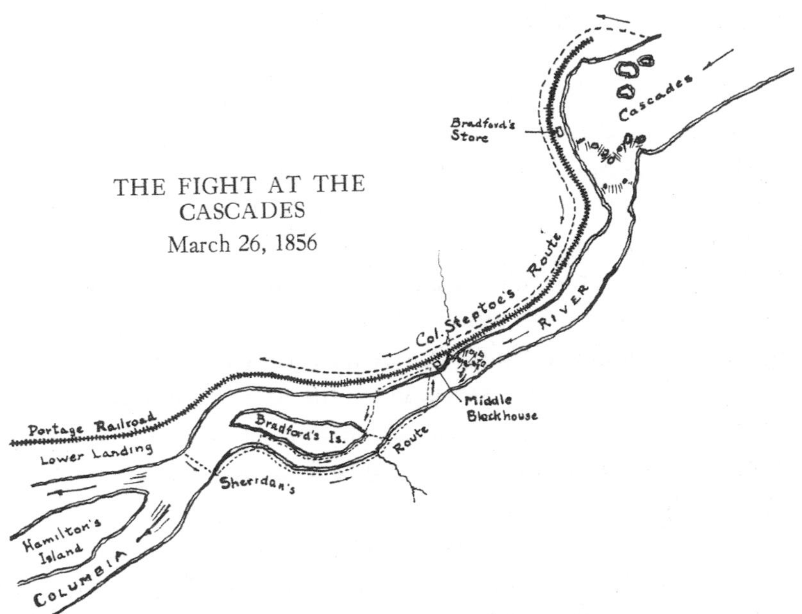

Key locations and troop movements at Cascade Rapids. From Rosebush, *Frontier Steel*, p. 194, and based on information found in *Personal Memoirs of P. H. Sheridan* (1888). Courtesy Eastern Washington Historical Society and Museum of Arts and Culture.

difficult for the besieged to tell, and most Indians remained hidden among the steep slopes above the settlements. They would periodically trade shots with the party barricaded in the Bradfords' store at the upper landing, and they made repeated attempts to set fire to it with burning pitch, to no avail. The siege continued for two days and nights.

Some members of the Cascade tribe had remained out of the fight and assisted in the escape of the people from the lower landing and the launching of the steamships to Fort Vancouver. Late on the 26th, the night of the initial attack, the *Belle* arrived at Fort Vancouver, picked up Lt. Philip Sheridan and a detachment of forty dragoons, and headed back upstream to the lower landing. Sheridan decided his first move would be to approach Fort Rains and free the men in the blockhouse.[26]

RESCUE AND "TRIALS"

Sheridan reported that as soon as the *Belle* landed on the 27th, the Indians, hidden in the forested bluffs, immediately began taunting the troops with "frequent shots, loud shouting, and much blustering; they, by the most exasperating yells and indecent exhibitions, daring me to the contest." For nearly a day Sheridan and his men fought at close quarters and long range; at one point, a bullet grazed his nose, then struck the soldier next to him, killing him. Keeping the main force of the Indians occupied with his howitzer, Sheridan planned to cross the south channel, land on Bradford's Island, and conduct a surprise attack. Before undertaking this risky venture, he wrote that he needed to assess the strength and position of the warriors, so he found a secure high spot and surveyed the scene: "From this point I observed the Indians running horse-races and otherwise enjoying themselves behind the line they had held against me the day before. The squaws decked out in gay colors, and the men gaudily dressed in war bonnets, made the scene most attractive, but as everything looked propitious for the dangerous enterprise in hand I spent little time watching them."[27]

Sheridan then embarked on a risky and shrewd maneuver. Using a small boat, he shuttled his force to the south bank of the river, intending to pull the boat through the rapids upstream to a point from which they would recross to the north bank at a spot behind the Indians' position. However, the rapids along the south bank were too turbulent to pull the boat through, so he took ten men partway back and crossed to Bradford's Island, in the middle of the south channel, where the water was fast, but smoother.

On Bradford's Island, they made little progress against the spring current, but came upon "a camp of old squaws who had been left on the island for safety, and had not gone over to the mainland to see the races." He noted, "We utilized them to our advantage. With unmistakable threats and signs we made them not only keep quiet, but also give us much needed assistance in pulling vigorously on the towrope of our boat." The women, of the Cascade people, reluctantly helped Sheridan. "I felt very grateful to the old squaws for the assistance they rendered," he wrote. "They worked well under compulsion, and manifested no disposition to strike for higher wages. Indeed, I was so much relieved when we had crossed over from the island and joined the rest of the party, that I mentally thanked the squaws one and all."[28]

Col. Edward Steptoe's force had been at Fort Dalles, and upon learning the news of the attack they boarded a steamboat and headed downriver toward the Cascades. While Sheridan was preparing his men for the crossing back to the north bank, Steptoe's force arrived and met him. By that time, the Indians had begun to retreat into the mountains, unintentionally warned away by a careless bugler in Steptoe's command.

Sheridan took thirteen prisoners, and while he waited for Colonel Wright to arrive, he not only had to guard the prisoners, he also had to protect innocent Indians from newly arrived Oregon volunteer militiamen. Arriving late to the action, the volunteers insisted on immediately shooting the prisoners in reprisal for allegedly killing a man named Seymour. Sheridan warned the militia to stay away, telling them that he would use lethal force to stop them. A while later Seymour emerged from the wilds, unscathed, where he had been hiding since the initial attack.[29]

Colonel Wright had learned of the attack at midnight on March 26th, when he was forty-five miles upriver at Five-Mile Camp. One of Wright's men, Joel Graham, later wrote, "Notwithstanding the lateness of the hour, this news was speedily communicated throughout the command, and by the blaze of the quickly replenished fires the soldiers could be seen flitting about in active preparation for the countermarch, and long before the dawn of day the column was clattering along the trail towards the steamboat landing, where the diminutive steamer *Mary Ann* was waiting and sputtering in nervous readiness."[30]

Hurrying to Fort Dalles, Colonel Wright ordered an artillery company with two howitzers aboard the *Mary Ann*, then filled the remaining space with the rest of the force. What Graham described as a "large, leaky scow" was jammed with dragoons and their horses. By four in the morning on March 27 the steamboat was heading downstream, but they made poor time because of problems with the boilers. By evening, the Cascades still lay ten miles further downstream, and not wanting to reach the battle site in the dark, at sunset Wright ordered his force to disembark. They resumed their journey early enough to reach the Cascades at first daylight.

The next morning, the 28th, as Wright's force of 270 men neared the upper landing, they heard gunfire, then spotted waving handkerchiefs in the windows of the Bradfords' store. Indians hiding in the forest opened fire on the *Mary Ann*, and the captain quickly rammed the bow into the bank to allow the soldiers to disembark. The howitzers began firing from the deck, raking the woods, and as the Indians fell back the infantry charged, quickly driving the Indians deep into the forest while taking prisoners. Graham wrote, "Soon four of them were picked up, and further on another lying prone beside a half-emptied whiskey barrel. Miserable victim of intemperance, he received no opportunity to take the pledge in this world."[31]

The soldiers continued along the shoreline, moving downstream, until they could hear shouts from the blockhouse. More firing could be heard nearby, which turned out to be Sheridan's force moving upriver toward the blockhouse. The combination of Steptoe's and Wright's forces moving downriver from the east and Sheridan's, fighting from the west, forced most of the remaining warriors to flee.

When the Yakamas and Klickitats fled, they left behind the Cascade warriors, some of whom had joined them in the fight. They denied participating in the killing of civilians, but Sheridan was not convinced and approached one man: "Putting my forefinger into the muzzle of his gun, I found unmistakable signs of its having been recently discharged. My finger was black with the stains of burnt powder, and holding it up to the Indian, he had nothing more to say in the face of such positive evidence of his guilt. A further examination proved that all the guns were in the same condition."[32]

After the evidence was collected on Sheridan's fingertip, he turned over the prisoners to Colonel Wright. Following what Sheridan termed "a trial by military commission," Wright declared them guilty of treason and ordered them executed. A rope was flung over a tree branch, two barrels placed beneath, one on top of the other, creating a "rude but certain substitute" for normal gallows. Each victim was made to stand on the top barrel, the bottom was knocked away, "and the necessary drop was thus attained." Sheridan reported that before being executed, they all confessed their guilt, and then "met their doom with the usual stoicism of their race."[33]

During Wright's questioning, Lawrence Coe acted as an interpreter. He later wrote his account of events:

> Old Chenoweth-Chief was brought up before Colonel Wright, tried, and sentenced to be hanged. The Cascade Indians, being under treaty, were adjudged guilty of treason in fighting. Chenoweth died game. He offered two horses, two squaws, and a little something to every "tyee" for his life; said he was afraid of the grave in the ground and begged to be put into an Indian dead-house. He gave a terrific war whoop while the rope was being put about his neck. I thought he expected the Indians to come and rescue him. The rope did not work well, and while hanging he muttered, "Wake nika kwass kopa memaloose" (I am not afraid to die). He was then shot.[34]

The treason charge was curious, since the Indians had never been considered to have citizenship equal to that of whites. Indeed, few whites would have considered Indians true citizens of the United States with rights equal to those of settlers, even if they were, as Coe said, "under treaty." To the warriors, they were engaged in a battle against an invader, not fighting their own countrymen or government.[35]

At least one innocent man was executed. Margaret Windsor Iman, a resident of the settlement at the Cascades, wrote:

> The device of the hanging was one end of a rope tied to a limb, the other to the neck. A whiskey barrel stood on end and one end of a

> rope about twenty feet in length, drawn through the bung hole of the barrel with a knot tied on the inner end, which served to jerk the barrel from under the condemned man. One among them was Jim Tassalo—he insisted that he had not been in the battle. My husband, some few days before their capture, while on his way to The Dalles, had met Jim and told him the Indians had already been killing the whites at the Cascades so he turned his skiff and sailed for the point from where he had come. He wanted those who held him in captivity, to hold him unharmed till Felix, my husband, came from The Dalles and if he said he was in the battle, he was willing to be hanged. This they refused to do and so hanged him and asked Mr. Iman afterwards; hence a life was taken from one for the crime he had not committed, for my husband said, "Men, you have done wrong, for Jim, I know, was not in the battle."[36]

Sheridan was preparing another man for execution when Indian Jack intervened, saying the man had not been involved; Sheridan promptly turned him loose.

Joel Graham witnessed the executions: "They all met their death stoically, with the exception of one burly fellow [Chenowith], who so excited the ire of an eccentric lieutenant that the latter discharged the contents of his revolver into the body while it was swinging from the scaffold. The dogs were kept constantly busy after the fighting ended in hunting up the victims of the slaughter. All were finally found, numbering about twenty-three."[37]

When the dust and ash settled, a tally was taken of the damage. All the buildings at the lower landing were burned to the ground, including the Fort Cascades blockhouse. The Fort Rains blockhouse at the middle part of the rapids still stood, but most of the buildings at the upper landing had been burned. According to Lawrence Coe's count, fourteen civilians and three soldiers were killed during the three days of fighting, and another dozen people were wounded. A casualty count among Indians has not survived history, other than the nine executed on Wright's orders. The army had learned, too late, the importance of the Cascades to the tribes. Joel Graham perhaps summed up the lesson for both sides in the fighting: "Many years were required to repair the damages and great suffering was entailed thereby."[38]

ANOTHER MASSACRE

Several days after Colonel Wright's hangings, Sheridan, still encamped at the lower landing, received a visit from Joseph Meek, frontiersman, mountain guide for wagon trains, and the man who as territorial marshal had hanged the Indians tried for the Whitman massacre. Meek asked if Sheridan had seen a Chinook Indian by the name of Spencer and his family. Sheridan wrote fondly of Spencer in his memoirs, noting that Wright not only had hired Spencer as an interpreter, but had taken his family to Fort Dalles during the current expedition so they could visit relatives. Due to his hasty return to the Cascades, Wright had to leave behind Spencer and his family, and shortly thereafter they had disappeared. Although Spencer was later found in good health, his family remained missing. Sheridan led a force into the forests and eventually found Spencer's family. They had been strangled; their bodies lay close together, "the mother, two youths, three girls, and a baby." They had been garroted with thin rope, and as there apparently had not been enough rope for all, the baby had been killed with a "red silk handkerchief." In a letter to Wright, Sheridan said, "The person of the young woman was undoubtedly violated."[39] In his memoirs, published in 1888, the emotional impact on Sheridan was still evident:

> They had all been killed by white men, who had probably met the innocent creatures somewhere near the blockhouse, driven them from the road into the timber, where the cruel murders were committed without provocation, and for no purpose than the gratification of the inordinate hatred of the Indian that has often existed on the frontier, and which on more than one occasion has failed to distinguish friend from foe. . . . It was a distressing sight. A most cruel outrage had been committed on unarmed people—our friends and allies—in a spirit of aimless revenge."[40]

Sheridan ordered his men to build coffins for the family and buried the "bodies of these hapless victims of misdirected vengeance."[41]

Although white suspects were identified—one Samuel Hamilton and members of an Oregon territorial militia—no one was ever arrested for the crimes. In San Francisco, the *Daily Alta California* ran an article about the murder of Spencer's family, pointing out the barbarity of some of the *white* people:

> The annals of Indian barbarity furnish no instance of cold blooded, diabolical, cowardly villainy, that can much transcend this act, which has stamped the character of our Territory with a foul blot, which will stick to it long after the perpetrators of that act and those who countenance it, are dead and damned. A few more such acts as this, and Oregon will be a by-word and a hissing among the civilized nations of the earth.[42]

A few weeks later, Colonel Wright returned to the Cascades to further investigate the violence, including the Spencer family murders. He wrote to General Wool, "I hope, for the sake of humanity, and our character as a civilized people, that it may turn out that this savage deed has been performed by Indians; but it pains me to say that from the reports and indications, it appears more than probable that the murder was committed by white persons. . . . Should this unfortunately prove to be the case it will embarrass me. Those Indians are faithful adherents to our cause, and they confidently rely upon my willingness, and power to protect them."[43]

The Cascades battle was of such significance that Wright's superior officer, General Wool, made the trip from San Francisco to Fort Vancouver and not only praised Sheridan's conduct, but sent a complimentary report to the commander of the army, Gen. Winfield Scott, who praised both Colonel Steptoe and Lieutenant Sheridan from headquarters in Washington, D.C. The commander in charge, George Wright, received no positive mention. It did not help Wright's case that he had irritated General Wool by disobeying his orders and marching into the Walla Walla

Valley, not the Yakima Valley. Wright's primary influence on events were the executions.

"A PERFECT FARCE"

The Cascades violence triggered another round of vitriol between General Wool and Governor Stevens. In a July 1856 letter to the army headquarters, General Wool accused Stevens and Curry of inciting war to help white businessmen who sold goods to the army. He wrote that if Governors Curry and Stevens and their followers put as much energy into making peace "as they did to make war and plunder the Indians of their lands, horses, and cattle, that the Army and settlers would be relieved of all trouble, and the United States of a very large expenditure of money." In the same letter, Wool accused Stevens and Curry of exaggerating the military's ineptitude at the Cascades to "promote their own ambitious schemes and that of pecuniary speculators." Furthermore, Wool wrote, "The reference to the massacres at the Cascades by these would-be military Chieftans will turn out no less unfortunate for them, when all the facts are made known; I think it will be discovered that they were the cause of that disaster, which came near producing what they most desired, a long war." While Wool privately admitted that leaving the Cascades undermanned was a strategic mistake, publicly he put all the blame on Stevens and Curry, accusing them of pressuring Wright. Wool noted that Stevens and Curry "strenuously urged the colonel [Wright] to disregard my instructions, and to adopt Stevens' magnificent plan of campaign, by way of the Walla Walla Valley." Instead of splitting his force, Wright had concentrated his nine companies on the south side of the Columbia, leaving the region north of the Cascades unguarded and the Cascades settlements woefully underprotected.[44]

In the letter Wool twice terms the violence at the Cascades as "massacres," rather than using the singular form of the word, the preference of other whites of the time and still the preference of many historians.[45] In the national media, there was no subtlety or balance. On June 23, 1856, the *New York Times* ran a letter from "A Washington Settler" that made it clear who was to blame for the brutality at the Cascades:

> Do your readers attach to the word "massacre" its full meaning? It is not merely indiscriminate slaughter, but such savage butchery as, thank God, has long since disappeared from the enlightened portion of the world—lurking now only in the dark recesses of Indian crime—such atrocities as reach us but in whispers, never to be recorded by the pen. The race that committed them are passing away forever—let the remembrance of their deeds go with them.[46]

The Cascades violence triggered debate in Congress. Representative James Patton Anderson, from Washington Territory, addressed Congress on August 6, 1856, offering a defense of the actions of the militia and a condemnation of General Wool. He praised the militia for their handling of the Walla Walla fight and the murder of Peopeo-moxmox the prior December and excoriated Wool for his management of Indian-white relations in the Northwest. In a long, vitriolic address concerning the murders of the Spencer family, he said of Wool, "He charges that white men violated a squaw and cruelly strangled a whole family of friendly Indians at the Cascades: I defy anyone to prove it."[47] The fact that none of the white witnesses at the Cascades expressed doubt about white culpability meant little in Washington, D.C. Anderson's defiance was indicative of the hardened attitudes spreading throughout white settlements in the Northwest. After the Cascades violence, little empathy remained for the tribes, and voices became louder for their removal, or in many cases, extermination.

The incident kept the attention of the government. Early the next year, in January 1857, George Gibbs wrote to James Swan expressing his views on the conduct of the Indian war in the Pacific Northwest. Gibbs's longtime affiliation with Stevens did not stop him from offering his candid assessment of Stevens's work, attributing a great deal of the blame for the Indian wars to him: "The governor's treaties had a great deal to do in fomenting this war there is no doubt. Those on the Sound were too much hurried, and the reservations allowed them were insufficient; but his grand blunder was in bringing together the Nez Perces, Walla Wallas, Yakamas, and others into one council, and cramming a treaty down their throats in a hurry."[48]

However, in the same report, Gibbs had even more harsh things to say of Colonel Wright's involvement at the Cascades:

> As to the conduct of the war on this side (that is, west of the Cascade range of mountains), it has been well managed. Captain Keyes and Colonel Casey, who succeeded him in command, acted with judgment and energy; but the war on the other side, directed by Colonel Wright, has been a perfect farce. He has proclaimed peace when it only exists because the whites have been driven from the country. He left his communications behind him unguarded, suffered the Cascades to be taken and burned, ran back, gave up an expedition on which he started, undertook another, sent back for more troops, and finally, at the head of eleven companies of regulars, after talking and feeding the hostiles on sugar and flour, marched back without taking a single one of the murderers, without killing an enemy in the field, without dictating terms, or doing any thing whatever to chastise or subdue those who were in arms. The result, is, that all communication by way of the Plains is abandoned; that other tribes, encouraged by the inefficiency of the troops, or, rather, of their commander, have joined; and that the Indians hold undisputed control over the country.[49]

Gibbs's report makes no mention of the fact that Wright had disobeyed General Wool's order to send troops into the Yakima Valley, but instead marched toward the Walla Walla Valley.

Following the battle at the Cascades, Wright ignored the criticism and focused on strengthening defenses along the Columbia River and into the plateau. He enlarged Fort Dalles and used it as his base of operations. That summer, one unidentified party complained to General Wool at headquarters, Department of the Pacific, that Wright had left the supply depot at Fort Dalles unguarded, "except for a few sick and disabled men." General

Wool's adjutant wrote to Colonel Wright about the accusation: "This the General does not believe to be true. With your ample forces there would be no necessity for leaving so important a post as The Dalles unprotected or without troops to defend it. A company, he thinks, would not be too large a guard for that post."[50] Wool did not want a repeat of the Cascades debacle and no doubt wondered why Wright, having seen what happened to an undermanned post along the river, had not strengthened defenses at Fort Dalles.

Wright did not seem particularly concerned about Wool's criticism: "With regard to my depot at Fort Dalles, it is, and has always been, perfectly safe," he wrote. Wright gave details of troop movements he had ordered to secure Fort Dalles and the Cascade Rapids and noted that the blockhouse at the central landing had been abandoned, since it had been deemed unnecessary and "the people living there keep the party of soldiers drunk all the time."[51]

The army continued to strengthen its forces in the Northwest. By the end of 1856, more than eighteen hundred regular troops were stationed in the Oregon and Washington Territories. The army presence was spreading outward from established settlements into land desired by settlers (and therefore territory ripe for conflict). New forts were constructed at the Cascades, in the Yakima Valley at Simcoe, at Port Townsend and Bellingham, and in the Walla Walla Valley. The number of settlers was growing, and along with them came requests for protection from Indians—and in many cases, demands for their extermination.

In his memoirs, Philip Sheridan noted the effect of hangings on the Plateau Indian population, starting with the executions at the Cascade Rapids in 1856: "The summary punishment inflicted on the nine Indians, in their trial and execution, had a most salutary effect on the confederation, and was the entering wedge to its disintegration; and though Colonel Wright's campaign continued through summer and into early winter, the subjugation of the allied bands became a comparatively easy matter after the lesson taught the renegades who were captured at the Cascades."[52]

As it turned out, Wright's work was anything but easy.

ECHOES

In 1878 construction began on a series of locks at the Cascades Rapids. They opened for use in November 1896, and most of the rapids upriver were tamed. The entire stretch was inundated in 1938 when the Bonneville Dam was completed. The dam bisects Bradford's Island, which had lain at the center of Sheridan's maneuvers during the fight. Visitors to the site will see no sign of the rapids, but the current still surges powerfully, albeit more quietly, through the narrow portion of the channel.[53]

Today, there are fourteen dams on the Columbia River. Winds funneling through the narrow gorge from Hood River to the Cascades are consistently strong, making it one of the world's most popular windsurfing destinations. Other than a few historical points of interest with interpretive signs, there are few obvious signs of human habitation prior to western settlement or of the 1856 carnage at the Cascades Rapids.

SIX

Big Dog and Crazy

While Col. George Wright was trying to establish the U.S. Army as the ruling force regarding Indian-white relations in Washington Territory, Isaac Stevens was trying to do the same with the territorial government and the volunteer militia. Like Stevens, Wright was ambitious, self-confident, and at times willing to interpret the law to fit his needs. However, while Wright was concerned with duty, Stevens was concerned with power. Stevens was sometimes overtly belligerent, while Wright was more quietly so. Although Governor Stevens had no military command authority over Wright, he sometimes acted as if he did. Perhaps a collision was inevitable.

The differences in the two men's temperaments were among the reasons their legacies would diverge. Wright would later be heralded as a hero by the white public, while Stevens alienated much of the public, both white and Indian, through his political overreach and impatient manner. Stevens's treaty councils harmed more Native people during the 1850s and thereafter, but George Wright's name evokes stronger reactions, in part because of the gruesome violence he conducted during his 1858 march.[1] Thus, Wright became the subject of a heroic public narrative, while Stevens and his councils became the subjects of books and symposia that focused on problems resulting from the treaties and Indian policy.[2] Today, when Stevens is praised, it is usually for his speed and effectiveness in opening the Pacific Northwest to settlement.

After the debacle at the Cascades Rapids, in order to intimidate the Native people, George Wright would tell the tribes that he was the "Big Dog" on the plateau.[3] Isaac Stevens would pressure George Wright to deal more forcefully with the tribes, while General Wool, knowing what Stevens was attempting, would warn Wright, "Governor Stevens is crazy and does not know what he's doing."[4]

In early March 1856, even before the violence at the Cascade Rapids, the feud between Wool and Stevens intensified, with Wright caught in the middle. Stevens sent a particularly scathing letter to Wool in which he took issue with a large number of Wool's statements and actions. For example, Wool had been critical of the militiamen who had killed Chief Peopeo-moxmox and dismembered his body.[5] In response, Stevens asserted that Wool had committed "blunders"; was "ignorant" of the facts; was "unfit for [his] position," and so on—his arguments and accusations waxing for more than three thousand words.[6] Wool responded with a lengthy letter to Gen. Winfield Scott at army headquarters in which he presented his case against Stevens. Scott forwarded the letter to Secretary of War Jefferson Davis with a note reading, "Indian affairs. Highly interesting. I have full confidence in General Wool's statement of facts, and fully concur in his views and sentiments."[7] Wool's answer to Stevens's long letter was to the point: he instructed his aide-de-camp to send it back to him without comment.

Just a few days after the Cascades tragedy, Stevens wrote to Colonel Wright: "The recent attack on the Cascades must convince all persons that this is no time for forms, but for vigorous, energetic, and united action."[8] To Stevens, that meant sending territorial militia into the field to supplement army regulars, but to Wright it meant combining policing techniques with threats and keeping the militia out of the way. Wright notified Stevens that the army was building two blockhouses, one at each end of the Cascades Rapids. Furthermore, Wright had ordered a detachment into the field with the charge of protecting settlers. Wright's tone in the letter to Stevens is confident, even triumphant. He credits his "sudden return" to the rapids for the dispersal of the Indians, then claims the workers at the Cascades should have been carrying weapons with them. He makes no mention of the

Gen. John Wool. Original in the author's collection.

soldiers that were withdrawn just a few days before the attack, which was one thing he could have controlled.

Colonel Wright also boasted to Governor Stevens that "I have given them a lesson which they will long remember. Ten [actually nine] of those Indians, including their chief, have been hung by sentence of a military commission. The residue, some forty men and seventy or eighty women and children have been placed on an island without any means of leaving it, and are under the observation of the troops."[9] It's unclear why Wright kept the families on an island, since few of the local Indians had been involved in the violence. They were probably kept as hostages, a tactic Wright and other officers sometimes used. Typically, after a designated period of time—sometimes up to a year—hostages would be released if no further violence occurred.

Colonel Wright and General Wool were clear about their feelings toward the territorial militias. On April 26 Wright received a letter from the Indian agent for the region, R. R. Thompson, in which he requested an armed force to protect Indians at The Dalles: "Some few have been furnished with passports to take fish at The Dalles of the Columbia river, on the Oregon side; and while thus peaceably engaged, have been fired upon by the Oregon Volunteers, who are encamped on the north side." Thompson noted that if Wright provided protection for the Indians, it would mean the tribes could be self-supporting, thus saving the government money. Thompson closed by commenting that the tribes needed protection from "our own people."[10]

Wright became concerned about worsening relations between the army and the militias. His early official letters are direct, with little emotion. However, by 1856, and increasingly during the following years, some of his letters became more impassioned, often sweeping into grandiosity and drama. In a letter to Governor George Curry of Oregon Territory, for example, Wright impressed upon him his respect for militia forces:

> Since thirteen years of age I have been a soldier; I have served in the east, the west, the north, and the south. I have no sectional

> prejudices; I am a citizen of the United States; I know that an opinion has obtained that soldiers are mere machines; that they have no feelings or sympathies in unison with civilians, and particularly that the regular army is hostile to volunteer troops. This is entirely a mistake, as far as my observation has extended. I have been stationed near large cities and in densely populated districts, and I have almost universally found the greatest harmony, friendship, and deep regret expressed when the social intercourse was broken off by the removal of the troops. With regard to volunteer troops, I have never seen any unkind feelings exhibited toward them by the regular army. On the battle fields of Mexico, side by side, we fought and conquered, and a friendship cemented in blood, in the hour of victory, will cease only with the last pulsation of a true heart.[11]

The first sentence summarizes a common theme in Wright's correspondence: he was first and foremost a patriot. In this, as with most of his correspondence, Wright was respectful and gracious, and unlike General Wool, would rarely make direct accusations.

Meanwhile, in Olympia, Stevens was about to face his own battle—not only with the Indians, but also with his own citizens. Peace complicated Governor Stevens's goals for the Pacific Northwest. He had a railroad to build, a territory to develop, and uncooperative Indians to move out of the way. The governor's impatience reached a crescendo on April 3, when he declared martial law in Pierce County in order to restrain or imprison anyone who might give support to, or participate in, hostilities against settlers. Many of his targets were white men with Indian wives or mixed-race citizens with unstated loyalties. Some were put in jail. The governor's justification rested on the premise that "there is no such thing in my humble judgment as neutrality in an Indian war, and whoever can remain on his claim unmolested, is an ally of the enemy, and must be dealt with as such."[12]

Stevens tried to seize complete power, including the judiciary. In May, with neutral noncombatants still in jail, Judge Edward Lander of the Territorial Supreme Court listened to Stevens's arguments as to why martial law should be continued. Although a supporter of Stevens's anti-Indian policies, the judge considered the declaration of martial law to be excessive, and he asked Stevens to rescind it. When Stevens defied him, the judge ordered "every able-bodied male over sixteen in the county to attend court the next day and function as a posse comitatus to protect the integrity of civil law."[13] In response, Stevens's agent, Lt. Col. Benjamin Franklin (Frank) Shaw of the territorial militia, gathered a force of twenty armed men and entered the courtroom. Shaw announced he intended to arrest the judge and take him to jail. The twenty armed militiamen stared down the thirty law-abiding, armed citizens, and with tension at a breaking point, the judge allowed himself to be taken to jail in order to avoid violence.

While the militia and prominent business and political leaders were aligned with the governor, the citizenry was appalled and took to the streets. Protest rallies were held, and citizens sent a letter to President Franklin Pierce, asserting that the governor was a "despot." Stevens's response, published in local newspapers, claimed that the imprisoned noncombatants were aiding the enemy, "in every way furnishing them with aid and comfort." However, not only was there no evidence that any neutral parties had been helping the tribes, there was evidence most had conscientiously avoided doing so, knowing they would be subject to reprisals.[14]

Another former Stevens ally, George Gibbs, quickly turned on him. In a letter to Secretary of State William Macy, Gibbs and other citizens wrote that Stevens was "a diminutive Napoleon," corrupted by a lust for power—and by drink: "Of naturally arrogant and domineering character, of overweening ambition, and even unscrupulous of the means required to effect his objects, he has been further inflamed by the immoderate use of ardent spirits, and in his fits of intoxication knows no bounds to his language or to his actions."[15] Other allegations of drunkenness hounded Stevens during his career; drunk or not, during 1856 his treatment of the tribes in Washington Territory became increasingly belligerent.

Military Campaigns, 1856–58

Battles
Hangman Creek
Forts
Major Cities
Mission
Wright Military Expedition Routes
Other Military Expedition Routes
Roads

Puget Sound
Pacific Ocean
Seattle
Olympia
Portland
Fort Okanogan, est. 1811
Fort Colville, est. 1859
PRESENT-DAY IDAHO
Columbia River
Spokane River
Area of Interest
Spokane Falls
Coeur d'Alene Mission
WASHINGTON TERRITORY
Wright, 1858
Mullan Rd
Steptoe Battle May 16–17, 1858
Colville Rd
Palouse River
Steptoe, 1858
Wright, 1856
Garnett, 1858
Fort Simcoe, est. 1856
Snake River
Fort Taylor, est. 1858
Fort Walla Walla, est. 1856
Whitman Massacre 1847
Fort Vancouver, est. 1824
Cascades Rapids March 1856
Fort Dalles, est. 1856
Columbia River
OREGON TERRITORY
Grande Ronde Massacre July 17, 1856
0 25 50 miles

Washington Territory
Seattle
Spokane
Columbia Plateau
Portland
Walla Walla
Oregon Territory
Utah Territory
Redding
Sacramento
San Francisco
California
Los Angeles

HARASSING THE TRIBES

Barely two months after the Cascades debacle, Colonel Wright marched into the Yakima Valley with a force of five hundred men, determined to make the Yakamas submit to his demands. He reported to General Wool that while in the valley he had listened to the tribes' grievances, which the previous year had led to the murders of the gold miners and Indian agent Andrew Bolon: "They seem to think, and say, that they had strong and good reason for the murders they have committed, both of the miners and Indian agent; the outrages of the former and the injudicious and intemperate threats of the latter, if true, I doubt not, maddened the Indians to murder them."[16] Wright's words seem to support claims by some historians that during the early part of his tenure in the Pacific Northwest he was sympathetic toward the tribes. Indeed, numerous letters written during the period 1856–57 reflect an officer as frustrated with white settlers and militia as he was with Indians. During the first part of his posting in the Northwest, he felt he could keep peace through a nonviolent show of force. However, as the months passed he became more belligerent with the tribes. Later events show that his early "sympathy" resulted more from a sense of duty than to a belief that the tribes deserved fair and equal treatment. If he had believed it was his duty, and a *necessity*, to use violence, he would have done so. As Wright would later show, he was well aware of necessity, the legal concept that defined the general conditions under which one could break the law without fear of consequences. It was important to him that he followed rules, and his ethics were based on rules and duty, not true empathy. His ethical base worked in a world in which society was relatively homogenous, with minimal disagreement about societal values and norms. The collision of cultures in the Pacific Northwest and resulting violence must have created dissonance, which sometimes shows up in his letters.[17] In the same letter in which he had related the stated reasons for the Indians' violence against the belligerent miners and Agent Bolon, Wright said, "I have about five hundred men with me, and as soon as I can cross the river

I shall advance to the We-nass and the fisheries; and if I do not bring the Indians to terms, either by a battle or a desire for peace on their part, I shall endeavor to harass them so much that they will find it impossible to live in the country."[18] Throughout his career in the Pacific Northwest and California, he would miss the irony in his words regarding Indians and whites: while he found it reprehensible that miners would commit "outrages," it was fine for Wright to "harass" the Indians until they had to move out of their country. It was a theme that would often appear in Wright's letters.

In April, Stevens again ignored the army's chain of command and began pressuring Wright to move a force into the Walla Walla Valley, where, Stevens insisted, the tribes were planning an uprising. Wright immediately responded that he planned to move into the Yakima Valley, and since his sources told him the Walla Wallas were at peace, he had no intention of changing his plans and marching against them. Stevens made another run at Wright in early May, and when that failed, he ordered a militia force into the Yakima Valley, headed by the loyal Frank Shaw, lieutenant colonel of the Washington Volunteers. Stevens wrote to Wright informing him that Shaw's orders were to join Wright in subduing Chief Kamiakin and the Yakamas, requiring of them "unconditional submission, and the rendering up of murderers and instigators of the war to punishment." In fact, one reason Stevens sent his volunteers into the field was to keep track of Wright's activities.[19] E. C. Fitzhugh of the Washington Volunteers reported to Stevens on Wright's councils with the tribes east of the Cascade Mountains: "Our Indians have informed us that Colonel Wright told all of them that he was the 'Big Dog' in this part of the world, and come a long distance to treat with them, and if they would only stop fighting, that all would be right." Fitzhugh also wrote that Wright had been "tickling the [Indian] community with the belief that he intended speedily to demolish all the Indians on the east side."[20]

In June 1856 Wright met with Chiefs Owhi and Teias in the Yakima Valley, while Kamiakin watched from the opposite bank of the Naches River. Wright reported that they all sent "friendly messages." Owhi told Wright that the cause of ill feelings among the Yakamas was the 1855 treaty council, and the resulting war could be traced directly to the way the Indians had been treated. Wright later wrote that he was impressed with Owhi, believing him to be intelligent and a man of conviction. Then, as Wright so often did after a conciliatory meeting, he changed his tone by "enumerating the disasters which must inevitably befall them: their warriors all killed or driven from their country, never to return; their women and children starving to death far to the north where the snow never melts." He added, however, that "if peace was restored they could live happily in their own country, where rivers and ground afford ample food for their subsistence, etc."[21]

Wright frequently showed that while he understood the words the chiefs spoke, he did not understand the meaning behind them, nor the depth of the speakers' feelings. His meeting with Owhi and Teias provides an example. During his first two-and-a-half years on the Columbia Plateau, Wright often used verbal threats in order to keep peace, but he failed to understand that the Indians' silence did not mean they were cowed and grateful. In several of his official reports, the colonel wrote of the effectiveness of his threats and the gratitude with which they were received. Of the council in the Yakima Valley, he wrote,

> I said, if they all desired peace they must come to me and do all that I required of them; that I had a force sufficient to sweep them from the face of the earth, but that I pitied the poor Indian; that I was willing to spare them to make them happy, provided they would comply with all my demands, etc. I have never seen Indians apparently more delighted than these chiefs were. They expressed their highest satisfaction with everything I had said to them.[22]

The chiefs had simply told Wright what he wanted to hear, as they had little appetite for a military confrontation. However, Kamiakin's skepticism was clear, and rather than join the other chiefs, he refused to cross the river to meet with Wright. Wright noted that "Kamiakin says but little, is proud, and very jealous of his rights. . . . He sent me the strongest assurances of friendship, and his determination to fight no more. This was confirmed by Owhi and Teias." Despite the assurances of the other chiefs, Wright realized Kamiakin was different. He wrote, "I must humble him, and make him feel that hereafter his position as chief can only be maintained by faithful adherence to our cause."[23]

As Isaac Stevens had learned at the Walla Walla council, and Wright would eventually learn, Kamiakin was not a man easily humbled. He was tall and physically imposing and carried himself with a great amount of dignity. Kamiakin's refusal to cross the Naches River to meet with Wright was indicative not only of a physical boundary, but of a metaphorical one as well; he held himself steadfastly apart from any white influence that threatened to harm him or other members of his tribe. Throughout his long life he was to earn both admiration and condemnation from whites for his principled stance. Virtually every politician and military leader (including Stevens and Wright) who knew Kamiakin was impressed not only by his physical appearance but with what could be described as his imposing demeanor, which demanded and gave respect.[24] In 1853 writer and adventurer Theodore Winthrop traveled through the region and wrote of his experiences. He called Kamiakin "regal and courteous," a view that was shared by many white men who met him.[25]

During the Plateau War, Kamiakin was frequently blamed for instigating any violence targeted at settlers, even if facts indicated otherwise. Politicians in the Northwest needed a chief they could demonize, in part to rally support from a frightened populace. On the west side of the Cascade Mountains, Stevens and the populace focused on Leschi until he was executed, and on the east side, Kamiakin became perhaps the most vilified. Kamiakin's legacy lasted long beyond the Plateau War. In a memoir quoted a century later, it was noted, "There was a time when his [Kamiakin's] name was terror in Washington Territory and small children were frightened into eating their vegetables by the threat, 'Kamiakin will get you.'"[26]

In the Yakima Valley Wright told Owhi and Teias they must gather their people and meet with him five days hence, "prepared to surrender everything which has been captured or stolen from the white people, and to comply with such other demands as I may then make." Wright was convinced the chiefs would submit and that they wanted peace. He wrote, "But I am in no hurry; they must be made to see and feel that they are completely in my power; that they are, as I told them, 'children in my hands.'"[27] However, when five days had passed and the chiefs did not appear, Wright was at first puzzled, since he had been convinced they wanted peace. He wrote to General Wool, "I do not despair of ultimately reducing these Indians to sue for peace. I believe they really desire it, and I must find out what outside influence is operating to keep them from coming in." In the same letter, Wright shows a bit of the concern he was famous for among his troops: "My men are in want of some articles of clothing, especially shoes, stockings, and overalls. . . . Shoes, particularly those pegged, last but a few days, marching over sharp rocks."[28]

In his response to Wright's report, Wool suggested that Stevens or one of his supporters had sabotaged Wright's peace efforts and that the colonel should be aware of more attempts to do the same. Wool warned Wright, "You cannot be too cautious or wary of your double enemy. If a defeat, or if any serious disaster should happen to your command, it would be a source of great rejoicing to scrip holders, and especially to those who are anxious for a long war, and who have proclaimed it a God-send to the people of the Territories of Oregon and Washington."[29]

Wright led his force northward into the Yakima Valley. On the afternoon of June 6, his force met up with the Catholic missionary Father Charles Pandosy and several Yakama chiefs. They were friendly and asked only that they be allowed to fish in their accustomed places. Wright agreed, but noted, "I shall require hostages for their good behavior and compliance with their promises."[30]

On June 21, after a meandering march up the Yakima Valley, Stevens's reliable militia commander, Col. Frank Shaw, found the camps of Colonels Wright and Steptoe. One of Shaw's officers, Capt. W. W. De Lacy, noted the militia's disappointment at missing a chance to fight:

> No Indians. Kamiakin had left. It had been Colonel Shaw's intention to attack at once had he found him in front of Colonel Wright's camp. Colonel Wright, on being asked, had nothing particular to send to Colonel Shaw. Kamiakin after feeling some time very comfortable at the expense of Col. Wright, agreed to treat. Col. Wright prepared a bower. Kamiakin left for parts unknown. Bower a dead loss.[31]

Wright had misread the mood of the chiefs, and Kamiakin in particular. In several letters to headquarters written during midsummer, he claimed that Kamiakin had fled: "Kamiakin, who plunged these people into war, and was continually boasting of what he would do, has basely deserted his people and fled, probably to the Palouse country. His career on this side of the Columbia is ended."[32] While Wright misread Kamiakin, he was starting to understand how the Yakamas lived. In July he wrote to General Wool that he "was at a loss to fix a position for a permanent military post. The whole country should be given to the Indians; they require it; they cannot live at any one point for the whole year."[33] In August he wrote again: "The whole country between the Cascade Mountains and the Columbia River should be given to the Indians; it is not necessary to the white people. The Indians can subsist themselves if they have it; the mountains, the plains, and the rivers, each in turn affords them food. In winter they are compelled to live in the valley, and one strong military post will insure their good behavior."[34] This passage has been quoted as proof of Wright's sympathy for the tribes. However, as Wright himself notes, he did not deem the land "necessary" to settlers. It is also noteworthy that Wright suggested the land "be given to the Indians." In fact, the land in question was lightly traveled by whites; there were no white settlements, and certainly from the standpoint of the tribes, the land already belonged to them. By suggesting the land be left to the tribes, he may have been trying to avoid more conflict with the strong and wide-ranging Yakamas.

In late summer and early autumn, Wright's reports from Fort Vancouver and the Yakima Valley were optimistic and confident. In July he reported that he was certain of "permanent friendship" with the Klickitats. Of the tribes in the Yakima Valley, he reported they were "very happy," and he was convinced they would "remain forever our friends." He had traveled the length and breadth of the region east of the Cascade Mountains to the Columbia River, and he claimed all was well, thanks to his diplomacy and the tribes' goodwill. Of a notable episode in the Kittitas Valley, he wrote that he had been holding Leschi, Nelson, and Kitsap, the chiefs from west of the Cascades whom Stevens had accused of murdering whites. Governor Stevens had requested that Wright keep the prisoners until they could be delivered back to the Puget Sound area, but Wright demurred: "I would not take any harsh measures without proof of their guilt. I can establish nothing against them worthy of death. I have no doubt that they have, during the course of the war, committed many murders—at least so we would designate their acts; but they look upon the killing of men, women, and children as a legitimate mode of warfare; even of this, I have no evidence."[35] The temporary protection of Leschi and the others was commendable, although it is unclear if Wright did it for reasons of justice. By keeping the prisoners out of Stevens's hands, Wright was not only fulfilling his duty; he was exercising a chance to annoy Stevens—which must have pleased General Wool.

In July Colonel Wright heard the tribes' account of what happened at the Cascades Rapids. Chief Tow-a-tax told him that Kamiakin had gathered a war party consisting of Yakamas and Klickitats, then recruited some of the Cascade tribe. Their plan had been to burn the steamboats and attack the settlements and posts along the five-mile stretch of rapids. All of the whites were to be killed, after which time Kamiakin would arrive with a large force and take permanent possession of that strategic stretch, an act that would have choked off travel for emigrants and the army's critical supply line.

THE GRAND RONDE

Since Wright told militia Colonel Shaw his volunteers were not needed in the Yakima Valley, Shaw and his Second Regiment headed east into the Walla Walla Valley. Stevens had instructed him to confirm the support of the friendly Nez Perce and Spokanes and capture the Palouses and Cayuses whom he believed were still stirring up trouble. Stevens ordered Capt. F. M. P. Goff of the volunteers to take 170 men to meet Shaw. In addition, Goff was to take flour, coffee, sugar, and other supplies to the Spokanes in order to hold their allegiance to the whites. Stevens continued his relentless pressure on the tribes, depending on his loyal militia to suppress them. To Colonel Shaw he wrote, "I trust you will be able to strike the enemy severely, and afterwards get them on terms of unconditional surrender."[36]

By early June, Shaw's force was encamped near Fort Walla Walla. A large number of militiamen were leaving the force, either by desertion or because their enlistment periods were up. Only two months earlier, Shaw had more than three hundred men under his command, but by July the number had dropped to two hundred, with more slated to leave within days. Colonel Shaw learned from scouts that Kamiakin and the Yakamas were not in the region or were, as De Lacy put it, "Beyond our reach." Shaw was determined to find a battle while he still had an effective fighting force, and on June 16 he led his men toward the Grande Ronde Valley, since, according to De Lacy, "He was well aware that it was the usual resort of the hostile tribes, and it was morally certain that a body of them would be found there at this time."[37]

Shaw's assessment was correct. The Grande Ronde is an area of deep valleys and mountains that range from the high curves of the Blues to the spires of the Wallowa range; it is one of the more isolated regions of the Columbia Plateau. It was a popular meeting place for tribes, including the Cayuses, Walla Wallas, Nez Perces, Shoshones, and Umatillas. Enemies would become friends, at least temporarily, in the land they called the "Valley of Peace." There were warm springs in which to bathe, as well as plentiful fish.[38] Since Shaw was known to be well informed of the tribes' habits, he would have understood that the people gathered there were anything but threatening.[39] The land along the Grande Ronde River was used not only as a fishing retreat, but also as a place for the elderly and infirm to recuperate. According to a later account written by a white resident in the Walla Walla Valley, the Grande Ronde Valley was where various tribes gathered "who were seeking a place of temporary shelter and refuge. . . . It was in no sense a war camp."[40]

The valley was a popular resting point for white travelers, and it is easy to find records of emigrants who had positive experiences in the area. Pioneer Celinda Hines wrote that it was "a fertile valley, eight miles across and twenty miles long, entirely encompassed by mountains and watered by the Grande Ronde River." She added, "We were thronged by Indians on ponies," which included a Nez Perce chief who "seemed very pleasant and spoke English. These Indians here seem more intelligent and happy than any we have seen."[41] A year earlier John Kerns noted that the Nez Perces in the area were "more intelligent, clean, and sociable than any Indians I ever saw." He wrote that the Grande Ronde Valley was "certainly the most beautiful place I have ever gazed upon. The soil is rich and is covered with luxuriant growth of grass, wild clover, and herd grass. The Indians are after us, yet to trade for cows. Oxen they will not have."[42]

It was in this peaceful and social place that Colonel Shaw intended to make a point. On July 14 he assembled a force consisting of six companies. With 190 men, a pack train, and rations for ten days, he marched south from the Walla Walla Valley at dusk and crossed the Oregon border headed toward the Grande Ronde Valley. As much as possible the force traveled in the dark, and when camped they built no fires. On July 17 scouts reported an Indian village lay along the Grande Ronde River, five miles ahead of the force. Shaw took four companies and moved atop a knoll, where he had a view of the village. He organized his men for battle and ordered them to move slowly forward. They stopped when a band of warriors appeared a half mile in front of them. Shaw's account to Isaac Stevens claimed, "At this moment a large body of warriors came forward, singing, and whooping, and one of them waving a white man's scalp on a pole. One of them signified a desire to speak. Whereupon, I sent Captain John to meet him, and formed the command in line of battle.

When Captain John came up to the Indians, they cried out to one another to shoot him, whereupon he retreated to the command, and I ordered the four companies to charge."[43]

As the militia attacked, the Indians "attempted to fight and individually did fight to the last, but all in vain. Every instant they fell before the deadly rifle and revolver. . . . Such was the impetuosity of the charge that many of their women even were unable to escape and were overtaken by the pursuit. None that were recognized were harmed, but were suffered to ride off free." When the fighting ended, at least sixty Indians were killed, perhaps many more, since the warriors carried off as many of their dead as possible. De Lacy reported that 120 lodges were burned and food and supplies destroyed.[44]

Later, in a letter to George Wright, Isaac Stevens did his best to present the fighting as necessary and honorable. He wrote that Colonel Shaw had attacked four hundred warriors. However, while there may have been that many Indians encamped along the river, there were not nearly that many warriors. Shaw attacked with fewer than two hundred men—just four of his six companies, one of which, commanded by the obstinate and mutinous Maj. Hamilton Maxon, disappeared, only to reappear later when the fighting was over. The rest of Shaw's command remained behind to guard the pack train and did not take part in the fighting.

Governor Stevens's view of the Grande Ronde affair was clear in this statement to Shaw: "In general orders of this date, thanks are returned to yourself, the officers and men of your command for their intrepid conduct at the battle of Grande Ronde and Burnt Rivers."[45] Shaw's summary of the Grande Ronde violence hinted at the truth by admitting some women were killed: "We killed about forty of the enemy at Grand Ronde, and among them four or five squaws, who were mistaken by the boys for bucks, in the dust and smoke. Whenever they were recognized as squaws they were suffered to escape. I understand the enemy report that we killed more squaws and children than men. This was not so, to my own knowledge." Shaw told Stevens of his plans for the survivors: "If they come in, let them come quickly.

If I have to hunt them up, I will know they are bad people and will wipe them out."[46]

Indian accounts of the Grande Ronde fight were quite different, as was an account by one of Shaw's own men. Captain De Lacy, as the official journalist for the campaign, wrote what appears to be a relatively unbiased description of the events, but his account was changed by Colonel Shaw and Governor Stevens to transform what was an unwarranted attack into a heroic battle. In doing so, Stevens could inflate his position, and by emphasizing George Wright's diplomatic and military failure in the Yakima Valley, could make the army look bad in comparison. A more accurate account was later taken by George Wright, who at least made the effort to seek out an Indian witness, Chief Howlish Wampum of the Cayuses. Wright's report was succinct, quoting the chief:

> When Colonel Shaw arrived in this valley I went to see him. Colonel Shaw said to me, that he had come to make peace; that he had thrown his arms behind him. I told him my heart was made happy. Soon after, Colonel Shaw marched for the Grande Ronde. The Cayuses were encamped there—that is, the women, old men and children, with a few of the young men. The chiefs were absent when Colonel Shaw approached. He sent Captain John, a friendly Nez Perce, to open a communication with the Cayuses. No persons authorized to talk were in the Cayuse camp. The women and children became alarmed at the advance of the volunteers, and commenced packing up. The volunteers then charged the camp, and killed several old men, women, and children.[47]

Even Colonel Shaw's report, as cleansed as it was, said that his force "destroyed about 150 horse loads of lacamas, dried beef, tents, some flour, coffee, sugar, and about 100 pounds ammunition and a great quantity of tools and kitchen furniture. We took also about 200 horses, most of which were shot."[48] Shaw's long report—more than three thousand words—says that more than forty Indians were killed—perhaps far more—but curiously leaves out the number of killed and wounded soldiers. A separate report filed by his command's surgeon and circulated with the official accounts, noted five killed and four wounded.[49] None of the official reports explained the apparent inconsistency between the alleged number of fierce warriors and the low casualty count among the volunteers. Shaw obviously wanted to present the conflict as a pitched battle when it was actually more of a massacre.

To make matters worse, Shaw's force had marched across land that had been designated under the 1855 Walla Walla treaty as reserved for Chief Joseph's band of the Nez Perce. Shaw also crossed adjoining land still in the legal possession of the Cayuses and Umatillas.[50] Word of Shaw's brazen attack quickly spread north along the rest of the plateau, increasing tension among the Spokanes, Coeur d'Alenes, Palouses, Yakamas, and others.

Concerned that the militia might cause more harm, General Wool wrote that "Colonel Wright was ordered with all possible dispatch to that country, with orders to arrest, disarm, and send the volunteers out of the country."[51] A month later, Wool again wrote to army headquarters with assurances that Wright was establishing a post in the Walla Walla Valley, to be under the command of Lt. Col. Edward Steptoe.

In July, having ordered a stronger presence in the Walla Walla Valley, Wool wrote that the war in the Northwest was nearly over. He wrote to Wright, "As the war is finished in Puget's Sound and Southern Oregon, it only remains to you to give it the finishing stroke." Wool again issued a warning to Wright about another dangerous enemy, the territorial militias: "The commanding general, in his opinion of the 16th June, cautioned you against the whites in your rear, from whom you have as much to apprehend as the Indians in your front."[52]

In August 1856 Wright carried out Wool's order, sending Lt. Colonel Steptoe and 250 men into the Walla Walla Valley with orders to fortify Fort Walla Walla. In advance of the mission, General Wool issued a public order that was intended to protect the tribes: "No emigrant or other white person, except the Hudson's Bay Company, or persons having ceded rights from the Indians, will be permitted to settle or to remain in the Indian country, or on land not settled, or not confirmed by the Senate and approved by the President of the United States."[53] The order did not apply to miners in the Colville mining district, an omission that would later have fatal consequences.

PLACING BLAME

In his message to the citizens of Washington Territory published in October 1856, Governor Stevens, in another of his self-serving statements, laid out the causes of violence in the Northwest: "The war had its origin in the Indians treacherously killing some of our best citizens, both east and west of the Cascade mountains, not sparing women and children, in the teeth of the faith of solemn treaties. It was not caused as has been falsely asserted by bad conduct on the part of the citizens, who have been habitually kind to the Indians."[54] Stevens's remarks in the document are assertive, clear, and full of condemnation for Indians and those whites who supported them. His venom and bluster surely had something to do with the thuggish behavior of the militia, as well as the alienation of the U.S. Army. In his General Orders, he instructed territorial volunteer Col. Edward Lander to "make war on the savages infesting the forests."[55]

In June 1856 Isaac Stevens's attitude toward George Wright began to sour. He believed Wright "emboldened the Indians, and has probably enabled them to effect a general combination of the tribes."[56] Four months later Stevens complained to Secretary of War Jefferson Davis again, claiming that his valiant efforts at coming to terms with the Walla Wallas had fallen apart since Wright had assumed command of the army's tactics on the Columbia Plateau. He then went after Wright with vengeance. In a long letter, he accused Wright of neglect in the Yakima Valley and of general incompetence in his dealing with tribes east of the Cascade Mountains. Stevens believed Wright not only should have sought to punish the murderers of Agent Bolon, but he also should have insisted on the "absolute and unconditional submission of the whole tribe to the justice and mercy of the government."[57]

Events in the Yakima and Grande Ronde Valleys had so intensified dissatisfaction among the tribes on the Columbia Plateau that Governor Stevens decided a second council was needed to restore calm. In his biography of his father, Hazard Stevens accurately credited Shaw's brutal victory in the Grande Ronde with demoralizing the region's tribes. They knew that resistance would be met with brutal force, but it was worse than that: even when engaged in peaceful pursuits, they were not safe from attack.[58] Governor Stevens wanted to gather the friendly tribes—Nez Perces, Spokanes, Coeur d'Alenes, and others—to impress upon them the importance of their alliance with the whites. He hoped unfriendly groups would also attend so that he could prove the intentions of the government were peaceful. Stevens asked Colonel Wright to accompany him, but instead Wright sent Colonel Steptoe and four companies of men. On August 19, Stevens and Steptoe left The Dalles accompanied by thirty wagons and nearly three hundred oxen, horses, and mules.

Compared with the 1855 council, the second session would be smaller and more hostile. On August 23 Stevens arrived at the site in the Walla Walla Valley from which Colonel Shaw had prepared for his incursion into the Grande Ronde. On September 8, the governor received a party of three hundred wary Nez Perces led by Chief Lawyer. Two days later, not expecting serious trouble, Colonel Steptoe set up camp eight miles away from the council grounds. However, as more Indians arrived, the mood became tense, and some even fired the grass around the council grounds. Stevens requested that Steptoe bring his force closer to the governor's camp; the colonel refused, in accordance with General Wool's standing order to have as little as possible to do with Isaac Stevens.

The Spokanes and Coeur d'Alenes declined the invitation to attend the council, ostensibly because the salmon were running. While this was true, there was another reason: Chief Garry of the Spokanes had enough experience with Stevens and his treaties to know that little good could come from another council, and he wanted to keep his people away from both Stevens's machinations and any potential violence. Garry sent a message to Stevens that when the salmon run was over, the governor should not expect to meet with his people, either; then it would be time to hunt buffalo.[59]

At the first Walla Walla Treaty Council, Stevens had claimed Chief Kamiakin of the Yakamas spoke for numerous tribes in central and eastern Washington Territory, and thus these tribes could be dealt with as a group. Stevens refused to listen to their protests at the time, and he had little patience for the same people making the same objections a year later. The treaty council quickly deteriorated when Chief Quiltenenock of the Sinkiuse people insisted his tribe not be included in the reservation designated for the Yakamas. Earlier in the year, Quiltenenock had complained to George Wright of the injustice, and Wright referred him to Governor Stevens. The chief was able to gather an impressive delegation that included Yakama chiefs Owhi and Kamiakin, who would present their claims that they had not spoken for the Sinkiuse people at the prior council, and thus the Sinkiuses should not be held to the treaty's provisions. They made little progress with the governor.[60] In a closing address to the tribes, Stevens had "expressed regret that I had failed in my mission—that no one said 'yes,' to my propositions, and I now had only to say, 'follow your own hearts; those who wish to go to war, go.'" He reminded them that he required their "unconditional submission." His dismissive, belligerent tone only served to further anger the tribes.[61]

On September 19 he departed with his escort and pack train. Angered by Stevens's rebuff, a force led by Quiltenenock, Qualchan, and Kamiakin attacked the governor's entourage. Stevens would later claim the attacking force consisted of more than four hundred warriors, including Yakamas, Walla Wallas, Umatillas, and Nez Perces. Stevens's force suffered one fatality and three wounded, a small number of casualties considering the alleged size of the enemy force. In the early part of the twentieth century, Judge William Compton Brown, whose research included interviews with Indian participants, estimated the true attacking force at no more than fifty warriors, with a large number of men and women watching from a distance. In any case, the second

Walla Walla council merely served to reinforce the tribes' belief that Stevens was interested only in moving them off land coveted by settlers and the railroad. It is not clear what Stevens intended to accomplish in his second council. It was hastily arranged and conducted, and when the chiefs showed up, Stevens seemed unable to deal with their anger. The governor pleased no one: not the tribes, the army, or the citizenry, at least in 1856. Even the normally Stevens-friendly *Olympia Pioneer and Democrat* ran a headline that shouted, "THE COUNCIL A FAILURE!" Of course, the paper laid the blame on the tribes, claiming, as did Stevens, that they were offered fair terms and rejected them in favor of war.[62]

Fortunately for Stevens, he had Colonel Wright as a scapegoat, and he went after him with full force. In a long letter to Jefferson Davis, he wrote, "I have failed, therefore in making the desired arrangements with the Indians in the Walla Walla, and the failure, to be attributed in part to the want of cooperation with me as Superintendent of Indian Affairs, on the part of the regular troops, has its causes also in the whole plan of operations of the troops since Col. Wright assumed command." As with his letters criticizing General Wool, Stevens's bullets became more directed as the letter continued. He accused Wright of doing too much talking,

> thus giving safe conduct to murderers and assassins. . . . I state boldly, that the cause of the Nez Perces becoming disaffected and finally going into the war, is the operations of Colonel Wright east of the Cascades—operations so feeble, so procrastinating, so entirely unequal to the emergency, that not only has a most severe blow been struck at the credit of the government and prosperity and character of this remote section of country, but the impression has been made upon the Indians that the people and soldiers were a different people.[63]

Once again, Stevens had made a fundamental error in dealing with the tribes. He had again insisted on grouping tribes together, often appointing one chief to speak for unrelated tribes. He believed it was the most efficient way to take care of a problem, but his method had an unintended result: being treated equally made it more likely the tribes would act in concert to fight the Americans. In other words, according to historian Wayne E. Lee, his actions "progressively altered Native American societies toward greater aggression and political unity, which in turn enhanced those societies' capacity to wage destructive war."[64]

George Wright's lack of effort to control Governor Stevens brought criticism from General Wool, whose "annoyance" stemmed from Wright's inability or unwillingness to stop Governor Stevens from holding a second council in the Walla Walla Valley. At the least, Wool complained, Wright should have attended the council himself, instead of turning over the escort responsibility to Steptoe: "Your instructions were too plain to be misunderstood," Wool wrote. "How, then, could you permit the agent [Governor Stevens] to precede the march of your column to Walla Walla, to treat with Indians you had been ordered to subdue?"[65] Wright's response, if any, does not appear in military records.

Stevens capped off the year with a statement that summarized his view of the year's events and that sounds as if he felt a need to defend his legacy: "History will present the fact with credit and honor to the Volunteer Force—that during the six months of active service of one thousand of the citizens of Washington Territory, not a single friendly Indian has been harmed in a volunteer camp, or scout—no Indian has been plundered or molested and the captured property of defeated savages has been, in every case, turned over to the proper officers and faithfully accounted to them."[66] In a particularly incongruous remark, even for Stevens, he claimed that the safety of the tribes was attributable to the same people that had caused much of their suffering: "It was not the strength of a few frail men, but the strength and courage of a whole population that secured to the Indians this immunity from right and wrong."[67]

Stevens was adept at altering his message to suit his audience, especially when he was angling for power. For example, a month later, he wrote to Secretary of War Davis, "It seems to me that we have, in this territory, fallen upon evil times. I hope and trust some energetic action may be taken to stop with trifling with our public interests, and to make our flag respected by the Indians of the Interior. They scorn our people and our flag. They feel they can kill and plunder with impunity. They denominate us a nation of old women. They did not do this when the volunteers were in the field."[68]

Stevens continued to lay blame on Colonel Wright, whom he claimed had "made a concession to the Indians which he had no authority to make—that, by so doing, he has done nothing but to get the semblance of a peace, and that by his acts he has, in a measure, weakened the influence of the service by having the authority to make treaties, and having charge of the friendly Indians. He has, in my judgment, abandoned his own duty which was to reduce the Indians to submission, and has trenched upon and usurped a portion of mine."[69]

By the beginning of the winter of 1856, Colonel Steptoe had completed the first phase of Fort Walla Walla, and Major Garnett was ensconced in Fort Simcoe in the Yakima Valley. The winter of 1856–57 was unusually cold, and everyone in the Northwest concentrated on survival. For a few months, at least, the plateau was free of widespread bloodshed.

SEVEN

A Tense Quiet

The calm that settled over Washington Territory for most of 1857 was deceptive. Early in the year, rumblings of a coming Indian war trickled through the region, attracting the attention of the national press. The *New York Times* reported on the front page that the Yakamas were moving their women and children out of the probable battle area to relative safety at the Cascades and that the army believed a war would start "as soon as the proper season opens."[1]

At Fort Walla Walla, Col. Edward Steptoe's men had constructed a lumber mill, and progress started on barracks and quarters for the officers. The growing fort made the Plateau tribes uneasy, and the Catholic missionaries among the Flathead and Coeur d'Alene people worked to avoid war. In April 1857 the missionaries were becoming concerned about rising tension between whites and the tribes, in particular the Palouses, Yakamas, and Cayuses. Father Adrian Hoecken of the Flathead Mission predicted a general outbreak in 1857. Thanks in part to the efforts of Fathers Joset, Hoecken, De Smet, and Ravalli, general bloodshed was avoided.[2] Father Hoecken accused the Nez Perces and Spokanes of trying to corrupt the Coeur d'Alenes, Flatheads, and Kalispels. He wrote that they "spread a bad spirit among the Indians who reside in the country below. They endeavor to communicate their hatred of the Americans; but our chiefs are firm."[3] Although individual members of many tribes were encouraging strong opposition to the invasion of their land, Father Hoecken's claim reflected a narrow view of intertribal influence. Had Father Hoecken lived among the Spokanes and Nez Perces, he may have had the view that the Flatheads and other tribes were trying to "corrupt" *them*. As whites (and Indians) in other parts of the territory had learned, familiarity often brought understanding and lessened fear.

In Oregon Territory some politicians and businessmen advocated for the annexation of Washington Territory into what would become the state of Oregon. An editorial in the *Olympia Pioneer and Democrat* asserted that such a combination was impossible, since the citizens of Washington Territory had been impoverished by the Indian war of 1856 and were opposed to the payment of taxes. In addition, the eastern portion of Washington Territory was in relative chaos, since, the paper noted, General Wool had "surrendered all that vast region of country to the demands of the Indians."[4] The paper's claims were exaggerations. The war had caused relatively little property damage, and while tension was high in the eastern part of the territory, it was far from "chaos." In fact, armed conflict tended to enrich the white businessmen who provided supplies to the army or militia, even if they often had to wait weeks or months for payment. With a lull in armed conflict with the tribes, the newspapers suspended some of their vitriol toward Indians and turned it toward Mormons in Utah Territory. Articles focused on the qualities of the Mormon man: his theology, morals, criminal tendencies, and polygamist practices. One paper published a list of the members of the Utah Legislature, noting their ages, physical condition, and number of wives.[5]

Travelers in eastern Washington Territory reported few problems with Indians. One miner wrote that the tribes were friendly, although the Spokanes and Pend Oreilles were "saucy."[6] Washington and Oregon territorial officials continued to pressure the army to remove General Wool, and in March Gen. Winfield Scott replaced him with Gen. Newman S. Clarke, a decorated veteran of the Mexican-American War. Although Stevens took at least some credit for Wool's removal, the general's letters reflect a man weary of the incessant battles with politicians in the Northwest. Given Wool's reputation in Washington, D.C., and the fact that he would later be given a prominent posting during the Civil War, his removal did his career no harm. It was more likely that the seasoned and canny Wool was fed up with Stevens and his machinations.

While the tribes tried to make the best of the turmoil and confusion resulting from the treaties, George Wright and the Ninth Infantry settled in at Fort Dalles, which had recently been expanded under the direction of the quartermaster, Capt. Thomas Jordan. Captain Jordan aimed to please his new commanding officer, telling his wife he hoped he was "giving not a little satisfaction to Col. Wright and others as quartermaster." Colonel Wright's new residence was luxurious for a military post, described as the "finest in all Oregon." Of Victorian design, it had two stories plus an attic and was approached by a wide carriage road designed to take in the view and present the house at its finest. The finishes included oak woodwork, a green marble fireplace mantle, and ceiling frescoes. Furniture was made on-site, most of it Victorian in design, to match the house. However, while the officers and their wives delighted in their luxury in the wilderness, George Wright's superior was not amused. Adjutant for the Department of the Pacific W. W. Mackall requested an accounting for the "enormous" expenses and transmitted General Clarke's order to reduce civilian employment in order to save money. One critic said it was a house "such as I have never seen occupied by a private gentleman except at or in the neighborhood of our large Eastern cities." Captain Jordan showed great concern about the fort's design and quality. An 1859 audit revealed the fort's total construction cost to have been about $240,000, an amount that appalled some civilians, who "censured Capt. Jordan for extravagance in erecting these neat cottages and necessary public buildings." One historian has defended the expenses, saying, "They were related to several ends. Wool's concepts of how the Indians should be handled were applied: Wright's Indian campaigns were in no sense massacres, and very few Indians were killed or executed."[7] The connection between the cost of the fort and the number of Indians killed is a curious one, and represents one way of trying to justify not only the construction cost, but Wright's actions against the tribes.

Colonel Wright's response included a range of reasons for the expense, from the need for a large logistical base from which to launch expeditions to the fact that the staff officers were working seven days a week. General Clarke visited the post in summer 1857 and in July issued an order in which he laid out guidelines for fort design and construction, including, "Such structures will be of the plainest kind, according to climate, in view of the health of the troops, and of the most convenient, and economical procurement of materials for construction."[8]

Wright's relatively elaborate quarters, coupled with his increasingly confident words to the tribes, political leaders, and to his own superior officer, reflect a man trying to make a distinct mark in the region, holding himself apart from, and in some ways above, both the tribes and the territorial political powers—a Big Dog not only to Indians but to whites as well.

THE BROWNE REPORT

In need of an independent appraisal of the state of Indian affairs in the Pacific Northwest, Congress appointed a special agent to investigate. In August 1857 J. Ross Browne arrived at the mouth of the Columbia on the steamship *Commodore* to begin a five-week tour of the Pacific Northwest.[9] Browne had a strong sense of curiosity about many things and enough passion to put it to good use. At fifty-four years old, his accomplishments were remarkable. In addition to a stint as minister to China, he became an expert on the whaling industry, mining, government waste, international diplomacy, travel writing, Indian affairs, and much more. As a writer and satirist he provided inspiration to writers such as Mark Twain and published frequently in *Harper's* magazine and other publications. Thus, his report on Indian affairs carried great weight both in the Northwest and in Washington, D.C. During his investigation he traveled two thousand miles visiting reservations and holding councils with the tribes. He audited government accounts and contractors' records, uncovering fraud and abuse in the reservation payment system. His conclusions were clear: the state of Indian affairs was abysmal, in great part due to a basic conflict between the tribes and the federal government. Having their way of life taken away, the tribes had few reasons to trust or obey Indian agents or anyone else who tried to convince them of what was in their best interests. Browne clearly understood the cause of the conflicts, but while he was extremely critical of how whites had treated the tribes, he had just as little patience with Indians. He felt the solution to the Indian problem in the Pacific Northwest was to keep Indians and whites apart, which meant improving the reservation system and enforcing restrictions on the tribes.[10]

In councils with Browne, the tribes listed their grievances, focusing on broken promises concerning treaties and the general poor health of their people. Browne assured them they would be paid for their land, and the government would make good on reparations and promises of food and medicine; but in return, he told them they must remain on reservations and be satisfied with what they were provided. He led the tribes to believe that the Walla Walla treaty signed in 1855 would be ratified and they would soon receive payment for the land taken from them.[11]

At least one white observer was aware of the growing tensions—and the reasons for them. In 1858 the Indian agent for western Washington Territory, M. T. Simmons, wrote of the Indians: "Their forbearance has been remarkable. While they had the power of crushing us like worms they treated us like brothers. We, I think, should return their kindness now that we have the power, and our duty is so plainly pointed out by their deplorable situation." Simmons believed the treaties needed to be ratified so that the tribes would have the tools, schools, medical help, and other assistance the pacts promised.[12]

Despite the turmoil around them, the Plateau tribes remained quiet, determined to withstand outside pressure peacefully. Peaceful influences on the tribes included chiefs like Garry of the

Spokanes; missionaries such as Father Joseph Joset of the Coeur d'Alene Mission; and the tribes' own generally peaceable cultures. Kamiakin, the Yakama chief, was often alleged to be inciting violence, but more often he was defending his people and their way of life from outside pressure. He no doubt had learned at the Cascades Rapids that attacking a small settlement like the Cascades accomplished little except provoking a rapid response from the army. Although Kamiakin had the standing to organize war parties, he did so infrequently compared to the number of attacks launched against his people. Regardless of the relative quiet, at the end of 1857 Commissioner of Indian Affairs J. W. Denver wrote in his annual report to Congress, "Our relations with the Indians in those Territories [Washington and Oregon] are in a very critical condition," and that an outbreak of violence was likely "from any disturbing cause."[13]

As tension built in the Northwest, Isaac Stevens began to plan for his departure from Washington Territory. In March, running as a Democrat, he easily won election to Congress as the territorial representative. In the autumn of 1857 he left the Pacific Northwest for good. However, distance was not a hindrance to Representative Stevens. From Washington he continued his work on the Northern Pacific Railway and continued his criticism of Colonel Wright and any member of the army who had disagreed with his policies. In addition, he kept pushing both territorial officials and the army to pursue and punish Indians who were resisting occupation by settlers.

Late in the year, George Gibbs reported that some Indians near Puget Sound had apparently received a visit from a Mormon emissary, who told them that "Choosuklee (Jesus Christ) had recently appeared on the other side of the mountains; that he was after a while coming here, when the whites would be sent out of the country, and all would be well for themselves." Gibbs assumed that the "Jesus Christ" referred to was actually Brigham Young.[14] Maj. Robert S. Garnett, in command of Fort Simcoe in the Yakima Valley, reported, "The Indian Chief 'Skloom,' brother of Kamiakin, has recently sent word to me, for the second time, that the Mormons, on one or two occasions since last summer, have sent emissaries among the Indians of the region to incite them to a union with the Mormons in hostility to the United States."[15] The perceived threat from the Mormons never materialized, and the year ended with an uneasy peace.

In 1858 the pressure would lead to an explosion that left behind death, broken hearts, and a crippled culture.

EIGHT

A Disastrous Affair

Just over there where yon purple peak,
Like a great amethyst, gems the brow of the desert,
I sprawled flat in the bunch-grass, a target
For those Indians, betrayed by this thing we call the State.

C. E. S. WOOD, *THE POET IN THE DESERT*

Father Joseph Joset played a key role during the fateful events of 1858. Years later, in 1874, he wrote to Rev. Joseph Giorda, "Your Reverend wishes me to give an account of the sad events of 1858; it is easy enough, for the times were so hot, that it would be difficult to forget anything about them."[1] Unlike Joset's more balanced recollections, in the white ethnocentric narrative that developed following the events of 1858, Col. Edward Steptoe and his men became heroes and the Indians criminals. The truth was something in between, but regardless, Steptoe's expedition was the proximate cause of George Wright's punitive 1858 campaign. The deaths of officers and soldiers on the Steptoe battlefield gave rise to a desire for vengeance among the public, the government, and the army.

In writing of the Plateau War, Lt. Lawrence Kip said, "An Indian war is a chapter of accidents."[2] Perhaps no other episode illustrates Kip's words better than Colonel Steptoe's expedition of May 1858, a march that ended in death and humiliation.[3] Steptoe's expedition plays a central role in the long narrative about the Plateau War, and the episode contributes a number of questions and mysteries. After 150 years, the central question remains:

Why did an experienced and respected officer like Steptoe take an ill-prepared force into land occupied by wary tribes?

TRANQUILITY AND TENSION

Edward J. Steptoe was a Virginian who was, by both blood and marriage, related to George Washington, James Madison, and other Virginia aristocrats.[4] He graduated from West Point in 1837 at the age of twenty-one, fought in the Seminole War (1838–42), and participated in the forced relocation of the Cherokee people, performing duty that one chronicler referred to as "emigrating the Indians to the West."[5] During the Mexican-American War, Steptoe was awarded two brevets for "gallant and meritorious conduct," the first to the rank of major, the second to lieutenant colonel. Steptoe's friendship with President Franklin Pierce, formed while the two fought together in Mexico, led to an appointment as governor of Utah Territory, succeeding Brigham Young. President Pierce held Steptoe in such high regard that he penned a five-page letter congratulating the colonel and pledging his full support.[6] Given the political and military tensions in Utah Territory, the appointment was one of the most important the president could make, but Steptoe was astute enough to avoid trying to manage relations between the U.S. government and a territory populated by the confrontational Mormons, and he turned down the appointment.[7] He was uneasy about the influence of the Mormon authorities over the Indian tribes in Utah Territory, and he asked that additional troops be sent to help police the region. Steptoe then headed back to his home state of Virginia, where he joined Colonel Wright at Fort Monroe and assisted in the formation of the new Ninth Infantry. In 1856 he accompanied the Ninth to Fort Vancouver, and after the battle at Cascades Rapids he led an incursion into the Yakima Valley that ended with little consequence.

In late summer 1856 Colonel Wright had directed Steptoe to establish a fort in the Walla Walla Valley. The isolation agreed

Col. Edward J. Steptoe. Original in the private collection of Greg Partch, Sr.

with Steptoe, as expressed in a letter to his sister, Nannie, dated October 27, 1856:

> Do you know where this place is? Look up the Columbia River on the map till you see its tributary, the Walla Walla, and on this latter "The Mission." About five miles above the last place I am erecting a Post. The Walla Walla River flows through a valley surrounded by hills & mountains. This valley being so shut in has a very fine climate, is

> very fertile and is intersected by streams everywhere. I find much to interest and amuse me. What with supervising the work, shooting grouse & catching trout, the time moves not unpleasantly along. My command embraces some 14 or 15 officers and five companies of troops. One want we feel much, and that is female society; but one officer is married & his family is absent.[8]

Steptoe's men would not have agreed with his assessment of life at Fort Walla Walla. During the harsh winter of 1857–58, they lived in huts made of mud, willow branches, and grass pressed together to form crude shelters. Floors were dirt and food was poor, with fresh vegetables often impossible to obtain. Their clothing was shabby and their shoes falling apart. As weather permitted, they worked on the construction of the new fort, which would eventually provide the simple comforts expected in an isolated outpost. While Fort Walla Walla took shape, Steptoe apparently ordered few drills; discipline was relaxed and his men were inexperienced not only in waging war, but also in their ability to effectively use the tools of war.

In the Walla Walla Valley, Colonel Steptoe was in a good position to gauge the mood of the tribes in the region. Even back in September 1856, not long after he arrived in the Walla Walla Valley, he sensed trouble. In a letter to Colonel Wright, Steptoe had requested an additional company of riflemen: "The necessity of controlling by a strong force the Nez Perces and Spokane tribes cannot be overestimated. . . . If they begin war, every inner tribe will necessarily unite with them."[9] Given the mood of the tribes in the wake of the Stevens treaties, there was little doubt Steptoe was correct.

Steptoe had been optimistic about the peace in the Walla Walla Valley until he learned that government investigator J. Ross Browne had met with Chief Lawyer of the Nez Perces and informed him that "Governor Stevens' treaty of the Walla Walla would *certainly* be ratified and enforced." Steptoe said of Browne, "He had no right to unsettle the Indian minds on a point respecting which his convictions are probably no stronger than the opposite belief of many others in daily intercourse with them.

. . . I will simply add that in my opinion any attempt to enforce the treaty will be followed by immediate hostilities with most of the tribes in this part of the country."[10] Steptoe suggested that a new commission be established in order to draw up a revised treaty that would be more acceptable to the tribes.

In addition to the Sahaptin-speaking tribes in the Walla Walla and Yakima Valleys and along the Snake River, the Coeur d'Alenes and Spokanes were likewise wary of the intentions of both the army and the territorial government. Events of the prior few years were pressing on them, and by the winter of 1857–58, Father Joset noted that "a great preoccupation prevailed among the Coeur d'Alenes; several times they questioned me as to whether the troops should come in the country next spring. I told them always that I considered it an idle tale." Joset knew of no reason for the army to march north of the Snake and enter the homelands of the Coeur d'Alenes, Spokanes, or Palouses. In fact, the only reason the missionary could imagine the army going anywhere in the region was to go to Colville, more than two hundred miles north of Walla Walla, "where I knew that since the introduction of whisky, there were some difficulties between the whites and Indians." Joset wrote, "I was told privately by an Indian of another tribe, 'Should soldiers come, the people will be awfully mad.'"[11] The warning made Joset nervous, and he decided to make the journey from the Coeur d'Alene Mission to Fort Walla Walla to let Colonel Steptoe know of the tribes' discomfort. In early April 1858, while the Coeur d'Alenes were spread over the region gathering roots and hunting, Joset started out with three companions. They rode south and before leaving Coeur d'Alene country they met Chief Vincent, who warned Joset that the Palouses were trying to stir up anger against whites. Joset decided to return to the Coeur d'Alene Mission without seeing Steptoe, telling Chief Vincent to let him know if any soldiers appeared north of the Snake River. Again, Joset told Vincent that he could think of no reason why the army would move into Coeur d'Alene land.

Events in Utah compounded the tension felt by army and government officials in Washington and Oregon Territories.

Mormons fighting the U.S. government had been attempting to recruit Indian allies; they had spread word through the Snakes to the Walla Wallas, Nez Perces, Cayuses, and other tribes that if they joined their fight, they would be supplied with arms, ammunition, horses, cattle, and other gifts.

From Washington, D.C., Congressman Stevens maintained an active hand in Northwest Indian policy. In a letter dated January 18, 1858, he wrote to J. W. Nesmith, superintendent of Indian affairs for Oregon and Washington Territories, updating him on Congressional action regarding the treaties with Indians in the Pacific Northwest. Stevens was aware of the tribes' dissatisfaction with the Walla Walla treaty, but as usual shifted blame elsewhere: "Our trouble will be with the Treaty with the Yakamas, the Treaty with the Nez Perces, and the Treaty with the Cayuses, Walla Wallas, and the Umatillas," he wrote. He was, as usual, frustrated with the army: "The Military have in the strongest manner urged that these Treaties be not confirmed," he wrote. "They are treaties very liberal to the Indians. Look on my map on file in your office and see how large and well adapted to the Indians the reserves are."[12] In fact, Stevens's map, or any map, could not show what was happening in the tribes' homeland. The savvy Stevens had to have known that the reservation lines meant little to whites who wanted Indian land.

The Washington Territorial legislature did not care if the tribes were unhappy. On January 29, 1858, they passed a bill creating Spokane County; the boundaries were formalized two years later. The county included the majority of the Columbia Plateau and was bordered by the Columbia River to the west, the Snake to the south, the Rockies to the east, and Canada to the north. Spokane and Walla Walla Counties—the territory that would later be conquered by Colonel Wright—encompassed virtually all of the Columbia Plateau, and then some. Thus, even before Steptoe and Wright began their expeditions, political wheels were already in motion to settle the land.[13]

In early 1858 rumors about an Indian uprising were widespread. A Portland newspaper again reported that Mormons in Utah were encouraging the Northwest tribes to attack white settlements, even going so far as to supply them with arms. A January 14 column stated, "It seems to be a universal sentiment among the Indians on our Northern and Western frontier that there is to be trouble in the approaching spring."[14] Two French-Canadian miners on their way to the Colville gold fields had been killed by Indians, stirring up fears of further violence. Also in early 1858 Chief Tilcoax of the Palouses had been active in stirring up the Spokanes, Kalispels, and some of the Coeur d'Alenes. It was primarily through the efforts of Chief Vincent and a few others that the majority of the Coeur d'Alenes remained peaceful. On April 12 a band of Palouses drove off cattle from a herd owned by a rancher in the Walla Walla Valley. A pursuit by soldiers from Fort Walla Walla proved fruitless. The incident served to incite territory-wide anger toward essentially all the Plateau tribes, and in particular Chief Tilcoax, who was regarded by the army and civilians as the cause of at least as much trouble against whites as Kamiakin.

Colonel Steptoe informed his new commanding officer, Gen. Newman Clarke, that he had heard that there was enough "excitement amongst the Pelouse and Spokane Indians as to make an expedition to the north advisable." He believed that tribes in eastern Washington Territory had been planning an uprising, allegedly to be led by Chief Owhi, his son Qualchan, and Chief Kamiakin, all of the Yakamas.[15] A group of whites in Colville, near the Canadian border, had asked for protection from local Indians. In mid-April 1858 Steptoe sent word from Fort Walla Walla to department headquarters, informing them that Palouse Indians were conducting raids and stealing horses and cattle. He intended to "investigate the matter thoroughly." In a follow-up letter to Major Mackall, General Clarke's adjutant, dated May 2, Steptoe added, "There appears to be some probability of considerable disturbance among the neighboring tribes [Coeur d'Alenes, Palouse, Spokanes, etc.], but I hope to check it."[16] He did not explain how he meant to "check" the tribes with his small force. Some historians have claimed that Steptoe was just doing reconnaissance, while others believe he intended his march as a show of force or an incursion to gather intelligence regarding the tribes. Perhaps there was some truth to all of the reasons that have been suggested, but in any case, Steptoe was unprepared.

ENGAGEMENT AND RETREAT

Steptoe started off from Fort Walla Walla on May 6 with a force of 152 soldiers and 7 officers.[17] They were accompanied by 30 civilian packers in charge of about one hundred pack animals. In addition to muskets and rifles, they took two twelve-pound howitzers with their folding carriages packed on horses.[18] The fighting force was made up of two infantry companies and three companies of dragoons, leaving a fourth company behind at Fort Walla Walla under the command of Capt. Frederick Dent.[19]

The dragoons left behind their sabers, which were useful in close fighting but were no use against firearms. The privates were required to carry muskets that fired a single ball with three pieces of shot, essentially a crude precursor to the shotgun. However, Steptoe's muskets, called musketoons, were useless beyond fifty yards, and even within that distance striking a target was due as much to luck as to skill. A survivor claimed, "The most effective sort of work with a blunderbuss like the musketoon was its use as a shillaleh."[20] One company carried Mississippi Jaeger (Yager) rifles, which were powerful but heavy and slow loading, particularly for soldiers on horseback. Lt. David M. Gregg's H Troop carried ten new Sharp's carbines, which had longer range than the musketoons but were untried in battle. In addition, at times a shot could emit so much smoke and flame it would temporarily blind the soldier firing it.[21]

Instead of heading north from Walla Walla to the Snake River and the Colville Road, Steptoe led his men fifty miles northeast and crossed the Snake at Red Wolf's Crossing. The land ahead was foreign to Steptoe and his inexperienced force, and scouts from Chief Timothy's Nez Perce band joined the force at the crossing. Also at the Snake River, Steptoe's force enlisted—or according to some accounts, forced—some Palouse Indians to help them cross the river in a turbulent stretch of water.[22]

Beyond the basalt cliffs along the Snake, the terrain consists of rolling hills, some quite steep; in spring it is lush with bunchgrass and prairie flowers. With plenty of good grazing for the horses, the force needed to find only water. Not far to the east of the river, the terrain rises into pine-covered foothills, then forested mountains beyond. Until 1858 relatively few whites had ventured north of the Snake River without permission from the tribes who lived there, including the Spokanes, Coeur d'Alenes, and Palouses. The land was unmapped, which makes Steptoe's choice of route all the more curious.

The mile-long string of soldiers, horses, and cattle moved slowly. Capt. Charles Winder, who commanded an artillery company, wrote that after departing Fort Walla Walla on May 6, the force traveled 150 miles in ten days.[23] Their route added at least thirty miles to their trip (compared to the Colville Road), taking them along the present-day border of Washington and Idaho. Along the way the troops had frequent contact with various Indians who had come to investigate the reason for Steptoe's incursion. Chief Vincent of the Coeur d'Alenes sent scouts; they noted the soldiers' rifles, muskets, and howitzers and questioned Steptoe about his intentions. On orders from Chief Vincent, they warned Steptoe that he was trespassing and told him he should withdraw south of the Snake River. At the same time, Vincent sent a messenger to Father Joset at the Coeur d'Alene Mission notifying him of the incursion.[24]

Although the route took the force into country unknown to Steptoe, he did not seem to lack confidence. Joel Trimble was a soldier in Steptoe's force and later a company commander in the Nez Perce War. His experience fighting Indians began in 1851 when he was involved in the Rogue River War, followed by the battle at Cascades Rapids in 1856, the Steptoe and Wright expeditions in 1858, the Civil War, the Modoc War in 1872–73, and the Nez Perce War in 1877. Years later Trimble claimed that Steptoe had seemed lackadaisical: "On the expedition Colonel Steptoe was in civilian attire and rode along carelessly and confidently, carrying in his hand a small riding whip." Furthermore, while Steptoe was a decorated veteran of the Mexican-American War,

Father Joseph Joset of the Coeur d'Alene Mission. Jesuit Oregon Province Archive, Gonzaga University Special Collections.

fighting Indians was a different matter. Trimble said that Steptoe lacked "craft," meaning that he did not understand Indians and frontiersmen: "You must know how to fight the way Indians do. You must know signs. You must watch the weather. You must be on your guard all the time. In fact, 'craft' becomes sort of an instinct or second nature." Later in life, Trimble addressed the failure of Steptoe's expedition, which he attributed both to Steptoe's poor leadership and to ineffective weaponry. He derided not only the muskets and rifles they carried, but also their pistols, which he had "often seen used as a policeman's club in the hands of a sturdy Irish corporal, but never as a weapon of war."[25]

Regardless of Trimble's assessment of Steptoe's Indian-fighting stills, the colonel's real failing might have been his ignorance of the tribes' mood. During the two years prior to Steptoe's incursion, the tribes had been subject to unprovoked attacks by the territorial militia, uncertain policing actions from the army, and the insulting councils conducted by Isaac Stevens. They viewed Steptoe's march as brazen intimidation.[26]

Steptoe's official report of the expedition, written a few days after his retreat, claimed that the Palouses were hostile and stated that as his force approached, "The enemy fled towards the north, and I followed leisurely on the road to Colville."[27] He was on the "road to Colville" only in the sense that he was heading roughly north, since by the time the Palouses had fled from him, the actual Colville Road lay at least thirty miles to the west. In fact, Steptoe was, for at least the early part of his journey, on the Lapwai trail. It was a main pathway used by Indians; other trails intersected with it. Further north it was sometimes referred to as the Colville trail, but it was not the same route as the Colville Road. The difference was critical: whites were unwelcome on the Lapwai trail without permission.

Later, Father Joset would write that Chief Timothy admitted that he led Steptoe into a trap. Timothy apparently wanted to engage the army in a fight with his enemy, Chief Tilcoax of the Palouses, so he led them on a path that would force a confrontation. Timothy figured Tilcoax would be with his people gathering food along a tributary of the Palouse River, near present-day

Chief Timothy of the Nez Perces. Drawing by Gustavus Sohon, 1855. Washington State Historical Society.

Moscow, Idaho. According to Father Joset's account, on May 8, Timothy, riding ahead of the troops, found the Palouse chief and confronted him, saying, "Telaxway [Tilcoax], very soon thy wives, thy horses, thy goods shall be ours."[28] Thus, Steptoe's force became unwitting pawns in personal and intertribal conflicts. Hearing from the Nez Perces that Steptoe was after Coeur d'Alene wives, horses, and goods, Chief Vincent sent a messenger to Father Joset at the Coeur d'Alene Mission. He then rode to confer with Chief Seltice, who was camped near the present-day Washington-Idaho border.[29]

Meanwhile, Steptoe's path curved back toward the northwest, heading into the central Palouse, inside the present-day Washington border. On May 14 his men camped along the Palouse River, then continued north, making camp on the 15th along Pine Creek, near the present-day town of Rosalia. The next day, Sunday, the march continued northwest, a direction that would eventually take them to the Colville Road. However, Steptoe was unaware that he was heading directly toward a seasonal village called Sila (Seelah) at which a large number of families were camped. In spring and summer the area was a harvest ground for bitterroot, a wild rose with edible roots that blooms in spring, as well as for camas bulbs, a food staple.[30]

Steptoe had no idea he was heading toward a village, nor did he know how unsettled his presence made the native people feel. Later, Father Joset wrote, "Think of the effect of it upon the young, who thought they saw in the movement of the troops a confirmation of that word; they were pursued, without any provocation on their part."[31] Thinking the troops intended to attack their village, the warriors quickly gathered, appearing so fast they surprised the soldiers. When the two sides were within shouting distance, they stopped and Chief Vincent of the Coeur d'Alenes and Chief Sgalgalt of the Spokanes rode forward and met Steptoe. Despite Steptoe's promise that he had only peaceful intentions, Vincent and Sgalgalt grew agitated. Instead of turning around, Steptoe ordered his force forward, intending to find a campsite for his tired troops and water for his horses. For the soldiers and packers in Steptoe's force, it was a harrowing experience. While some soldiers believed there were at least one thousand Indians allied against them, others put the figure closer to five hundred. Regardless, Steptoe was far outnumbered. Captain Winder, commander of the artillery, later wrote that on Sunday, May 16, "we found ourselves opposed by a body of Indians, painted and dressed for war, bows strung and guns loaded. . . . They were painted and dressed in the most fantastic and savage style; their horses painted and dressed. We formed for defense, and marched two miles or more to water, they charging around us, yelling, whooping, shaking scalps and such things over our heads, looking like so many fiends."[32]

Coeur d'Alene chief Andrew Seltice, who had been working with Vincent and Joset for peace, watched the force withdraw, later saying, "The marching column looked like a sorrowful, slow-moving procession."[33] The colonel and his men were exhausted. To one of his men, Colonel Steptoe looked "like a man in a coma."[34] Steptoe had been ill periodically for several years, but physicians had been unable to make a diagnosis. He suffered from transitory strokes and other "spells" that left him partially paralyzed and seemingly dazed.

Father Joset, having been warned of the situation, had left the mission on the 15th, braved rough terrain and streams swollen with snowmelt, and arrived at Sila on the evening of the 16th. Steptoe's troops were camped no more than eight miles away. Joset was discouraged to learn that the tribes were organizing war parties, and he talked with the chiefs, telling them they must not fight. Joset wrote that his words had little effect, and the warriors spent the night "yelling their war songs."[35]

Early the next morning, May 17, Joset rode out of Sila and caught up to Steptoe, whose force had been on the move since first light. One of Steptoe's men recounted, "So sudden was his appearance that he seemed to have dropped from the clouds. His black cassock and strikingly pale face strongly suggested the spectral to many of us, and his escort also looked unnaturally unsavage—each decked with a large cross and other churchly emblems." After Steptoe assured Joset he had no violent intentions, Joset suggested a council with some of the chiefs. He could only find Vincent and some of his subchiefs. Joset interpreted as Vincent questioned Steptoe's motive: "If you are going to Colville on a peaceful mission, why do you have so many men all carrying rifles, with a fully loaded pack train, and with large guns? Why didn't you go straight to Colville instead of coming around this way?"[36] They were making progress in their talks, so much so that Levi, one of Timothy's scouts, believed they were about to lose their chance for the army to engage Timothy's enemies in battle. Levi lashed Vincent, saying, "Proud man, why do you not fire?"[37] Vincent admonished him but otherwise did not react, and a brief, uneasy peace followed.

Steptoe, Vincent, and Joset agreed that if Steptoe would head directly back to Fort Walla Walla, the warriors would not attack. As they were talking, Vincent's uncle arrived and warned them that the Palouses were threatening to attack. The meeting quickly broke up, and Steptoe's force continued its retreat. Joset returned to Sila, where he intended to rest before heading back to the mission. Later, Coeur d'Alene chief Seltice said that Qualchan had been trying to convince a small group of Palouse and Yakama warriors to attack. When they were slow to respond, Qualchan fired into Steptoe's ranks at close range and was quickly joined by other warriors. Soldiers returned fire, initially with deadly results. The first clash resulted in the death of three Coeur d'Alenes, including Chief Victor, brother-in-law of Vincent. Word quickly spread of Victor's fall, inciting more anger among the assembled warriors.

Steptoe led his troops up the side of a ravine and established a defensive position, allowing his men to regroup. Capt. Oliver Taylor and Lt. William Gaston were ordered to protect the left and right flanks, exposing themselves to fire. Indians gathered on a nearby, higher hill, and Gaston led his men toward them, separating from the main force. Coeur d'Alene warriors, seeing an opportunity to catch Gaston's men alone, swept down the hillside toward them. While Gaston counterattacked, Captain Taylor hit the warriors from the opposite side. The fighting was fierce and close. Victor DeMoy shouted, "My God for my saber!" shortly before suffering fatal wounds. While Gaston's and Taylor's forces were engaging the warriors, Steptoe was able to move the main force south towards a slope overlooking Pine Creek, where they waited. Both Taylor and Gaston were killed.[38]

The fighting continued in a series of running skirmishes, with Steptoe's force trying to move south as quickly as possible while fighting off repeated charges by groups of warriors. Winder wrote, "The scene beggars description, 1,000 of those infuriated devils, painted and dressed as I said, charging in all directions, yelling, and whooping, and firing on us. . . . The firing was hot and heavy."[39] In addition to Taylor and Gaston, fatalities included five enlisted men; thirteen more were wounded.[40] The number of Indian dead and wounded was unclear, although various accounts place the dead at a dozen or more, and perhaps twice that number wounded. Steptoe's men were so inept with the howitzers that one of the Coeur d'Alenes later told Father Joset that they made "harmless noise and provoked [our] laughter."[41] Women of the tribes worked on the periphery, preparing weapons for the warriors and taking care of the wounded. One passed along a story of the battle in which a soldier on a horse pursued a warrior and killed him; several warriors chased after the soldier and returned a while later with his head. When Lieutenant Gaston's remains were recovered three months later, his head was missing.[42]

Steptoe's force was exhausted, nearly out of ammunition, and surrounded. On the slope, the men formed a wide circle around the pack train, facing the warriors, some of whom were watching, some of whom made periodic charges, more to stir up the soldiers than mount a serious attack. Thomas Beall, the chief pack master, later described how the men prepared for what they believed to be a devastating attack:

> We had built a little fortification about two feet high, of packsaddles, sacks of flour, bags of provisions, etc. Into this little shelter we had brought the wounded men and here the officers were in command. The soldiers were scattered in the bunchgrass round about. Late in the afternoon Colonel Steptoe had directed me to collect all

ammunition from the men on the inner lines and redistribute it to the men on the outer line, who had the most firing to do.[43]

Around sunset on May 17 Steptoe received a message that Chief Timothy had found a gap in the circle of Indians through which the troops could escape. One of the officers warned Steptoe that Timothy might be leading the soldiers into a trap, to which Steptoe reportedly replied, "But gentlemen, what can we do? Our ammunition is gone, we are surrounded and greatly outnumbered, and if we stay here until morning we shall be killed."[44]

The howitzers were buried and their carriages sunk in the creek. After strapping the wounded to saddles, most of the command made their way down the knoll, across the creek, and up a hill on the opposite side. Sgt. Michael Kenny chose three men to help him retrieve and bury Captain Taylor's body, which lay outside their modest fortification. They had tried to preserve ammunition during the running battle, using it only from close range, but now some of the men had only one bullet left and were pondering what one officer believed would be the "general massacre of the command."[45]

A different account was later given by Chief Seltice. The warriors circled and made camp, their cries and songs rising and falling. As the last trace of light faded, flames from dozens of campfires flickered, forming a circle with a half-mile diameter. Chief Vincent had taken command of the tribes and ordered them to stop firing in order to save ammunition. He held a conference with Father Joset and Chiefs Seltice and Wildshoe. According to the account handed down by Seltice, Father Joset was instrumental in convincing the chiefs not to order an attack. They agreed to open a passage across the creek, on the south side of the hill. Seltice and Sebastian crawled up the hill with a note for Steptoe. It had been written by Joset and signed by Chiefs Seltice, Vincent, and Wildshoe. The note read, "The Coeur d'Alene Chiefs are in deep sympathy for you and your remaining troops. There is an opening made for you down the slope that hits the creek so you can make a getaway." Seltice recalled that "Vincent then ordered all the Indians to beat their drums and sing war songs until midnight. He knew that this noise would drown out the sounds of

Painting of Steptoe's defensive stand, based on historical accounts. Painting by Nona Hengen. Courtesy of the artist.

retreating soldiers, and that by midnight their retreat would be complete."[46] Father Joset's account makes no mention of the plan described by Seltice, and none of the officers or soldiers mentioned it in their accounts. Joset implies that the Coeur d'Alenes were surprised that the force escaped, writing that the warriors "in the morning seeing they were gone, forbore to pursue; may be less the spoils should fall into other hands."[47]

In any case, after dark the wounded were lashed to saddles, and at ten P.M. the force began moving down the hill. In Seltice's account, the troops "found the Coeur d'Alene Indians all kneeling on one knee, with the butt of their rifles on the ground and the end of the barrel in the air. No rifle was pointing at them, as their sorrowful procession passed along the Coeur d'Alene lines. The Indians no longer thought of rifle firing, but instead could feel commiseration with the wounded carried on the horses. There was even the farewell gesture of a hand-wave between both sides, the mutual respect of two fighting foes that turned bitterness into honor."[48] It is possible that stories handed down by Indians overstate the tolerance and respect shown by the Coeur d'Alenes, given the strong animosity shown only a short time earlier. None of the accounts told by soldiers said anything about a "farewell gesture," or for that matter, having any contact at all with Indians during the retreat; yet, it seems nearly impossible that Steptoe's force could have escaped without help from some of their former enemies.

One variation of the heroic narrative claims that Steptoe's force made a daring escape, sneaking through the lines and dashing for freedom. That claim has survived, at least in some minds, perhaps in part because it makes an impressive story. However, the hillside on which Steptoe and his men huddled is in plain view of the adjacent hills on three sides and the flat land at its base. Vegetation was limited to bunchgrass and possibly a few pines, but there were no natural features that would have provided a screen. The moon was in its first quarter, but even in the darkest night, it is highly unlikely that a force the size of Steptoe's—especially with horses—could sneak away with perhaps a thousand warriors surrounding them.

Yet, fifty years after the fact, at least one of Steptoe's officers claimed that the command had indeed escaped without help. The commander of the dragoons, Lt. D. M. Gregg, wrote that he, Captain Winder, and the surgeon, Dr. John Randolph, suggested to Colonel Steptoe that an escape be attempted. At first Steptoe refused, saying that escape was impossible and telling Gregg, "It only remains for us to meet our fate like brave men." A company of dragoons took the lead, followed by infantry mounted on mules. Gregg was to lead a dragoon company at the rear of the procession, but the retreat was so quiet he did not realize it had started. He had been "collecting [his] skirmishers who were lying in the grass, and some of whom had fallen asleep from exhaustion." Gregg also recalled that the Indian rifle fire came from beyond the low part of the hill, to the east. He did not believe the hill was surrounded, which, if true, would have given him reason to believe the soldiers had escaped, rather than being allowed to escape.[49]

Steptoe's force quickly moved south, heading toward the Snake River, covering the eighty miles by ten that night. A group of Nez Perces headed by Chief Timothy greeted them and protected their camp while they rested. The next day, May 19, while Steptoe marched toward Fort Walla Walla, Chief Lawyer of the Nez Perce met him with 120 warriors and asked him to join him in an attack on the Coeur d'Alenes. Steptoe's army was in no shape to fight, and he continued on toward Fort Walla Walla and safety. The men were physically and emotionally exhausted. Captain Winder wrote to his brother-in-law, "I can't tell you my feelings or thoughts during the fight, and march afterwards, while balls were whistling freely around, and yells ringing in my ears. For two or three days after did I ever hear the same."[50]

WARNINGS AND RECRIMINATIONS

The day following the battle, Father Joset had confronted some of the Coeur d'Alenes and admonished them for fighting. In a letter to his superior, Father Congiato, dated June 27, 1858, he wrote, "I asked them if they had taken scalps. They told me no, with the exception of a small piece that had been taken by a half-fool. I asked them, also, if they had interred the dead. They replied that the women had buried them, but that the Pelouses had opened the graves which were at the encampment." Having had several weeks to interview participants in the events, Joset laid much of the blame for the confrontation to the Nez Perce scout, Timothy, who had been both helping and hindering Steptoe: "I see no other way to explain his conduct," Joset wrote, "than to say he laid a snare for the Coeur d'Alenes, whom he wished to humiliate, and that seeing afterwards the troops fall in the ditch that he had dug for others, he has done everything possible to draw them from it." Joset considered the possibility that it had been Steptoe's idea to offer his force's pack train and its spoils to the Coeur d'Alenes in exchange for safe passage through the siege line. "He foresaw, without doubt, that the Indians on the one hand had let him take the advance, and on the other tempted by the booty abandoned the pursuit; so that if the troops have escaped, they owe it to the sagacity of the Colonel."[51]

When Father Joset and the Coeur d'Alenes reached the mission, they faced a tempestuous situation. The mother of Zachary, one of the warriors killed in battle, "by her wailings was exciting the men to vengeance." Four white men traveling through the area were targeted by some of the angry Coeur d'Alenes, but they were saved through the efforts of Father Joset and several Indians, including one "Old Francis," who helped the men by "running as fast as his age would permit, through brushes and swamps, succeeded in warning the men of the danger; they took to the mountains."[52]

At the mission, Joset gathered the chiefs and warriors and "explained to them the necessary consequences of their folly." In attacking the whites, especially after agreeing to let them retreat, they assured a "fearful revenge." Joset put the place of the Coeur d'Alene people in context of the white world: "You are bewailing the loss of three of your men; the whites would not be the least dismayed had they lost 3,000; should you have killed as many immediately, 30,000 others would come, and so on until not a single Coeur d'Alene would remain." Joset showed them a map of the United States, "pointing to the little spot representing their country to let them understand how insignificant they were."[53]

After the violence ended, Joset set out for Fort Walla Walla, hoping to advocate for peace on the upper plateau. He felt he had failed with the Coeur d'Alenes and thought of abandoning the mission. He detoured around Palouse country to Fort Walla Walla and was warmly received by Steptoe. Traveling down the Columbia River, he was likewise warmly greeted at Fort Dalles. Joset continued downriver, past the Cascades Rapids, to Fort Vancouver, where he met with General Clarke, who encouraged the priest to continue his work at the mission.[54]

As the news traveled east, the reported scope of Steptoe's battle expanded, adding drama and tragedy. The August 1858 issue of *Harper's New Monthly* magazine reported that the colonel had taken four hundred men and engaged fifteen hundred warriors, with fifty-three killed in Steptoe's force. After the affair, Steptoe wrote, "The savages appear to have been excited by rumors that the Government intends to take possession of their lands, and the Act of the last Congress to lay out a military road from Walla Walla to the waters of the Upper Missouri fully satisfied them of the truth of the rumor."[55] Steptoe's words imply that prior to his expedition, he had perhaps been unaware of the tribes' uneasiness about their land being taken, which seems odd since it had been the primary topic of discussion across the plateau ever since the treaty council of 1855, and he had addressed the issue in his own letters.

In July 1858, two months after Steptoe's defeat, the *New York Times* published correspondence from him in which he still did not express a clear purpose: "The objective of my visit was to talk with the white people and Indians, and try to effect a more harmonious intercourse between them."[56] Even murkier was a claim he made soon after the expedition, in a letter to Maj. W. W. Mackall dated May 28; in praising the actions of the officers who were mortally wounded in battle, Steptoe wrote, "It was, no doubt, due to the severe punishment which, by their [the officers'] exertions, the enemy received, that we were not pursued and attacked at the crossing of Snake River, where a bold attack would have been disastrous for us."[57] In fact, the tribes did not feel they had received "severe punishment" and had not pursued his force in part because they had made their point and in part because many were divvying up the considerable animals and supplies Steptoe had abandoned in his retreat. The warriors were anything but impressed.

Steptoe's defeat sent a shockwave up the chain of command. Colonel Wright, General Clarke, Secretary of War Scott, and President Buchanan were all incensed. General Scott's reaction was concise: "This is a candid report of a disastrous affair. The small supply of ammunition is surprising and unaccounted for." Scott ordered reinforcements into the region, and from San Francisco, General Clarke ordered that all available troops in California move north to Fort Vancouver in preparation for movement onto the plateau.[58]

Clarke acted swiftly. On June 2 he sent a dispatch to the army headquarters in New York relaying his decision to go to Washington Territory to take command of the conflict. He diverted troops from Utah, where tension with the Mormons had subsided. On July 23, from his new headquarters of the Department of the Pacific at Fort Vancouver, Clarke wrote Lieutenant Colonel Thomas at army headquarters of his plans. He summarized his objectives: prevent a confederation of tribes from forming and enter into negotiations using a "frank and kind demeanor, and have caused presents to be made." He added, "I desire medals may be sent for distribution to friendly chiefs." Clarke, at this point still showing sympathy for some Indians, noted that Spencer, the man whose family was murdered at the Cascades Rapids in 1856, was worthy of a medal "by reason of his misfortune of losing his whole family by the whites, a massacre either through wantonness or by misapprehension, nevertheless he continued in his friendship." Clarke also hoped to "procure him some compensation for his misfortunes."[59]

On May 31, 1858, before Representative Isaac Stevens had heard the news of Steptoe's defeat, he asked Congress for reimbursement for expenses incurred by Washington and Oregon citizens in fighting the tribes. In addition to his laudatory remarks about the heroism of the volunteer militia, he again singled out George Wright for criticism of events at the Cascades two years earlier: "I shall insist that the nineteen [the actual count was seventeen] dead bodies left on the ground at the Cascades, [were] in consequence of Colonel Wright advancing upon the Walla Walla, and leaving his rear unprotected and insecure. . . . He did not leave a sufficient garrison at the Cascades."[60]

The *New York Times'* editors took note of the Steptoe disaster and published a scathing editorial. They criticized Steptoe's "defective preparation," his "obstinate skepticism," and lack of discretion. The column ended with a final shot, comparing Steptoe to another failed expedition from a century earlier: "There is great reason to believe that Colonel Steptoe is as little fitted for Indian service as the ill-fated Braddock."[61]

More than a month after Steptoe's defeat, in a letter to Judge B. F. Yantis, Isaac Stevens could not hide his satisfaction with the army's failure: "The news of Steptoe's defeat has made a very deep impression at the War Dept., and has shown that something was 'rotten in Denmark.' I quietly observed *'The Indians who whipped Steptoe, the Volunteers whipped'* [Stevens's italics]. But it being a case of Volunteers, it was pronounced a cultus [worthless] affair." In the same letter, Stevens notes his satisfaction with the mining possibilities east of the Cascade Mountains. He also notes, "The defeat of Steptoe, the discovery of rich gold fields, the rush of miners, and the rapid filling up of population will all help the war debt. There will be a large emigration next year."[62]

Stevens's criticism of the army was relentless. He wrote to Colonel J. W. Nesmith, "Steptoe's defeat has made a great sensation here [Washington, D.C.], and the true mode of managing our Indians is greatly acknowledged. The sentiment of condemnation of the temporizing measures of the military is universal and overwhelming. The officers whose commands have led to it, have pretty much lost all the reputation they ever had." Representative Stevens claimed to have the government on his side: "All the officers from Gen. Scott down, the Secretary of War and the President expect a change, and that the present war will be crushed out with a strong hand. The War Dept. has taken energetic measures."[63]

The "great sensation" referred to by Stevens was caused in large part by the congressman himself, and it is likely that many of the opinions about the army's failure were based on Stevens's self-serving criticism. There is little evidence that any of Stevens's criticism injured the reputations or careers of his various targets, including Wool and Wright.[64]

In many of the accounts recorded by non-Native historians, Steptoe has been treated as a good officer who suffered betrayal at the hands of the Plateau tribes. Many accounts assert that his primary mistake was his failure to supply his men with adequate arms and ammunition, and at least a few historians have blamed that shortcoming on packers who, without Steptoe's knowledge, pulled cases of ammunition off the pack train to reduce the burden on the pack horses. Over time, Steptoe's fight and retreat attained nearly legendary status, with some asserting that only brave action by the colonel prevented a massacre equal to that of Custer's. Like Custer, Steptoe made a "last stand" on a hillside, and his men prepared to use all their ammunition, save one bullet each—for their own heads.

It is unclear if Steptoe's unknown medical condition impacted the planning and execution of his expedition, but his physical condition was clearly noticeable to his men. More importantly, his illness was of great concern to Dr. Randolph, who accompanied both the Steptoe and Wright expeditions. In April 1861 Dr. Randolph recalled that a few months after the May 1858 campaign, Steptoe showed signs of "nervous debility" and "mental trouble." In addition, Steptoe's sister, Nannie, wrote that "he was *paralyzed* in the fall of 1861."[65] For years he had suffered from what his physician referred to as "palsy," periodic strokes that left him temporarily incapacitated due to paralysis.[66] His condition seems to have been more than transient strokes, and Dr. Randolph wrote that he had seen only one other case like it, a judge in San Francisco. The individual in question, a Judge Thornton, died of "paralysis." If Steptoe suffered transient strokes, it is unlikely that Randolph or Steptoe himself would have been mystified by the illness, as strokes were fairly well known at the time. However, diseases such as MS and ALS had not been identified as such, and it is possible that Steptoe suffered from one of those illnesses or another disorder of the central nervous system. One medical observer has suggested that Steptoe may have been suffering from syphilis, the symptoms of which can masquerade in different forms, including mimicking strokes. In any case, Steptoe's condition affected his physical and mental condition during 1858 and thereafter.[67]

Steptoe returned to the east coast in 1859 and was married the following year. For the next five years he tried to regain his health, living for a time in Cuba for the weather, in Philadelphia for treatment, and in Canada to see if the northern climate would help. In 1861 he resigned from the army, in part because of his health and in part because he felt torn between his loyalty to his native Virginia and his commitment to the causes of the Union. He died in Lynchburg, Virginia, on April 16, 1865, at the age of forty-nine. His only child, a daughter, had died the year before.

In response to the disaster and Steptoe's report, Colonel Wright wrote a letter to headquarters of the Department of the Pacific. In it Wright was characteristically clear about his desire to punish the tribes: "They [the northern tribes] are numerous, active, and perfectly acquainted with the topography of the country; hence a large body of troops will be necessary if, as I presume, it is designed to bring those Indians under subjection, and signally chastise them for their unwarranted attack upon Colonel Steptoe." Wright then suggested a command of "one thousand troops should be sent into that country, thus enabling the commander to pursue the enemy in two or three columns." Wright emphasized the need to "prosecute it [war] systematically, with an ample supply of the *personnel* and *material* to guard against a possibility of failure."[68]

Edward Steptoe passed into history as a tragic hero, a man still frequently spoken of today with sympathetic respect. In his 1856 letter to Nannie, he wrote of his regret at not marrying early in adulthood: "You may be sure that with a heart so warm in its feelings memory is often thus, and then it is that I experience probably the keenest sorrow of my life. Well, Nannie, age and death must overtake us all sometime, and if we have striven diligently to perform our duty in the sphere allotted to us, perhaps the retrospect of *this* will obscure the other."[69]

One more curious event marked the tragic life of Edward Steptoe. In September 1860 Colonel Wright reported that the once-proud Virginia aristocrat and colonel was absent without leave. In December, Wright reported again that Steptoe "has been 'absent without leave' since May 4th, 1860." Steptoe had taken a leave of absence and at least according to Wright had been expected to rejoin his regiment. Perhaps Steptoe had become too ill to resume service, and it is possible that given the challenges of distance, there had been a misunderstanding. In any case, Edward Steptoe's legacy is one of misfortune and tragedy.[70]

ECHOES

One result of the turmoil on the plateau was the suspension of Lt. John Mullan's work on the military road he intended to build from Fort Walla Walla, Washington Territory, to Fort Benton, Dakota Territory, on the Missouri River. The tribes, particularly the Coeur d'Alenes, had been nervous about the road for some time, since they knew it would run directly through their homeland. While Steptoe was engaged with the Indians, Mullan was at The Dalles preparing his surveyors and laborers for the long journey. They were to join a military escort at Fort Walla Walla, but the plan was put on hold.

Four months later, during Wright's campaign through the region, a contingent of men headed by Lt. Mullan visited the site of Steptoe's final battle. Mullan wrote a detailed account of what the men found: "Having arrived near the battlefield, we came upon the bones of many of our men that had laid bleaching on the prairie hills for four months, and that had, in this interval, been scattered and dragged in every direction by the bands of wolves that infested the place." Mullan's men were accompanied by a Coeur d'Alene man who had participated in the battle. When the fighting had ended, he had found Lieutenant Gaston's body and covered it with brush in an effort to protect it from scavenging animals. The remains of Gaston and four others were recovered, including "Captain Taylor, a half-breed, and two of the dragoons." The remains were taken to Fort Walla Walla, where some were buried and some sent back east to relatives. Mullan's men found a gun shaft that they used to make a cross, which they placed "as a Christian token to the honored dead, and to point the stranger to the spot where brave men met their fate; and as each officer and soldier lingered near the spot, and heard rehearsed the sad recital of that memorable defeat, the silent tear stole down many a bronzed cheek that had confronted death." Mullan's men returned to their camp, where they sat in silence and toasted their fallen comrades with a bottle of brandy Colonel Wright had sent along for the purpose. Mullan makes no mention of the Indian warriors, living or dead, except to remark on the "unmistakable signs of a relentless savage who had determined on the utter annihilation of this small command."[71]

Steptoe's expedition, the fighting, and his escape, quickly became support for a heroic narrative. Several accounts written decades after the events note that had Steptoe's command been massacred while they were pinned on the hillside above Pine Creek, the disaster (for whites) would have been second only to that at the Little Big Horn. Steptoe's escape inspired patriotic and religious feelings like the following, written in the early twentieth century:

> Whether or not the hand of God may be seen in the delivery of the command either for itself or as the starting point for the things that have been accomplished through succeeding years in the land that bore witness to its trials, the escape of Colonel Steptoe from an army of savages sufficiently numerous to overwhelm his own force, and who possessed every advantage which the situation could offer, with no force that could attempt a rescue within a hundred miles, has not a parallel in the history of American Indian warfare.[72]

A stone obelisk now stands at the site of Steptoe's last defensive position, with words honoring the men who fought and died with him. No mention is made of the Indian warriors who

Monument honoring the dead at Steptoe Battlefield State Park. Author photo.

fought and died.[73] At the dedication in 1908 more than two thousand people were in attendance. The festivities began with a parade of soldiers and bands. One honored guest was Col. Lea Feabiger, the commanding officer at Fort George Wright. Colonel Feabiger gave an impassioned speech about the high moral status of the conquerors, claiming, "Even the religion of the gentle Christ has found its most potent missionary in the soldier." Washington's Governor Mead spoke of the need to honor the state's soldiers and pioneers: "Had it not been for the sacrifice of such men as served under Colonel Steptoe, the settlement of the Inland Empire might have been postponed a quarter century or more and we might not have had an opportunity to build cities and develop our wonderful resources. . . . In fact civilization and all of its concomitant advantages would have long been deferred."[74]

The Steptoe battle continues to live in American Indian histories. One story tells of an aging Coeur d'Alene warrior living near the Cataldo Mission who heard of the fighting and wanted to join the other warriors. Everyone at the mission told him to stay home: his wife, his friends, and the priests. He insisted on going. He rode to the battle site, but found that the fighting was over:

> And everywhere, there were pots, blankets, horses, a big mess. But no battle to fight. So he loaded up a horse with all kinds of war booty and went back to his village near the Mission. When he arrived back at his village, his wife and the priests were angry, and insisted he return the goods to the Army. "But these things are won by me, my honors; if I try to return them, the soldiers would kill me!" The priests insisted, as did everyone else.
>
> So he loaded his things onto his horse and headed to the nearest fort, Fort Walla Walla, many miles away. It took him a long time to travel there, and he knew he'd be shot as soon as the soldiers saw him. But he went anyway. Finally he arrived close to the Fort.
>
> He hung his head down. His horse knew something too. It hung its head down and slowly they approached the gate. All the soldiers were at the wall looking down. He knew he'd be shot soon. But he

continued. His horse knew as well. Slowly they entered the fort, with all the soldiers' rifles pointed at them. He got off his horse and laid out a blanket. On it he laid all the things he had taken from the battle site. After he had done this, and without a word, he got back on his horse and headed out slowly. He knew he'd get shot. Slowly he rode out of the fort. All the rifles were still pointed at him. After he had got out of firing range of the rifles, he held his head high, and as if his horse knew they were out of danger as well, they galloped over the hill and back to the Mission.

But this time, when he arrived, expecting the same cold shoulder, everyone cheered him. And the priests welcomed him back to the church. This was indeed a brave deed![75]

In 2001, Supreme Court justice David Souter referred to the Plateau Indian War in the court's opinion that assigned, in effect, ownership of the southern portion of Lake Coeur d'Alene to its namesake tribe. In *Idaho v. the United States, et al.,* he wrote:

> The Tribe had shown its readiness to fight to preserve its land rights when in 1858 it defeated a force of the United States military, which it misunderstood as intending to take aboriginal lands. . . . Congress was free to define the [Coeur d'Alene] reservation boundaries however it saw fit; the goal of avoiding hostility seemingly could not have been attained without the agreement of the Tribe. Congress in any event made it expressly plain that its object was to obtain tribal interests only by tribal consent.[76]

Justice Souter was acknowledging the fact that because the tribe was willing to fight for its land, both the government and the tribe were best served by negotiation, rather than fiat.

Today, the wind frequently sweeps across the hillside where the Steptoe expedition fought and lost. An aging concrete railroad trestle passes over Pine Creek, and a highway runs past five hundred yards to the east. The town of Rosalia sits close by, invisible from the base of the hill. Other than the monument and the small patch of lawn surrounding it, bunchgrass covers the ground, as it would have in 1858.

NINE

"An American Way of Small Wars"

He was a genuine soldier and a soldier's friend. . . . Among all the men who led other men in the struggle between civilization and savagery on the frontier of old Oregon, none was more efficient, none more respected and beloved by those under him than Colonel (later General) George Wright.

JOEL GRAHAM TRIMBLE

The Plateau War was gaining international attention. In England, the *Illustrated London News* reported that Colonel Wright and nine hundred troops were on their way to "severely chastise the savages for their attack on Colonel Steptoe's command." The *News* attributed the army's campaign to a desire for revenge and predicted that a "bloody war or speedy submission of the red skins was anticipated."[1]

In the Pacific Northwest, the Steptoe affair had provided newspapers new ammunition with which to criticize both Indians and the army. The *Weekly Oregonian* claimed that the expedition proved that "the Indian character is universally false, deceptive, and cruel. . . . The Indian is cunning and shrewd enough to know that there is a general feeling of sympathy and confidence felt by the regulars toward them."[2] The writer noted one thing rarely admitted by civilians in the Northwest: that indeed, many army officers and soldiers felt sympathy for the tribes. The restraint that the army showed, at least prior to 1858, had resulted in councils and other peaceful interactions between army regulars and Indians. Such relationships tended to emphasize common interests—primarily, limiting bloodshed—and temper the dehumanization engaged in by so many whites.

There were no uncertain voices in Wright's chain of command, however. In a letter dated June 18, 1858, General Clarke's instructions to Wright were clear: "Kamiakin and Qualchan cannot longer be permitted to remain at large or in the country, they must be surrendered or driven away, and no accommodation should be made with any who will harbor them; let all know that asylum given to either of these troublesome Indians, will be considered in future as evidence of a hostile intention on the part of the tribe."[3]

In June 1858 J. W. Nesmith, the superintendent of Indian affairs for Washington and Oregon Territories, asked Indian agent John Owen to investigate the Steptoe affair and determine how many Indians, and which tribes, had been involved. In late June, Owen traveled to Fort Colville and was disturbed to find several hundred Indians in war paint, dancing and chanting. Capt. Oliver Taylor's blood-stained saddle was on display, and Owen noted that a number of horses at the scene were from Steptoe's command. Owen suggested that Hudson's Bay Company officials at Colville had obtained some of Steptoe's horses and mules from the Indians and had probably supplied arms and ammunition to the tribes. While at Fort Colville, Owen heard claims from some Indians that the Jesuits at the Coeur d'Alene Mission had supplied arms for the Steptoe battle, a claim that would prove false. On July 16 Owen traveled fifty miles south and attempted to hold a peace conference at Spokane Falls, but it turned out to be "one of the blackest councils, I think, that has ever been held on the Pacific Slope. . . . Five hundred fighting men were present, elated with their recent success; the dragoon horses were prancing around all day; the scalp and war dance going on all night."[4] Owen quickly lost interest in discussing peace and focused instead on getting out of the Spokane Valley alive. His friends, Chiefs Garry and Polatkin of the Spokanes, could do little to help. His path was blocked by unfriendly tribes on three sides, so he headed north and then east around Coeur d'Alene country. Eventually, his party found help at Lake Pend Oreille with the Kalispels and further east with the Flatheads. In a conversation with Steptoe and Nesmith, Owen repeated the rumors he had heard that implicated the Jesuits in supplying arms to the tribes. In part because Owen made no effort to disavow the stories, they spread, causing no little trauma among Father Joset and the other Jesuits. No evidence was presented that supported the claim, and Father Joset vehemently, and convincingly, denied the accusation. Owen's experience shows the tension that existed on the plateau after Steptoe's defeat. His desire to escape the Spokane Valley and its dangers reflects how little the tribes feared intervention by the army.

One of Colonel Wright's most notable military accomplishments with his 1858 campaign was his success in instilling fear in the tribes through use of precise, fierce tactics. Wright engaged in what has been termed "an American way of small wars," created by "a loose body of theory, doctrine, thought, and precedent."[5] One scholar believes the lack of formal doctrine was because "military leaders looked upon Indian warfare as a fleeting bother. Today's conflict or tomorrow's would be the last, and to develop a special system for it seemed hardly worthwhile."[6] Thus, military strategists spent little time pondering grand strategies and planning tactics unique to Indian warfare. The primary purpose of the army was to police Indians and settlers, trying to keep them from killing one another. The army's vision, at least in the 1850s in the Northwest, was primarily limited to reacting to violence or threats of violence. A notable exception occurred in present-day Nebraska, where in 1855 William Harney's force attacked a Sioux village, killing about one hundred men, women, and children.[7]

New weapons made Colonel Wright's defeat of the tribes in 1858 easier for the army. In December 1856 Secretary of War Jefferson Davis had informed Congress of progress in developing more effective small arms: "The operations at national armories have been restricted to the completion of new models for small arms; the alteration of old models for the exclusive manufacture of the adopted new model, of which many of the parts have been fabricated. This model, which is common in its general principal to our small arms, is a rifled arm (such as is commonly called the Minie rifle.)"[8] In addition to the rifles, Wright's men made efficient use of their portable howitzers. The barrel and carriage weighed five hundred pounds and were made to be broken down and transported on three horses or mules. They could launch a nine-pound explosive shell one thousand yards with devastating results. According to some Indians, and to Father Joset, the howitzers were at least as effective as rifles in killing and scattering the warriors. In the Steptoe fight, however, the inexperience of the soldiers meant the howitzers did little more than make noise and evoke derision from the warriors.[9]

THE INVASION BEGINS

The Yakama, Nez Perce, Walla Walla, and other Sahaptin tribes had suffered insult and injury during treaty councils and attacks by militias; they had retaliated at the Cascades Rapids and at the battle against Steptoe's forces. Now it was time for the army to enter the heart of the tribes' land, to deal not only with the Yakamas and Palouses, but with the elusive Spokanes and Coeur d'Alenes as well. General Clarke had ordered Wright to "make their punishment severe, and persevere until the submission of all is complete." To the tribes, Wright's expedition would be an invasion and Colonel Wright the conqueror.[10]

By mid-1858 one-sixth of the standing U.S. Army had gathered in posts along the Columbia River, ready to join the fight against the Plateau tribes. In July General Clarke laid out his plan of attack. While Colonel Wright was marching north from Fort Walla Walla, another force under the command of Maj. Robert Garnett would move north from Fort Simcoe, located in the Yakima Valley on the east side of the Cascade Mountains. Garnett's initial target was the Yakamas, and in particular the Indians who had attacked a party of miners in the Yakima Valley. If the tribe failed to deliver the culprits to the major, then Garnett was instructed to "drive the whole [tribe] to submission by severe punishment." In his orders, Clarke took a new, firmer stance in regard to Indian affairs in Washington Territory. He warned Garnett, "Arrangements for temporary neutrality are of no avail; both parties live in a state of distrust and every accident is likely to produce war. This state of things can no longer be tolerated; the Indians must not only promise to be peaceable under such regulations as the government may think proper to make for them, but they must give in hostages, that the army may not again be needed to insure its performance."[11]

Garnett began his march on August 11. As it turned out, most of the warriors Garnett was seeking to engage in the Yakima Valley had dispersed; some had headed east to join the Spokanes and Coeur d'Alenes in preparing to meet Wright's force. Several days out, Garnett heard of an Indian village located near present-day Cle Elum, on the east side of the Cascade Mountains. Garnett sent out a detachment led by Lt. Jesse K. Allen, who carelessly attacked the village at three in the morning. The inhabitants, mostly women and children, suffered no fatalities, but Lieutenant Allen was accidentally killed by gunfire from one of his own men. The village was burned, cattle and horses were confiscated, and five men were captured and tied to trees. Four were executed by gunfire, and one, unknown to Garnett's men, survived.[12] Garnett split his force, with one command headed by Capt. (later general) George Crook moving farther north, burning lodges and food supplies and taking more cattle and horses. Near the present-day town of Leavenworth, Crook ordered five prisoners taken. In his journal he wrote, "The whole business was rather distasteful to me, and as my second lieutenant Turner rather enjoyed that sort of thing, I detailed him to execute them which was done . . . by firing squad."[13]

While Garnett was marching north from Fort Simcoe in the Yakima Valley, Chiefs Owhi, Moses, Teias, and their families were gathered near the confluence of the Columbia and Wenatchee Rivers.[14] Hearing that Garnett was moving toward them, some of the men decided to avoid a confrontation with him and headed east to join the force being organized by Kamiakin to fight George Wright's troops. Warriors from other tribes also decided to join the confederation, including some from the Okanogan and Kettle

(Colville) tribes, as well as from the Flatheads, a designation that included the Kalispels and Kootenais.[15]

Meanwhile, Wright's expedition prepared for its own march. Some of the men in his command had served in Steptoe's force under Gaston or Taylor, and they were especially anxious for revenge. Along the Pacific coast, army regulars were eager to avenge the army's embarrassing loss. Lt. Michael Ryan Morgan, who would play a key role in later events, was one of the officers sent from California to join Wright's force. Years later, he recalled, "Going on board the steamer in San Francisco I saw ex-captain William Tecumseh Sherman, at the gangway, look at us, of his old regiment, marching on board and going up to Washington Territory to discipline those savages, Spokanes, Coeur d'Alenes, etc., who killed our comrades."[16]

"PERFECT CONFIDENCE"

In a letter dated August 14, 1858, and addressed to General Clarke, commanding officer of the Department of the Pacific, Wright wrote,

> Sir: I march hence tomorrow against the hostile Indians beyond the Snake River. I have a body of troops, both officers and men, in the highest order, and on whom I feel that I can rely with perfect confidence; yet with all these circumstances in my favor, I am greatly apprehensive that the results of the campaign may fall short of what is expected by the general and by the country. From all that I can learn, we must not expect the enemy to meet us in a pitched battle; although haughty, insolent, and boastful now, when I approach he will resort to a guerrilla warfare, he will lay waste to the country with fire, and endeavor by every means in his power to embarrass and cripple our operations.[17]

Wright ordered his men to drill in two-hour stretches three times a day. Dragoons and artillerymen were trained as light infantry, and one boy was assigned responsibility for every five dragoons, standing ready to take their horses should they need to dismount.

Before setting out from Fort Walla Walla, Wright held a council with the Nez Perces to reiterate his peaceful intentions with them and to get their commitment to stay out of the fighting. A contingent was formed consisting of thirty Nez Perce warriors and three chiefs to serve as scouts, including Spotted Eagle and Utsinmalikan (about sixty-five years old at the time). They were given army uniforms, and Lieutenant Kip observed, "Like all Indians, they are particularly delighted with their clothes, and no young officer just commissioned, thinks as much of his uniform as they do. They insist, indeed, upon having every minute portion, even to the glazed cap covers."[18]

As events unfolded, the Nez Perces fought against the confederated tribes and some were specifically mentioned for their heroism, including Utsinmalikan. The inclusion of Nez Perces in Wright's army was disconcerting to some of their tribesmen, and today the memory still lives among some tribal members and occasions some intertribal teasing about the acts of ancestors.[19]

On August 7 Capt. Erasmus Darwin Keyes left Fort Walla Walla with one company of dragoons and six companies of artillery—with two howitzers—to establish a base camp at the Snake River, forty-two miles north. The march from Fort Walla Walla was through grassland recently burnt by Indians, who were trying to destroy food available for the army's horses.[20] On August 10 Keyes's force reached the Tucannon River and marched seven miles to Dry Creek, where they found plenty of grazing and water. The next day the march covered fourteen miles, ending in the lush Touchet Valley, in which the moist grass had not been burned. The fourth day after leaving Fort Walla Walla, the party reached a point three miles above the mouth of the Tucannon River, along which was plentiful grass. While Captain Keyes and a topographical officer scouted for the best place to build the base camp, two Indians believed to be spies were captured. They were taken into custody but quickly escaped, avoiding the volley of bullets fired by the soldiers. A party of mounted soldiers pursued and spotted the two in the river; Lt. John Mullan dismounted, ran after one, fired his pistol, and missed. The warrior went after Mullan and tried to wrest the pistol from his grip. When that failed, he began throwing rocks at him, then grabbed his coat. An observer said, "As he [the Indian] was a powerful man and Mullan very small, he would doubtless have killed the latter, when the Indian made a misstep and got into a hole over his depth, and turned away. They were left, and finally made their escape across the Snake River."[21]

At the confluence of the Snake and Tucannon Rivers, Keyes and his men built an outpost, naming it Fort Taylor after the officer killed in the Steptoe fight. Lieutenant Kip noted that the location of Fort Taylor "seems to have been used as an old Indian burial-place, for we are surrounded by graves."[22] Over the next several days, Indians watched from the cliffs, occasionally firing guns to no effect other than to fray the soldiers' nerves. On August 13, Father Joset arrived, informing Keyes that the Spokanes and Coeur d'Alenes were not interested in peace; they were "ready for war and did not wish peace, but a war of extermination."[23] A Dr. Perkins, who had been at Fort Colville and witnessed the mood of the tribes along with Indian agent John Owen, reported that an Indian had waved Lieutenant Gaston's sword in his face, having taken it during the Steptoe battle, in which Gaston was killed. According to Kip, the tribes claimed to be well armed with plenty of guns and ammunition, "and when their ammunition gave out, they would poison their arrows and fight with them."[24]

Colonel Wright arrived at Fort Taylor on August 18 along with the supply train. The fort, a simple stone rectangle with two guard towers, was nearly complete. The four-hundred-mule pack train was readied; all equipment would be carried by animals, as the terrain was too rough to allow passage of wagons. Lieutenant Mullan's surveying cart would be the only wheeled vehicle on the march. The force that would leave Fort Taylor included 190 dragoons, 400 artillerymen serving as infantry, and a rifle brigade with 90 men. In addition to the 680 officers and soldiers, the 33 friendly Nez Perces were organized under the command of Lieutenant Mullan. Support was provided by 200 civilian packers and herders responsible for the mule train and horses. At the time, it was the largest army force to have embarked on a military expedition in the West.

Colonel Wright's preparations had been meticulous. On August 18 he issued a written order detailing the Order of March and Rules of Conduct. Dragoons would lead the way, followed by the howitzer company, artillery company (infantry), rifle brigade, part of the pack train, another infantry company, the rest of the pack train, and more dragoons guarding the rear. No detail was too small. The dragoons were to remain within four hundred yards of the main force. Men were ordered to carry arms at all times, expect daily inspections, and sleep with their weapons and ammunition belts. On August 24, Wright issued further orders, adding more detail. He ordered that after the last signal of the day, at eight P.M., lights were to be extinguished, "after which no noise or loud talking will be allowed."[25] The command included buglers and drummers, who would be crucial for maintaining discipline in camp and communicating orders during battle.

Jesuit missionary Pierre-Jean De Smet described the land over which Wright would march and the land through which he would conduct his "march of destruction":

> The distance from Fort Walla Walla to the Great Spokane Prairie, through which the Spokane River flows, is about 150 miles. This whole region is undulating and hilly, and though generally of a light soil, it is covered with a rich and nutritious grass, forming grazing fields where thousands of cattle might be easily raised. It is almost destitute of timber until you are within thirty miles of the Spokane Prairie, where you find open woods and clusters of trees scattered far and wide; this portion, particularly, contains a great number of lakes and ponds with ranges of long walls, of large basaltic columns and beds of basalt. The country abounds in nutritious roots (bitter-root, camas, etc.), on which principally the Indians subsist for a great portion of the year. The Spokane Prairie is about thirty miles from north to south and from east to west, bounded all around by well-wooded hills and mountains of easy access.[26]

Three days of rain delayed the march, but on the morning of August 25, the first part of Wright's command began crossing the Snake River, which Kip and Morgan referred to as the "Rubicon."[27] During the previous few days, several Indians had appeared at the fort to see Wright, including Spokanes and at least one Palouse. They expressed their desire for peace and warned the colonel that a large fighting force awaited at the Spokane River. Wright told one Spokane man that if he turned over his weapons, he would be spared; otherwise, he would be shot, "which would be the fate of every Indian taken with arms."[28] The man refused and rode away unharmed. The last part of the command crossed the Snake the next day, the 26th. An inspection followed the crossing, and the men prepared to march northward.

On August 27 they traveled along the Palouse River for fifteen miles. Lt. Kip wrote that the men were "all on alert, as any hour may find us in face of the enemy." His words indicate a cautious reliance on Colonel Wright: "We suppose, indeed, that our commander can have no definite plan, as we are entering a country almost entirely unknown to us, but he will have to be guided by circumstances." Kip implies that in a force the size of Wright's, communication did not always flow clearly down the line, and speculation sometimes filled in the blanks. In regard to marching through foreign country, he noted that "camp talk is, that we have stores for only forty days, during which time we must find and beat the enemy."[29]

The procession sometimes extended two miles or more; much of the time the soldiers and packers trudged single-file because of the narrow, rocky trail, which was impassable for wagons. The procession would have been noisy, dusty, and smelly, with mud forming from animal waste.[30] Each evening, the force would have spread out over an acre or more just to unpack, feed, and water the animals; the camp itself would have covered at least several acres. Indian scouts were dispatched to find water, which was critical not only for the horses, but for the hot, exhausted infantry and artillery companies as well, who had to trudge along on foot, earning the label "worm crushers."[31] Despite the complicated logistics and hostile land, one soldier wrote of Colonel Wright, "No worry, confusion, or doubt was ever discernible in our commander, and everything went forward with alacrity and confidence."[32]

Over the next few days, the command made its way over basalt scabland and hills covered with bunchgrass and scrub. Water was scarce, and the men were overwhelmed by heat, dust, and smoke from grassfires set by Indians. Every so often warriors would appear and fire at the troops, although from too far to do any damage. Twice during the campaign Capt. Edward Ord sent Lieutenant Morgan out to draw fire, in order to determine the position of the warriors. Morgan would later find some amusement about his duty as a target.[33]

Every morning and evening was a logistical production. The morning routine for breakfast and preparing for the day's march took two hours, as did setting up camp and preparing the evening meal. Reveille was at three A.M., followed by drills, breakfast, and breaking camp. Each day's march started promptly at five o'clock. Captain Keyes, Wright's second-in-command, wrote that on one occasion his men were delayed by, at most, three minutes. Keyes reported that he had to "answer a brisk demand, through a staff officer, to explain why my column did not move at the time appointed."[34]

The late summer weather that year was dry early in the month, although they experienced at least one severe thunderstorm with heavy rain. When it rained, mud clung to everything: animals, equipment, weapons, men. In the dry scablands, water enough for bathing was not easy to find. It was a miserable march, but optimism prevailed—driven in large part by a desire for revenge.

BATTLE OF FOUR LAKES

On August 30, near present-day Fish Trap Lake in the basalt scablands, the advance guard engaged in a minor skirmish with a small group of warriors. While Lieutenant Kip called the camp

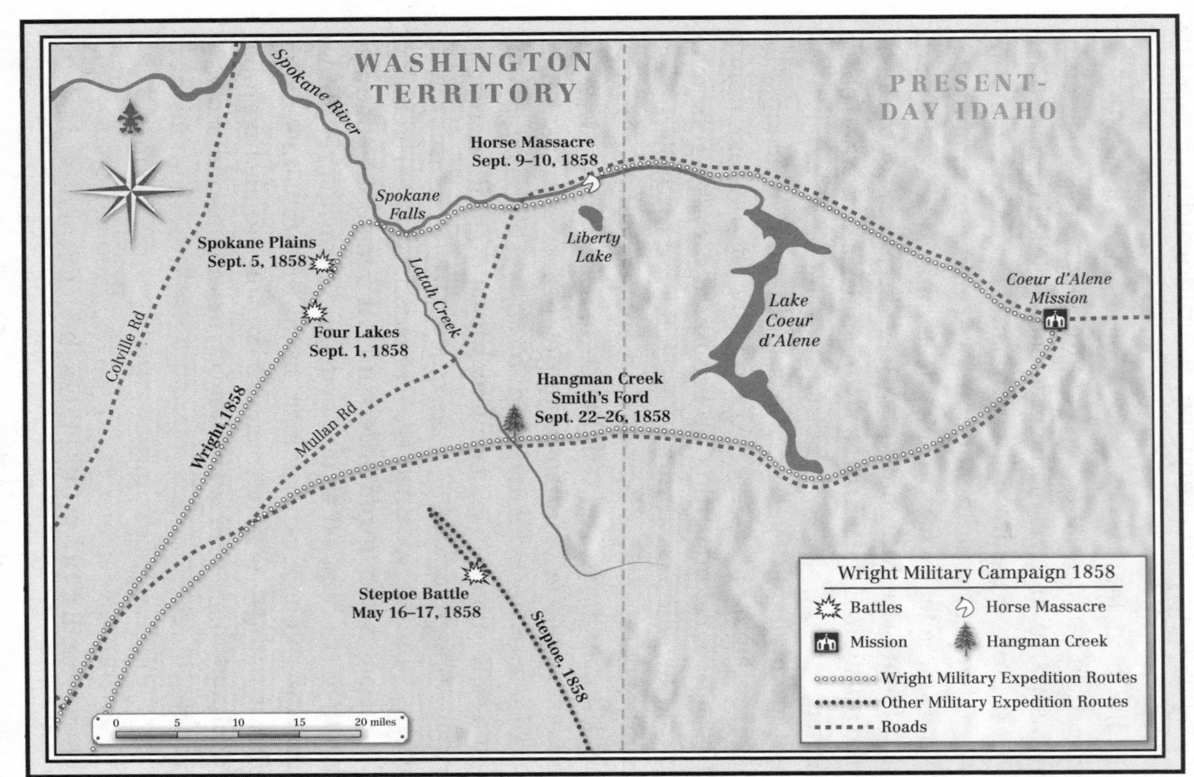
WASHINGTON
TERRITORY
PRESENT-
DAY IDAHO
Spokane River
Horse Massacre
Sept. 9–10, 1858
Spokane
Falls
Liberty
Lake
Spokane Plains
Sept. 5, 1858
Four Lakes
Sept. 1, 1858
Latah Creek
Colville Rd
Wright, 1858
Mullan Rd
Hangman Creek
Smith's Ford
Sept. 22–26, 1858
Lake
Coeur
d'Alene
Coeur d'Alene
Mission
Steptoe Battle
May 16–17, 1858
Steptoe, 1858
0
5
10
15
20 miles
Wright Military Campaign 1858
Battles
Horse Massacre
Mission
Hangman Creek
Wright Military Expedition Routes
Other Military Expedition Routes
Roads

"Pedrigal," it quickly became known as "Poison Camp," since eight soldiers became ill from eating poisonous roots and two died.[35] Morgan wrote, "On the 30th of August we had a harassing day, because of the heat, the absence of water along the trail and because the enemy hung close to us, firing upon us but doing no damage. We suffered greatly from thirst. I remember passing a small marsh where you could wet your throat by getting down on your face and sucking up moisture."[36] On August 31 the force marched eighteen miles, tailed and harassed by warriors nearly the entire time. That evening they camped near a lake, exhausted and hoping for rest.[37] From the top of a nearby hill, warriors watched. That night messages went around to the tribes in the region, and they began to assemble a fighting force.[38]

The morning of September 1 was clear, the rising sun illuminating a hilltop at least a mile away. The crest of the hill stands four hundred feet above the plain, and Kip wrote that warriors had gathered on the hilltop, "their manner defiant and insolent."[39] Wright had sent out his Nez Perce scouts, and they reported that in addition to the gathering on the hill, a large number of warriors waited on the plain below. Wright had wanted to rest his exhausted men and horses for a day, but he knew that his camp in the lowland was vulnerable to attack. The assembled warriors were obviously ready to fight, so Wright ordered his men to prepare for battle and began to move out at 9:30 A.M. The procession consisted of two squadrons of the First Dragoons under Brevet Maj. William N. Grier, four companies of the Third Artillery commanded by Captain Keyes, two rifle battalions of the Ninth Infantry under Capt. Frederick Dent, one mountain howitzer commanded by Lt. J. L. White of the Third Artillery, and the friendly Nez Perces, led by Lt. John Mullan. First, howitzer fire scattered Indians gathered at the top of the hill. More than two hundred mounted and foot soldiers began moving toward the hill; another force headed toward the plain, moving out of sight behind one of the great Palouse dunes. As the dragoons neared the top of the hill, the Indians moved down, some hiding behind trees and rocks. During the climb, Wright received a message from Major Grier that approximately five hundred warriors were waiting in the plains to the north and east. Wright ordered a rapid ascent to the hilltop, finding that the Indians had descended into cover behind trees and rocks.

One of the soldiers provided a description of the view from the top of the hill:

> Now we on the top got an idea of the country and the enemy's force. At our feet, to the left of the hill top and west, were three pretty little lakes, embowered in pines and rocks; another larger and longer one lay just at the foot of the high bare hill, on which we found ourselves; and to the north, beyond it, rose another series of bare, gritty hills rolling away eastward and northward. To the northwest, lay for miles, a plain. In the distance, spits of timber, and still farther, a line of black pine covered mountains made a fit border to this wild picture. On the plain beyond and between the ponds, among the pines which bordered them, and in all the gullies and shelters at our feet, to the northwest, were the wily and wild warriors of the famous *Coeur d'Alenes*, or " Hearts of Arrows," the *Pelouses*, the *Spokanes* and *Yakamas* going hither and yon on their fleet ponies, keeping up a wild and exciting yell and song, by turns.[40]

From the summit, Lieutenant Kip described the scene:

> On the plain below us we saw the enemy. Every spot seemed alive with the wild warriors we had come so far to meet. They were in the pines on the edge of the lakes, in the ravines and gullies, on the opposite hillsides, and swarming over the plain. They seemed to cover the country for two miles. Mounted on their fleet, hardy horses, the crowd swayed back and forth, brandishing their weapons, shouting their war cries, and keeping up a song of defiance.[41]

He described the warriors as "gaudily painted and decorated with their wild trappings. . . . Their plumes fluttered above them, while below skins and trinkets and all kinds of fantastic embellishments flaunted in the sunshine." Even their horses were painted, and feathers adorned their tails, giving them a "wild and fantastic appearance."[42]

Captain Keyes surveyed the scene through his field glasses, describing "a thousand or more savage warriors who were riding furiously hither and thither. . . . The barbarous host was armed with Hudson Bay muskets, spears, bows and arrows, and apparently they were subject to no order or command."[43] One indication of how impressive the sight must have been is the fact that Keyes's count of the enemy was more than double Wright's official count of approximately four hundred, most of which were Spokanes and Yakamas, with smaller numbers of Palouses, Coeur d'Alenes, Kalispels, and warriors from Columbia River Salish bands.

Lieutenant Kip was inspired enough to compose a verse:

> By heavens! It was a glorious sight to see
> The gay array of their wild chivalry.[44]

The battle was, indeed, dramatic. Army dragoons and infantry gathered at the top of the hill, preparing to advance. The cry of bugles signaled a charge by colorfully dressed dragoons, who galloped down a hillside into the sea of brightly painted warriors who were brandishing bows and muskets. Ranks of infantry advanced, firing deadly new rifles. Smoke and dust swirled, soldiers and Indians cried out, and hoof-beats from more than a thousand horses thundered amid rifle reports, the noise of drums and bugles, and eventually, the victorious shouts of soldiers as the warriors picked up their dead and wounded and rode into the distant hills.[45]

Wright's plan was to snap closed the claw his forces had made, pushing his enemy downhill into the dragoons, who would drive them into the open. Captain Keyes ordered several companies to deploy as skirmishers, which they did with great enthusiasm and accuracy, surprising the Indians, most of whom fled. Later, Dandy Jim, one of the Yakamas, gave an account in which he noted the confidence of the soldiers. Yet, he said, the warriors still felt confident, saying of Wright's men: "They appeared to be hunting a fight, but we felt sure they were ours. . . . As soon as the soldiers got close enough to us they opened fire with their guns at once, point-blank. Indian flesh and blood could not stand it. We broke in utter confusion and fled."[46]

Major Grier's force moved two miles from camp up to Granite Lake and confronted an Indian force on a hill on the east side of Willow Lake. The warriors fled east, then joined more of their number on the plain to the northeast of the butte that by now Wright's force had taken. The colonel ordered rifle pits dug near the top, in case they had to fend off an assault, but a combination of charging dragoons and devastating fire from the infantry's long-range rifles quickly broke the warriors' ranks, and the fighting turned into a series of skirmishes that only minimally threatened the soldiers.[47]

One participant described the battle:

> Every move could be seen, and might be likened to 500 little boats playing in the San Francisco harbor, seen from Telegraph Hill. The Indians (whose force outnumbered ours), skirmished rapidly and with courage—advancing at a run, wheeling and delivering their fire, with such quickness and so irregularly, each on his own hook, scattered, yet numerous—that it was almost impossible for musketeers to pick them out, though our men kept their lines, advancing steadily, and as soon as they got range, aimed. Till then the Indians had, for half or three-quarters of an hour, kept the dragoons pretty busy.
>
> But as soon as the Minie balls from our line began to unsaddle them—first, one; then two or three; then their horses caught it; then some half a dozen more swerved in their seats, fell, and were picked up; then they broke, especially those near the line of infantry. The dragoons now got the long awaited word, "Charge the d—d rascals," from "Old Scootum" (Major Grier), and such a race as we witnessed from the top of that hill! By George the sight would have done you good. From the pines, and glens, and open plain, a stream of their ponies poured up that high hill to the north; away after them followed the dragoons, who had been longing to avenge the Steptoe attack; uplifted hands and shrieks for mercy were unheeded as the rear of the Indians was overtaken.[48]

Lieutenant Kip noticed the men who had served under the two officers killed in the Steptoe expedition: "Taylor's and Gaston's companies were there, burning for revenge, and soon they were down on them. We saw the flash of their sabers as they cut them down. Yells and shrieks and uplifted hands were of no avail, as they rode over them."[49] Captain Keyes observed, "Lieutenant Gregg, who was a splendid *sabreur,* overtook one of the flying rascals and with a blow of his blade split his skull in two."[50] After the initial charge down the hill to drive the enemy onto the plain, superior weaponry took over. Instead of muzzle-loading weapons, the infantry was armed with long-range Sharps carbines, which could fire deadly Minie balls. The army had been testing the rifles since 1851, and while a few of Steptoe's men had carried the new arms during his failed expedition, at Four Lakes the rifles were used on a large scale for the first time.[51] In addition to the Sharps, the artillery (fighting as infantry) carried Springfield .58-caliber rifled muskets. Instead of engaging in close fighting, as the Indians preferred, the men were able to accurately hit targets from a hundred yards or more, far out of range of the Indians' muskets and bows and arrows. Still, even with the superiority in weaponry and training, it took nearly four hours for the dragoons to chase away the last of the defenders, pushing them north and east into pine trees growing in earth broken by basalt crags, a distance of four miles.[52]

Indian casualties were reported to number about twenty killed and fifty wounded, with at least that many more horse casualties. The only casualty in Wright's force was one injured horse, despite the fact that not only were the soldiers facing an enemy equal in numbers, but the terrain on which they fought was extremely rough, even on the grassland. In great part, the lack of army casualties was because the conflict was more of a rout than a pitched battle. The warriors tried to regroup after the cavalry charge, signaling each other by waving blankets and shouting. However, rifle fire drove them further off, and the fight ended.[53]

Another version of the conflict, told years later by Thomas Beall, agrees with other accounts in some respects, but adds a significant element. In a 1916 interview, Beall told a less valorous version of events. He claimed that at sunset, the warriors left the top of the hill. Wright ordered the howitzers to be placed on a knoll, positioned so they could "throw shells into the teepees on

Fanciful and heroic depiction of the Battle of Four Lakes. Note the American flag rising in the center of the battle. From Brackett, *History of the United States Cavalry*.

the lake not over a quarter mile distant." The next morning two companies of infantry were positioned behind the artillery, with four dragoon companies behind them. Beall was with the pack train, asleep, when the howitzers began firing. "I was awakened by the noise of the shelling. When the shells struck those teepees the Indians came out like bees out of a hive. Then the dragoons charged and made quite a slaughter." Beall did not say if he witnessed the shelling of the village, or if his information was second hand. Accounts by Kip, Keyes, and others do not mention a village being shelled.[54]

Wright's forces were in high spirits over the next several days as they remained in camp resting for the next stage of the campaign. The men were so happy with their victory and the new rifles that Kip wrote, "Three hearty cheers" were first given to their "gallant commander, Colonel Wright," and more cheers were added for the new rifles.[55] The battle took on mythic proportions almost immediately, due in part to the army's lack of casualties and in part to the dramatic versions told by Kip and others in Wright's force and by Indian warriors.

Depiction of the Battle of Four Lakes based on witness accounts. Painting by Nona Hengen. Courtesy of the artist.

History books written in the decades following the battle present a grandiose view of the fighting. One drawing, called "The Charge of Major Grier's First U.S. Dragoons," shows a great tangle of soldiers and warriors engaging in hand-to-hand combat, the American flag standing tall at the center of the action.[56] Descriptions of events appeared in newspapers around the country, and in some cases the drama seemed to grow as time passed. In 1912 a Spokane newspaper printed a version that was not unusual. The dragoon charge at Four Lakes was described thus: "Out thrust the sabre in the mellow sun of autumn and began its brutal task of drinking the lifeblood of the laggard."[57]

On September 5, while camped at Four Lakes, John Mullan wrote a long, passionate letter to Charles Mix, the commissioner of Indian affairs in Washington, D.C.: "Like an immense monster of desolation to these Indians the waves of civilization are fast approaching them, and ere long, unless prompt and speedy measures be taken for their security and safety, must engulf and destroy them." Mullan tells Mix that the Four Lakes battle was "a memorable never to be forgotten fight; since he [Wright] killed, discomfited, and drove in dismay the enemy from the field without sustaining a single loss to his command."[58]

After the battle one of the soldiers wrote that Colonel Wright, "anticipating our needs, ordered the small supply of stimulant that had been brought along to be equitably distributed. . . . A little artificial life received at such a time well supplemented our tough bread and bacon, and no doubt reinforced many an aged veteran and slender recruit."[59] In the meantime, the Indians sent messengers to surrounding tribes, calling for reinforcements, preparing for the next battle.

BATTLE OF THE SPOKANE PLAINS

Over the following four days, the men had an uneasy rest. On the morning of Sunday, September 5, Wright's men broke camp and headed north toward the Spokane River. After the company marched for an hour, groups of Indians began riding parallel to the pack train, their numbers steadily increasing. On the right, Kamiakin headed up the Yakamas and Palouses; the Coeur d'Alenes were in the center, and the Spokanes on the left. There appeared to be greater numbers than in the prior battle; certainly, according to the soldiers, there were more than one thousand. This time, the grass was torched in an attempt to panic the train. Lieutenant Dandy wrote that the fires were "accompanied by horrible yells, war whoops and battle cries of a hideous nature, at least to our new recruits." The packers gathered the train tightly, then started a backfire in order to stop the advance of the flames.[60]

Instead of retreating, Wright's men charged through a gap in the blaze and began firing, with the same result as at Four Lakes. Major Grier led his dragoons through the smoke and drew harmless fire from bows and muskets. As the troops spread out, firing their deadly rifles, warriors took shelter behind hillocks and pine trees. Lieutenant White's howitzer was particularly lethal, killing several charging Indians with one blast. One shot ripped a branch off a pine tree, which fell onto a group of Indians, including Chief Kamiakin, who was severely injured. Later, Lieutenant Dandy spoke with several warriors, who told him they were afraid of the howitzers, which they called "the guns that went off twice" because of their exploding projectiles.[61]

Skirmishes continued past five o'clock that evening. Again, to their amazement, Wright's troops had suffered no fatalities, and only one man received a minor injury. The army had traveled twenty-five miles, fighting more than half the distance. When they finally set up camp along the Spokane River, they were exhausted but jubilant. In a letter to the *New York Times* sent from the campaign, Lt. Robert Ogden Tyler wrote that during the September 5 battle, an Indian was shot from his horse, then captured by soldiers. On him they found a pistol that had belonged to their beloved Lieutenant Gaston, who had been killed in the Steptoe battle. Tyler did not mention what happened to their captive; undoubtedly he was quickly executed. It is unknown how many wounded Indians were left on the battlefield, since the warriors typically tried to retrieve their fallen comrades, but the soldiers took no prisoners.[62] According to Indian accounts gathered by one historian, "Every Indian that was wounded and fell into the hands of the soldiers, or had been taken in flight had been immediately dispatched. No Indian was spared who surrendered."[63]

News of the two battles spread across the west. On September 26 the *San Francisco Daily Alta California* printed what was described as a "private letter," dated September 3. The unidentified author, a soldier in Wright's force, gives a vivid description of the Battle of Four Lakes and the sentiments of the men. The correspondent noted that the Nez Perces allied with the army returned from chasing the fleeing warriors, bringing back "trophies—such as Hudson's Bay guns, blankets, bows and quivers—for many of the Indians were armed with both bows and rifles—and I think, from what I can learn, that these swarthy allies of ours have surreptitiously brought in some half dozen scalps. I rather think the prestige (if any was gained) of their having driven Steptoe back, is gone, and now all we have to do is to keep whipping them." He summed up the immediate effect of the Battle of Four Lakes: "There was an energy and a gleaming satisfaction seen through the dusty, sweaty faces of our soldiers—quite cheering." The writer outlined plans to follow up the successful start to the campaign: "We mean to follow it up by pitching into their corn crops, fish caches, potato patches, and domestic affairs generally; and show them that war is not quite so pleasant a pastime as they thought, when bullying Steptoe's small party."[64]

ECHOES

The combination of aggressive battle tactics and modern firepower were later to prove devastating during the Civil War, when both sides used what were then old-style tactics with new weapons. Close-quarters fighting worked with bayonets and muskets, but not rifles and grapeshot blasted from howitzers. After Wright's 1858 campaign, an article in the *Washington (D.C.) Union* noted the effectiveness of the new weapons: "Col.

The 1926 dedication of the monument at the Battle of Spokane Plains, with special guest Alice Garry, great-granddaughter of Chief Garry of the Spokanes. Museum of Arts and Culture, Spokane.

Wright's command used the Sharpe [*sic*] rifle, and the difference in result is most striking. Says one account of the Battle of Four Lakes: 'We have killed and wounded more than forty-seven of the enemy, and not one of us hurt. I tell you the Indians were astonished when our fellows perched them off at four and five

Monument at the site of the Battle of Four Lakes. Author photo.

hundred yards. They won't let a single man now approach them nearer than half a mile.'"[65]

On October 20, 1935, the community of Four Lakes hosted the dedication of the granite monument that noted the army's success against the local tribes. First, the band from the state "custodial" school played. Next, Mrs. Leo Buteau, a pioneer living in Four Lakes, pulled red, white, and blue banners away from the stone, revealing it to the assembled gathering. Four young women christened the stone with water taken from each of the Four Lakes: Meadow, Silver, Willow, and Granite. Washington's governor made a speech, as did at least six others, including the man who carved the stone. Mrs. Charles Goodsell led the crowd in singing "America the Beautiful."[66]

There was no notice of Native people in attendance, unlike the unveiling of the monument to mark the Battle of Spokane Plains.[67] At that dedication, a smiling Miss Spokane—Alice Garry—stood next to the monument commemorating the army's victory. Miss Garry was Chief Garry's great-granddaughter. Accounts of the ceremony do not indicate if anyone noticed the irony.

TEN

Exulting in a Bloody Task

Following the Battle of Spokane Plains, George Wright sent a letter to the headquarters of the Department of the Pacific in which he expressed his appreciation for help his troops had received: "A kind Providence again protected us, although at many times the balls flew thick and fast through ranks, yet, strange to say, we had but one man slightly wounded."[1] Providence is mentioned frequently in accounts written by Wright and his men, always in a matter-of-fact tone, as if there was never any doubt that their mission was being guided by a force more powerful than their enemy.

The day after the Battle of Spokane Plains, September 6, 1858, Wright's force rested, keeping a wary eye on Indians across the Spokane River. That afternoon several crossed over and offered their friendship; Wright questioned a few and sent them on their way unharmed. The tribes' will to fight was nearly broken; only a few of the young warriors wanted to continue.[2] The ferocity of the soldiers had unnerved them and destroyed their confidence. Some battle participants literally fled to all points on the compass: the Yakamas to the west, the Kalispels to the north and east, and the Coeur d'Alenes east and south.[3] However, an unknown but significant number of Indians did not travel far, intending to regroup and try to raise another force.

The dry, warm weather took a toll on everyone. Captain Keyes gives us an account of what he felt after the Battle of Spokane Plains:

The country fought over was without water, and when we reached the Spokan River, and pitched our camp, twenty-five miles distant from the former, the whole command, men and animals were nearly exhausted. It was estimated that I had ridden eighty miles on the same pony of incredible endurance. I kept my saddle till my tent was pitched; then I dismounted, took a glass of wine, gave orders not to disturb me, and lay down on my back to rest. For half an hour I did not move a muscle, and felt the whole time that if I did move one I should die. At the end of an hour I was restored, and no one had noticed my debility. Never before, or since, was I so nearly finished by the toil of war.[4]

Expedition camp on the Spokane River, September 6, 1858. Wright's camp is center-right. The location is near present-day Fort George Wright, three miles northwest of downtown Spokane. Drawing by Gustavus Sohon. Sohon Drawings Collection, Manuscripts, Archives, and Special Collections, Washington State University Libraries.

"I CAME HERE TO FIGHT"

Now, after the military part of the campaign was largely over, Wright shifted into the next stage of the war. On September 7 the march east began, and the expedition moved along the south bank of the Spokane River, passing the falls in the center of present-day Spokane, described by Kip as "a high, narrow basaltic canyon where the whole river passes over an inclined level of rocks, with a fall of between forty and fifty feet. The view from every point is exceedingly picturesque."[5] During the salmon runs tribes from all over the Inland Northwest would gather at the falls to catch fish for the winter. There were several fisheries along the river. At one near the present-day Washington-Idaho border, weirs were built to obstruct the flow of salmon, which were speared. A hundred or more people might gather at one spot, every day hauling out more than a thousand fish, some weighing more than forty pounds.[6]

Not far from the falls, on land that is now part of downtown Spokane, a group of Indians on the north bank of the river signaled that they wanted to talk. Through a Nez Perce interpreter, Wright instructed them to meet him two miles upriver at a ford. One was Chief Garry of the Spokanes, a man trusted and respected by nearly all who knew him, including whites. When he was a boy the Hudson's Bay Company had selected Garry to attend the Red River School in Manitoba, an institution started by missionaries from the Church of England. As a result, Garry not only could speak English, but for many years had also felt conflicted about his spiritual beliefs and his role in the Indian world. He had found his voice three years earlier at the Walla Walla Treaty Council, when he stood up for all the tribes who were being pushed aside. "I think the difference between us and you Americans is in the clothing," he said at the treaty council. "The blood and body are the same."[7] But now, along the Spokane River in his homeland, Garry was a defeated man willing to pay Wright's price for peace.

The forty-seven-year-old chief started by telling Wright that he had always wanted peace but that he had been overruled by other chiefs and some of the younger warriors. Wright was not interested in listening and launched into a speech that Lieutenant Kip reported was "by no means pleasing." Later, in the official report that Wright sent to Fort Vancouver, he wrote what he had said to Garry:

> I have met you in two bloody battles; you have been badly whipped; you have had several chiefs and many warriors killed or wounded; I have not lost a man or an animal. I have a large force, and you, Spokans, Coeur d'Alenes, Pelouzes, and Pend d'Oreilles may unite, and I can defeat you as badly as before. I did not come into the country to make peace; I came here to fight. Now, when you are tired of war and ask for peace, I will tell you what you must do. You must come to me with your arms, with your women and children, and everything you have, and lay them at my feet. You must put your faith in me and trust to my mercy. If you do this, I shall then tell you the terms upon which I shall give you peace. If you do not do this, war will be made on you this year and the next, and until your nation shall be exterminated.[8]

Wright told Garry to spread his message throughout the tribes in the region, and that if they obeyed, no lives would be taken. In a letter to headquarters dated September 15, he said, "The chastisement which these Indians have received has been severe but well merited."[9]

Such thinking was difficult for the tribes to understand, and it terrified them. That afternoon, as Wright's men were making camp, nine Indians approached the opposite bank, laid down their guns, and swam across. Wright learned that one was Polatkin, a chief who was present at the Steptoe battle in May and had been the head war chief of the Spokanes during the Battle of Spokane Plains. Polatkin was accompanied by Jo-hout, a Palouse warrior suspected of being involved in the murder of two miners earlier that year, an incident that preceded Steptoe's ill-fated march. Wright ordered two of the Indians to swim back across the river and bring over the guns. Upon reaching the opposite bank, one fled, but the other returned to Wright with the rifles, which were stamped "London, 1847"—the type sold by the Hudson's Bay Company.[10] Wright was not pleased; not only had there been bad feelings between the United States and Britain because of an ongoing territorial dispute in Puget Sound, but also the Hudson's Bay Company had been selling alcohol and guns to the Indians through trading posts throughout the Northwest.[11] Wright took Polatkin and Jo-hout prisoner and told the others to leave and spread the message that anyone who had been involved in the fight against Steptoe must surrender to him.

Along the way, Lieutenant Kip's friend Cutmouth John continued to entertain and irritate the troops. John had been "saved" by missionaries some years earlier and alternated bible reading with wild drinking binges. On this expedition he served as one of the scouts under the command of Lieutenant Mullan. It was said of John, "No other in Mullan's force secured more scalps than he, and no one perhaps was entitled to fewer."[12] Unlike the friendly Indians who accompanied the Steptoe march earlier in the year, the Nez Perce on Wright's campaign were brave and extraordinarily helpful under the command of Lieutenant Mullan. Wright even praised the friendly Indians in his official report on the battle.[13]

The next day, September 8, as the troops marched along the south side of the Spokane River, Wright's men spotted a cloud of dust. After moving ahead another eight miles, the two artillery companies and one company of dragoons took defensive positions. The balance of the force headed toward the dust, the dragoons galloping, the infantry running behind. Captain Keyes reported, "I marched my foot-soldiers eighteen miles at quick-time, without a halt, to the top of a range of hills."[14] From high ground, the soldiers saw a lake and broad meadows over which ran hundreds of horses, many of which were mares and colts. They were told by their Nez Perce scouts that Indians were driving a great herd of horses into the hills, intending to scatter them out of reach of the whites. The dragoons dismounted and gave chase, engaging in a skirmish that drove away the Indians.

The troops managed to capture about nine hundred horses and drove them back to the river, where the main part of the

Spokane Falls. This stretch of the Spokane River runs through the heart of present-day Spokane. Drawing by John Mix Stanley. Courtesy Washington State Historical Society.

force had made camp. The men set about building a large corral, with some of the soldiers and packers working to keep the captive horses together. The heat, dust, smell, cries and scramble of the horses would have been daunting for even the most trail-hardened soldier. Nearly two thousand horses, mules, and cattle were at the encampment, with the captured horses penned into a tight area between a low embankment and the river.

It was the dry season, and although the water was fast moving, it was not deep. Hence, crossing it was not a problem to men and animals. That day, two of Polatkin's sons appeared on the opposite side of the river and shouted for their father to be released. Soldiers under the command of Capt. Edward Ord (for whom Fort Ord in California was later named) fired on them, killing one horse and wounding both men. They escaped into a thicket of trees, and were not heard from again. About this same time, a group of peace-seeking Spokanes sent over a negotiator named Amtoola, who, holding a white flag, swam across the river with his horse. For some unknown reason, the soldiers fatally shot him. Wright makes no mention of the incident in his official reports, just as there is no mention of executing wounded prisoners on the battlefield. According to witnesses, there were more such executions on the trek east, but the details have been either ignored or lost in time.[15]

At dusk the camp was settled, and Colonel Wright ordered that Jo-hout, the Palouse captive, be delivered to him. Wright conducted one of his soon-to-be infamous "trials," which consisted of the colonel asking a few questions, then hanging the alleged perpetrator. Wright determined that Jo-hout had been involved in the killing of two miners earlier in the year, and sentenced him to death. Jo-hout was placed on Lieutenant Mullan's surveying wagon and a rope was thrown over the branch of a poplar tree. Soldiers climbed on the wagon with Jo-hout, holding him while Tom Beall adjusted the noose. The cart was then driven from under him, and he strangled to death. None of the hangings Wright ordered used the five- to ten-foot drop that severs the spinal cord, providing a nearly instant death; rather, after the noose was placed around the victim's neck, he was left to slowly strangle, remaining in excruciating consciousness for up to twenty minutes.[16] Wright had the resources to build a scaffold for a quicker death (after all, his men built a corral fence for the horses), but he chose not to use them. Later events proved that he intended for the theatrically macabre nature of the executions to be a warning to others. Execution by hanging was often used not only as a means of killing an offender, but also as a warning to others. It was a gruesome way to intimidate and display the power of the executioner. The sight of the victim struggling at the end of the rope, his judge standing nearby, indifferent to the man's suffering, sent a clear message to those watching.[17]

After sunset Wright sent out a force to capture a herd of the Indians' cattle, but the livestock escaped into the mountains. He sent out another group of soldiers to find lodges and food stores and burn them—a task with which they had great success. September was a critical time of year for the tribes, for it was when they harvested wheat and other crops to store for the long, cold winters. The loss of their sustenance would have been particularly devastating. Mullan, Kip, and other men in Wright's expedition made note of the destruction of the Indians' food stores. On September 9, for example, Kip wrote, "This morning at daybreak, three companies of dragoons were sent out, and destroyed seven lodges used by the Indians as storehouses of wheat."[18] Packer John Smith reported that the force passed through an abandoned village on the south bank of the Spokane River from which the inhabitants had fled, leaving "many of their lodges and considerable of their property," which the soldiers destroyed. While at the site, Captain Ord's men shot at a group of Indians gathered on the far side of the river, killing some of their horses.[19] The troops destroyed grain fields, root caches, and canoes and boats they found on small lakes. One man recalled, "It was a most enlivening sight, at times, to see the long line of cavalry strung out by file ascending the mountain, each trooper buried in the midst of some half-dozen enormous sheaves of rye or wheat, carried along for horse food, as the grass was now dry and scarce."[20]

During the march along the Spokane River the soldiers and packers burned caches of wheat, oats, and hay and destroyed stones used for grinding grain. Cattle were killed for meat, and according to Seltice at least several ponies belonging to Indian children were shot. Wright's troops killed so many people and animals on his trip that in many historical accounts, the destruction of food stores pales in comparison, receiving only a sentence or two. However, if not for the Jesuits helping the tribes (in particular the Coeur d'Alenes), and if not for the departure of the army in late September, there is no doubt that starvation would have added more victims to Wright's tally. The destruction of their villages and food supply was so complete that in the weeks and months afterwards many Indians went east to the Coeur d'Alene Mission, both for protection from Wright and for sustenance. The devastation caused by the destruction of the Indians' food was compounded by the fact that the prior winter had been particularly cold, and food supplies were already limited.[21] Later it was learned at the mission that one of the storage buildings that burned contained the carriage that had carried one of the howitzers that the Indians had taken from the battlefield after

Colonel Steptoe's escape, a fact that ratcheted up the anger in some of the men.[22]

The next day was, for many Indians, the worst of Wright's thirty-day march. The colonel and his officers had the problem of the horses. Captain Keyes wrote, "At first Colonel Wright and the others were not disposed to kill the horses thinking them too valuable. I told him I should not sleep so long as they remained alive, as I regarded them the main dependence and most prized of all the Indians' [possessions]."[23] Wright appointed Keyes to head a board of officers to determine what to do with the creatures. The board decided that each officer and the quartermaster could keep one horse for his own use and each of the Nez Perce scouts could take two. A total of 130 were kept, and two contingents of soldiers were assigned to slaughter the remainder. Another corral was built from poplar and cottonwood logs, the animals were gathered in groups, and from there, they were lassoed a few at a time and dragged out to a gravel bar in the river. The older ones were shot in the back of the head, while the colts were clubbed in the head. Lieutenant Kip wrote, "It was distressing during all the following night, to hear the cries of the brood mares whose young had thus been taken from them."[24] Lieutenant Dandy reported it to be "a pitiable sight; but it was undoubtedly a necessity of war."[25] Years later, one witness wrote, "None of us who are still alive will ever forget this unpleasant and mournful sight. The neighing of horses and calling of colts and dams made the nights hideous during our stay at this place."[26]

As the slaughter progressed, Indians watched from the hills, shocked by the brutality towards defenseless creatures the Indians considered to be spiritual beings. Horses were critically important to the tribes, as they depended on them to hunt, travel, fight, and carry food, and they were used as currency. In an oral history, one Coeur d'Alene woman quoted her grandfather as saying, "You'd just look out there and they [the hills] would be just dark with herds and herds of horses."[27] They were the most important possession an Indian could have; without horses, life became very tenuous. A herd as large as the one captured by Wright's men represented great wealth, since at that time,

The horse massacre along the Spokane River as described by witnesses. Painting by Nona Hengen, courtesy of the artist.

Hudson's Bay Company posts were selling horses to whites for up to one hundred dollars a head.[28] However, the long-term economic impact was secondary to the immediate emotional blow delivered to the tribes. Several of the soldiers' journals and letters express justification for the slaughter. In his journal, John Mullan wrote, "I know not when I have witnessed a more disturbing sight but it was actually an act of humanity. For it was the means of saving our own men, and the lives of parties passing through the territory but it was of such character as to strike dismay into the heart of the enemy. . . . To see 700 beautiful mares, colts and horses in one slaughter pen was truly awful."[29]

After the better part of a day 270 horses had been killed, but the job was taking too long. The soldiers starting shooting into the corral in an effort to make the slaughter go more quickly. Still, it took two days to kill them all. Years later, Lieutenant Morgan recalled, "Company after company, in turn, marched up and fired into them until the muskets became fouled, when the company marched off and was succeeded by another, until the ponies were all slain."[30]

Years later one soldier remembered that when given the order to kill the horses, the men "almost mutinied," but apparently all followed Wright's directive.[31] Indians watching from a distance were devastated by the killing of animals they valued so highly, since it emphasized both the brutality of their enemy and the hopelessness of their defense. Years later Morgan wrote, "While this judicious slaughter was going on, the Indians were assembled on the distant hills looking on at the destruction of their wealth. This was their Gettysburg."[32] Keyes recalled, "It was a cruel sight to see so many noble beasts shot down. They were all sleek, glossy, and fat, and as I love a horse, I fancied I saw in their beautiful faces a plea for mercy. Towards the last the soldiers appeared to exult in their bloody task; and such is the ferocious character of men."[33]

In Captain Keyes's disturbing description of the soldiers' behavior there are clues to Wright's state of mind. For example, there is no indication in Keyes's account—or in any other account of the episode—that Wright was disturbed that his men "appeared to exult" while they slaughtered animals. In historical accounts of the horse slaughter, some historians have excused the bloodshed as an unfortunate but necessary part of warfare. This argument oversimplifies the situation. Equating living animals to inanimate machinery softens the emotional trauma to the participants, but in this case that argument is based on a false premise: that the army intended for Wright to kill the creatures. The "evidence," according to one historian, consists of a letter from army headquarters to General Harney concerning Wright's 1858 expedition. The historian asserts that the orders contained in the letter "indicated that the destruction of the Indian herds was to be part of his task." However, Wright could not have been aware of the orders, since the letter was sent from Washington, D.C., on September 14, a day on which Wright's force was fighting its way through dense forest on the way to the Coeur d'Alene Mission. Not only had the horse massacre already occurred, but the letter would not reach Harney until after the campaign ended.[34]

To Wright and at least some of his men, the slaughter was a strategic decision, part of their overall plan to so cripple the tribes that they would not have the resources to keep fighting. The primary reason for the horse massacre was to create terror. John Mullan admitted, "As our desire was to strike a blow that should teach the Indians a never-to-be-forgotten lesson, it was decided to kill them."[35] Later, Father Joset would write to his superior that Wright had shot the horses "as they were a bother to the party." He added, "He shot them all: this added not a little to the fright of the Indians."[36]

In Wright's official report of the incident, he claims that the horse slaughter not only dealt an economic blow to the tribes, it also served as retribution. His letter to General Clarke explains: "As I reported in my communication of yesterday the capture of 800 horses on the 8th instant, I have now to add that this large band of horses composed the entire wealth of the Palouse Chief Til-co-ax. This man has ever been hostile; for the last two years he has been constantly sending his young men into the Walla Walla Valley, and stealing horses and cattle from settlers and the government. He boldly acknowledged these facts when he met Colonel Steptoe, in May last. Retributive justice has now overtaken him; the blow has been severe but well-merited."[37] At least some, maybe all, of the horses belonged to the hated Tilcoax, but others have suggested they belonged to Poyahkin and Penockahlowyun, Palouse chiefs from Wawawai, along the Snake River.[38] In 1961 Judge William Compton Brown claimed that Wright had intentionally assigned the horses to Tilcoax, knowing that destroying that chief's herd would elicit high praise from General Clarke.[39] Wright's report on the horse massacre ended with an expression of regret, invoking the moral and legal principals of "dire necessity." It was possibly the only time during his years on the Columbia Plateau that he expressed remorse over one of his actions, and it had nothing to do with human beings.[40]

Wright's command of the incident raises a question about his leadership: If he was so convinced that killing the animals was "dire necessity," why did he not just give the order? Instead, Wright perhaps unconsciously used a tactic that social scientists have identified in similar situations: he diffused the responsibility for the slaughter.[41] He appointed a board of officers and the quartermaster to make the final decision; they then selected soldiers to do the killing. Up until this point in the trip, he had shown no hesitation; his men admired him for his steadiness and discipline, yet in this case he apparently hesitated. He told the officers, in effect, to make the decision for him, thereby absolving himself of some of the responsibility. Then, in his report to headquarters, when a difficult decision was not at stake, he assumed total responsibility, which of course was expected of the commander of a force. Besides, he wanted to show General Clarke how viciously he was punishing the tribes.[42] The Indians, the human victims, had already been dehumanized, making it easier to kill them. The fact that the victims in this case were animals made little difference. When Captain Keyes noted that he "saw in their beautiful faces an appeal for mercy," he was attributing more of a human quality to the animals than most of the men in his force ascribed to Indians.

Arguments about the horse massacre have continued to more recent times. In 1988 Wright's biographer stated, "It was army policy to destroy horses, and so he did that. . . . It's still the army's policy to destroy the other guy's transportation." While it is true that enemy horses were often killed or stolen, it was "practice" more than "policy." Wright's horse slaughter stands out more than perhaps any other in the West for two reasons: its size and its gruesomely theatrical nature. The killing took place in an open area next to the Spokane River. At that point, the Spokane Valley is only about a mile across, with hills running east to west, parallel to the river. The Spokanes, Coeur d'Alenes, Palouses, and other tribal members had a clear view of the killing, not to mention the sounds of gunshots, dying animals, and shouting men. It was as if the scene was being played out in a great amphitheater. Wright knew tribes were watching and he knew the effect the killing would have on them. The drama unfolded; the horse killings were another of the colonel's spectacles, intended to impress and terrify.[43]

The collective narrative includes claims that Wright's actions did not violate the "rules of war." Whether or not Wright's actions fit within the rules of war was of little concern to him, although the concept of formal restrictions on violence in war was not foreign to him. In 1847 during the Mexican-American War, Gen. Winfield Scott introduced military tribunals intended to punish violators of "the laws of war," which one scholar has called an example of "emerging standards regarding proper conduct of warfare."[44] However, the laws of war did not address destruction of property.

At least a few of the civilian employees working in the pack train tried to keep horses for themselves. Only a few miles from the massacre site, controlling the additional animals became burdensome, and the quartermaster began taking the extras away. John Smith wrote, "The officers thought these horses would take up too much time, require too much attention, so they gathered them all, and killed them there." There is no record of how many animals were killed in the second slaughter, but it could easily have been one hundred or more.[45]

From the horse camp Wright wrote a letter to Father Joset, to be delivered by "the faithful Sebastian," a Coeur d'Alene Indian close to Joset. The letter, uncharacteristically written by Wright himself rather than an aide, tells Joset, "Kind fortune has favored us far beyond our most sanguine expectations. . . . I am truly happy that these poor people are brought to a sense of their true position." Wright then added a statement that was to later infuriate his commanding officer, General Clarke. Wright promised to spare anyone who came to him in peace, and Clarke wanted no such promises. The fact that Wright would later break that promise is still a source of anger and sadness to some people today, particularly Native Americans.

> The Indians who have not joined the hostiles at any time, have nothing to fear; let them remain perfectly quiet with their women and children around them—I now speak to all Indians, whether Coeur d'Alene or belonging to other tribes, who have taken part in this war—if you are sincere and really desire peace you must all come to me with your guns, with your families and all you have and trust entirely to my mercy—I shall then say to you what I require you to do, if we are to have peace now and forever hereafter, I promise no life shall be taken for acts committed in this unhappy war. If you do all I require you shall have peace—If you do not, the war will be prosecuted this year and next, until you are all killed or driven from your country. This from me, who never yet told a lie to the Indians.

Wright then promised Joset that the Palouses had nothing to fear: "I shall prosecute the war against the Palouses, but if they want peace, they can have it on the same terms I offer the Coeur d'Alenes."[46] That, as it turned out, was not true.

As the force prepared to head further east, Tom Beall recalled more destruction near the camp: "After the killing it was discovered by the scouts that there was quite an Indian village just around a point of mountain a short distance from our camp. A detachment was sent to destroy it. Most of the houses contained grain, and some not, but they were all destroyed by the torch. The hostiles did not know what to think of this kind of warfare, and it was the cause of completely subduing them."[47]

While Colonel Wright was still at the Horse Slaughter Camp, a courier arrived with a message from Father Joset, who was at the mission. Joset said the Coeur d'Alenes desired peace, and he offered to help. The plea was futile. In the early hours of September 11 the force packed up, and at five A.M., headed east across a grassy plain dotted with pines. They were bound for the Coeur d'Alene Mission in present-day northern Idaho, a distance of forty-five miles from what some of the soldiers called "Dead Horse Camp." As they moved through the Spokane Valley, they were "burning fences and fields, and every vestige of improvement by the roadside, when the Indians sent in one of the Fathers to sue for peace."[48]

Keyes wrote that "desolation marked our tracks."[49] The dragoons located grain caches, which were taken for the army's horses; what they did not keep, they destroyed. Wright's belligerence with Chief Garry and the others who had tried to talk peace was probably a result of his growing arrogance, which became more apparent in his letters as the campaign continued. In any case his actions were risky, since it was now autumn, his force was exhausted, and they were moving further away from their base, Fort Walla Walla. Although they had soundly defeated the Indians at Four Lakes and the Spokane Plains, perhaps only five percent of the warriors had been killed or wounded. Many of the braves, especially the younger ones, had retreated to the hills to figure out their next move. If the confederation had been successful at recruiting from other tribes—the Kalispels, for example—Wright's force could have marched right into a trap. The reason he did not had less to do with his military strategy and more to do with the work of Father Joset, who, more than Wright or anyone else, convinced the Coeur d'Alenes to stop fighting.[50] The troops knew the Indians were disheartened, and some believed their mission was completed. Lieutenant Tyler reported that the Indians had headed into the mountains, "where they are living in fear and trembling lest we follow them."[51]

By now, news of the campaign was trickling east, thanks to letters sent out by Lieutenant Tyler and others. Eastward-bound mail was given to a messenger, who would ride with it to Fort Taylor or Fort Walla Walla. From there it would travel by courier to The Dalles, by steamer to Fort Vancouver, and by ship to the east coast. Accounts of the campaign started to appear in Pacific coast newspapers in late September, and a month later in the east, where accounts were published in the *New York Times* and other publications. The events of mid-September were reported in the December 1858 edition of *Harper's New Monthly* magazine, which noted, "The soldiers are destroying the grain fields and provisions of the savages, who are reduced to great distress."[52] On the west side of Washington Territory, the *Puget Sound Herald* (located in Steilacoom) printed an unintentionally ironic article praising Wright and General Clarke: "The column under Col. Wright has marched into the very heart of the hostile tribes, destroying hundreds of their stock, burning lodges full of grain, caches of camas and berries, and striking terror into the bravest of their warriors. . . . [General Clarke] will adhere to his determination of altering the entire aspect of our Indian relations, and convince them that the friendship and goodwill of the hitherto despised Bostons is all important to their welfare."[53] ("Bostons" was a term some Indians used for setters from the east, since in the early days of expansion so many came from New England, and sailed from that city.) Despite the article's assertion, the Indians were having a hard time appreciating Wright's "friendship and goodwill." The sentiment expressed in the newspaper was a common one of the day, a kind of dysfunctional mutation of Puritanical thinking in which sinners need to be punished in order to achieve salvation, or in this case, survival.

Wright's strategy of death and devastation was not impulsive. As a career army officer and graduate of West Point, he had been exposed to what was referred to as the "feed fight," which had become a common strategy used against Indians. One historian points out, "Devastation as a deliberate choice was not only indiscriminate in its treatment of the land and the property within it, it also opened doors for individual soldiers to make more drastic choices about the people and property they encountered."[54] In other words, as the violence continued, the men became less sensitized to it, which made it easier for them to engage in further actions, sometimes more violent. Some of Wright's officers wrote of the food destruction in matter-of-fact tones, with little of the emotion they felt at watching the horses be killed. Some clearly had mixed feelings about the destruction. Lieutenant Kip wrote, "At noon, we came across four Indian lodges filled with wheat, which we burned. Some caches, filled with dried cake and wild cherries, were also discovered and destroyed. This outbreak will bring upon the Indians a winter of great suffering, from the destruction of their stores."[55] It is difficult to tell how much empathy Kip might have felt at the plight of their victims, but certainly he and the rest of Wright's command were well aware of the impact their actions would have on all Indians, not just the warriors they had come to fight.

The march Wright's force made to the Coeur d'Alene Mission was the most difficult of the campaign. The route from the Horse Slaughter Camp to the mission passed through dense forest. They crossed one mountain pass and literally hacked their way through conifer forests. Moving the pack train proved exceptionally difficult, with some men cutting trees and boughs, while others pulled and pushed heavily laden mules. Lieutenant Mullan, the surveyor, had to disassemble his surveying cart, and the limbers for the howitzers were abandoned. Heat and dust exhausted the men, and Lieutenant Kip noted that the burden was so great that every so often a soldier would collapse. The affected man would be attended to by one of the physicians, and if unable to walk, would be placed on a horse. Kip described the density of the forest like that of a cavern, and wrote that "we wound our way in a twilight gloom."[56]

When they were able gain a view, the soldiers, most of who had been stationed at various posts in the west, were awed by the scenery, thinking it was some of the most beautiful they had ever seen. On this march Kip expressed a sentiment that showed appreciation for the natural beauty and some empathy for the Indians: "This is a splendid country as a home for the Indians, and we cannot wonder that they are aroused when they think the white men are intruding on them. . . . When the Indian thinks of the hunting-grounds to which he is looking forward in the Spirit Land, we doubt whether he could imagine anything more in accordance with his taste than this reality."[57]

While Wright's force was burning its way east, Father Joset was trying to determine how to stop the destruction and bloodshed.

THE COEUR D'ALENE MISSION

In 1740 Chief Circling Raven of the Coeur d'Alenes foresaw the coming of the Black Robes. His prophecy was fulfilled a century later when Father De Smet arrived in the Flathead country, just to the east of the Coeur d'Alenes.[58] During his 1840 visit De Smet told the people that he would send another Black Robe to them. In 1842 Father Nicholas Point arrived and began directing the work of building a mission. Three years later Father Joseph Joset arrived in present-day northern Idaho. Joset was born in 1810 in the village of Courfaivre, Switzerland. At the age of thirty he elected to become a missionary among the American Indians. A year after his arrival in Idaho, the earnest and capable priest was appointed vice-provincial and given responsibility for all missions in the Pacific Northwest. The courage and endurance Father Joset displayed during the Steptoe affair would again be called upon to help Colonel Wright.

Unlike some of the missionaries who had come to the Inland Northwest, Joset did not hold himself above or apart from the Coeur d'Alene people. He lived in a log cabin he built with their help, but he ate the same food as they and insisted on doing his share of the work. When offered fish, he once turned it down, telling them, "I will continue to get my own supply of fish."[59] In contrast, Chief Seltice noted that the 1847 murder of Marcus Whitman would not have happened if Whitman's attitude toward the tribes had been more open. Seltice said, "Had he come into our country determined to heal our sick and respect our church, we would have welcomed Dr. Whitman." Seltice described Whitman as "negative towards the Indians in his looks, his actions, his medicines, and his beliefs."[60] Wright's second-in-command, Capt. Erasmus Keyes, visited Rome years after the Plateau War. He interviewed the general of the Jesuits, who explained why Jesuit missionaries had been relatively successful with Indian tribes, at least compared to some of the ill-fated Protestant efforts. St. Ignatius Loyola had taught his followers the importance of learning about the characteristics of the people among whom they were to live. "They were required to acquaint themselves clearly with the impulses, modes of thought, and all the peculiarities of the heathen, and of all unbelievers of every nation and sect, and then to lead them out of their errors into the Catholic Church. In that manner they succeeded in civilizing, converting, and preserving many savage tribes, and arresting infidelity."[61] Joset clearly took Ignatius's message to heart, and his interpretation had generally positive effects on the daily life of the Coeur d'Alenes. George Wright also acquainted himself "with the impulses, modes of thought," and so on, of the tribes, and turned them against the people, using enough force to inflame fear, in line with his goal of suppression, rather than conversion. While some may not like the church's aim of turning native people away from their own spiritual beliefs, few would argue Wright's way was better.

Lt. George Dandy observed that the Coeur d'Alene Indians at the mission were "good, practical Catholics and adept in all the observances of the church. . . . Every evening while we

The Coeur d'Alene Mission in present-day northern Idaho. Drawing by Gustavus Sohon. From Mullan, *Report on the Construction of a Military Road* (1863), in the author's collection.

encamped here, we could hear the Indian men and women at or near the chapel, intoning vespers, and their voices, while sounding somewhat weird, were sweet, and their chanting agreeable to the ear. The hostiles who ventured to come to our camp, having been treated with forbearance, took heart and became humble supplicants for peace."[62]

In 1853 Jesuit missionaries had opened the new Sacred Heart Mission after closing the old one at the south end of Lake Coeur d'Alene. The new mission sat at Cataldo, located in the middle of a wide valley twenty miles east of the lake. The mission church was built on a knoll covered by lawn and shaded by maples. The valley around it was pristine, with wide meadows crossed by streams and densely forested mountains all around. In this part of the Coeur d'Alene basin, the river enters a wide floodplain, sending off branches that curve roughly parallel to the main channel before they dead-end as small lakes or rejoin the river's trunk. The river originates in the Silver Valley, just to the east, and continues westward and drains into Lake Coeur d'Alene, which in turn is drained by the Spokane River, which flows west to the Columbia.

When he and his force arrived at the mission, Colonel Wright wrote to General Clarke, "For the last eighty miles our route has been marked by slaughter and devastation; 900 horses and a large number of cattle have been killed or appropriated to our own use; many horses, with large quantities of wheat and oats, also many caches of vegetables, kamas, and dried berries have been destroyed. A blow has been struck which they will never forget." Throughout the expedition he failed to indicate concern for his actions; when he did comment on his treatment of the Indians, it was only to note, as in a later message to General Clarke, "I have treated these Indians severely, but they justly deserved it all. They will remember it."[63]

Shortly after their arrival at the mission, Lawrence Kip saw women "weeping bitterly. . . . Some were mourning for those who had fallen in battle, others for the hostages who were to be taken by us."[64] Kip believed only about 40 Natives were living at the mission at the time of Wright's visit, but five years earlier, Father Joset had counted 320 living there. A great part of the difference can be attributed to the dispersal of the people avoiding Wright's force.[65]

At the mission the soldiers were able to relax, their concerns turning to other matters, such as the mail. On September 15, Lieutenant Tyler sent a letter from the Coeur d'Alene Mission that was later printed in the *Hartford* (Connecticut) *Times.* He wrote, "We are in the very heart of the enemy's country, and the dangers which beset this letter are very great. The only way we can get the mail through is to entrust it to the good faith of the Indians who fought us the other day."[66]

Wright's men, although exultant, were beginning to suffer from the effects of their rugged march. One officer wrote, "We are now in the mountain fastness; weather cold at night; short rations. Men almost barefoot, but the command in good spirits, for our successes have been unprecedented in Indian warfare. . . . Colonel Wright thus far has received the encomiums of all, and that a kind Providence and a prudent, discreet, sound judgment on his part may hereafter guide the remainder of his acts while on this expedition is the only wish of us."[67] During the stay at the mission the Indians and soldiers got along well, trading shirts and blankets for moccasins and bows and arrows. The soldiers enjoyed their stay, many forming fondness for the people.

The Coeur d'Alene people were discouraged. Some expressed surprise that the soldiers were so friendly after the battles, which Father Joset explained to them: "The soldiers were like lions in war and lambs in peace."[68] The soldiers relaxed their attitudes enough to transcend the violence and at least some of the emotional strain of past weeks. The Indians turned over a myriad of goods they had taken after Steptoe's retreat. Lieutenant Tyler reported they returned "tin pans, cups, spurs, pistols . . . even a skein of thread and needle."[69]

Years later, in an interview with Joel Trimble, the interviewer reported Trimble's memory of Wright at the mission: "Kindness and benevolence showed on his [Wright's] open, manly face. One trait in him was, however, preeminent—his love of justice. As the Major [Trimble] talked quietly of the man who had defeated the Indians and slaughtered their horses and hanged their rascals, and who yet had retained their admiration and respect, he gave the key to his achievement in one brief phrase: 'He was very just.'"[70]

With the considerable help of Father Joset, Colonel Wright consummated a treaty with the Coeur d'Alenes that included provisions that whites would have "free passage" through Coeur d'Alene land, that they could build roads, and that hostages would be taken in order to ensure compliance with the provisions. From the tribe's perspective, it was a one-sided treaty that in effect meant Wright and the army were the conquerors and the tribe the conquered. Nonetheless, the Joset-managed council stopped the Coeur d'Alenes from engaging in war with Wright's force, which would have ended even more tragically for the Native people.[71]

Of the opening of Coeur d'Alene lands to whites, Kip predicted, "As soon as the stream of population flows up to them, they will be contaminated by the vices of white men, and their end will be that of every other tribe which has been brought into contact with civilization."[72]

In his account of the Plateau War, Father Joset wrote, "From the first, the Colonel knew how to disable them that, by their own admission, they cannot war anymore. . . . He has terrified the bad Indians by his severity as much as he won the hearts of the good ones by his clemency." In one historical account published in 1992, those words were quoted to indicate Joset's approval of Wright's tactics. However, in that account, the following words were truncated from Joset's observations: "They [the Coeur d'Alene Indians] are like men tied hand and foot, who cannot move."[73] Placing Wright's victims in the position of prisoners gives a different context to the claim that Wright "won the hearts of the good ones." If they had retained free will, no doubt the attitude of the tribes toward the army would have been decidedly different.

ECHOES

In 1877, the year of the Nez Perce War, Gen. William T. Sherman made a swing though Coeur d'Alene and Spokane country and established a fort in present-day Coeur d'Alene; some of the buildings still stand. In 1883 he returned, and an aide-de-camp, Col. John C. Tidball, kept a journal of the trip. From Coeur d'Alene, Sherman headed west along the Spokane River, reversing Colonel Wright's course. Sherman's army crossed to the south side of the Spokane River where Idaho Territory gave way to Washington Territory, then continued west toward the town of Spokane Falls (present-day Spokane). The yellow jackets were so aggressive that Sherman's horse, frantic to escape, threw him to the ground. In early August Colonel Tidball wrote, "About two miles below the bridge, on a slender neck between the road and river we passed the 'boneyard,' so named from piles of bones, the remains of Indian ponies captured and killed in 1858 by Colonel Wright, when at war with the Spokanes."[74] In 1878 George Dandy revisited the site of the horse massacre. Bones lay piled about, and Dandy "fancied that [he] could hear the report of the rifles and the whinny of the mares for their colts as they were shot down."[75]

In 1865 Father Joseph Cataldo arrived in Spokane and established the Mount St. Michael's Mission. Seeing a need for a Jesuit mission school to educate Indian boys, in 1881 he purchased land along the Spokane River. White residents of the region requested that the school be established for white boys, and when it opened in 1887 no Indians were allowed to attend. Father Joset arrived to register two Coeur d'Alene boys, but the college's president, Father James Rebmann, refused to admit them. The college, named after Father Aloysius Gonzaga, is now Gonzaga University.[76]

For many Native Americans, the tragedy of the horse massacre lives in the past and present. In Sherman Alexie's novel *Reservation Blues*, set on the Spokane reservation, the character Big Mom—who lives both in current time, and across time—hears a gunshot that "reverberated in her DNA." She then witnesses the horror: "There, she saw the future and the past, the white soldiers in blue uniforms with black rifles and pistols. She saw the Indian horses shot and fallen like tattered sheets. Big Mom stood on the rise and watched the horses fall, until only one remained." Big Mom watched as an officer "stepped down from his pony, walked over to the colt, gently touched his face, and whispered in his ear. The colt shivered as the officer put his pistol between its eyes and pulled the trigger." Alexie then ties the image to the present: "That colt fell to the grass of the clearing, to the sidewalk outside a reservation tavern, to the cold, hard coroner's table in a Veterans hospital." In this part of his novel, Alexie connects the trauma of the past with the trauma of the present for Native people.[77]

Today, the Coeur d'Alene Mission still sits in a pastoral setting, although Interstate 90 passes by it less than a quarter-mile away. The chapel stands comfortably on a knoll in the middle of a wide valley, surrounded by meadows and forests through which flows the Coeur d'Alene River. A network of streams spreads through wetlands and groves of pines, cedars, and cottonwoods. Today,

Monument at the site of the 1858 horse massacre along the Spokane River. Author photo.

from a certain vantage point, the mission chapel looks much the same as it did in the mid-nineteenth century, and it does not take much imagination to envision the long-gone log structures and teepees that surrounded the settlement in the time of George Wright. The setting was so peaceful that Lt. John Mullan wrote, "It has always proved to the weary traveler and destitute emigrant a St. Bernard in the Coeur d'Alene Mountains."[78]

A stone marker along the Spokane River designates the location of Horse Slaughter Camp. In the early twentieth century, piles of bleached bones could be found. Most were picked up a century ago and ground for fertilizer. In 2000 an effort was made by a few non-Native citizens to commemorate the historic aspect of the massacre. Native Americans chose not to participate, preferring more private commemorations, in accordance with their traditions. At least for some, the massacre is remembered in accounts passed down through generations. One Coeur d'Alene man recalled hearing stories from his great-grandmother, who had picked huckleberries in the hills above the site of the slaughter. She recalled that from afar, the mass of bones would "shimmer like a lake."[79]

ELEVEN

A Peculiar Way of Asking

A sailor wrecked on a barren coast came at length in sight of a gallows. "Thank God," said he. "I'm getting into a civilized country."

OLYMPIA PIONEER AND DEMOCRAT, 1858

On September 18, 1858, after leaving Coeur d'Alene, Wright headed southwest, taking more hostages along the way. As one man was removed from a Coeur d'Alene village, he looked back at his family and cried. Lawrence Kip observed, "It was a scene very different from the pictures of Mohegan indifference given by Fennimore Cooper."[1] Kip's discomfort with the scene is an example of a common problem that Ethan Allen Hitchcock had pointed out while he was the commander of the Pacific Division in 1854: "It is a hard case for the troops to know the whites are in the wrong, and yet be compelled to *punish* the Indians if they attempt to defend themselves."[2]

On September 22 Wright's force marched eighteen miles across rolling hills studded with pine trees, making camp at Smith's Ford on Latah Creek, twenty-five miles south of present-day Spokane. One soldier reported that they were met by "107 Indians, Spokanes, Ils-despierres, Sun-poils, Nez Perces, and others—all asking for peace."[3] The assembly included Chiefs Polatkin and Garry of the Spokanes. More Indians appeared, and by the next day at least two hundred were at the site.

After the Battles of Four Lakes and Spokane Plains, Wright's march of destruction up the Spokane River, and the September 9 hanging of Jo-hout, the chiefs had been uneasy about meeting him at Latah Creek. But although Wright's actions had been violent, his words expressed peaceful intentions. In addition, Father Joset had made the trip from the mission, and his presence added some calm. Word quickly spread among the tribes that Wright was being conciliatory, and more Indians joined the ones already gathered. On the morning of the 23rd, the attending chiefs agreed to a treaty with essentially the same provisions as the one agreed to by the Coeur d'Alenes a few days earlier. Before the signing, Wright demanded that each of the chiefs show their subservience. Later, he wrote, "They acknowledged their crimes, and expressed great sorrow for what they had done, and thankfulness for the mercy extended to them."[4]

That evening, Wright had an unexpected visitor: Chief Owhi of the Yakamas, who had heard of the council and wanted to talk peace with Wright. Owhi, like Kamiakin, was respected not only by his own people, but by a number of non-Natives as well. Adventurer Theodore Winthrop had met Owhi five years earlier and expressed admiration for him, calling him "magisterial."[5] Two years earlier, Wright had praised Owhi, writing, "Owhi is a very intelligent man. He speaks with great energy, is well acquainted with his subject, and his words carry conviction of truth to his hearers."[6] However, Wright had never gotten over Owhi's snub in the Yakima Valley, when the chief had promised to meet with Wright, then did not appear. Now Wright thought of him as "semi-hostile," and that opinion, along with the fact that he was Qualchan's father, was enough to have the chief placed in irons. Pack master Tom Beall wrote that Wright's intention was to take Owhi to the Presidio in San Francisco, where he would be held as a hostage for a few years, ensuring good behavior by the Yakamas. Beall claimed Wright wanted to do the same thing with Garry and Kamiakin. However, Kamiakin could not be found, and Wright had decided Garry was not a threat.[7]

Beall was in Wright's tent that night and heard Dr. John Hammond tell the colonel, "Hadn't you better send word to Qualchen to come in and he would not be hurt?" Wright replied,

"Hurt—I'll hang him in fifteen minutes after I catch him."[8] Wright ordered that a message be sent to Qualchan: if he did not show himself before Wright within four days, Owhi would be hung. Wright told this to Owhi, and according to one witness, Owhi began sweating profusely, fell to his knees, took out a "book of prayers," and looked to Father Joset.[9] While the missionary had worked to bring the tribes together for peace talks and had earned Wright's gratitude and respect, he had little influence over Wright's decisions, at least away from the mission. Considering himself a friend of the Indians, he surely would not have approved of Wright's conduct with Owhi or of the events of the following days.

The next morning Captain Keyes noticed "two braves and a handsome squaw" riding toward the camp. The Indians were wearing a "great deal of scarlet, and the squaw sported two ornamental scarfs, passing from the right shoulder under the left arm. She also carried, resting across in front of her saddle, a long spear, the staff of which was completely wound with various colored beads, and from the ends of which hung two long round pendants of beaver skins."[10] The men held rifles, and one carried a tomahawk covered with ornaments. The braves were Qualchan and Lo-kout, his brother; the woman was Qualchan's wife, Whist-alks (Chief Polatkin's daughter). Qualchan was dressed in "a calico shirt, leggings, breech-cloth, blanket, and beaded belt, moccasins, and was bareheaded. He wore a blanket over his shoulders."[11]

Wright talked with him for a few minutes and concluded that the messengers he had sent earlier had not reached Qualchan. Rather, Qualchan had heard a rumor that Wright wanted to talk, so he had come of his own accord. Wright told Qualchan that his father was already in the camp, pointing out the prisoner. Captain Keyes was standing near Wright and Qualchan as they talked and later claimed that Qualchan seemed stunned that his father was in Wright's custody. "His eyes watered and he appeared stupefied," Keyes wrote.[12]

Wright called for an interpreter, but Beall claimed Wright was simply buying time so guards could arrive; the colonel had little intention of talking. Wright asked the interpreter to talk with Qualchan to distract him: "Tell him anything, lie if necessary."[13] While Qualchan was talking with the interpreter, Wright ordered soldiers to seize him. "He had the strength of a Hercules," wrote Keyes. It took six men to hold him and tie his hands and feet, despite an unhealed wound in his abdomen from an earlier battle. Keyes admired the way Qualchan fought his captors: "He was still young, not over twenty-five years of age, and his physical constitution was apparently perfect—that, and his renown as a prince and warrior, gave to his life a charm and value which he was unwilling to surrender."[14] As the men dragged Qualchan toward the pack train to tie him up, he tried to pull out a pistol he had hidden under the blanket he was wearing. Hearing the disturbance, Wright ordered Qualchan hanged immediately. A rope was tossed over a pine tree branch, the noose placed around his neck, and "he was pulled up to the limb by the soldiers in attendance." According to Tom Beall, Owhi witnessed the execution and said Qualchan "was a bad man and of a murderous disposition, and that he had murdered not only white people but some of his own."[15] In a letter to General Clarke, Wright's description of the event amounted to one sentence: "Qual-chew came to me at 9 o'clock this morning, and at 9 1/4 A.M. he was hung."[16]

Keyes recalled that while Qualchan was struggling, Whist-alks was also defiant. Using a knife, she fought the soldiers, and once her husband was dead, she jumped on her horse and "in a frenzy of chagrin dexterously twirled her decorated lance over her head, and uttering a shrill cry drove it into the ground, where she left it and rode away."[17] Lo-kout, the brave who had ridden in with Qualchan and Whist-alks, was permitted to leave, since at the time Wright did not know that he was Qualchan's brother, or he likely would have suffered the same fate as his brother. Mary Moses, one of Qualchan's younger sisters, was camped with two of Qualchan's other brothers, Whist-alks, and other Yakamas when the trio had left to visit Wright. In later life (she died in 1939 at the age of 112) Mary clearly recalled Spokanes coming into their camp in mid-September to tell the band about

Qualchan, son of Owhi, as drawn by Johnson Kelly Duncan in 1853. Lieutenant Duncan was part of the Northern Pacific Railway exploration expedition (1853–55) lead by Isaac Stevens. Duncan portrayed many of his Indian subjects with dour or angry expressions, unlike Sohon's portraits. National Anthropological Archives, Smithsonian Institution, MS 130305 EE.

Wright's request for the Indians to meet him at the creek for peaceful talks.

Some of Wright's men felt conflicted about the events, and expressed quiet discomfort about the lack of a trial for Qualchan. While understanding that Qualchan had indeed engaged in violence and murder, it bothered them that an enemy had come to Wright voluntarily to talk with the commanding officer and had been executed without a trial.[18] One of the solders claimed that when Qualchan was being hanged, "The whole Indian camp re-echoed, 'just,' 'just,' chanting their approval of the execution."[19] Indeed, Qualchan had enemies not only among whites, but among the tribes. The Indians witnessing his execution were no doubt worried that Wright might turn his attention toward them, whether they were accused of a crime or not.

Wright's duplicity also worried the assembled Indians. In his appeal for their voluntary surrender, the colonel had told the Indians, "Put your faith in me and trust to my mercy," but after the Qualchan episode they felt double-crossed.[20] Yet they were powerless to do anything of substance about it. Wright's strategy of humbling and dispiriting the Indians was having its desired effect.

Tom Beall told a slightly different version of the execution of Qualchan:

> I was standing by the Colonel's tent when an Indian woman rode into camp on a fine brown horse. She had in her hand a lance covered with solid beadwork. She rode up to the colonel's tent, stuck the lance in the ground, and rode off. It was a mysterious incident that none in our camp understood, not even the scouts. The woman proved to be the wife of Qualshin, and a short time later he rode into camp on a large spotted cayuse, with a boy mounted behind him. He was arrested and bound hand and foot, after he had tried to draw a six-shooter from under his blanket. Colonel Wright ordered him hanged, which was done after the murderer had been in camp not more than 10 minutes.[21]

In Beall's account Qualchan was dragged some distance away from Wright's camp, where Beall was preparing to hang him. In the tense moments before Qualchan's execution, Beall claimed Qualchan offered him a "band of horses" if he let him go. However, in another account Beall made a point to say that Qualchan did not understand English. Thus, at the moment of the hanging, it is unclear if Beall would have been able to understand what Qualchan was saying. In any case, in the struggle, Qualchan tried to bite Beall's thumb, and a nearby soldier cried out for Beall to hit him, shouting, "Paste him one in the mug!" Beall claimed he stood up for Qualchan, saying to the soldier, "That would be a most cowardly act, this Indian has his hands tied and is fighting for his life." Beall also claimed Qualchan "cried like a child before he was executed." If Qualchan was indeed crying—not singing the plaintive death song, as was more likely—Beall said he could not tell if it was from "fear or hatred."[22]

Qualchan, Owhi, and Kamiakin were remembered by some Native people as having superhuman strength. In 1908 Smith Luc-ie, of the Yakama tribe, related this about Qualchan and Owhi:

> Quach-lum [Qualchan], son of Owhi, was a great strong man, who like Owhi and Kamiakin, could not be affected by a bullet. In one instance he mounted and rode circling a band of soldiers, receiving their concentrated fire without any evil effects. Completing the wild dash he rejoined his friends with his shirt perforated with bullet holes. Removing his belt numerous bullets dropped to the ground, flattened as though they had been fired against the surface of a rock. . . . Owhi, on one occasion, performed a similar feat, followed by a small band of warriors all of whom were alike impervious to the bullets of the enemy. There were about thirty warriors, all told, who could not be harmed by a bullet.[23]

Mary Moses later recalled that Lo-kout and other members of Chief Owhi's family hid in the mountains, since "we were all very much afraid." After they were sure Wright's army had left the creek, two of her sisters went to the site and found Qualchan's body buried in a shallow grave: "My sisters dug a deeper grave and took up the body, wrapped it in a blanket and put moccasins on the feet and buried it again, and put some shells on the grave."[24] This account of Mary Moses's was supported by other Indians and by comments made by some of Wright's men. Wright's statements and implications that any of the chiefs or warriors coming to see him would be treated peacefully has become a permanent part of the collective narrative. Today, many people, both Native Americans and others, if they know nothing else about Wright have heard about the army officer who called a council and executed some of the attendees.

On September 24, while Wright was dealing with the Indians at Smith's Ford, he sent three companies of dragoons to the site of the Steptoe debacle, located ten miles south. The party returned midday on the 25th with the remains of Gaston and Taylor, along with the bones of other victims. Their arrival inflamed Wright and his men and certainly had a bearing on events of that day and the days following. Also on the 25th, members of the Palouse and Walla Walla tribes rode into camp, unaware of Qualchan's fate and the imprisonment of Owhi (who was still in irons). Wright identified fifteen who had engaged in battles against Steptoe, selected six, and promptly ordered them hanged. Since there were only three ropes, half the group had to wait while their comrades were executed. Lt. George Dandy, an eyewitness, recalled, "The three Indians who were obliged to wait while their comrades were being dealt with . . . smiled cheerfully as they looked up at those who were suffering the agonies of death." While the ropes were being adjusted on the necks of the second trio, they danced and hopped around, singing their death songs. "They went cheerfully to their fate," according to Dandy.[25] Wright said he conducted a "thorough investigation," prior to the executions, but witnesses noted that his "investigations" consisted of asking a few questions then, if the party was adjudged guilty, immediately executing him. During all of his executions, Wright apparently made no pretense of providing a dignified death. In fact, as with Owhi and the Palouse council on September 30, he made sure family members watched as their loved ones died in anguish.[26]

The other nine Indians in the party were put in irons. Wright's force left Latah [Hangman] Creek on September 26, heading south toward Fort Walla Walla. On the 27th he met up with Chief Slow-i-archy and a small group of his Palouse people. Ordering that the chief and two others be placed in irons, Wright told the remainder to gather their tribe and meet him at the Lower Palouse River in three days' time. On September 30 about one hundred Palouses gathered at Wright's camp; most of the rest were with their chiefs camped near Spokane. Wright told them he did not need to make a treaty with them, but instead "addressed them in severe language, enumerating their murders, thefts, and war against the United States."[27] When he demanded that they produce the men who had murdered two miners earlier in the year, one man was identified and put forward. Later there were claims that the Indians had offered up an innocent victim only because they were afraid of reprisals. Wright then took more hostages: one chief plus four men and their families. By that time, Wright held hostages from the Spokane, Coeur d'Alene, Yakama, Walla Walla, and Palouse tribes. He told the assembled Palouses that if they remained peaceful, he would come back in a year and conclude a peace treaty with them. In the meantime, he threatened, if they were hostile to whites, he would not only hang the hostages, but, as he wrote to General Clarke, he would return and "annihilate the whole nation."[28] Wright then selected four warriors from among his prisoners. They were not accused of committing specific crimes but had allegedly participated in the fight against Steptoe's force. Their hands were tied behind their backs. Lt. Mullan's surveying wagon was positioned under a tree and the four men placed on top. They were hanged in full view of the gathered Palouse people, their bodies squirming at the ends of their ropes while Wright continued talking to the others as if the display was nothing more than a backdrop in a theatre.

Kip's journal entry for the day included another of his slightly cynical comments about Wright's conferences and interrogations. In this case, Kip wrote, "The Indians assembled in front of his [Wright's] tent for a 'talk.'" Then Kip said Wright told an interpreter to give the assemblage "the following complimentary and gratifying address," which began, "Tell them they are a set of rascals, and deserve to be hung; that if I should hang them all, I should do no wrong." The message ended with a threat to "hang them all, men, women, and children."[29]

On October 1 Wright's force reached Fort Taylor on the Snake River, where the commanding officer, Maj. F. O. Wyse, had prepared for them a feast of "bunch-grass fed beef (the best in the world), prairie chickens, vegetables, and . . . a basket of champagne, which disappeared down our thirsty throats like water in sand."[30] The men were relieved not only that the campaign was nearly over, but also that there had been only two casualties—the two members of the artillery who had eaten poisonous roots.

On October 3, after crossing the Snake River, Lt. Morgan was escorting Chief Owhi, riding close to him along the trail. As they began to cross the Tucannon River, Morgan said, Owhi

> cut me repeatedly across the eyes and face with his whip, and cutting his pony, quickly crossed over the creek, and I, getting over my surprise, put after him, drawing my revolver, cocking it and shooting at him. My horse belonged to the Government and was not the best. I kept near the fugitive, angry because I feared he might escape, and that would end my military career. I put three bullets into him. . . . Some of the dragoons rushed toward me, the one nearest being Sergeant Ball. Owyhee sat motionless on his pony between me and the Sergeant. I had exhausted all the charges in my pistol and told Ball to shoot the Indian, which he did, Owyhee falling from his pony."[31]

Sergeant Ball shot Owhi in the left temple; the bullet exited from the right temple. Chief Owhi lived up to his reputation as a tough warrior. Despite being shot four times, once in the head, he lived until sunset. The incident with Owhi made an impression on Morgan and witness Tom Beall, both of whom more than sixty years later spoke of Owhi with tones approaching reverence.[32]

Paul Lumli, a Nez Perce packer in George Wright's force, talked with Owhi shortly before his escape attempt. He recalled Owhi's sadness: "I know that they are going to hang me, and I might as well die now as a brave man. I am going to ride for the hills and if I once pass over yonder ridge, it will be good-bye, for they will see me no more. . . . I am going to try to get away from these soldiers. They shall never hang me!"[33]

A CHAPLET RICHLY WON

The force reached Fort Walla Walla on October 5, sixty days after leaving. Their entrance into the fort was a formal affair, with the dragoons entering first, the artillery battalion last. Two days later a formal burial service was held for Gaston, Taylor, and the other men who had died during the Steptoe expedition. Three years later, the remains of Captain Taylor and Lieutenant Gaston were disinterred and taken to the cadets' cemetery at West Point.

Wright had planned for his campaign to last forty days once all the troops had gathered and departed from Fort Taylor. It took thirty-nine-and-a-half days, which had as much to do with happenstance as planning. In any case, the apparent precision added to Wright's reputation as a careful commander and strict disciplinarian. Wright's work was completed on October 9, when he called a council of Walla Wallas. He asked any of them who had been in any of the recent battles to stand; thirty-five did so. Selecting four, he ordered them immediately hanged. The hangings in the 1858 campaign became more than justice dealt out to men he saw as criminals; after the two battles, the hangings became the central part of his military strategy to crush the tribes. However, as one scholar points out, "Needless to say, the army used capital punishment unilaterally—against Indian 'criminals' but not against whites accused of crimes against Indians."[34] Certainly during the 1858 march Wright engaged in his usual tactic of asking a few questions of his prisoner, then, if the answers were not to his liking, hanging him. Lt. Lawrence Kip, in his journal of the 1858 expedition, offers one view of what it was like to be interrogated by Wright: "The Colonel has a peculiarly nervous way of putting questions."[35] Another soldier wrote, "The power to procure information possessed by Colonel Wright was truly wonderful." The same soldier makes an observation and admission about the "councils" Wright convened, saying, "These councils were really investigations."[36]

Officials in Washington, D.C., took note of Wright's success. In his report to Congress that December, Secretary of War John B. Floyd credited the executions with contributing to Wright's success:

> The campaign was prosecuted with great activity and vigor by Colonel Wright, of the 9th Infantry, who gave battle to the Indians

> on several occasions, always routing them completely. After beating their forces, capturing many prisoners, and destroying large amounts of property, and laying waste their country, the Indians surrendered at discretion, with their wives and children, and sued abjectly for peace. The criminal offenders amongst them, heretofore guilty of murder and rapine, the chief instigators of all dissatisfaction amongst the tribes, and the immediate cause of the recent hostilities, were surrendered, tried, and executed.[37]

Floyd's remark about "great activity and vigor" was the highest praise he offered Wright, and he refused to approve a promotion for the colonel. As tensions increased between the North and South, Floyd, a Virginian, began to snub northern officers in favor of southerners. He split General Clarke's Department of the Pacific in two, giving command of the northern portion, consisting of Washington and Oregon Territories, to Gen. William S. Harney, also a southerner. Harney was a difficult man to get along with, and he started off in his new position by insulting Colonel Wright and the expedition he had recently completed. Keyes wrote, "The Harney clique spoke in derision of our battles, in which no soldier was killed, and only one slightly wounded. Their prejudices inclined them to withhold all credit from Wright and his associates, a great majority of whom were Union men."[38]

Regardless of the views of detractors, Wright's legacy received a boost from the region's newspapers. In a triumphant summary of Wright's campaign, the *Olympia Pioneer and Democrat* said, "Colonel Wright, has, then, finished one war, and all that his friends and warmest admirers could ask, is that a kind Providence may grant him long life to wear and enjoy a chaplet he has so richly won."[39]

In October 1858 Father De Smet traveled the path that George Wright had taken just a few months before. Sailing up the Columbia River from the Pacific Ocean, De Smet noted, "The Savages, formerly numerous along the coast and the river, have almost entirely disappeared. Every approach of the whites thrusts them back, by force or otherwise; they go upon reservations, in a strange land far removed from their hunting and fishing grounds, and where drink, misery and diseases of every sort mow them down by the hundreds." At Fort Walla Walla, he heard from Father Congiato "reassuring news about the disposition of the savages." De Smet talked with the hostages Colonel Wright had taken during his march, many of whom knew De Smet from his 1847 trip into the Coeur d'Alene homeland. The prisoners had "managed during their captivity to gain the good will of the officers and soldiers of the fort, by exemplary and Christian-like conduct." De Smet and Congiato, with the fort's commander, decided De Smet would leave with the hostages, while in the meantime Congiato would send a request to General Harney asking for permission to do so. By the time Harney received the request and sent back a response, De Smet and the newly freed prisoners would be at the Coeur d'Alene Mission. De Smet and the Indians promised to return to Walla Walla if Harney objected to their release, but in the end, the general approved. Of course, the Indians were thrilled to be going home, and De Smet wrote, "Whatever their detractors may say, Indians know how to appreciate a kind act and to be grateful for a favor received."[40]

The same year that Wright conducted his violent expedition, on the opposite side of the country a high-level official offered a critical view of events in the Pacific Northwest. Commissioner of Indian Affairs Charles Mix summed up the state of Indian policy since 1850. Mix's remarks were highly critical of the treatment the tribes had received at the hands of local politicians and settlers, saying their actions had been "repugnant alike to the dictates of humanity and the principles of natural justice." Mix noted that they had encouraged white settlement while disregarding the impact on the tribes. In addition, no process was in place to compensate the Indians for land taken. As a result, Mix wrote, the tribes had been "intruded upon, ousted of their homes and possessions without any compensation, and deprived, in most cases, of their accustomed means of support. . . . It is not a matter of surprise that they have committed many depredations on our citizens, and been exasperated to frequent acts of hostility."[41]

In addition to officers like General Harney questioning whether or not Wright's campaign was much of a military victory, one twentieth-century historian claimed, "It had all been flags and sabers, foam-flecked horses and a confusion of musketry; the game of war with an illusion of danger, an illusion of dedication."[42] While it is true that the battles were one-sided, they were not just "an illusion of danger." Conditions were challenging, and the tribes had been formidable foes in other battles. Both the warriors and the soldiers were surprised at the effectiveness of the new long-range rifles. From the army's viewpoint Wright succeeded in fulfilling the most basic lesson of Indian warfare taught at West Point. While at the academy in the early nineteenth century, Wright had studied under military theorist Dennis Hart Mahan, who taught cadets the proper way to make war against Indians: "Strike such a blow that it shall be handed down as memorable in the traditions of the Tribe."[43]

It is unclear how many of George Wright's victims were guilty of crimes. Certainly some were hanged because Wright viewed them as leaders or instigators in the attack against Steptoe, and some, like Qualchan, may well have been. However, there was no formal process to evaluate the circumstances of the attacks or to consider justification. In any case, the hangings Wright ordered were of a particular nature, intended to be a drawn-out display that was excruciating to the victim and meant to instill terror in those who watched. In some cases, Wright made sure there was an audience, and in several cases with multiple hangings, he made the condemned men watch as they awaited their own executions.

DIRE NECESSITY

Were Wright's actions legal under existing law and rules of war? At the time, the law of nations provided the primary guide as to what could be considered a war crime, and those guidelines were so open-ended that they provided little protection for alleged criminals, such as Wright's victims. Before 1863, when the Civil

War prompted the revision and codification of rules of war, the U.S. Army had no clear laws relating to tribunals or other forums in which to try alleged perpetrators of violence during wartime. Article 65 of the 1830 revision of the Articles of War provided that breaches of military regulations be handled by a court-martial, but the law did not directly apply to civilian wrongdoers. Before the Civil War the only other type of military tribunal under existing law was the court of inquiry, which had no power to judge the accused or pass sentence. During the Mexican-American War, Gen. Winfield Scott issued an order declaring martial law in war zones and authorized the use of military commissions to try Mexican civilians accused of crimes of violence or property against U.S. soldiers, as well as to try U.S. personnel for crimes against each other or against civilians. In addition to Scott, Generals John Wool and Zachary Taylor also used military commissions to try U.S. personnel accused of crimes against each other. Scott also began to use "councils of war," intended to try those accused of breaking the "laws of war," including encouraging desertion or committing acts of espionage.[44]

Thus, during Wright's tenure in the Northwest there was no formal definition of war crimes, nor had Congress established a legal structure upon which a military commander could conduct an inquiry or trial. Like Scott had done in Mexico, Wright could have stretched Article 65 to cover accusations against his enemy. But even if he had been inclined to establish that questionable legal justification, he would have run into another problem: Article 65 forbid the officer calling a court-martial from acting as judge.

In any case, in the absence of a regulatory structure or other oversight, Wright was free to take hostages or execute prisoners at will. His reports claimed his actions were done out of "dire necessity," an argument not uncommon among officers of the time. The concept of "necessity" as expressed by Wright had its legal foundation in Greek, Roman, and European law. It provided a justification for breaking the law in cases of "necessity," of which "dire necessity" was the most extreme kind. In Wright's case, he seemed to use the term to justify his actions, as if to give them a cloak of legality. Since governmental policies regarding treatment of Indians were either conflicting or nonexistent, Wright was left to establish his own rationale for his actions. According to legal historian Carol Chomsky, the executions carried out by Wright "seem to represent individual action rather than government policy."[45]

Wright conducted his 1858 expedition in what historian Wayne E. Lee calls a "context generated by calculation." The army command structure allowed selective forms of violence to be used against the tribes, and their decisions "created [an] atmosphere of permissiveness."[46] Orders from commanding officers were often clear as to intent but vague on details. General Clarke ordered George Wright to "attack all the hostile Indians you may meet, with vigor; make their punishment severe, and persevere until the submission of all is complete."[47] Clearly Clarke allowed Wright to use any means necessary to achieve the somewhat nebulous objectives of "punishment" and "submission." Lee writes that actions like Wright's were due in part to "social authorization." According to Lee, social authorization "assured individual soldiers that they would not face censure from their peers for such violence. It did not require that they act violently, but it swept away the restraints that might otherwise govern an individual's choices about violence."[48]

The other legal issue that confounded the tribes was the question of sovereignty. When it suited politicians and military leaders in the Northwest, the tribes were treated as sovereign nations, as during Isaac Stevens's treaty councils. At other times—as during the conflict at the Cascade Rapids—they were treated as citizen-traitors to the United States and executed for their actions. During his 1858 expedition Wright worked both sides of the issue, making treaties with the tribes as if they were nations, but executing individual "criminals" for violent acts committed in wartime. In short, in the absence of clear legal restrictions and military regulations, and given the physical isolation of his troops, he used enough punitive force not only to ensure that the tribes were dissuaded from more fighting, but also to ensure that he could return to Walla Walla safely, free of harassment or attack.

Was there an alternative to military action on the plateau? Secretary of the Interior Jacob Thompson had offered an alternative. In his December 1857 report to Congress, he noted that the tribes in Washington and Oregon were "still restive and belligerent." Thompson was concerned that the tribes did not respect the "ability of this government to punish them for trespasses committed upon our settlements." That was, in essence, the same conclusion reached by many politicians and military officials, but Thompson believed Indian minds could be changed "by peaceful means" rather than by force. He recommended that a delegation from each tribe be taken on a tour of the eastern United States, visiting Washington, D.C., and other cities. He thought that "when they carried the story of our greatness and power to their people, a change would come over their minds, and we might then reasonably hope for the establishment by treaties, of good understanding and perpetual peace between us." In recommending treaties, it sounds as if he is referring either to new treaties or to revisions of existing ones, ostensibly more fair to the tribes than those executed in the Walla Walla Valley. Nonetheless, his suggestion was not acted on, and only a few months later the tribes and army were at war.[49]

A more recent commentator put a relatively positive light on the hangings: "Although harsh, the executions should be seen as substitutes—given the goal of asserting military strength—for battlefield casualties and preferred alternatives to the losses of a full-scale war of the sort desired by settlers. That the Indians of the eastern Washington region thereafter remained at peace was proof to the army of the wisdom of its traditional approach."[50] However, official records provide no evidence that during the 1858 campaign Wright considered his actions to be "substitutes" for battle deaths. Wright's reports refer to the hangings as punishment and retribution meant to create fear, not as a military strategy. Nor do records support the notion that his superior officers strove to minimize bloodshed. Their letters and orders were clear: the objective was to punish and cripple the tribes, thus ensuring whites free access to Indian land.

Monument near the site of Qualchan's execution on Latah (Hangman) Creek. Author photo.

In 1988 Wright's biographer wrote, "To Wright's credit he never made predawn attacks or raids under a white flag of truce on Indian villages."[51] This sentiment has become part of Wright's heroic legacy: he was not as violent as he could have been, or as violent as were some other officers. The same historian defends Wright's executions thus: "Indians expected to die when caught. . . . In fact, captivity was the greatest ignominy forced on them by white settlers. By the same token, Indians showed no mercy to whites they captured, which is why I re-emphasize thinking in terms of how things were done by military men of that time."[52]

However, while Wright's hostages may have *feared* they would die in captivity, there is no evidence they *expected* to. Quite the contrary. At Latah Creek, Wright claimed that if the chiefs came in peace, they would be safe, and Owhi, Qualchan, and others were angered and frightened at the betrayal. Likewise, it is far from certain that prisoners taken by Philip Sheridan in 1856 at the Cascades Rapids expected to die by virtue of being taken prisoner; one was innocent, and perhaps more. Did they expect to die? As for murders committed by Indians, there were times when whites taken by Indians were killed and times when they were not.[53]

While some historians have concluded that the hangings served to reduce future bloodshed, some have seen them in a different light. In 1992 William B. Skelton wrote, "A surprisingly common practice, at least in the Pacific Northwest, was the execution of Indian captives, either summarily or after hasty military trials. Although the ostensible purpose was to punish specific crimes, officers intended the deaths to serve as warnings to terrify other tribesmen into submission."[54] While one may claim that terror can limit bloodshed, it is an argument that carries little weight with Wright's victims, their descendants, and with many people of any ancestry living on the Columbia Plateau today.

ECHOES

One insightful observation of Wright's actions came years later from Isaac Stevens's son. As a boy Hazard Stevens had traveled extensively with his father and had witnessed treaty councils. Of the hangings of Qualchan and the others, he later wrote, "Wool and his parasites, so vociferous in denouncing the slaying of Pu-pu-mox-mox [Peopeo-moxmox] under like circumstances, raised no voice in rebuke of the merciless severity of Wright." Stevens was probably correct: General Clarke and other army officers—including Wright himself—might well have condemned Wright's violent march if it had been orchestrated by militia commanders like James K. Kelly and Benjamin Shaw.[55]

Several of Wright's men attempted to put the events in a perspective that perhaps reduced their emotional dissonance over their participation. Some, like Gen. George Dandy, wrote about events late in life, when they had the benefit of time and introspection:

> The Indians who were executed during this campaign under the orders of Colonel Wright, were outlaws and criminals, from the point of view of our government. They were mostly of a class that robbed and murdered of their own volition and for their own personal benefit and advantage. Doubtless the majority of the chiefs and warriors, in attempting to drive out our settlers and to keep the country for their own use, regarded themselves as patriots. They banded together, believing that they could rid their territory of an invading enemy who, if not driven out, would take possession of their ancient lands, build roads through their hunting grounds, destroy the game on which they had subsisted and revolutionize the mode of life in which for many years they had been contented and happy. This was to them ample cause for war. They got the worst of it, and had to submit to the penalty which comes to the conquered.[56]

Like Mullan, Kip, Keyes, and others who wrote of the plight of the Indians, Dandy expressed little bitterness or hatred of them. He was moved, to at least a modest degree, by their predicament, but he attributed their fate to destiny. In fact, among the known journals and reminiscences of Wright's officers and soldiers, all contain the usual cultural biases of the time, but none uses the kind of ugly rhetoric common in the region's newspapers.

One of the most telling echoes of Wright's actions comes from Native American cultural history. In 2001 Rodney Frey wrote of the impact of the hangings on one family, who are descendants of one of Wright's victims. While the warrior sat on a horse, waiting to be executed, he sang this song, described as being "somewhere between a death song and a medicine song for our young people." It is entitled "Don't Be Sad":

> If things are going bad and your people are suffering and your children are crying, this song will heal you. So don't be sad because of the death around us, because these men who are being hung were fighters and they faced the soldiers. Don't be sad that the young girls who followed the battle and some of them even getting involved with killing the soldiers. When they get old and they are

feeling bad for what they had to do, sing this song. When your children and grandchildren are hurting or having hard times, then sing this song.[57]

WASHINGTON IS THE ONLY STATE with a permanent gallows, which is located at the state penitentiary in Walla Walla. Those condemned to death may select hanging or lethal injection. Two other states allow hanging in rare circumstances: New Hampshire and Delaware.[58] By one count, 425 Indians have been executed in the United States, its colonies, and territories since 1639. Their most common crime was murder. The great majority were executed by hanging. The first recorded hangings in Washington Territory occurred in 1849, when two Indians, Cusass and Quallahworst, were hanged in Pierce County, in western Washington. The army had recently established Fort Nisqually, and it was attacked by a band of Nisqually Indians. One soldier was killed and one wounded. Six Indians were tried, and Cusass and Quallahworst convicted.[59]

Perhaps the most infamous hanging in Washington's history was February 19, 1858, when Chief Leschi was hanged at the order of Isaac Stevens. Even at that time, when friends of the Indians were few, a substantial portion of the non-Native populace questioned the sentence, and some were outraged. George Wright was assigned temporary custody of Leschi, and he hesitated to turn the chief over to law enforcement authorities, understanding Leschi's probable fate. In Leschi's first trail he was found not guilty since the alleged crimes occurred in wartime. A second trial resulted in his conviction, in part because his lawyers were not allowed to introduce evidence that would have absolved him. Shortly afterward, one observer wrote, Leschi, "the unhappy savage, ill and emaciated from long confinement, and weary of a life which for three years had been one of strife and misery, was strangled according to law."[60] In 2004 the Washington Legislature passed a resolution absolving Leschi of guilt, acknowledging that he was wrongly executed.

Perhaps the most sobering, and least changed, place along the route of George Wright's 1858 march are the flats on which his army camped alongside peace-seeking Spokane Indians September 22–26, the ground on which he hung Qualchan. Hangman Creek still winds beneath pine-forested bluffs. Old Kentuck Trail is now a paved county road, bridged across Smith's Ford. The flats—where the peace treaty was signed—are covered with prairie grass, chokecherry, yarrow, and coyote willow. Many of the pine trees predate Wright's camp, but the one from which Qualchan was hung is gone. According to lore, it washed away in a flood decades ago.

TWELVE

"I Will Weather the Storm"

After George Wright's march across the Columbia Plateau, the Northwest's anti-Indian newspapers trumpeted the repression of the tribes. In an editorial dated October 1, 1858, the *Olympia Pioneer and Democrat* marveled at the past and future of Washington Territory:

> Ten years ago Washington was a terra incognita, containing a few people speaking English, a few speaking French, numerous petty tribes of wandering Indians; her coasts unknown; her coasts rarely frequented; her markets the most distant from supplies; having no organization, no laws, no exports, no imports; her territory unexplored, the base of her population—with but few American exceptions—a mixed race, unlettered, indolent and unsettled; her future yet to be shaped and moulded.[1]

In case Indians continued to resist settlement, the *Pioneer and Democrat* suggested a solution learned from Colonel Wright's expedition: "Kindness to the tribes was child's play. . . . Wholesome terror should be instilled into the minds of the Indians."[2] The *Portland Standard* celebrated the death of Qualchan, calling him "the master demon of remorseless rapine and unpitying slaughter. . . . With him, at least, we are done forever."[3] However, Wright would have little opportunity to bask in glory. His military life after the 1858 Plateau Indian War became a series of assignments that left him discouraged and bitter. Yet, given the circumstances, for most of the last years of his life he would conduct himself with grace and skill.

On September 13, 1858, while Wright's force had been marching east along the Spokane River, the Department of the Pacific was split into two parts: the Department of California, commanded by Gen. Clarke in San Francisco, and the Department of Oregon, commanded by Gen. William Harney. Thus, Wright arrived back at Fort Walla Walla to a hero's welcome, but he had been stripped of his command. Within a few months of the expedition, Wright began to be publicly criticized for not punishing the tribes more severely. One California newspaper was satisfied that Harney would not be as "soft" as Wright: "The great Indian fighter [Harney] . . . would chastise the hostile Indians severely, whether they sue for peace or not. After they have been sufficiently punished to make them appreciate the fact that we are masters, then he will listen to their overtures for peace, treat them with the utmost kindness, and protect them fully in all their rights."[4] The paper's ironic message—punishing the Indians as a condition for kind treatment—provides an example of the kind of muddled messages Wright, and the U.S. Army, sent the tribes during the mid-nineteenth century. It was a theme Wright would continue to express during his late career.

One historian has described Harney as "a cross between a pantomime villain and a puffed-up pirate." His behavior was sometimes erratic, cruel, and illogical. He once had an officer arrested for addressing a letter "Fort Vancouver, W.T." instead of using the official name, "Headquarters, Department of Oregon." He sometimes showed little concern for his men and frequently expressed contempt for Indians. Shortly after taking command Harney, like Stevens had earlier, alienated the tribes by allowing settlers to establish homesteads on Indian land that should have been made available only when the 1855 treaties were ratified. No doubt the tribes knew that if they resisted settlement, the army's response would be devastating. Congress finally ratified the treaties in March 1859, but by that time the Indian tribes had lost what little trust they might still have had in the treaty process, and talk about an Indian uprising began to spread.[5] In June 1859 General Harney closed Fort Simcoe in the Yakima Valley and ordered Wright to move from Fort Dalles, where the colonel and his wife had been enjoying his infamously comfortable house, to Fort Walla Walla. In the Walla Walla Valley, Wright would be able to react quickly to any threats of violence by the same tribes he had defeated earlier. However, no significant threats to Wright's authority occurred.

By May 1861 Harney's infamous temper and obstinacy resulted in conflicts with Maj. Gen.Winfield Scott, an official reprimand from the secretary of war, and his removal from the West. Wright was appointed to replace Harney as commander of the Department of Oregon and transferred to Fort Vancouver. As Wright worked on plans for a spring campaign against the tribes in present-day southern Idaho, the Civil War broke out and national attention focused on the East.[6]

In his new command, in addition to Indian-white relations, Wright had to deal with an ongoing boundary dispute in Puget Sound. The United States and Great Britain each had established posts on San Juan Island, and in the early years of the dispute war between the nations very nearly broke out. When the southerner Harney was in command of the region, he had treated the British so disrespectfully that at least one historian has claimed he was trying to incite war with Great Britain. Such a war could have been disastrous for the Union, since the North would have been forced to fight two wars. Wright's political skill reestablished peaceful relations with the British.[7]

In June 1861 Wright ordered Capt. George Pickett's garrison to remain in place on San Juan Island, partly to enhance the defense network of the northern coast, but mostly to keep a strong U.S. presence in the face of the boundary dispute. On July 2, after Wright learned that Pickett had resigned to join the Confederate Army, he ordered Capt. T. C. English and Company H of the Ninth Infantry to replace him. Pickett traveled to Fort Steilacoom on Puget Sound, where he was ordered to "turn over his command and public property."[8] Pickett conducted himself with more aplomb than did Harney, and when the time came for him to leave the Northwest, he did so without inflaming tensions.[9]

George Wright, ca. 1863. Washington State Historical Society.

CALIFORNIA DISCONTENT

While George Wright was dealing with challenges in the Pacific Northwest, his former subordinate and confidant Erasmus Keyes had been promoted to brigadier general and was appointed adjutant to General Scott at the Headquarters of the Army.[10] In early 1861 Keyes had heard that the newly appointed commander of the Department of the Pacific, Albert Sidney Johnston, was a Southern sympathizer, and he requested a meeting with Scott and Secretary of State William Seward.[11] Secretary Seward recommended that Keyes go west to evaluate Johnston's loyalty, and Keyes suggested that Wright be named Johnston's replacement. Although Scott at first agreed, a day later Keyes was dismayed to learn that Scott had changed his mind. Instead, Scott ordered Gen. Edwin Vose Sumner to travel to San Francisco and relieve Johnston of his command. Scott never directly said that he did not want Wright to assume a higher command. However, Keyes wrote, "He knew my partiality for that noble old soldier, Colonel George Wright. . . . This was probably his main reason for detaining me in Washington."[12] In his memoir, Keyes notes the large number of disputes and feuds Scott had been embroiled in with various people in and out of the army, but he expresses no specific issue between Scott and Wright. Scott's rejection of Wright seemed based more on a tepid discomfort rather than a strong objection. At least one historian suggests that Scott was punishing Wright for his allegiance to Gen. William J. Worth. Until 1847 Scott and Worth had been close friends, and Worth had named his son after Scott. During the Mexican-American War, while planning the attack at Molino del Rey, Worth had wanted to modify the battle plan to reduce casualties. However, Scott insisted on the direct assault, which was led by George Wright, then a major, and resulted in heavy casualties.[13] Worth was so incensed, he changed his son's name from Winfield Scott to William. However, there is no evidence to show that fifteen years later Scott punished Wright because of his dispute with Worth.

During 1861 Wright began to chafe at being overlooked for promotion and a command post in the eastern battle zones. Some of his letters began with a hopeful tone, but as his frequent requests for promotion were denied or ignored, his words gradually slid from pride into bitterness. His disappointment was tempered by the presence of his friend (and brother-in-law) General Sumner, who in April had arrived to assume command of the Department of the Pacific, which, due to a consolidation of the departments of Oregon and California, now included the entire Pacific Coast.[14] The following month Wright wrote to Secretary of War Simon Cameron. He asked for a promotion and included "a memorandum of my military antecedents," in which he summarized his military accomplishments, particularly his success in Washington Territory.[15]

In the meantime, Sumner ordered Wright to take command of Southern California and suppress the pockets of Southern sympathizers, who had begun to stir unrest. Wright immediately traveled from Fort Vancouver to San Francisco, canceled leaves of more than twenty-four hours, and ordered all commanding officers to make weekly reports containing the condition and number of their command. He ordered his officers to "enforce the most rigid discipline" and to "maintain the supremacy and due observance of the Constitution and the laws of the United States, as well as of the State of California." He ends his order with, "The undersigned, having served for more than nine years on the Pacific Coast, appeals with confidence to the patriotic Union-loving citizens of Southern California for their cordial assistance and co-operation in preserving their beautiful country from the horrors of civil war."[16]

While Wright had often written with a grandiose tone, from 1861 into 1865 his words soared with patriotism, defiantly condemning enemies of the Union. He frequently pledged his allegiance to God and country, and, perhaps most tellingly, in letter after letter he included at least a few remarks about his past accomplishments. In some instances he wrote at length about his experience, sacrifice, and sense of duty. During these final years of his life he began to sound increasingly desperate.

In June 1861 he wrote an impassioned letter to an old friend, Sen. James. W. Nesmith of Oregon, who had played a prominent role in the Pacific Northwest, having served as superintendent of Indian affairs for Oregon and Washington in the mid-1850s. "I have no sectional prejudices," General Wright wrote. "I love the whole country, North, South, East, and West, and will fight to preserve this Union. I have no sympathy with any man, no matter from what section he may come, who is not for the Union, now and forever, one and indivisible." As in many of his other letters, he next turned to his experience:

> I have served thirty-nine years in the army, and whether battling with the savage foes in the far West, or deadly hummocks of Florida, or contending with the hosts of Mexico on many a well-fought and always victorious field, I have always turned with affection to my native land, and offered up a heartfelt prayer for the Union—God grant this struggle may soon cease, and that peace may be restored, and our glorious banner, with its thirty-four stars, proudly wave on every housetop from Maine to Texas, and from the Atlantic to our own loved Pacific shore. . . . I was made a *Colonel* on the bloody battlefield of Molina Sept. 8, 1847, but it was only a *Brevet* until March, 1855. But I have not rested very tranquil, under certain *Brevets* of my juniors, over me, and I shall not do so.[17]

Wright believed that sectional bias had kept him from promotion, a claim that reflected the fact that many Southerners held key posts in the army and government prior to the Civil War. One was John B. Floyd, the former governor of Virginia and secretary of war who had been lukewarm about Wright's success in the 1858 expedition. In the same letter to Nesmith, Wright lays out his complaint:

> Had I hailed from south of Mason and Dixon's line, I might have obtained a *Brevet* in 1858; but unfortunately, I was born in the frozen regions of the North. I cannot, however, now consent to be brought into active service without advancement; not that I could for a moment abandon my flag or country in this, her hour of peril, but I would prefer fighting in the ranks, to occupying a position without looking forward to preferment.
>
> With great regard, very truly your friend, G. Wright.[18]

At the end of September 1861 the army issued Special Orders No. 160, which upended officer assignments and changed army administrative regions. Sumner was ordered east and for a few weeks Wright's professional fate was uncertain. Sumner recommended that Wright take his place, saying, "The safety of the whole coast may depend upon it."[19] Although ready to replace

Sumner, Wright still wanted to go east, and he wrote army headquarters to reconsider. Then again, the very next day, he telegraphed: "Again, most earnestly requesting that I may be ordered to the east."[20]

Wright's appointment as commander of the Pacific was intended to be temporary, since Scott wanted Gen. J. W. Denver to have the permanent post. However, political objections to Denver's appointment resulted in a cancellation of his orders, and Brig. Gen. J. K. F. Mansfield was appointed commander of the Department of the Pacific. On September 28 Wright was appointed brigadier general of volunteers and directed to move back to the Northwest to assume responsibility for a newly created command: the Columbia River District. However, until Mansfield arrived from the East, Wright was to assume temporary command of the Department of the Pacific.

Wright's promotion to brigadier general of volunteers was a disappointment, since it was not the same as attaining the rank of general in the regular army. Frustrated and bitter, Wright sent a letter to Sumner, dated October 26, 1861. It is perhaps the most personal of his known correspondence, emotional and penned by his own hand rather than by a clerk. The writing begins in tight script and ends in a scrawl, some of which he underlined for emphasis.

> My Dear Friend,
>
> The blow has fallen, I am crushed, Mansfield is assigned to this command and I am appointed a Brig Genl of Volunteers & ordered to command the Columbia River District, having a few companies of Volunteers, scattered over an immense region of country, and over this not an independent command, but a dependency of the Dept—as the senior Col. Of Infantry, & in fact of the whole regular army, on duty, this appointment gives me hardly any additional rank, had it been in the Regular army I should have regained nearly my position at the commencement of the War—I never asked for, or sought a commission in the Volunteers, had it been given me five months since, it would have been better, but to make me a Brig, now, when

San Francisco. Ca. Oct 26. 1861.

My dear friend,

The blow has fallen, I am crushed, Mansfield [?] is assigned to this command, & I am appointed a Brig Genl of Volunteers, & ordered to command the Columbia River District, having a few companies of Volunteers, scattered over an immense region of country, and even this not an independent command, but a dependency of the dept — as the senior Col of Infantry, & in fact of the whole regular army, on duty. this appointment gives me hardly any additional rank, had it been in the Regular army. I should have regained nearly my position at the commencement of the war — I never asked for, or sought a commission in the Volunteers, had it been given me four months since, it would have been better, but to make me a Brig, now, when more than a hundred have been appointed, junior officers of the army and civilians, it looks as if I was to be victimized at all hazards — I had the strongest documents, and the united influence of several [?]

delegations from different States, and it was
looked upon as a settled matter that I was to
be appointed in the Regular Army — I have
met with opposition, and it must have been
from high quarters and powerful; they
have succeeded and I am down for the
present, but I shall not remain quiet,
cost what it will, I am bound to ferret
out this business.

I am peculiarly situated, I cannot decline
even this appointment, without sacrificing all
my future prospects — The night is dark,
& the winds howl, but with a stout heart,
and strong arm I will weather the storm.
I love my country, I love the Union,
and I will sacrifice all, life if necessary,
to guard our old flag, under which you and
myself, fought & won some little honor on
the bloody fields of Mexico.

No fancied personal injustice can lessen my
love for my country.

Your friend,
G. Wright

Genl Sumner.

P.S. I wrote to-day to Senators Collamer & Nesmith

Letter from George Wright to his friend and brother-in-law Edwin Vose Sumner, after Wright was passed over for promotion. The emotion and emphasis are typical of many of Wright's late-career letters. Courtesy of the Northwest Room, Spokane Public Library.

more than a hundred have been appointed, young officers of this army and civilians, it looks as if I was to be victimized at all hazards—I had the strongest documents, and the united influence of several delegations from different states, and it was looked upon as a settled matter that I was to be appointed in the Regular Army—I have met with opposition, and it must have been from high quarters, and powerful; they have succeeded, and I am down for the present, but I shall not remain quiet. Cost what it will, I am bound to ferret out this business.

I am particularly situated, I cannot decline even this appointment, without sacrificing all my future prospects. The night is dark, & the winds howl, but with a stout heart, and *strong arm I will weather the storm.* I love my country, I love the Union, and I will sacrifice all, life if necessary, to shield our old flag, under which you and myself, fought & won some little honor on the bloody fields of Mexico.

No fancied personal injustice can lesson my love for my country.[21]

Once again, Wright refers to a conspiracy to block his promotion. Wright's claim is repeated in several histories written over the years, but other than his own words, there is little to support it. Some historical accounts have suggested that Wright tended to irritate his superiors by not adhering strictly to orders, thus slowing his promotions. However, such cases were for the most part limited to relatively small issues, such as sending a man to a hospital without permission and building the expensive house at Fort Dalles. In 1856 Wright had annoyed General Wool on at least two occasions and disobeyed a key order, but records indicate that Wool's criticism was directed more at Isaac Stevens than at Wright. It certainly was not unusual for officers to irritate their superiors, and unless a transgression was particularly egregious, one's career suffered little, if at all. The average age of brigadier generals at the time was thirty-seven, and Wright, twenty years older, just may have been considered too old for a battle posting.[22]

Wright, who again had requested a field command in the East, asked that the order to the Columbia River district be reconsidered. In a letter to the headquarters of the army, he wrote, "I beg leave, most respectfully, but earnestly, to request the General-in-Chief may be pleased to reconsider. . . . I have served on the Pacific Coast more than nine years; six of them passed in dark valleys of the Columbia River, or in pursuing the savage foe in the mountain fastness on the eastern borders of Oregon and Washington."[23] Wright signed as "Colonel, Ninth Infantry," and the next day, he telegraphed again to army headquarters, again "most earnestly requesting that I may be ordered to the East." This time he signed, "Brigadier General, U.S. Volunteers."[24]

When General Scott retired in November 1861, Gen. George McClellan became general-in-chief of the army. McClellan, having served with Wright in the Northwest, thought more highly of him than did Scott. Mansfield's appointment was canceled and McClellan appointed Wright to the permanent post of commander of the Department of the Pacific. It would prove to be his longest appointment, lasting until July 1864. Although he remained a brigadier general of volunteers, he was still not promoted above his regular army rank of colonel of the Ninth Infantry. In this command he would show remarkable fortitude, although his letters sounded increasingly like pleas from a wounded soul.

During his tenure as commander of the Department of the Pacific, Wright was responsible for all states and territories west of the Rocky Mountains, which covered five hundred thousand square miles. To keep peace in his command, an area greater than that of the Confederacy, he initially had only twenty-four hundred officers and soldiers. One of his highest priorities was to raise more volunteers to augment the regulars.[25] One of McClellan's first orders to Wright came on November 2, 1861: "Send by telegram condition of your troops. Report by letter fully and frequently."[26] In what was perhaps an attempt to curry favor with McClellan, in a forty-day stretch between November and December Wright sent no fewer than five reports—including letters to McClellan's adjutant on December 9, 10, and 20—in which he used the same verbiage: his troops were receiving "instruction and discipline."[27]

Also in November 1861 Wright sent a letter to Nevada territorial governor J. W. Nye concerning protection of the overland mail route. Wright expressed concern regarding Indians along the route—he feared they might rob the mail, and he worried they might starve during the winter. Then, midparagraph, he switched to a favorite topic: his passion for duty and love for his country: "The Union-loving people of this coast are vastly in time ascendant, their fiat has gone forth, and no secession doctrine can flourish here," he wrote. He then shifted the focus to his experience, stating that he was "ready at all times to enforce a due respect and observance of the Constitution and laws of our country." He ended with a reminder of his patriotism: "If it becomes my duty to act, I shall do so fearlessly, and without regard to personal consequences."[28]

Wright acted quickly to send a message to anyone in California who might question his efforts to stamp out anti-Union sentiment. One of his first acts as commander was to telegraph Gen. Lorenzo Thomas, the new adjutant general of the army: "Can I disregard writs of habeas corpus in case of political or state prisoners?" The response was simply, "You cannot disregard writs."[29]

During the Civil War, California was rife with political intrigue. It was difficult to discern rumor from fact or to determine the loyalty of individuals to either the North or South. Some newspapers and local political figures criticized the army for not doing enough to stamp out pockets of Confederate loyalists, while others were critical of efforts to do so. Wright sometimes found himself caught between conflicting passions and had to make decisions that would often make no one happy.

As the Civil War heated up, Wright's critics in California became more vociferous. Some of the harshest critics were Union loyalists who sparked rumors, then fanned them into wildfires. In 1861 a Confederate army fourteen thousand strong was rumored to be heading out of Texas (or perhaps, some said, from Sonora, Mexico) toward California. Thousands of armed insurrectionists were gathering in various parts of California, claimed another. Yet another alleged that gunboats patrolled the coast and would soon enter San Francisco harbor.

HOSTILE FEELINGS

The events of the 1850s seemed as if they were rarely far from Wright's mind. In a March 1862 letter to Commissioner of Indian Affairs William Dole, he blamed the Indian wars in great part to whites settling on Indian land. He wrote, "Such acts had, of course, a tendency to create a hostile feeling against the white people." He particularly criticized the 1855 Walla Walla treaties. Although they had finally been ratified in 1859, the government had not fulfilled its obligations to the tribes. Wright's assessment was blunt: "For ten years past the system of managing our Indian affairs on this coast has been a miserable failure."[30] He made no mention of his possible culpability in the "failure." Also in March, Wright reported that four white men had apparently stolen horses from four Mono Indian men: "The result was that the Indians were all killed. Reports from that country represent that the whites were in the wrong; probably they were, but I cannot let the innocent suffer for the guilty."[31] Thus, while he expressed some understanding about what the tribes were facing, his duty and enforcement requirements were clear: punishment for Indians extended not only to the perpetrators (or alleged perpetrators) but to their families or other members of their tribe as well. Punishment of white criminals, if it was applied at all, was restricted to the perpetrators.

Policing the Indians became less of a responsibility and more of a bother. His answer to Indian problems found two solutions: hanging them or shipping them offshore. In April 1862 Wright instructed Capt. George Price to take a company and investigate disturbances near Honey Lake, California: "The main object of sending you is to restore peace between the white people and the Indians. Should you capture any of the latter who have been guilty of murder, robbery, etc., execute summary justice on them. I have generally found that by hanging a few of the worst Indians peace and quiet is soon restored."[32] In response to concerns about Indians expressed by citizens of Arcata, California, Wright tried to reassure them: "I have an officer in command there in whom I place the highest confidence. I have sent him instructions to prosecute the campaign against those Indians with the greatest vigor, and to hang on the spot all who have been engaged at any time in hostilities."[33]

Wright knew that "hanging a few Indians" in order to terrorize the tribes was only a short-term solution. He wrote of his concern with the relocation of the Indians once they were subdued. If they were placed on reservations near their ancestral homes, they would simply move back, so Wright had a solution: create a reservation "on some of the islands near this coast."[34] The best location, he concluded, was Catalina Island. He investigated the idea at length, but logistical issues, the distractions of his other duties, and a lack of enthusiasm from his superiors pushed the idea into the background.

During the later years of his life, when Wright seemed to be fighting for credibility, he sometimes appeared to be concerned that he might appear weak. In November 1862 he wrote to army headquarters, asking permission to move the headquarters of the Department of the Pacific inland from San Francisco to Sacramento. During his time in the west he was frequently afflicted with asthma and perhaps had recurring bouts of malaria. In his November 1862 letter, he was careful to point out that his affliction would not be a problem if he were to be moved east: "During a few months past I have been suffering with the asthma, the only affliction I ever had, and this only in San Francisco. Anywhere removed from the coast I am perfectly well."[35]

In California, where events demanded his immediate attention, he was impatient. One week after penning the letter to Commissioner of Indian Affairs Dole, he wrote to Col. Francis Lippitt of the Second Infantry, commanding the District of Humboldt: "The Indian difficulties in the Humboldt District have been growing worse and worse for years, and I am determined to settle them now for the last time. Every Indian you may capture, and who has been engaged in hostilities present or past, shall be hung on the spot. Spare the women and children."[36] On May 2, 1862, Wright sent an order to Col. Ferris Forman: "I wish a command of mounted troops dispatched for the Owen's Lake country to chastise those Indians and protect our people.

. . . Expect those Indian difficulties to be brought to a speedy termination, and such punishment inflicted on the guilty as will prevent another Indian outbreak in that quarter."[37]

At times, Wright had little patience for the whites, either, and he used strong rhetoric to condemn them. Soldiers had been deserting to seek their fortunes in the goldfields, leaving white settlements without adequate protection. On May 24 Wright wrote to George Hanson, superintendent of Indian affairs for the Northern District of California, noting that he had received demands for soldiers to protect women and children from Indians, since so many men had left their homes. To Wright, it was "a very poor argument." He added, "There is either no danger from Indians or the men who will thus abandon their wives and little ones for the gold fields deserve death."[38] However, given his other orders while in this position, it is highly unlikely that an actual Indian threat would have gone unpunished.

Some of Wright's letters from late in his career became bogged down in poetic sentiments, with vague intent. An example is the long letter to General Thomas, which ostensibly was an update on the state of affairs in California. However, most of Wright's words were about himself. He begins:

> I have served on the Pacific Coast for ten years, the last year in command of this department. My duties have called me to nearly every section of this great country; from the sunny plains of the south to the farthest bounds of our possessions in the north. I have been called, either to battle with our savage foes, or to aid in the preservation of this beautiful land from the horrors of civil war. During this long period I have had ample opportunity of judging of the character of the people and the value to the Union of these remote possessions of the United States.

After a lengthy account of the settlement of the west, with its conflicts and challenges, he again returned to his accomplishments:

> I saw at once that to overcome all these threatening difficulties it was necessary to be watchful, vigilant, and firm; not create unnecessary

alarm in the public mind by hasty and ill-advised acts, but to pursue the even tenor of my way, regardless of personal consequences, and feeling assured that such a course could not fail to secure the respect of political parties of every complexion, and ultimately redound [rebound] to the honor of our Government and country. If what little I have done has contributed in the smallest degree in preserving intact our glorious Union and maintaining unsullied our flag, I shall feel more than repaid. It affords me high satisfaction to inform the General-in-Chief that during all the period of my command in this department I have received the most cordial approval and assistance from the Governors and State officers, as well as from the most prominent citizens.

Very respectfully, your obedient servant,

G. WRIGHT, Brigadier-General, U. S. Army, Commanding.[39]

A key sentence in the letter is "I have been called." In his letters, a clear message comes through: George Wright believed he served a special purpose. Other officers had obvious interests and foibles, but not Wright. Ulysses S. Grant was interested in business deals, George McClellan departed for world travel and politics, Philip Sheridan was known for his social side, Ethan Allen Hitchcock and John Wool preferred to spend time with books and the world of ideas, and so on. In addition, those officers had one thing in common that George Wright lacked: they had held positions of respect and power in the battle zones during the Civil War. In fact, during the Civil War twenty-one of the men who served with Wright became generals for either the Union or Confederacy.[40]

YET ANOTHER MASSACRE

Wright's attitude toward Indians continued to harden, and in November 1862 he wrote to army headquarters that attacks along the Humboldt River and against overland mail routes proved that "retributive punishment [was the] only way to deal with those savages."[41] He ordered Col. P. E. Connor, commanding the

Third Infantry of California Volunteers, to the Utah district to take measures to stop Indian attacks on the overland mail routes, particularly along the Bear River, just north of the present-day Utah-Idaho border. On January 29, 1863, Connor and a force of two hundred California Volunteers attacked a Shoshone village and engaged perhaps three hundred warriors in a battle that was at first fierce but quickly turned into a massacre. The volunteers went on a rampage, using axes to kill women and children. The militiamen followed the carnage by burning food supplies and houses and stealing two hundred horses. When it was over, hundreds of Indians lay dead. Shortly after the massacre, three settlers traveling through the area counted nearly 400 bodies, and a Danish immigrant, Hans Jasperson, counted 493 men, women, and children. In his journal nineteen-year-old Jasperson wrote, "I turned around and counted them back and counted just the same."[42] In his official report to army headquarters, General Wright reported the volunteers suffered 15 dead and 53 wounded. Seven of the wounded later died. Unlike in the Northwest with the Grande Ronde attack, Wright apparently made little effort to investigate the circumstances of the battle. The massacre was no secret: immediately afterward, stories circulated through Salt Lake City describing the bloody details, and in a telegram a few days after the attack, Connor reported "Enemy's loss very heavy. Destroyed their camp."[43] General Wright praised Connor's force, saying, "Of the good conduct and bravery of both officers and men, California has reason to be proud." With Wright's support, General-of-the-Army Henry Halleck promoted Connor to brigadier general.[44] None of Wright's letters refer to an investigation of the Bear River Massacre.

"A BLESSED MARTYR"

One way Wright sought to protect the Union was to inspire the citizenry. He wrote a number of letters that appealed to the patriotic zeal and obligations of the population, like this one from April 1863, which ends with an ominous tone:

To the Citizens of the Pacific Coast:

You are far removed from the scenes of war and desolation; a war which has drenched in blood the fairest portion of our beloved country; a war to preserve our Union and our free institutions against the assaults of traitors—traitors to their God and traitors to their country; who, disregarding the example and precepts of the great Washington, seek to destroy our very existence as a nation. During the war which has been raging for the last two years in the Eastern States you have enjoyed all the blessings of peace and prosperity within your borders. No family hearth has been made desolate. The wailings of the widow and orphan are rarely heard in this favored land. So far you have been exempt from the scourge of war. Are you prepared, then, to sacrifice all these blessings, to prove recreant to yourselves, to the nation, and to the high and holy trust transmitted to you by the founders of our Republic? No. Already I hear the welkin ring with shouts of acclamation: "The Union shall be preserved." Although the great mass of the people on the Pacific Coast are eminently patriotic and devoted to the Union, yet, fellow-citizens, we must not disguise the fact that we have traitors in our midst who are doing all in their power to involve this country in the horrors of civil war. To all such persons, I say, pause, and reflect well before plunging into the yawning abyss of treason; an indignant people will rise in their majesty, and swift retributive justice will be your certain doom.

Done at the headquarters of the Department of the Pacific this 7th day of April, 1863.[45]

In July 1863 Wright became involved in political turmoil with national consequences. President Lincoln ordered the army to seize the New Almaden quicksilver mine, near San Jose, California. The mercury extracted from the quicksilver was used in armaments and the mining industry, and the president wanted to establish a dependable supply for the war effort. Wright was ordered to take a cavalry company and infantry detachment to seize the mine. Strong protests arose from owners of other mines, in addition to opposition from California political figures. Wright telegraphed General Halleck: "Respectfully submitted that the President's order to take possession of Almaden Mines be deferred for the present. If seized now, great excitement will result."[46] That same day Lincoln telegraphed his emissary and friend Leonard Swett and the Republican candidate for California governor, Frederick Low: "Consult together and do not have a riot or great difficulty about delivering possession."[47] Low replied to Lincoln, "If not already done, telegraph General Wright to suspend execution by military force in regard to Almaden Mine. . . . The results will be deplorable if the order is carried into immediate execution."[48]

Wright's challenges during his tenure on the Pacific coast often seemed relentless. In addition to his normal military duties, he had to deal with often-antagonistic newspapers, politicians, and citizens. There were sporadic conflicts with Indian tribes across the west, shortages of military personnel and supplies, and, as he reported to army headquarters in September 1863, even disruption in his senior staff: "I am greatly pained at an accident which happened to Maj. R. W. Kirkham, quartermaster, who accompanied me on my tour. At Carson City he unfortunately walked out of an open doorway at the end of a hall where there was no balcony, and falling some fourteen feet bruised himself much and fractured his thigh bone. I brought him back with me, but he will probably be laid up eight or ten weeks."[49] With all the dangers Wright and his officers faced while traveling around the American West, Major Kirkham's mishap is the only one that Wright notes in his official correspondence. Wright's own son, Maj. John Montomgery Wright, had been seriously wounded at Gettysburg two months earlier. The juxtaposition of his son's wounds—incurred in the midst of the war where Wright so badly wanted to be—with a careless accident with one of his senior officers must have raised some dissonance in Wright's mind.[50]

By early 1864 Wright had alienated powerful people: some believed he was too strident with his restrictions on trade and civil liberties, and some thought he was too lax. Rumors spread that he held treasonous views, and despite support from his allies, on April 11 it was reported that he had been replaced by Gen. Irwin McDowell. Wright was placed in charge of the District of California, with his headquarters in Sacramento.[51] In

August 1864 General Grant became concerned about McDowell's effectiveness and wrote to Secretary of War Stanton suggesting that McDowell be removed and replaced with Halleck or, once again, Wright. Stanton responded that he had heard there had been "frequent applications for the removal of General Wright" and that McDowell was adequate for the job. Grant acquiesced, and McDowell remained in the post. At the same time, Stanton admitted, "You know as I do that no man can please all sides in any department, much less in California."[52]

In his dramatic farewell address, printed in a California newspaper in 1864 when Wright was unhappily being transferred from San Francisco to Sacramento, he concluded by quoting Wolsey's farewell speech to Cromwell from Shakespeare's *Henry VIII*:[53]

> Be just and fear not;
> Let all the ends thou aimest at be thy country's,
> Thy God's and truth's.

However, Wright omitted the last part of the speech:

> Then, if thou fallest, O Cromwell,
> thou fallest a blessed martyr.
> Act 3, Scene 2

Whatever might have been lost by omitting the last two lines had been made clear in his letters over the prior years, in which he told Generals Sumner, Thomas, and others of his self-sacrifice for God and country. Wright's demotion pleased some, including the *Los Angeles News*. The paper bid good riddance to him, referring to him as "the old granny with buttons on his coat." In a backhanded compliment, the paper attributed Wright's shortcomings to his advancing age, "and not to any fault of the old man's heart."[54]

Despite being moved aside, Wright continued to inspire the California citizenry with exhortations to uphold the principles of the Union. In November 1864 he addressed the Lincoln and Johnson Club in Sacramento and was greeted with "the heartiest applause." With rhetoric just as strong as he had once applied to Indian tribes in Washington Territory, he attacked enemies of the Union, calling them "haughty traitors" who would "drench this fair land of ours with human gore."[55] In December 1864 he was awarded the rank of brevet brigadier general of the regular army, for "Long, faithful, and meritorious services."[56] The promotion order was signed by yet another of Wright's onetime subordinates, Inspector General Col. James A. Hardie. During the 1858 expedition Hardie, then a captain, had been in charge of an infantry company.[57]

THE DOOLITTLE REPORT

In November 1864 a Colorado territorial militia led by Col. John Chivington attacked a village of Cheyennes and Arapahos, killing more than one hundred people. Some of the elderly and children were used for target practice, and corpses were desecrated. Chivington encouraged the murder of women and children by telling his men, "Nits make lice." Horror was widespread across the country, and among the resulting investigations was one conducted by a Joint Committee of Congress chaired by J. R. Doolittle. In March 1865 Congress began a two-year investigation of conditions among the Indian tribes across the West. The intent of the investigation was to evaluate the condition of the tribes and make suggestions for improvements in regard to their treatment. The report gathered facts using a questionnaire that consisted of twenty-three questions. Some were specific: "What diseases are most common and most fatal among them, and from what causes?" Many asked for more complex assessments: "What proportion of the children are orphans, and to what extent would it be practicable for the Indian Bureau to place Indian children in the families of Christian white men, to be trained and educated in the English language and in the habits of civilized life?"[58] Some of the country's most experienced army officers and Indian agents participated, including Col. Kit Carson, Maj. Gen. John Pope, Inspector General R. B. Marcy, and twenty others. Because of his experience in dealing with the tribes, George Wright was asked to participate. His response, dated one month before his death, reads like a brief autobiography of his professional life. His replies are imbued with the settled wisdom of a man who knew his duty and had no regrets about the consequences of his actions over the preceding forty years. Wright's response to the questionnaire was one of the last official tasks of his life. An inventory of his experience, knowledge, and prejudices, it was his final offering before stepping onto the deck of the *Brother Jonathan.*

The words and tone of Wright's answers stand in sharp contrast to those provided by most of the others, including Colonel Carson and Major General Pope. Nearly all of the respondents sound informed (by nineteenth-century standards), detailed, and often impassioned, at least compared to Wright. Carson wrote, "Humanity shudders at the picture of the extermination of thousands of human beings until every means is tried and found useless for their redemption." Pope, addressing the decline of the Indian population, listed the causes: "By disease; by wars; by cruel treatment of the part of the whites—both by irresponsible persons and by government officials; by unwise policy of the government, or by inhumane and dishonest administration of that policy; and by steady and relentless encroachments of the white emigration toward the west, which is everyday confining the Indians to narrower limits, and by driving off or killing their game, their only means of subsistence."[59]

All of the responses reflected the ethnocentrism and stereotypes of the era. However, Wright's remarks about his own experiences and accomplishments are lengthier than any of his responses about how to improve the condition of the tribes. In answer to a question about whether Indian reservations should be established by law, treaty, or by "regulation by the department," the sum total of Wright's answer was: "Let it be done by law and enforced by arms; make it a military colony." To the question about how to provide better education for Indian children, Wright noted only, "Schools have a good effect. Provide for a Protestant minister on every reservation, having under him assistants to teach schools."[60] Other respondents, some with far less experience than Wright, offered suggestions and comments that in many cases amounted to more than five hundred words for each question. In addition to the officers working with the Doolittle Commission, other officers expressed concerns about the tribes. In March 1864 Brig. Gen. James H. Carleton, commander of the Department of New Mexico, reported to General Wright: "It will require the greatest effort and most careful husbandry to keep the Indians alive until the new crop matures." He ordered his troops to work with the Indians, "plowing, spading, and hoeing up ground."[61]

At the end of the Civil War, the army was reorganized into five divisions and eighteen departments. Wright assumed command of the Department of the Columbia, consisting of the state of Oregon and Washington and Idaho Territories. One of Wright's last official actions in California was to write to the sheriff of Shasta County, informing him that it was his "duty as a loyal citizen and sheriff of the county, to arrest all persons publicly exulting over the death of the President."[62]

Wright's new headquarters were to be at Fort Vancouver, and on July 28, 1865, he and Margaret, with all of their possessions, boarded the *Brother Jonathan.*

ECHOES

If Wright expressed remorse for any of his actions, we will probably never know. What might have he said in private, to Margaret, or to a close friend? In Alexie's *Reservation Blues,* Wright, Sheridan, and Armstrong are record producers trying to take advantage of a Native American band. Tiring of Sheridan and Armstrong's machinations, Wright leaves the record offices and tells a cabbie to take him home. Home, as it turns out, is the cemetery in Sacramento where George and Margaret Wright are buried. At his grave, he stands looking at the monument, "remembering the ship that went down in the Pacific and the water rushing into his lungs."

> "Margaret," Wright said as he lay down on top of his grave. "I'm home. I'm home. I'm so sorry. I'm home." Margaret patted his head as he wept and remembered all those horses who had screamed in that field so long ago . . . "I was the one . . . I was the one. I was the one who killed them all. I gave the orders."
>
> The horses screamed in his head.
>
> "Shh," Margaret whispered. "It's okay, I forgive you."

In Alexie's story, Wright repents:

> "Oh God," Wright sobbed to his wife on their graves. The grief rushed into his lungs. "I'm a killer. I'm a killer."
>
> "You've come home," Margaret whispered. "You're home now."[63]

THIRTEEN

Legacy

Twenty-five years after the Plateau Indian War, one of Wright's men voiced feelings shared by many who served with him:

> We read much of the exploits of this or that commander, who has followed the footsteps of General Jackson or General Harney, in Indian warfare. I will try, in a plain way, to extol one whose name I have never seen quoted as a modern Jackson or Harrison, but whose deeds I do not think have been excelled by any who have worn the army uniform since those illustrious Indian fighters have passed away. His name is General George Wright.[1]

Once the Civil War broke out, the plight of Indians in the faraway Pacific Northwest became irrelevant to the great majority of the white population. Still, settlers began to trickle into the Inland Empire, and the tribes were faced with their own immediate concern: how to survive in a rapidly changing region.

For those looking to make a new home in the region, Wright's 1858 campaign was remembered in small ways. In 1861 a small party of settlers was traveling along the Columbia River near its confluence with the Snake when some of their horses were stolen by "Snake River Indians," probably Palouses. Sixteen-year-old William P. Gray, as the eldest healthy male in the group, was sent after them. After a twelve-mile chase, he confronted the horse thieves at their camp. Outmanned and outgunned, he chose to conjure the spirit of George Wright.

> I rode up to the big tent where I could hear the tom-tom and the sound of Indians dancing. . . . Some years earlier General Wright had inflicted severe punishment upon the Indians by killing a large band of their horses. I rode up to the tent, dismounted, threw the tepee flap back and stepped into the entrance. The Indians stopped dancing and looked intently at me. I talked the Chinook jargon as well as I did English, so I said, "Some of you Indians have stolen my horses last night. If they are not back in my camp an hour after I get there I'll see that every horse in your band is shot." There was utter silence.[2]

Mr. Gray departed with his horses, but one wonders what bitterness lingered after his departure.

A few hundred white settlers lived in "Spokane Falls" in 1880. However, by 1890, the population was ten thousand, and by the turn of the century the region's population was nearly forty thousand.[3] Newcomers began building homes, lumber mills, and businesses next to Spokane Falls, one of the key Indian fisheries in the region. The tribes began to struggle, trying to keep some of their old ways while striving to live with the new American culture. White society demanded they become "civilized," and stripped away their food sources and lifestyle. In addition to being subjected to theft, fraud, and general abuse, many Indian parents were powerless to stop government officials from taking their children to boarding schools. They had become unwelcome people in their own land.[4]

With some of the Native people living near or in towns, white citizens had to take notice. Toward the end of the nineteenth century, expressions of sympathy for Indians became more frequent, and in some cases, more public. In 1892, a writer for the *Spokane Spokesman-Review* said that the local Indians were "wanderers upon the face of the earth, landless in a land that was once entirely theirs." The writer continued with a lament that ends tragically:

> [Garry's] people are either dead or scattered, and of all that wild array that gathered upon the luxuriant plains of the Spokane to hurl defiance to the invader, but a miserable remnant remains, broken

> in health, poor in the wealth most prized by Indian character, and doomed to an early extinction. It would have been better, perhaps, if they had made a firmer stand in their fight for the retention of their native land—if they had abided by their defiance of war to the death sent by the "black robe" from the Coeur d'Alene Mission, and fallen in a single desperate struggle for their homes and native land. . . . Annihilation under those heroic circumstances appeals more strongly to the patriotic impulses of the race.[5]

The writer's cultural bias is clear, but perhaps there is a hidden, darker issue: Is the writer projecting onto Indians his own regret that they survived? Would it have been better for the tribes if they had not survived at all and easier for the culture that displaced them not to witness the struggles of people they mistreated?

While Indians were trying to make the best of their new lives, the rest of the population seemed unsure about what to think of the people they displaced. In the early twentieth century newspaper articles with sympathetic sentiments appeared periodically. The *Spokane Spokesman-Review*'s 1892 obituary of Chief Garry noted his passing with regret: "Alas poor Garry! The story of his life, interwoven with that of the death of his people, might well be made a theme of poetry; to endure long after the last Spokane has vanished from the land."[6]

Five years later, another article raised the "Noble Savage" ideal and included a heavy dose of wishful thinking—that is, that the conquest of the tribes was good for everyone: "Colonel Wright's brilliant campaign of three months against the Northern Indians accomplished a lasting peace through all of eastern Washington. The Spokane braves who participated in those memorable scenes are now nearly all passed away, and their children are many of them today advancing in the arts of civilization."[7]

As the twentieth century began, the narrative depicting Wright and his legacy became more inconsistent. Often it seemed that the white community could not quite make up its mind about Wright's legacy. Praise for his actions was typically based on a superficial, ethnocentric view at his expedition: Colonel Wright led a fighting force through hostile territory, conquered the tribes, and made the land safe not only for whites but for Indians as well. The narrative supporting a heroic legacy carried a common theme: he committed violence in order to limit violence. The heroic legacy was boosted by the fact that he made it plain in his letters that he was guided by zealous patriotism, a strong sense of duty, and religious piety.

One of the best examples of Wright's mixed legacy came in a 1902 *New York Times* article that suggested that Wright's success might provide a defense for an accused U.S. war criminal. In 1901, during the Philippine-American War, Gen. Jacob H. Smith was accused of ordering the massacre of at least two thousand civilians. The argument in the *Times* was that Smith's actions were no worse than Wright's, and in the context of war they were acceptable. Thus, if Wright had not been prosecuted for war crimes, perhaps General Smith should likewise be spared. The article drew a direct connection from Wright's to Smith's actions by declaring that Wright's report describing his 1858 march into the Columbia scablands "sounds as if he were starting off to-day for a campaign across Samar." The *Times* used Colonel Wright's official reports, focusing on a few of his more arrogant comments, such as, "The chastisement which these Indians were suffered has been severe but well-merited, and absolutely necessary to impress them with our power." The article notes that Wright hung prisoners without trials and that his only critic was his commanding officer, General Clarke, who reprimanded him for not being severe enough. In other words, nearly a half-century later the *Times* uses Wright's "brilliant" Indian campaign to justify the actions of another commander, General Smith, who committed a savage act that drew condemnation from many, both in and out of the army, and ended in a war-crimes trial.[8]

At times, at least some segments of white society were trying to redefine their relationship with the past in ways that were troubling to the Native people. Some whites found it advantageous to take on characteristics of the tribes—or *their* version of the tribes. As the "Noble Savages" faded away, some of the newer residents of the Inland Northwest decided to adapt aspects of the nobility to their own purposes. Local chapters of the Order of the Red Man formed, in effect allowing whites to "play Indian." In 1901 an article in the *Spokesman-Review* boasted that Palouse Tribe No. 58 of the Improved Order of the Red Man took on twenty-three new members, called "palefaces." The paper said, "The affair was one of the most elaborate ever witnessed here and was participated in by members of seven tribes, including J. Thomas of Farmington, who claims the record of the oldest Red Man in the State, having been a member for thirty-three years." The paper reported that one local chapter, the Palouse Tribe, "opened the hall and prepared the forest, after which the 'braves,' headed by the Palouse band, marched to the hotel, where the visiting Red Men were captured and adopted into the tribe, after which Palefaces Lemon and Harper were each given the full three degrees of the order. . . . The affair was one of the most pleasant in the history of Palouse secret society circles." At the time of the evening's festivities, there might have been more *white* Red Men than there were real Palouse Indians, most of whom were living a few miles south, at the ancestral village of Palus at the confluence of the Snake and Palouse Rivers.[9]

All of the region's tribes were suffering. In the last half of the nineteenth century, to the Indian tribes Wright's legacy was irrelevant, since they were trying to survive. Some were nearly finished off by smallpox in 1890, and although they struggled to farm as they had been taught, they were faring poorly. Cold winters drove them to starvation, especially during the winter of 1858–59, when their food supplies had been burned by Wright's command. White ranchers and farmers had destroyed their root grounds. They had always preferred to take salmon from the rivers, but commercial salmon fishing at the mouth of the Columbia had decimated the supply upstream. Conditions were so poor that in 1897 Lewis T. Irwin, Indian agent for the Yakamas, recommended that "they [the Palouse] be forcibly removed to either the Nez Perce, Umatilla, or Yakima Reservations." In 1905 the order was carried out, and nearly all members of the tribe left the village of Palus and their homeland at the confluence of the Palouse and Snake Rivers.[10]

The Red Men stand in contrast to another white man, George Hunter, who worked with Indians to help them acquire and keep land. He lived near the Palouse tribe and became a close friend of many. In 1877, Hunter worked as an interpreter for Gen. Oliver O. Howard during the Nez Perce war. After the war General Howard, like Hunter, supported the rights of Indians to homestead on open land and asked Hunter to assist the Indians with land claims. The Palouse made Hunter an honorary member of their tribe, which was a tribute to his friendship and ensured the tribe had an ally among the local whites.[11]

There have been influential public voices supporting a heroic legacy for George Wright. In 1907 photographer Edward Curtis began publishing the volumes making up *The North American Indian* series. His photographs of Native people were accompanied by observations gathered during his travels. In writing of the Plateau tribes, he expressed a sentiment that has been used by non-Native historians to defend Wright's actions: "Whatever may be thought of the harshness of Wright's methods in this campaign, it must be admitted they were eminently successful. If in the march of civilization the Indians were to be disposed of their lands, conflict was unavoidable, and decisive measures were more humane for all concerned than the temporizing policy of the army in the trouble with the Yakima."[12] Thus, Curtis added his voice to those who claimed that Wright, just one man in the march of Manifest Destiny, foresaw the inevitable outcome and did his best to limit bloodshed.

In the early twentieth century a few old soldiers remembered the Plateau War as an unqualified success. In 1907 George Dandy, a lieutenant during the 1858 campaign, remembered the fight in romantic terms, his sentiment similar to those expressed by many settlers and politicians over the preceding fifty years:

> This [Wright's] expedition has made possible the "Empire of the Columbia" by completely subduing the hostile tribes who had divided it among themselves and hoped to exclude all others. It may truthfully be affirmed that but for this conclusive victory over these tribes, and the valuable lessons it taught them, the country would have

> remained for many years a howling wilderness, instead of the happy and prosperous country it has since become. It would still have resembled an unweeded garden instead of a "land flowing with milk and honey," containing prosperous modern cities and towns, the homes of wealth, culture and refinement—enabling every man to sit under the shadow of his own vine and fig tree, with none to molest or make him afraid.[13]

In 1922 the issue of extermination again appeared when a newspaper writer summarizing the conflict between cultures used an old quote from Chief Garry: "The tragedy, the romance, the past and the present of the Spokane country are all bound up on one pathetic sentence uttered by the poor old chief of the Spokanes, a sentence he repeated many times: 'This country was all mine and my people's.'"[14]

MILITARY LEGACY

George Wright's heroic legacy was enhanced by the actions of officers who learned from him. In 1997 one historian wrote that by their example, army officers passed their knowledge to succeeding generations. Thus, "When Col. George Wright applied techniques of devastation and retribution that he had first observed in the Second Seminole War, his actions were not lost on young 2d Lt. Philip H. Sheridan, who would himself apply devastation as a weapon against southern and Native American regulars over the next thirty years."[15]

Sheridan, having learned well from Wright, devastated the Shenandoah Valley during the Civil War. After the war, Sheridan's words and actions would sometimes echo those of his old commander. Like Wright, he could be sympathetic at times and cruel at others. While he expressed outrage about the murders of Spencer's family at the Cascades in 1856, he later advocated total destruction of combatants and civilians alike. Of the post–Civil War conflicts with the Plains tribes, he said, "The people must be left nothing but their eyes to weep with after the war." In 1868 he ordered an attack on a Cheyenne village in the Washita Valley, Oklahoma Territory. George Armstrong Custer led the primary assault, in which a large number of noncombatants were killed. In addition, Custer gathered about eight hundred of the Indians' ponies and had them shot. After the war in the plains in 1868–69, Sheridan expressed regret. He attributed conflict with Indians to "the government breaking every promise it had made to the Indians." Yet, during a trip to Prussia in 1870, Sheridan told a dinner audience that in regard to their French enemies, the Prussians should "hang the insurgents and burn their villages."[16]

However, after the Sioux War of 1876–77 Sheridan again spoke sympathetically of the tribes, saying, "We took away their country, and their means of support, broke up their mode of living, their habits of life, introduced disease and decay among them, and it was for this and against this that they made war. Could any one expect less? Then why wonder at Indian difficulties?"[17]

Sheridan's respect for Wright extended beyond his former commander's strategic violence. In 1888, more than thirty years after serving under Colonel Wright, Sheridan was the first signatory on a petition to Congress to grant a pension for Wright's daughter, Lizzie, who spent the last years of her life in poverty and ill health. Sheridan and nine other high-ranking officers wrote that Wright was a "gallant, noble, heroic, spotless man and soldier whose deeds and fame will ever be remembered and cherished in our service."[18]

Today, the U.S. Army's historical accounts refer to Indians as insurgents. The military science program at Eastern Washington University teaches students that Wright's campaign was a "counterinsurgency operation."[19] Princeton University's Wordnet defines an insurgency as an "organized rebellion aimed at overthrowing a constitutional government through the use of subversion and armed conflict."[20] The words "insurgency" and "rebellion" refer to "rebels . . . rising in active revolt," acting in "open resistance to an established government."[21] The concept is offensive to many Native Americans, who point out *they* were the established government in their homelands, and that the soldiers were the invaders.[22]

NATIVE AMERICAN LEGACY

Over the generations native people have kept alive the events of 1855–58, particularly the circumstances involving the treaties, and of course, Wright's actions during his expedition. Erratic and negligent U.S. Indian policy has enlarged the legacy at various times in history due to government investigations and legal actions brought by the tribes to enforce treaty provisions.

In 1915 Chief Weninock of the Yakamas gave testimony in a lawsuit concerning fishing rights. In doing so, he drew on the events of the Plateau War: "I was at the Council at Walla Walla with my father, who was one of the Chiefs who signed the treaty. I well remember hearing the talk about the treaty. There were more Indians at Walla Walla than ever came together at any one place in this country. Besides the women and children, there were two thousand Indian warriors, and they were there for about one moon." Weninock remembered Kamiakin saying, "I am afraid that the white men are not speaking straight; that their children will not do what is right by our children; that they will not do what you have promised for them."[23]

In 1919 Owhi, grandson of the Chief Owhi who was killed while in Wright's custody, spoke about the war and its aftermath. He told of Wright's desire to find Qualchan and Kamiakin and spoke of the Spokane messengers Wright sent out to request the presence of the chiefs at Smith's Ford. Chief Owhi was warned by friends to stay away, but trusting Wright, he traveled to the encampment, where he was taken captive. This is the narrative handed down through generations of Native people, and it squares in most details with accounts of eyewitnesses, both Indian and white. Lo-kout, who traveled to see Wright with Qualchan and Whist-alks, recalled that they rode into Wright's camp having been told by an Indian they met that Owhi was at the camp "having a good time with his friends." When they reached Wright's tent, the colonel greeted them cordially, but handed a hastily scribbled note to a soldier, who jumped on a horse and rode off toward the soldiers' camp. An armed contingent soon arrived to take Qualchan into custody. Shortly after Qualchan

Chief Hoosis-moxmox of the Palouses, ca. 1908. The chief fought against both Steptoe and Wright. Photo by Benjamin A. Gifford. Gifford Photographic Collection, Oregon State University Libraries Special Collections and Archives Research Center.

Chief Garry in old age. Courtesy of Spokane Museum of Arts and Culture.

was hanged, Lo-kout was slated to be next, but he fought until a Nez Perce intervened and Wright let him go.[24]

One Palouse chief and warrior, Hoosis-moxmox (Yellow Hair), lived until 1909, when he was about ninety years old. Hoosis-moxmox fought against both Wright and Steptoe, and as he aged he bore the weight of sadness, but he expressed little bitterness. He spoke of his grandfather, a chief who had met Lewis and Clark and befriended them. The explorers left behind a gift for the chief: a U.S. flag, which meant a great deal to him. When Hoosis-moxmox's grandfather died, the flag went to Hoosis-moxmox's father, who valued it highly. Hoosis-moxmox had attended the Walla Walla council, and in 1903 spoke of the tension there between the chiefs and Stevens and later spoke of Wright's march and the horse massacre. Despite the tragedies, he refused to condemn Wright or any of the participants. Late in life he said, "You stand on this ground—Boston-man. I stand on this ground—Indian. The same Father made Boston-man and made Indian. We are brothers."[25]

Today, Dr. Roberta Paul, a direct descendant of Utsinmalikan, one of the Nez Perce chiefs present at the council, notes that Stevens "failed to recognize the significance of the Nez Perce entrance. Our Nez Perce ancestors were not only honoring him as an important person, they were also demonstrating that the Nez Perce are a strong and important people who expect to be treated as equals."[26] Bill Matt, preservation officer of the Spokane tribe, points out that a frequent issue with the government's treatment of the tribes was the lack of respect shown in councils and other face-to-face interactions. The treaty councils at Walla Walla and along the Spokane River were just a few of many examples.[27]

To the tribes of the Inland Northwest, Wright's legacy lives on in contemporary expressions of his actions. In place-names, literature, art, music, and academic research the Native people who directly suffered the impact of political and military suppression are remembered, and their experiences are used to help today's Native people honor ancestors and deal with challenges.[28] Some native people are frustrated that Wright's memory is treated with respect by so many non-Natives. One tribal member recently said, "We don't want to dwell on the past, but it's frustrating to be around people who don't at least acknowledge it. How can we, as a community, move forward if we don't take an honest look at the past?"[29] Charlene Teters, the Native American artist and teacher, emphasizes the importance of empowering younger generations. "We must help young people believe in themselves,"

Indian Congress, 1926, Spokane. Courtesy of the Northwest Room, Spokane Public Library.

she says. "They need to understand that our culture is intact. . . . We won the war."[30]

Michael Holloman, who runs the Plateau Center for Native American Studies at Washington State University, points out that Native Americans commemorate historical events differently than many non-Natives, particularly in regard to traumatic events. "The place is a witness to the event, and as such it carries special meaning," he says. Visiting such a place creates powerful emotions that are best honored by ceremonies or private remembrances rather than stone monuments.[31]

Some Native Americans are working to increase understanding of the Indian wars for the general public. Albert Andrews, a member of the Confederated Tribes of the Colville Reservation, is of Palouse and Nez Perce ancestry. He looks toward the future. As a consultant to the National Park Service, he is actively involved in the process of creating meaningful and accurate educational programs at historical sites from Washington to Montana. Andrews believes that Native American involvement in historical education is important, because "it helps us, our ancestors, and our descendants." Plateau Indian culture recognizes that the past, present, and future cannot, and should not be, separated.[32]

The Coeur d'Alene tribe still has a U.S. Army saber taken from the Steptoe battlefield. Rodney Frey of the University of Idaho recalls seeing it in 1996. A warrior, after striking down a soldier, had taken the saber, and his family has kept it ever since. It is brought out on special occasions to honor both "the soldier who had given his life for it and the Indian men who took it from the soldiers, who met the soldiers with only a bow and arrow and maybe a musket."[33] The saber is on display in a cultural exhibit at the tribe's entertainment complex on the Coeur d'Alene reservation. In modern times the late artist George Flett of the Spokane tribe painted vibrant images of horses and native people, using old ledger paper as a canvas. One is called "Comes Charging with his Captured Saber," based on the event at the Battle of Pine Creek.

Periodically, members of the Coeur d'Alene tribe still honor the fighters in the Steptoe battle. The Memorial Warriors Horse Ride begins on the Coeur d'Alene reservation and ends at the battle site adjacent to the town of Rosalia. "At the end of the ride, families share stories, song, meals, and sweat prayers at a tipi encampment."[34]

HISTORICAL MEMORY

While some view Wright as a revenge-minded military commander, others know him only as a name—a historical figure honored by the naming of Fort George Wright, which opened in 1899 and was used by the military until 1957. Fort George Wright Drive runs alongside the campus of Spokane Falls Community College and the old buildings of Fort George Wright. In 1994 a group of Spokane Falls Community College students proposed changing the name of Fort George Wright Drive to "Sintul-mena," an Interior Salish term representing two different bands of the Spokane tribe. The vote was for advisory purposes only, as the action had no legal strength; the final decision would be made by the city planning commission. The side favoring the change included some Native people, a group of students, the Peace and Justice Action League, and a group of nuns at a convent located on the drive. One college staff member, a woman with Chippewa-Cree heritage, favored removing Wright's name, saying the change would be a "symbolic gesture toward sensitivity." The *Spokane Spokesman-Review* printed a letter from a reader claiming the proposed change was the result of "hysterical political correctness."[35]

A faculty member opposed the change, saying that leaving Wright's name would be a reminder of the mistakes made during the colonization period and a reminder to avoid similar errors in the future. One opponent of the change used a claim that is often repeated about Wright—that he was "less offensive in his dealings with the area's tribes than were many other military men of his time."[36] That stance assumes that a family left destitute by the army's destruction of their food supplies and horses would care if Wright was not as bad as he could have been. The fort's name, and the name of the street along which it sits, remains unchanged. Today the fort is owned by Education Corporation Mukogawa Gakuin of Japan and is operated as the Fort Wright Institute, a branch campus of Mukogawa Women's University.[37]

Over the years since the Plateau Indian War, there have been attempts by some citizens in the Inland Northwest to reconcile the region's past with the present. In some cases attempts to add balance to the region's history with Native people have been awkward. In 1933 the Spokane Brewing and Malting Company ran an ad for their new Gilt Top Coburger beer. The message was superimposed over a profile of Chief Garry. The text read, "Chief Garry: great friend of the white man, was mourned by whites and Indians alike when he passed away in 1892, one year after Gilt Top came into existence."[38]

In the mid-twentieth century, other advertisements invoked Wright's campaign, offering differing views. A 1957 newspaper advertisement for a funeral home featured an image of a soldier shooting at Indians; it claimed Wright's force battled "screaming Indians" and "fought their way through ambush after ambush."[39] Newspaper editorial content continued to skew accounts of a hundred years earlier. The first line of a 1958 newspaper column read, "Intoxicated by their victory over Steptoe's dragoons, hostile Indian tribes became more arrogant."[40] Yet seventeen years later an ad for a local bank featured much different text, which referred to Wright as "ruthless" and made clear he executed Indians without trials.[41]

Controversy over geographic place-names forms part of the legacy of Wright's expedition. For example, in 1934 the Spokane County Pioneer Society petitioned the state legislature to change the name of Latah Creek to Hangman Creek, one of several reversals in the name of the waterway. A representative of the society said, "Indians and whites alike called it Hangman Creek because of the hanging of Qualchan and other Indians on its banks, September 17, 1858. The hangings marked the end of the Indian wars and brought permanent peace and a feeling of safety to the whites of this territory for the first time."[42] The sentiment in the statement reflected one of several changes in attitudes toward Wright's march. In fact, there were very few settlers in the region when Wright conquered it, and complaints about Indian depredations were few. Perhaps it sounded more honorable, however, to attribute Wright's actions to a need for "protection" rather than revenge for Steptoe's defeat—or the desire for land acquisition. The claim of "permanent peace and a feeling of safety to the whites" represents one of the most compelling chapters in the heroic narrative. It is a claim that dismays and angers Native people in the region, especially when it is espoused in current times.[43]

In 1997 an attempt was made to change the name of Hangman Creek back to Latah Creek, but the U. S. Board of Geographical Names refused, saying, "There is no historical reason to change it."[44] Another unsuccessful attempt was made in 1999. There is not a uniform feeling about the name in the Native American community or in the general community. Some people prefer the name to remain "Hangman" as a reminder of the executions. Some members of the Spokane and Coeur d'Alene tribes favored Hangman, while the county commissioners sided with the Nez Perce and Yakama tribes, who favored returning the name to "Latah," meaning "grove of trees."[45] One prominent member of the Spokane tribe believes the term "Hangman Creek" is a reminder of the arrogant treatment of the tribes. Yet it is more important to her that today's young Native Americans "believe in themselves" in order to understand and strengthen their culture.[46] Albert Andrews, when asked about his feelings about using the name Hangman Creek instead of one of the old names, such as Latah or Nedwauld, paused, then said, "You know, I don't think about it." Andrews is focused on a larger landscape: the misconceptions about past events.[47]

In 1990 the Spokane Parks Board recommended that a planned golf course be named the "Creek at Qualchan" to honor Wright's best-known victim. The course straddles Hangman Creek and sits a few miles downstream from another course, called Hangman Valley Golf Course. The Qualchan name was selected over that of professional golfer Rod Funseth, a Spokane native. A suggestion was made to erect a sculpture of Qualchan, to complement a Japanese garden meant "to remind golfers of the Japanese-American vegetable farms that have become a part of the valley's history."[48] The golf course was built, but other than the name there is scant evidence of the real Qualchan—which is fine with at least some Native Americans.

Until 1973 the mascot of Eastern Washington University—located only a few miles from the Four Lakes battlefield—was the "Savages." A swath of bricks bearing a "savage" caricature became the object of a three-decade controversy, which lasted until the school's mascot was changed and the bricks were sandblasted to remove the Indian caricature. As recently as 2013 an unofficial student athletic organization adopted the "Savage" mascot until directed by the university to cease.[49] At Wellpinit High School, on the Spokane Indian Reservation, the mascot is the "Redskins." The student body is over ninety percent Native American. While the term "savage" is offensive to a great majority of Native Americans (and many non-Natives), the term "redskins" does not trouble some Native people if used in a respectful context.[50]

In 2009 Washington state's junior senator, Maria Cantwell, cosponsored a resolution in the U.S. Senate to apologize to Native Americans for a "long history of official depredations and ill-conceived policies imposed on Native Americans by the Federal Government."[51] Senator Cantwell was a member of the Senate Indian Affairs Committee. The resolution was included as part of a defense appropriations bill. President Obama signed the bill in December 2009, but it was not read publicly until May 2010 when Sen. Sam Brownback of Kansas read it at a ceremony at the Congressional Cemetery in Washington, D.C. There was little coverage and discussion in the national media. Lise Balk King wrote a column for the Indian Country Today Media Network website entitled, "A Tree Fell in the Forest: The U.S. Apologized to Native Americans and No One Heard a Sound."[52] In contrast, in 2008 Prime Minister Stephen Harper of Canada delivered a formal apology in the House of Commons, focusing on the forced removal of Native children to boarding schools. Harper said of the government, "These institutions gave rise to abuse or neglect and were inadequately controlled and we apologize for failing to protect you."[53] The apology was telecast across Canada, and it started a national conversation about the treatment of the First Nations.

The City of Spokane has a minor league baseball team called the "Indians" and a hockey team called the "Chiefs."[54] In 2006 the Spokane Indians baseball organization collaborated with the Spokane tribe to create a new logo incorporating the Salish language. During some games in 2015 the team began wearing uniforms bearing the new logo. The tribe sees the cooperation with the Indians baseball team as one way to help keep the Salish language alive and perhaps pique interest among younger people who may want to learn it.[55]

Present-day Salish version (*right*) of Spokane Indians baseball team logo (*left*). Courtesy of the Spokane Indians Baseball Club.

Despite varying, often antagonistic views from the non-Native community, many Native Americans in the region have transformed the tragedy of their violent suppression into a vehicle to teach their young people about the past while helping them prepare for the future. Mark Stanger, a Coeur d'Alene member, works to keep traditions alive. Among the lessons Stanger teaches to young members of the tribe is how to find water potatoes, a root that lives in mud next to waterways. He also teaches them about Plateau Indian culture, including ceremonies, hunting, spirituality, and environmental issues. His work reaches out not only to people with Native American ancestry but also to those who want to understand more about Native American culture and history.

Efforts continue in Spokane to raise awareness of the continuing impact of the army's actions in 1858. In 2014 the City of Spokane and the Spokane tribe agreed to designate a public plaza in downtown Spokane as the "Spokane Tribal Gathering Place." The plaza is adjacent to Huntington Park, which lies on the south side of Spokane Falls, where tribes once gathered to fish. In the summer of 2015 Ryan Feddersen, an artist and member of the Confederated Tribes of the Colville reservation, worked with

Spokane Arts to create in the plaza a collaborative art project, called *900 Horses*. Feddersen stenciled the outlines of nine hundred horses across the plaza, and provided visitors paints and brushes to color them in. Her intent was to "show the scale of what happened, and the impact it had on the tribes," she said.[56]

Also in 2015 a newspaper article again raised the issue of Wright's legacy, in particular with regard to place-names like Hangman Creek, noting the controversy over his actions. In the article Dr. Robbie Paul says that George Wright believed Native people were "heathen." "That's the legacy that we're still trying to undo," she says. "We're not less than. We're just as equal."[57]

Conclusion

The narrative that traces George Wright's legacy follows an uneven arc through history, from hero to human. To Euro-Americans, Wright's legacy was at first perfect in its portrayal: a son of New England imbued with patriotism and passion for God and country, who acted heroically in battle and removed Indians as an impediment to the destiny of a great nation. During the nineteenth century few criticized that heroic theme. The twentieth century brought increasing attention to the plight of disenfranchised Indians—but little help for them. Historians like William Compton Brown published books strongly supporting the tribes and condemning the actions of the government. Over the decades the tone shifted in newspaper columns and advertisements across the inland Pacific Northwest. By the latter half of the twentieth century, geographic place-names honoring Wright and school mascots objectifying Indians became the focus of controversy. In the twenty-first century, educational efforts are raising awareness of why historical events are still important.

In the mid-nineteenth century, when communication was limited to newspapers and word-of-mouth, rumormongers found it easy to manipulate or exaggerate information and inflame angry passions, and calmer minds found it difficult to disprove rumors. If a newspaper reported that Indians were murdering women and children, would you be more likely to take steps to eliminate the potential attacker or take your chances that the report was wrong? Likewise, when Indians heard that a heavily armed U.S. Army patrol was crossing into tribal land, was it better to wait to see if they were hostile or to take action, knowing that to wait might invite death and destruction? Add to that the knowledge in both cultures that the whites were colonists and invaders, many of whom were living on land the tribes had ceded under often questionable circumstances—or, in many cases, had not ceded at all.

In such an environment conflict was inevitable. During the nineteenth century (and today), many tribal members respected the common soldiers who fought. Not only did they value courage in battle, they realized that in some circumstances the whites were fighting for their lives. For that reason, today some tribal members, particularly the Coeur d'Alenes, honor the soldiers in Steptoe's force, who were in a sense victims of circumstance. They view George Wright's expedition across the plateau much differently: it was a march of conquest, and the strategy he used was terror. Their victory over Steptoe was won against a relatively honorable foe, while their later defeat was at the hands of an officer set on violent retribution.

Today, the Steptoe battle site is a well-maintained state park with a monument to the soldiers killed in combat. The site of George Wright's biggest battle, at Four Lakes, bears a much smaller historical marker sitting in a vacant lot at the end of a lane. One reason the monuments are so different is because white blood was spilled at Pine Creek, while the Battle of Four Lakes ended without serious injury to white participants. The Steptoe monument stands on consecrated ground, while the Four Lakes monument stands not as a memorial to the dead but as a monument to a hero with a now-unsteady legacy. As I neared the end of this project, it occurred to me that one reason the memorial at Four Lakes has been neglected was perhaps expressed by University of Kansas professor James Mayo: "Commemoration through war memorials mirrors not only what a society wants to remember but also what it wishes to forget."[1] The depth of passion that accompanies some stories of Wright's actions perhaps indicates a defensiveness that compensates for an unwillingness to admit that U.S. western expansion came at a high human price.

What of the cultural context? Today, is it unfair and misleading to "evaluate Wright's conduct by modern standards" as one historian claims?[2] Maybe the answer lies in the answer to another question: When it comes to the infliction of emotional and physical pain, are "modern standards" different than those of a century-and-a-half ago? I believe they are not, and Colonel Wright, by admitting his intent was to strike fear into the tribes, showed that he understood the power of cruelty.

Regarding the actions of historical figures, historian John Lewis Gaddis writes, "While context does not directly *cause* what happens, it can certainly determine consequences."[3] Scholar Wayne E. Lee says, "The army leadership, partly out of calculation (of how to win), made choices about forms of violence, and those choices created an atmosphere of permissiveness."[4] While conducting his theatrically gruesome executions, Wright could act without fear of punishment, and it is clear from his letters that he expected credit for his widely praised military accomplishments. Gaddis writes, "Nothing apart from the passage of time is inevitable. There are always choices, however unpromising these may have seemed at the time. Our responsibility as historians is as much to show that there were paths *not* taken as it is to explain the ones that were."[5] Gaddis believes that looking at history in such a fashion is "an act of liberation" from a rigid examination of history that expresses historical events as fixed.

If we look at George Wright as a human being having the ability to make choices, he becomes more real—even if the choices he made created unnecessary pain and trauma. He was not a hero, and at times he was cruel; he was a man created by a culture that valued conquest. His life's purpose may have been set by his temperament, education, upbringing, and military experience, but his choices—humane and inhumane—were his alone. If Wright believed that he was committing violence to limit widespread bloodshed, he could have done so by using trials that showed the tribes that he was serious about justice, rather than the injustice and insult of his "trials." How does one justify the destruction of food supplies and villages, knowing the result would be hardship for people who depend on the land and the seasons for sustenance? It is not enough to claim that such actions were acceptable in warfare or according to the rules of war. Nor is it fair to claim Wright was acting in the context of the time. Wright chose to listen to the voices that supported his worldview and acted accordingly. Others living in the same era and faced with the same cultural circumstances, made different choices.

The tribes felt betrayed, and those feelings linger. In many cases they were tolerant of newcomers and willing to share land if they were treated with respect and honesty. Conflict happened when miners, ranchers, and railroads began to take land; the tribes' goodwill ended. When asked how old enemies might bridge gaps in understanding that still exist, Colville tribal elder Albert Andrews thought a moment, then said, "I want all of us to walk through the past—all of us, Indian and white, together." Andrews used the phrase "through the past," to denote the importance of stepping back in order to move forward. Once clear and honest observations about the past are complete, it does little good to live there. In *A People's History of the United States,* Howard Zinn writes, "Those tears, that anger, cast into the past, deplete our moral energy for the present."[6]

George Wright was not more cruel or violent than many other people of the time, or of any time. Social scientists of the past half century have tried to answer the question of why normal people engage in cruelty. Phillip Zimabardo and Stanley Milgram are among those who have demonstrated that in certain circumstances, nearly anyone is capable of the kinds of acts orchestrated by Wright—regardless of the time in which they lived. It is the circumstances of location, authority and individual temperament that can result in violence.[7]

Perhaps the change in Wright's legacy can be described by the words of the nineteenth-century theologian Theodore Parker, who wrote, "The arc of the moral universe is long, but it bends toward justice."[8] It is time to see George Wright not as an angel and not as a devil, but as a human being who, through a combination of conditions, committed cruel and unjust acts. While it is fair to illuminate and condemn some of Wright's actions, we should not distance ourselves too far from him.

The legacy left by George Wright, with all of its imperfections and contradictions, can be a curse or it can be a gift. Which one to embrace is a choice to be made by future generations.

Epilogue

SEPTEMBER 2, 2012.

The road from Spokane to Wellpinit, on the Spokane reservation, passes over a high prairie on the northern edge of the Columbia Basin, then winds down past basalt cliffs to the Little Falls Dam on the Spokane River. On the other side of the river, pine trees begin to appear over clusters of yellow balsamroot, and a few miles farther on, the air is infused with the fragrance of pine and sagebrush. At Wellpinit, you land in front of a campus of reservation management buildings, including a health clinic and various other facilities. Turning left, you see a modern tribal headquarters building; down the road is the newly remodeled combination middle school–high school. Take a right turn, go a quarter mile, and you find the Catholic church, built in 1943 and boasting a fresh coat of paint. Down from the church are the fairgrounds, at which the annual powwow is held every Labor Day weekend. It features the food and craft booths you see at any country fair, but the focus is on traditional dances, music, and camaraderie.

One booth exhibits prints by George Flett, the Spokane man famed for his vibrant ledger art. At another, among the books for sale are several by Sherman Alexie, whose stories are set on the Spokane and Coeur d'Alene reservations.

At the Spokane powwow the master of ceremonies quiets the crowd in the pavilion. "In 1858," he begins, "George Wright and his soldiers came to our land, and our ancestors fought them. The army was too powerful, there were too many, with weapons better than ours. Our people suffered, and hostages were taken, and some were hanged. When the first man was hanged, he was asked if he wanted to say anything; he said no. The second man was asked, and he began to sing, and we will now honor him and all of our ancestors who suffered. This is the Death Song." A chorus of voices begins, slow and low, rising in volume and pitch, the sound swirling gently against the roof of the pavilion, curling around, gliding down through the crowd of perhaps three hundred people, nearly all Native American. The drums begin beating, softly, then more strongly, the circle sending out ripples of sound and power. Everyone, Native or not, is transfixed as the song rises in a crescendo before trailing off, sad, but not fearful. In the crowd, some people stare, many close their eyes, some sing, some hum, and the drums pound like a chorus of amplified heartbeats.

More than a century and a half later, George Wright's victims are honored.

Notes

PREFACE

1. "Peace Memorial on Indian Battle Site Unveiled," *Spokane Spokesman-Review,* Oct. 21, 1935.

2. "A Flattering Compliment to a Faithful Officer," *San Francisco Daily Alta California,* Aug. 11, 1864.

3. Robinson, "The Ordeal of General George Wright," 153.

4. Keyes, *Fifty Years,* 285.

5. "Garry of the Spokanes: An Indian Chief's Career," *Spokane Spokesman-Review,* Nov. 25, 1917.

6. Burns, *Jesuits and the Indian Wars,* 277.

7. "Indians Honor Dead: Pilgrimage Is Made," *Spokane Chronicle,* Sept. 9, 1970.

8. "General Wright to Be Superseded," *Los Angeles Star,* Jan. 23, 1864.

9. Smith, "George Wright: Peacemaker," 161.

10. Officers in state or territorial volunteer militias were, in many cases, undisciplined and violent. Officers in the regular army, many of whom attended West Point, often looked down on volunteer units as little more than thuggish gangs. This issue is taken up later in this book.

11. Wright to Price, Apr. 25, 1862, in Scott et al., *War of the Rebellion: A Compilation of the Official Records of the Union and Confederate Armies,* ser. 1, vol. 50, pt. 1, correspondence (hereafter cited as *OR,* followed by series, volume, and part number, corresp.).

12. Smith, "George Wright: Peace Maker," 165.

13. "Precedents in Indian Wars for Gen. Smith: Col. George Wright in 1858 Hung Prisoners without Trial," *New York Times,* May 1, 1902. The remark appears in an article comparing Wright's actions to those of Gen. Jacob H. Smith during the Philippine-American War. General Smith was in charge of the Ninth Infantry, the same unit commanded forty-four years earlier by Colonel Wright. In September 1901 a band of Filipino guerrillas, in an intricately designed ruse, attacked a unit of the Ninth Infantry. Of the seventy-six U.S. soldiers attacked, fifty died immediately or as a result of injuries; another twenty-two were injured. In retaliation General Smith ordered widespread attacks on people and

property, decreeing that everyone over the age of ten be killed. An estimated two thousand Filipino civilians were massacred.

14. Pinker, *Better Angels of Our Nature*, 483.

15. Author conversation with Rob McDonald, May 21, 2012.

16. Author conversation with Dr. Laurie Arnold, May 3, 2015.

17. Geographic Names Information System entry for "Hangman Creek," http://geonames.usgs.gov/apex/f?p=gnispq:3:0::NO::P3_FID:1505370.

PROLOGUE

1. Henry had formerly been the territory's surveyor general.

2. Dennis M. Powers, *Treasure Ship: The Legend and Legacy of the S.S.* Brother Jonathan (New York: Citadel, 2006), 62–66.

3. Although Wool had enemies in high places, he was known for his intellect and experience. During the decade of the Plateau War—the 1850s—Wool showed his skill at defeating political enemies by letting them think *they* had beaten *him*, knowing he would have a chance to turn his enemy's dagger around. He would not hesitate to bait his nemesis, Isaac Stevens, by accusing him of incompetence, fraud, and stupidity. Stevens's vitriolic responses often made him appear petty, leaving Wool relatively unscathed. For more information about Wool and Stevens, see Richards, *Young Man in a Hurry*, 238–65; "A Sketch of the Life and Public Services of Maj. Gen. John E. Wool," *Democratic Review*, Nov. 1851, 1–30; "Obituary of Major General John E. Wool," *New York Times*, Nov. 11, 1869.

4. "New Steamship Brother Jonathan," *San Francisco Daily Alta California*, Mar. 3, 1851.

5. J. Mayne Baltimore, "Fate of General George Wright," *Spokane Spokesman-Review*, Apr. 29, 1900.

6. The gold carried on the *Brother Jonathan* would be worth over $50 million today. Several salvage attempts have been made with only partial success. Numerous legal battles have been fought over ownership of the wreck and its treasure. While a salvage company worked to retrieve gold and artifacts from the wreck (which had drifted two miles from the original wreck site), the state of California claimed ownership and fought for rights to anything taken from it. In 1998 the U.S. Supreme Court ruled in favor of the salvage company. The state continued its battle in lower courts and as a settlement received 20 percent of the value of goods recovered. For more information about the salvage efforts and legal battles, see Powers, *Treasure Ship*; and Q. David Bowers, *The Treasure Ship: S.S.* Brother Jonathan, *Her Life and Loss, 1850–1865* (Wolfeboro, N.H.: Bowers and Merena Galleries, 1999). In addition to the gold, the payroll for soldiers at Fort Vancouver and other northwest military posts totaled $200,000 in cash. In 1999, 1,006 recovered coins were auctioned for $5.3 million. In total, only 1,265 have been recovered, leaving a fortune still on the bottom of the Pacific.

The wreck of the *Brother Jonathan* still ranks as one of the most deadly civilian ship disasters on the West Cost.

7. "Brigadier General Wright," *San Francisco Daily Alta Vista,* Aug. 4, 1865.

8. "The Remains of General Wright," *Sacramento Daily Union,* Oct. 18, 1865. Other accounts date the body's discovery to the 29th or 30th, but accounts of the place of discovery are consistent.

9. "Funeral of the Late George Wright," *San Francisco Daily Alta California,* Oct. 22, 1865. The *Alta California* and one of its advertisers were not above making money on the disaster. Barely two weeks after the tragedy, the paper ran an ad that read, "Fearful Loss of Life—We venture to say that everyone on board the Brother Jonathan would have been saved if they had had Houston, Hastings, & Co.'s life-preserving vests, and the price places them within reach of all."

10. "Gen. George Wright," *New York Times,* Sept. 7, 1865.

11. Curtis, *North American Indian,* 7: 33.

12. Brown, *Indian Side of the Story,* 306.

13. An excellent account of Kamiakin's life can be found in Scheuerman and Finley, *Finding Chief Kamiakin.*

14. "Old Garry Is Dying," *Spokane Spokesman-Review,* Jan. 10, 1892.

15. "The Life of Garry," *Spokane Spokesman-Review,* Jan. 17, 1892.

16. Ibid.

17. Ibid.

CHAPTER 1

Epigraph: George Gibbs to James Swan, Jan. 7, 1857, reprinted in Swan, *The Northwest Coast,* 429. Gibbs was a geologist and ethnologist who worked for a time with the Smithsonian. Washington Territory Governor Isaac Stevens hired him to act as an interpreter and advisor during the railroad survey of 1853–54 and during some of the Pacific Northwest treaty councils.

1. Boundaries of the Columbia Plateau, Inland Empire, and Inland Northwest vary according to source. I have used the regional delineations found in Morrissey, *Mental Territories,* and Meinig, *Spokane and the Inland Empire.* The USGS defines the Columbia Plateau as consisting of 63,000 square miles, while figures from other sources range from 50,000 to 100,000 square miles. No matter which boundary one uses, the region covered in this book falls within it.

2. For example, the map of Wright's 1858 expedition contains several similar, vague references. It was surveyed and drawn by John Mullan, Theodore Kolecki, and Gustavus Sohon. While too large to be reproduced here in its entirety, it can be viewed at www.sos.wa.gov/legacy/maps_detail.aspx?m=150.

3. Meinig, *Great Columbia Plain,* 18. Meinig was raised in the town of Palouse, in the heart of the region once inhabited or frequented by the Palouse, Nez Perce, Coeur d'Alene, and Spokane Indians, among others.

4. Hoopes, *Indian Affairs*, 69.

5. Raymond Lasmanis, *The Geology of Washington: Rocks and Minerals*, vol. 66, no. 4 (1991): 262–277, www.dnr.wa.gov/researchscience/topics/geologyof washington/pages/columbia.aspx.

6. Among sources used for information on the geology of the Columbia Plateau are Meinig, *Great Columbia Plain*, 3–25; Victor R. Baker, "The Channeled Scablands: A Retrospective," *Annual Review of Earth and Planetary Sciences*, Dec. 30, 2008, 6.1–6.19, http://ice.tsu.ru/files/paul/Baker_-_Review.pdf; "Geology of the Palouse," from *GeoNote*, online publication of the Idaho Geological Survey (University of Idaho), http://geology.isu.edu/Digital_Geology_Idaho/Module13/Geology_of_the_Palouse_geonote_09.pdf; and Soennichsen, *Bretz's Flood*, 82–93.

7. "A Review of Oral History Information of the Confederated Tribes of the Umatilla," attachment 2, p. 6 (hereafter "Umatilla Oral History," followed by page number).

8. Steptoe Butte is fifty miles south of Spokane. The term "steptoe" is now used worldwide to designate a landform protruding from a basalt base: see "Umatilla Oral History," 6–7. John Mullan reported that the Spokane and Coeur d'Alene peoples used the Salish term "Se-emp-tee-ta," and the Sahaptin-speaking Nez Perces and Palouse "E-o-mosh-toss," as noted in Elliott, "Steptoe Butte and Steptoe Battlefield," 285–314.

9. For a discussion of J Harlan Bretz's work, see Soennichsen, *Bretz's Flood*. Bretz used the letter *J* as his first name, with no period.

10. Clark, *Indian Legends*, 116–17.

11. "Umatilla Oral History," 5–6.

12. Ibid., 7–8.

13. Ibid. Eells was the son of Cushing and Myra Eells, who in 1838 established the Tshimakain Mission near present-day Spokane. The protestant mission was cofounded by Elkanah and Mary Richardson Walker.

14. Ibid., 6–8.

15. Kolecki to Mullan, Feb. 8, 1860, in Mullan, *Report on the Construction of a Military Road*, 104.

16. The relationship between Northwest Indians and the land is addressed in a number of documents and books, including Clark, *Indian Legends*; Ruby and Brown, *Spokane Indians*; and Trafzer and Scheuerman, *Renegade Tribe*.

17. Remarks from Sla-hal conference, Seattle Pacific University, May 6, 2012, attended by the author.

18. Hunn, "Columbia Plateau Indian Place Names," 6–7. Tribes using Sahaptin-based languages populated roughly half of the plateau.

19. Trafzer, "The Legacy of the Walla Walla Council," 404.

20. Frey, *Landscape Traveled by Coyote and Crane*, 8. Frey notes that Catholic missionary Joseph Joset referred to all Coeur d'Alene people as the Schitsus, although at one time the term may have referred to one band of the tribe. Frey is professor of ethnography at the University of Idaho.

21. Trafzer and Scheuerman, *Renegade Tribe*, 98.

22. Ruby and Brown, *Spokane Indians*, 21.

23. Author interview with Mark Stanger, Coeur d'Alene tribe, May 13, 2014.

24. Joseph Joset Personal Papers, Jesuit Oregon Province Archive, Gonzaga University Special Collections, Foley Center Library, Spokane, Wash., 2:2 (hereafter referred to as Joset manuscript). Father Joset wrote at least three accounts of the Plateau Indian War. While they are nearly identical, there are a few inconsistencies and errors. In this case, Joset notes the year of the meeting on the Spokane River as 1854, instead of the correct year, 1855. Given the nature of events and the number of participants, various versions of events exist. Father Joset was in a position to view both sides, and his accounts seem to relate the events without vilifying or canonizing participants.

25. USGS Survey Fact Sheet 036-00, http://pubs.usgs.gov/fs/2000/fs036-00.

CHAPTER 2

Epigraph: Washington Irving, *A History of New York*, book 1, 65–66.

1. The town of "Norwhich" had been established on July 5, 1761, by the proclamation of King George III. At the time, it was located in the province of New Hampshire; Vermont would become a republic in 1777 and a state in 1791.

2. Swanton, *Indian Tribes of North America*, 18–19; also see, Hoxie, *Encyclopedia of North American Indians*, 1–4.

3. Partridge, *History of Norwich, Vermont*, 35.

4. Ibid. Wheelock had operated Doctor Wheelock's Indian School in Lebanon, Connecticut, before moving to the wilds along the Connecticut River.

5. *Native Languages of the Americas*, s.v. "Abenaki," www.native-languages.org/abenaki.htm.

6. Wright apparently did not have a middle name or initial. Neither Norwich town records nor West Point records show a middle initial, and he never used one in his correspondence. He has sometimes been confused with George B. Wright, a Civil War–era general from Ohio. During Wright's career there were at least two army officers named George M. Wright; neither was any relation. In his memoir, Erasmus Darwin Keyes incorrectly attributes to Wright a middle initial of *H*. A younger officer, George H. Wright, was posted in Montana and in at least a few instances has been confused with George Wright. Some references in the California State Archives attribute a middle initial of *F*, but it does not appear in primary sources, and the references may have been referring to George F. Wright, a California attorney who worked with several tribes. For a short time, the *George Wright*, a steamboat named after Wright, traveled the Columbia River. One post on a genealogy site assumes the middle initial *S*, but there are no records in support. The *George S. Wright*, an ocean steamer that traveled the Pacific Northwest coast from 1860–1873, was named after a man not related to the subject of this book.

7. New England Congregationalism of the time often was, and sometimes still is, referred to as Puritanism.

8. J. Bremer Francis, *Puritanism: A Very Short Introduction* (New York: Oxford University Press, 2009), 2–3.

9. Keyes, *Fifty Years*, 87, 83. Keyes was born in Massachusetts in 1810 and spent part of his youth in Maine. He graduated from West Point in 1832, ten years after Wright. In referring to Puritanism, Keyes wrote that he included "Presbyterians, Congregationalists, Methodists, and Baptists—all of whom I class together as Puritans in their relations to political and civil life," ibid., 83–84.

10. Partridge, *History of Norwich*, 35.

11. Skelton, *American Profession of Arms*, 318–19.

12. Wright to Jones, June 11, 1856, HED 1, 34th Cong., 3rd sess. (1857), 161.

13. Wright to Mackall, Sept. 9, 1858, Report of the Secretary of War, SED 32, 35th Cong., 2nd sess. (1859), 25.

14. Schlicke, *General George Wright*, 9.

15. Bogle, "Sylvanus Thayer and Ethical Instruction," 63. Bogle is an associate professor at the U.S. Naval Academy.

16. Skelton, *American Profession of Arms*, 122–23.

17. Bogle, "Sylvanus Thayer and Ethical Instruction," 79, 64.

18. Ibid., 65.

19. Vattel, *Law of Nations*, 335; Wright to Mackall, Sept. 10, 1858, quoted in Manring, *Conquest of the Coeur d'Alenes*, 213–14.

20. The term "necessity" as justification for possibly illegal official acts appears frequently in official letters written by other army officers.

21. Weidenbaum, *Necessity in International Law*, 114.

22. Vattel, *Law of Nations*, 456.

23. Ibid., 348.

24. Kip, *Indian War*, 117.

25. Wright to Mackall, Sept. 30, 1858, in Manring, *Conquest of the Coeur d'Alenes*, 254.

26. William Paley was the archduke of Carlisle. His *Principles of Moral Philosophy and Natural Theology* was required reading at Cambridge well into the mid-nineteenth century. Charles Darwin was strongly influenced by Paley's writing, and he carried *Principles of Moral Philosophy* with him on the *Beagle*. Paley's work and that of Charles Lyell (*Principles of Geology*) were instrumental in Darwin's rethinking the concept of creation: interview with Cynthia Cutler, Eastern Washington University Professor of Leadership and Integrative Studies.

27. Paley, *Principles of Moral Philosophy*, quoted in Bogle, "Sylvanus Thayer and Ethical Instruction," 72.

28. Wright's tactics and their validity are addressed in chapter 12; on necessity and the punishment and subjugation of the tribes, see chapters 8–10.

29. Paley, *Principles of Moral Philosophy*, 465.

30. Irving, *History of New York*, 76.

31. Paley, *Principles of Moral Philosophy*, 474, 467.

32. Irving, *History of New York*, 76.

33. Bonura, "French Inspired Way of War," 8.

34. Lee, *Barbarians and Brothers*, 220–21.

35. Bonura, "French Inspired Way of War," 10–19.

36. Skelton, *American Profession of Arms*, 167.

37. Bogle, "Sylvanus Thayer and Ethical Instruction," 72ff; and Schlicke, *General George Wright*, 8–13.

38. In February 1832 Cantonment Leavenworth became Fort Leavenworth. Kansas City was officially founded in 1838, www.kancoll.org/books/cutler/leavenworth/leavenworth-co-p2.html.

39. Wright to Bliss, Mar. 18, 1829, in Jensen, "Wright-Beauchampe Investigation," 133–43. The letter was written from the Cabannes Trading House near Council Bluffs.

40. Ibid.

41. *Kansas: A Guide*, 240.

42. Margaret Wallace Forster's ancestors settled in Pennsylvania in the early eighteenth century Margaret's last name incorrectly appears as *Foster* in some historical records; Schlicke, *General George Wright*, 22.

43. Egle, *Pennsylvania Genealogies*, 219; Schlicke, *General George Wright*, 65.

44. Wright wrote at least three letters to army headquarters from Norwich in November and December, 1836. In each he reported himself on leave of absence, as was required of him: National Archive Military Records, Letters Received, www.fold3.com/image/" \l "291545995. In his biography of Wright, Schlicke documented three children (41–46).

45. Grant, *Memoirs*, 36.

46. Halswelle, *Poems by Thomas Moore*, 421.

47. Causes of death are not noted. Roswell's information is from the *Army and Navy Chronicle* 2, no. 13 (Mar. 31, 1836), 201. James Heron's death was reported in the *Chronicle* on July 31, 1837.

48. In 1830 there were 592 officers in the army, but by 1860 the number had doubled: see Skelton, "Army Officers' Attitudes," 113.

49. A brevet was an award for "gallant and meritorious" conduct in war. It was a precursor to medals for heroism and valor. While in his home regiment, a subordinate officer would not retain his brevet rank; hence, in the subsequent Mexican-American war Wright would carry his rank as captain: see Hemphill, *West Pointers and Early Washington*, 20.

50. For more about Wright's early military career, see Schlicke, *General George Wright*.

51. Wright to Townsend, Mar. 10, 1864, in "Indian-White Relationships in Northern California," Bleyhl Collection, Meriam Library, California State University–Chico, #3321, 1106, www.csuchico.edu/lbib/spc/bleyhl.

52. Schlicke, *General George Wright*, 95–103.

53. "Indian-White Relationships in Northern California," #1999, 472.

54. The Ninth Infantry regiment was originally formed in 1798, then disbanded shortly thereafter. It was reformed for the War of 1812, disbanded, reformed for the Mexican-American War, and then disbanded again.

55. George Dandy, "Reminiscences," monograph written by General Dandy in 1907, when he was seventy-eight. From a typescript in Manuscripts, Archives and Special Collections, Washington State University, William Compton Brown papers, cage 196, box 14, file 144.

CHAPTER 3

1. Annual Report of the Department of the Interior, HED 2, 35th Cong., 1st sess., vol. 1 (1857), 62; the quotations in the following paragraph are from this source.

2. Boyd, *Coming of the Spirit of Pestilence*, 3.

3. Stevens, *Life of Isaac Stevens*, 2: 17–23.

4. Gibbs to McClellan, Mar. 4, 1854, in Joseph Henry et al., *Reports of Explorations and Surveys to Ascertain the Most Practicable and Economical Route for a Railroad from the Mississippi River to the Pacific Ocean* (Washington, D.C.: A. O. P. Nicholson, 1855–1860), 402ff.

5. Isaac Stevens, Washington's territorial governor and Indian agent, conducted a census published in 1857. At the time Stevens kept detailed population counts to include in his treaty reports. The figures are taken from the appendix found in Hazard Stevens, *Life of Isaac Stevens*, 503–504. Stevens's tally included 3,300 Nez Perces; 3,900 Yakamas, Palouses, and "Columbia River" and nearby tribes; 2,200 Spokanes; 500 Coeur d'Alenes; and 2,250 Flatheads and other tribes.

6. Ruby and Brown, *Indians of the Pacific Northwest*, 30.

7. See, for example, Ray, *Cultural Relations in the Plateau*; Ruby and Brown, *Indians of the Pacific Northwest*; Trafzer, *The Palouse Indians* and *The Chinook*; and Scheuerman and Finley, *Finding Chief Kamiakin*.

8. Walker and Sturtevant, *Handbook of North American Indians*, 12: 11ff.

9. Ray, *Cultural Relations in the Plateau*, 40–51.

10. De Smet to S. F. Tappan, May 1870, in De Smet, *Life, Letters, and Travels* 4: 1224.

11. Ray, *Cultural Relations in the Plateau*, 35.

12. Verne Ray writes of the incident in *Cultural Relations in the Plateau*, 35. Among the Nez Perce, Coeur d'Alene, Spokane, and other tribes, some chiefs were more pacifist than others, influenced by both tribal culture and individual temperament.

13. For comprehensive synopses of Northwest tribes, see Ruby et al., *Guide to the Indian Tribes.*

14. Ruby et al., *Guide to the Indian Tribes,* 381.

15. Ray, *Cultural Relations in the Plateau,* 13. "Sanpoil" (sometimes "San Poil") is attributed to an Okanogan term meaning "gray as far as one can see." Some attribute it to the French *"sans poil,"* meaning "without fur"; see the website for the Confederated Tribes of the Colville Reservation, www.colvilletribes.com/keller_district.php.

16. On such a trip in 1843, Elijah, the son of Walla Walla chief Peopeomoxmox, was murdered by an American at Sutter's Fort. The incident nearly started a wide-ranging war, but over time tempers cooled.

17. Garth, "Early Nineteenth-Century Tribal Relations," 43–45.

18. "Spokanes Loath to Leave Site their Ancestors Loved," *Spokane Spokesman-Review,* Apr. 9, 1916.

19. Ray, *Cultural Relations in the Plateau,* 13.

20. Garth, "Early Nineteenth-Century Tribal Relations," 52–54.

21. Ray, *Cultural Relations in the Plateau,* 34.

22. Numerous books give comprehensive accounts of Plateau tribal culture, including those by Ruby and Brown, Trafzer, Scheuerman, and Cebula.

23. Cox, *Adventures on the Columbia River,* 180.

24. Parker, *Journal of an Exploring Tour,* 293.

25. Unruh, *Plains Across,* 158, 184–86. For a detailed analysis and discussion regarding emigrant travel, including fatalities, see Unruh, *Plains Across,* 379–416. "Mountain fever" was a term used to describe a number of diseases, including tick-borne illness, malaria, and typhus; for information about diseases in the Pacific Northwest, see Boyd, *Coming of the Spirit of Pestilence.*

26. Unruh, *Plains Across,* 177, 395.

27. Report of the Secretary of the Interior, Dec. 5, 1853, appendix to the Cong. Globe, 33rd Cong., 1st sess. (1858), 26.

28. The *Truth Teller* was a short-lived paper printed in Steilacoom, Washington Territory. It was established to investigate the abuses involved in the arrest and execution of Nisqually chief Leschi. The paper was published by "Ann Onymous," who was actually Lt. August Kautz. He was assisted in his endeavor by his brother, Fred Kautz, and by William Fraser Tolmie, who was the chief factor for the Hudson's Bay Company at Fort Nisqually on Puget Sound.

29. For more about Hitchcock's experiences, see Hitchcock, *Traveler in Indian Territory.*

30. Skelton, "Army Officers' Attitudes," 119. While this group of officers is a small sample, it is noteworthy that Wool did not attend West Point; Hitchcock attended before the installation of the new curriculum; and Sherman, while a graduate of West Point, showed distinct disdain toward the strictures at the academy. Sherman's grades were exceeded by his willingness to attract demerits.

31. Coffman, *Old Army,* 73.

32. An in-depth account of the Whitman events can be found in Ruby and Brown, *Cayuse Indians.*

33. Victor, *River of the West,* 493–96. Joseph Meek had an Indian wife, and their daughter, Helen, had become stricken with the measles before the Indian attack; Dr. Whitman had said that he did not expect her to live.

34. On Scott's instructions and warnings to Hitchcock, see Croffut, *Fifty Years in Camp and Field,* 380–82. The fare for the journey was $330, but with related expenses, including those necessary to cross the Isthmus of Panama, the cost would total more than $400, equal to approximately $11,400 in 2015 dollars: see Minneapolis Federal Reserve Bank, Consumer Price Index Estimate, 1800–2015, found at www.minneapolisfed.org/community_education/teacher/calc/hist1800.cfm. Data is from U.S. Department of Labor sources. Benicia is located between San Francisco and Sacramento. The Pacific Division headquarters was established there because of its proximity to both San Francisco Bay and to those parts of northern California that tended to experience frequent conflict between Indian tribes and settlers.

35. Croffut, *Fifty Years in Camp and Field,* 389. Hitchcock's library was shipped at a cost of $200 and took nine months to arrive in California.

36. Townsend to Wright, Feb. 21, 1854, in "Indian-White Relationships in Northern California," 766.

37. Joel Graham Trimble, quoted in Will J. Trimble, "Soldier of the Oregon Frontier," 47.

38. In 1832 Wool toured Europe in order to evaluate military strategies and their possible application within the U.S. Army.

39. Wool to Calhoun, undated, referring to inspection report of Dec. 12, 1819, quoted in Skelton, "Army in the Age of the Common Man," 95.

40. Heitman, *Historical Register,* 49.

41. Prucha, *Documents of U.S. Indian Policy,* 12.

42. Annual Report of the Commissioner of Indian Affairs, Nov. 1852, SED 1, 32nd Cong., 2nd sess. (1852), 293.

43. Prucha, *Documents of U.S. Indian Policy,* 89–90.

44. The murder of Chief Peopeo-moxmox of the Walla Wallas provides one example: see Brown, *Indian Side of the Story,* 128; and Trafzer and Scheuerman, *Renegade Tribe,* 69.

45. "A Walla Walla Pioneer," in Washington Pioneer Project, *Told By the Pioneers: Reminiscences of Pioneer Life in Washington,* W.P.A. project no. 5841 (1938), vol. 2, 35.

46. *Portland Weekly Oregonian,* Oct. 20, 1855.

47. Utley, *Frontiersmen in Blue,* 101.

CHAPTER 4

Epigraph: Kent Richards, "Isaac Stevens and Federal Military Power in Washington Territory," 82.

1. Gibbs to Swan, Jan. 7, 1857, in Swan, *Northwest Coast,* 427.

2. Richards, *Isaac I. Stevens*, 26.

3. Ibid., 293. The wording in the Richards account about the injury seems to indicate that Wright helped Stevens from the battlefield, but Wright was the injured party. Later, during the Mexican-American War's final battle, Stevens was shot in the foot, a painful injury that became infected and nearly took his life.

4. For current essays on the impact of the Stevens treaties, see Alexandra Harmon, ed., *The Power of Promises: Rethinking Indian Treaties in the Pacific Northwest* (Seattle: University of Washington Press, 2008). West of the Cascades, the Medicine Creek Treaty was perhaps the most controversial. A comprehensive account of that treaty can be found in Kluger, *Bitter Waters of Medicine Creek*.

5. "Indian Wars of 1855," *New York Times*, Mar. 24, 1856.

6. Kip, *Indian Council*, 190. Kip kept a journal during the 1858 expedition. He attended West Point but did not graduate. During the Civil War he served on General Sheridan's staff. He received three brevets for bravery during the war and until his death in 1899 was known as "Colonel Kip." From "Col. Lawrence Kip Dead," *New York Times*, Nov. 18, 1899. The term "Snake Indians" referred to bands of Shoshones, Bannocks, or Northern Paiutes.

7. Josephy, *Nez Perce Indians*, 294.

8. Kip, *Indian Council*, 16.

9. Ibid., 17. Lewis and Clark referred to the Nez Perce as the Choppunish.

10. Josephy, *Nez Perce Indians*, 317.

11. Kip, *Indian Council*, 19.

12. James Doty, *Digest of the Journal of James Doty*, Manuscripts, Archives, and Special Collections, Washington State University Libraries, cage 196, box 14, folder 144, 5.

13. Kip, *Indian Council*, 19.

14. Ibid., 20.

15. Kluger, *Bitter Waters of Medicine Creek*, 111–12.

16. For more on Stevens's strategy, see Josephy, *Nez Perce Indians*, 319.

17. Doty, *Journal of James Doty*, 5.

18. Kip, *Indian Council*, 25.

19. Ibid., 28.

20. Clark, "Military History of Oregon," 28–29.

21. Kip, *Indian Council*, 18.

22. Ibid., 32.

23. Ibid., 34.

24. Ibid., 35.

25. Ibid., 36–37.

26. Ibid., 39.

27. Josephy, *Nez Perce Indians*, 365.

28. Kip, *Indian Council*, 39–40.

29. *Indian Affairs Laws and Treaties*, vol. 2, SED 452, 37th Cong., 1st sess. (1903), 524.

30. The first article of the treaty, Article 1, also made clear that ratification was required for white settlement: "The said tribes and bands agree to remove to and settle upon the same within one year after the ratification of this treaty, without any additional expense to the Government other than is provided by this treaty, and until the expiration of the time specified, the said bands shall be permitted to occupy and reside upon the tracts now possessed by them, guaranteeing to all citizen[s] of the United States, the right to enter upon and occupy as settlers any lands not actually enclosed by said Indians."

31. The proclamation by Stevens was dated Mar. 18, 1855, and was run periodically throughout the year.

32. *Olympia Pioneer and Democrat,* July 13, 1855.

33. Letter from the Secretary of War, Mar. 3, 1859, HED 114, 35th Cong., 2nd sess. (1859), 2. Secretary of War John Floyd wrote that much of Cram's report was "irrelevant" and included "animadversions upon public functionaries" [inappropriate criticism].

34. Cram, *Topographical Memoir,* 84.

35. The same accusation was made after the Medicine Creek Treaty in western Washington Territory: see Kluger, *Bitter Waters of Medicine Creek.*

36. The reservation established under the treaty is managed by the Confederated Salish and Kootenai Tribes, headquartered in Pablo, Montana, in the Mission Valley, north of Missoula.

37. The council took place at the confluence of the Missouri and Judith Rivers, approximately five hundred miles east of present-day Spokane.

38. *Olympia Pioneer and Democrat,* Jan. 25, 1856.

39. Stevens to Nesmith, June 25, 1858, in Todd, "Letters of Governor Stevens," 442.

40. Stevens to the House of Representatives, May 31, 1858, appendix to the Cong. Globe, 35th Cong., 1st sess. (1858), 490.

41. Fort Colville was established in 1859 by the U.S. Army. Prior to that, in 1825 "Fort Colvile" was established by the Hudson's Bay Company as a trading post. The earlier fort was located fifteen miles west of the army post. The site was inundated by the Columbia River after the completion of Grand Coulee Dam. For a discussion about the death of the miners, see Richards, *Young Man in a Hurry,* 236; and Brown, *Indian Side of the Story,* 131–34.

42. "The Indians—East and West," *Olympia Pioneer and Democrat,* Oct. 12, 1855.

43. Quoted in Kluger, *Bitter Waters of Medicine Creek,* 124.

44. Lee, *Barbarians and Brothers,* 222.

45. Cram, *Topographical Memoir,* 85–88.

46. Old Fort Walla Walla was also known as Fort Nez Perce. It was located near the confluence of the Walla Walla and Columbia Rivers.

47. Nesmith to Curry, Nov. 22, 1855, *Journal of the House of Representatives of the Territory of Oregon,* Dec. 3, 1855–Jan. 31, 1856 (Salem: Asahel Bush, printer, 1856), 78.

48. Lyman, *History of Old Walla Walla,* 15.

49. Coone, "Reminiscences," 17.

50. Trafzer and Scheuerman, *Renegade Tribe,* 69.

51. Betty Lou Gaeng, "Chirouse: The Reverend Father Eugene Casimir Chirouse, a Pioneer in Oregon and Washington Territories" (2011), 23–24, www.rootsweb.ancestry.com/~wasigs/CHIROUSE.pdf.

52. See the official website for the Confederated Tribes of the Umatilla Indian Reservation, http://ctuir.org.

53. See the official website for the Confederated Tribes and Bands of the Yakama Nation, www.yakamanation-nsn.gov.

54. Ruby, Brown, and Collins, *Guide to Indian Tribes,* 310; for more on the Nez Perces, see Josephy, *Nez Perce Indians.*

55. Nabakov, *Native American Testimony,* 129–133.

56. Author interview with Paul Wapato, Mar. 20, 2015.

57. A detailed history of relations between the U.S. Government and the Coeur d'Alene tribe can be found in the June 2001 Supreme Court opinion in *Idaho v. United States, et al.,* concerning ownership of the southern portion of Lake Coeur d'Alene and the St. Joe River. The court held that title to the contested area belonged to the U.S. government, in trust for the tribe. In other words, it was, and is, considered part of the reservation.

58. The Colville Confederation includes the following tribes: Arrow Lakes, Methow, Wenatchi, Palus (Palouse), Okanogan, Sanpoil, Colville, Nespelem, Entiat, Chelan, Moses-Columbia, and Nez Perce (Chief Joseph): see the Colville Confederated Tribes website, www.colvilletribes.com/index.php. A detailed history of the Colville reservation can be found in Ruby and Brown, *Indian Tribes of the Pacific Northwest.*

59. The statistics are from Columbia River Inter-Tribal Fish Commission website, www.critfc.org/member_tribes_overview/nez-perce-tribe.

CHAPTER 5

1. De Smet, *Life, Letters, and Travels,* 3: 753–54. De Smet writes that the suppression of the Columbia tribes and the army's incursion into the Yakima Valley stirred up fear among the Plateau tribes.

2. France is 211,000 square miles, while the Columbia's watershed, 15 percent of which is in Canada, is 260,000 square miles. The data are from the USGS website, http://vulcan.wr.usgs.gov/Volcanoes/Washington/ColumbiaRiver/description_columbia_river.html.

3. De Smet, *Life, Letters, and Travels,* 2: 555.

4. For a summary of the forces shaping the Cascades, see David Wilma, "Landslide Blocks the Columbia River in about 1450," www.historylink.org/index.cfm?DisplayPage=output.cfm&file_id=7797; and Richard Hill, "A New

Look at an Old Landslide," http://landslides.usgs.gov/recent/archives/1999bonneville.php.

5. Ruby, Brown, and Collins, *Guide to the Indian Tribes,* 379.

6. Ibid., 379.

7. See Ruby, Brown, and Collins, *Guide to the Indian Tribes,* for more information.

8. Lewis and Clark, *Travels to the Source of the Missouri River,* 2: 295–305, Lewis journal Oct. 29–Nov. 1, 1805. The sacacommis is an evergreen berry bush that bears bitter red berries used for medicinal purposes. If eaten raw, they are somewhat bitter, so they were often cooked for consumption.

9. Ibid., 3: 123.

10. De Smet to Father Provincial, letter 19, written from Fort Walla Walla, July 18, 1846, in De Smet, *Oregon Missions,* 228–29. The term "Great Cascades of the Columbia" was sometimes also used in reference to Celilo Falls, about fifty miles upstream from the Cascades Rapids.

11. De Smet, *Oregon Missions,* 232.

12. Ibid., 231. The Indian narrative matches the view of modern geologists: the Cascade Rapids were formed by great landslides. For more on this, see note 4, this chapter.

13. "Diary of John S. Zeiber, 1851," *Transactions of the Forty-Eighth Annual Reunion of the Oregon Pioneer Association,* July 1, 1920 (Portland: Chausse-Prudhomme, 1923), 333.

14. Origen Thompson, "Crossing the Plains: Narrative of the Scenes, Incidents, and Adventures Attending the Overland Journey of the Decatur and Rush County Emigrants to the 'Far Off' Oregon, in 1852" (Greensburg, Ind.: Orville Thomson, 1896).

15. Unruh, *Plains Across,* 342–44.

16. From the diary of Elizabeth Dickson Smith Greer, quoted in Lancaster, *The Columbia,* 44.

17. Lancaster, *The Columbia,* 90; and Bancroft, *History of Washington,* 145.

18. Townsend to Wright, Jan. 19, 1856, HED 1, 34th Cong., 3rd sess. (1856), 163–65.

19. Burns, *Jesuits and the Indian Wars,* 142. A *kepi* is a French military cap with a bill and round top.

20. Sheridan, *Memoirs,* 1: 70–71.

21. Stevens *Message of the Governor,* 67. The "dog in the manger" refers to one who keeps something from someone else, just for spite.

22. A bateau is a flat-bottomed river boat.

23. Accounts of the Cascades battle here are derived from sources involved in the fighting: Lawrence Coe (in a letter to Putnam Bradford; see note 35, this chapter), James Elgin, and Sgt. Robert Williams. Coe and Elgin were among the besieged in the store, and Williams was one of the soldiers trapped in the blockhouse at the middle landing. See Williams, "The Cascades Massacre," 69–89; and James Elgin letter, *Portland Oregonian,* May 9, 1886.

24. Diary of Lawrence W. Coe, from "History of Early Pioneer Families of Hood River, Oregon," compiled by Mrs. D. M. Coon, http://freepages.genealogy.rootsweb.ancestry.com/~bryajw/HoodRiverPioneers.

25. Ibid.

26. Sheridan, *Memoirs,* 1: 74. Dragoons were mounted soldiers skilled in fighting at close quarters. They normally carried carbines and sabers.

27. Ibid., 75.

28. Ibid., 57.

29. Ibid., 83.

30. Graham, "Massacre on the Frontier," 233.

31. Ibid., 234.

32. Sheridan, *Memoirs,* 1: 82.

33. Ibid., 84.

34. Lawrence Coe, quoted in Hines, *Illustrated History,* 214.

35. Coe's full account can be found at www.columbiagorge.org/wp-content/uploads/docs/Coe's_Letter_of_Cascade_Massacre.pdf.

36. Iman, "My Arrival in Washington," 254–60.

37. Graham, "Massacre on the Frontier," 234–35.

38. Ibid., 236.

39. Sheridan to Wright, quoted in Boyden, *Warrior of the Mist,* 237.

40. Sheridan, *Memoirs,* 1: 89.

41. Sheridan would earn an enduring reputation during the Civil War and later would become known as a relentless Indian fighter. However, during his short stay in the Pacific Northwest as Wright's subordinate, he took an Indian wife. Elizabeth Gilliam Jones had settled in Oregon Territory with her parents and knew Sheridan: "I knew Sheridan's squaw wife, who was the daughter of Chief Harney of the Rogue River Tribe, and who had been at our house a number of times. She was a bright little woman, very good looking, and quite likable. Sheridan had always been good and kind to her, and taught her to read and do many things. They had no children, and when he went back to Washington and left her, it almost broke her heart."

Sheridan's wife, whom whites called Frances, had an opportunity to go to Washington, D.C., as part of a government-paid trip. Upon her return, she visited Elizabeth Gilliam Jones and reported that while in Washington, she had an opportunity to see Sheridan. According to Mrs. Jones, "He came and shook hands with them all, and took her hand and asked about her welfare and then took them all upon the rostrum and introduced them. After that she never saw him again." Jones also reported, "It was no uncommon thing for a white man to have a squaw wife in those days." See "Lieutenants Grant and Sheridan's Indian Wives," L. V. McWhorter Papers, Manuscripts, Archives, and Special Collections, Washington State University Libraries, box 24, file 205.

42. *San Francisco Daily Alta California,* May 1856; column reprinted from the *Argus,* an Oregon Territory newspaper.

43. Wright to Wool, Apr. 18, 1856, quoted in Boyden, *Warrior of the Mist*, 238. Wright used the word "embarrass" to mean to interfere with, or, as Webster's 1828 dictionary put it, "to entangle."

44. Wool to Thomas, July 1, 1856, HED 1, 34th Cong., 3rd sess. (1857), 153–55.

45. Some scholars, including Scheuerman and Finley, use the term "Battle of the Cascades": see *Finding Chief Kamiakin.*

46. "The Indian War in Washington Territory," *New York Times*, June 23, 1856.

47. Speech of the Hon. J. Patton Anderson (Democrat) on the Indian War in Washington and Oregon, Aug. 6, 1856, appendix to Cong. Globe, 34th Cong., 1st sess. (1856), 1191.

48. Gibbs to Swan, Jan. 7, 1857, http://washingtonhistoryonline.org/treaty trail/aftermath/gibbs-report.htm. Gibbs was also a naturalist and later contributed much of his extensive collection of minerals, plants, insects, and animals. For ten years he worked at the Smithsonian studying Indian languages.

49. Ibid.

50. Mackall to Wright, July 3, 1856, HED 1, 34th Cong., 3rd sess. (1857), 163.

51. Wright to Mackall, July 18, 1856, ibid., 180.

52. Sheridan, *Memoirs*, 1: 89–90.

53. Elliott, "The Dalles-Celilo Portage," 134.

CHAPTER 6

1. Stevens's strongest supporter was his son, Hazard, who wrote a two-volume, adulatory biography after his father's death, *The Life of Isaac Ingalls Stevens* (1900).

2. For example, see Alexandra Harmon, ed., *The Power of Promises* (University of Washington Press, 2008). The volume is a collection of scholarly papers regarding the treaties. In 2005 Washington's governor was a key speaker at a symposium at Evergreen State College concerning treaties and Indian rights.

3. Fitzhugh to Stevens, June 20, 1856, in Stevens, *Message of the Governor*, 3.

4. Wool to Wright, Aug. 4, 1856, HED 1, 34th Cong., 3rd sess. (1857), 168.

5. Wool to Stevens, Feb. 12, 1856, in Stevens, *Message of the Governor*, 141.

6. Stevens to Wool, Mar. 20, 1856, ibid., 143–51.

7. Scott to Davis, May 2, 1856, SED 66, 34th Cong., 1st sess. (1856), 61.

8. Stevens to Wright, Apr. 2, 1856, in Stevens, *Message of the Governor*, 164.

9. Wright to Stevens, Apr. 10, 1856, ibid., 166.

10. Thompson to Wright, Apr. 26, 1856, *Journal of the House of Representatives of the Territory of Oregon during the Eighth Regular Session* (Salem, Ore.: Asahel Bush, printer, 1856), 45–46.

11. Wright to Thompson, May 19, 1856, ibid., 48.

12. Stevens, *Message of the Governor*, 5.

13. Kluger, *Bitter Waters of Medicine Creek*, 170.

14. Ibid., 171–73.

15. Ibid., 172.

16. Wright to Jones, May 30, 1856, SED 5, 34th Cong. 3rd sess. (1857), 152.

17. Bornstein, *How to Change the World,* 49–50. Bornstein believes that empathy-based ethics became necessary as cultures began intermixing in the late nineteenth and early twentieth centuries. Rather than being guided by rules, people had to become self-guiding using rules of behavior based on empathy.

18. Wright to Jones, May 30, 1856, SED 5, 34th Cong. 3rd sess. (1857), 152.

19. Stevens to Wright, June 18, 1856, ibid., 69.

20. Fitzhugh to Stevens, June 20, 1856, ibid., 339.

21. Wright to Jones, June 11, 1856, HED 1, 34th Cong., 3rd sess. (1857), 161.

22. Ibid.

23. Ibid.

24. For more about Kamiakin's life after the Plateau war, see Scheuerman and Finley, *Finding Chief Kamiakin,* chapter 7.

25. Winthrop, *Canoe and Saddle,* 294–95.

26. "Aged Kamiakin Lives with Past and Present," by Robert Browning, *Seattle Post Intelligencer,* Mar. 1, 1953.

27. Wright to Jones, June 11, 1856, HED 1, 34th Cong., 3rd sess. (1857), 161.

28. Wright to Jones, June 20, 1856, ibid., 163. The letter was written from camp on the Yakima River in the "Kittetas" (Kittatas) Valley.

29. Mackall to Wright, July 3, 1856, HED 1, 34th Cong., 3rd sess. (1857), 166. Civilians supplied the army with food and other supplies and were paid in scrip guaranteed by the federal government. Wool openly accused Stevens of encouraging violence in order to line the pockets of businessmen, virtually all of whom supported the governor.

30. Wright to Jones, June 20, 1856, ibid., 175.

31. De Lacy, *Diary of the Yakima Indian War Kept By W. W. De Lacy, Captain, Engineers and Acting Adjutant, Washington Territorial Volunteers,* www.nachestrail.org/media/pdf/DELACY%20Indian%20War%20reports%201856.pdf. The transcription has no page numbers but it is searchable. In referring to a "bower," De Lacy meant a treaty council. De Lacy prepared the official report of the campaign for Governor Stevens. According to historian Alvin Josephy, De Lacy's account is more accurate than the report prepared by Stevens for public consumption: see Josephy, *Nez Perce Indians.*

32. Wright to Jones, July 9, 1856, HED 1, 34th Cong., 3rd sess. (1857), 176.

33. Wright to Mackall, July 18, 1856, ibid.

34. Wright to Mackall, Aug. 3, 1856, ibid., 199.

35. Wright to Mackall, July 25, 1856, ibid., 187. For an account of the Leschi incident, see Kluger, *Bitter Waters of Medicine Creek.*

36. Stevens to Shaw, July 21, 1856, *Message of the Governor,* 260.

37. De Lacy *Diary of the Yakima Indian War,* July 13, 1856.

38. "A History of the Grande Ronde Valley," Union County Chamber of Commerce, www.unioncountychamber.org/pages/Heritage.

39. De Lacy, *Diary of the Yakima Indian War*; the July 13–15 entries provide details of preparations and the attitude of Colonel Shaw.

40. Brown, *Indian Side of the Story*, 158.

41. "Diary of Celinda E. Hines," Sept. 5, 1853, *Transactions of the 46th Annual Reunion of the Oregon Pioneer Association*, June 20, 1918 (Chausse-Prudhomme Printers, 1921), 118.

42. "Journal of Crossing the Plains to Oregon in 1852, John T. Kerns," Sept. 2, 1852, *Transactions of the 42nd Annual Reunion of the Oregon Pioneer Association*, June 25, 1914 (Chausse-Prudhomme Printers, 1917), 182.

43. Shaw to Tilton, July 24, 1856, in Stevens, *Message of the Governor*, 43.

44. De Lacy, *Diary of the Yakima Indian War*, July 17, 1856.

45. Stevens to Shaw, Aug. 2, 1856, *Message of the Governor*, 265.

46. Shaw to Stevens, Aug. 1, 1856, ibid., 267.

47. Brown, *Indian Side of the Story*, 159–60.

48. Report of Colonel Shaw, July 24, 1856, in Brown, *Indian Side of the Story*, 162. "Lacamas" is the French term for the camas bulb, one of the food staples for the Plateau tribes.

49. Brown, *Indian Side of the Story*, 165.

50. Josephy, *Nez Perce Indians*, 369.

51. Wool to Thomas, Aug. 19, 1856, HED 1, 34th Cong., 3rd sess. (1857), 180.

52. Mackall to Wright, July 3, 1856, ibid., 165.

53. Lang, *History of the Willamette Valley*, 463.

54. Stevens, *Message of the Governor*, 2.

55. General Orders No. 4, Feb. 25, 1856, ibid., 39.

56. Stevens to Davis, June 8, 1856, ibid., 82.

57. Stevens to Davis, Oct. 22, 1856, ibid., 91, 92.

58. Hazard Stevens, *Life of Isaac Stevens*, 2: 202–03.

59. Ruby and Brown, *Spokane Indians*, 104–15.

60. Brown, *Indian Side of the Story*, 66–77. In early accounts the Sinkiuse are sometimes referred to as the Isle de Pierres. According to Brown, Quiltenenock apparently had permission of other tribes to present their cases, including the Entiats and Chelans.

61. Stevens to Davis, Oct. 22, 1856, *Message of the Governor*, 89.

62. *Olympia Pioneer and Democrat*, Oct. 10, 1856.

63. Stevens, *Message of the Governor*, 91, 92.

64. Lee, *Barbarians and Brothers*, 163.

65. Mackall to Wright, Oct. 19, 1856, HED 1, 34th Cong., 3rd sess. (1857), 202.

66. "Substance of the Remarks of Gov. Stevens at the Dinner given to Col. Shaw and the Volunteers," *Olympia Pioneer and Democrat*, Nov. 7, 1856.

67. Stevens, General Orders No. 7, Oct. 30, 1856, *Message of the Governor*, 48.

68. Stevens to Davis, Nov. 21, 1856, *Message of the Governor*, 94.

69. Ibid., 94–95.

CHAPTER 7

1. *New York Times*, July 13, 1857.

2. De Smet, *Life, Letters, and Travels*, 4: 1241.

3. Ibid., 4: 1248–49.

4. "Oregon and Washington," *Olympia Pioneer and Democrat*, Jan. 9, 1857.

5. The *Olympia Pioneer and Democrat* during the first half of 1857 contained numerous articles about Mormons, most of which were critical. In the February 7 issue, for example, an inventory of Mormon leaders noted that a great many were "crippled and nearsighted."

6. "Fort Colville Mines, Indians, etc.," *Olympia Pioneer and Democrat*, Aug. 7, 1856.

7. Knuth, "Picturesque Frontier," 5–6, 9, 73. Of the four houses built by Jordan only the surgeon's house remains; it is home to the Fort Dalles Museum. Colonel Wright's house burned down in 1865.

8. Ibid., 8.

9. The *Commodore* became the *Brother Jonathan*, the ship on which, in 1865, George Wright met his end.

10. Goodman, *Western Panorama*, 124–25.

11. Ibid., 125–26.

12. "Report of M. T. Simmons, Indian Agent for Puget Sound District," HED 2, 35th Cong., 2nd sess. (1858), 583.

13. J. W. Denver, Report of the Commissioner of Indian Affairs, Nov. 30, 1857, HED 1, 35th Cong., 1st sess. (1858), 299.

14. Manring, *Conquest of the Coeur d'Alenes*, 58–59.

15. Garnett to Mackall, Jan. 30, 1858, SED 1, 35th Cong., 2nd sess. (1858), 339.

CHAPTER 8

Epigraph: Charles Erskine Scott Wood, *The Poet in the Desert* (Portland, Ore.: n.p., 1915), 103. Wood fought in the 1877 Nez Perce War, and later became friends with Chief Joseph. After that war Wood expressed deep regret and anger about how the government treated the tribes.

1. Joset manuscript.

2. Kip, *Indian War*, 51. According to *Merriam-Webster's Dictionary*, a "chapter of accidents" is "an unforeseen sequence of events."

3. Joset manuscript.

4. Manring, *Conquest of the Coeur d'Alenes*, 267. Manring states that Steptoe's middle name was Jevnor, but other accounts have it as Jenner.

5. Cullum, *Biographical Register*, 540.

6. Pierce to Steptoe, Jan. 6, 1855, copy in private collection of Greg Partch, Sr.

7. Biographical history of Edward J. Steptoe, www.accessgenealogy.com /virginia/biography-of-colonel-edward-j-steptoe.htm.

8. Manring, *Conquest of the Coeur d'Alenes,* 270–71. Steptoe was close to his sister and wrote frequently, one time telling her he was interested in going into the turpentine business.

9. Steptoe to Wright, Sept. 18, 1856, HED 1, 34th Cong., 3rd sess. (1856), 198.

10. Steptoe to Mackall, Oct. 19, 1857, HED 2, 35th Cong., 2nd sess. (1858), 332.

11. Joset manuscript.

12. Stevens to Nesmith, Jan. 18, 1858, in Todd, "Letters of Governor Stevens," 427–28.

13. Prosch, "Evolution of Spokane," 25–26.

14. *Portland Standard,* Jan. 14, 1858, reported in the *Olympia Pioneer and Democrat,* Jan. 22, 1858.

15. Scheuerman and Finley write that Owhi's sister was Kamiakin's mother; for more, see *Finding Chief Kamiakin.*

16. Steptoe to Mackall, Apr. 17 and May 2, 1858, HED 2, 35th Cong., 2nd sess. (1858), 344–45.

17. Basic details of the expedition described below are derived in part from Steptoe's official report (Steptoe to Mackall, May 23, 1858, HED 2, 35th Cong., 2nd sess. [1858]); Manring, *Conquest of the Coeur d'Alenes,* 66–110; Joset manuscript; and Kriebel, "Battle of To-hots-nim-me."

18. The howitzers and carriages were designed to be broken down and carried on mules or horses. There are varying accounts as to whether Steptoe's force used mules or horses in the pack train.

19. Dent was Ulysses S. Grant's brother-in-law.

20. Canis, "Steptoe's Indian Battle," 162. A "shillaleh" or "shillelagh" is a stout Irish walking stick that could be used as a club.

21. Rosebush, *Frontier Steel,* 209–10.

22. Kowrach, *Saga of the Coeur d'Alenes,* 98–99. According to an account told by Coeur d'Alene chief Joseph Seltice, "It was a sorrowful occurrence, because a young Palouse woman drowned with her two babies, while Steptoe's troops laughed and shot at the Indians fleeing across the river." The incident does not appear in Steptoe's official account or in the accounts of Steptoe's men. Shortly before his death in 1949, Chief Joseph Seltice finished writing his account of the oral histories concerning the Coeur d'Alene tribe. Joseph was the son of Chief Andrew Seltice, who participated in the battles and negotiations with the army.

23. Winder, "Account of a Battle," 57.

24. Joset manuscript; and Burns, *Jesuits and the Indian Wars,* 196–97.

25. Trimble, "Soldier of the Oregon Frontier," 46–47.

26. Birtle, *U.S. Army Counterinsurgency,* 65. During 1858 Lt. (later general) George Crook was serving in Wright's command in the Yakima Valley. The famous (and infamous) General Crook would incorporate psychology in his operations against the tribes. He wanted his officers to be "Indian thinkers,"

rather than "Indian fighters." For more on Indian views, see Burns, *Jesuits and the Indian Wars*; and Brown, *Indian Side of the Story*.

27. Steptoe to Mackall, May 23, 1858, HED 2, 35th Cong., 2nd sess. (1858), 346.

28. Joset manuscript. Father Joset refers to Tilcoax as Telxaway, as did the Coeur d'Alene people.

29. Burns, *Jesuits and the Indian Wars*, 204–206.

30. Father Joset wrote of meeting the tribes at Sila. Research by historian Mahlon Kriebel places the village at present-day Stubblefield Lake in the Turnbull National Wildlife refuge. Native people still harvest camas in the area: see Mahlon Kriebel, "Battle of To-hots-nim-me," in *Bunchgrass Historian* 24, nos. 2, 3, special double issue (2008) 1–63.

31. Joset manuscript.

32. Winder, "Account of a Battle," 57.

33. Kowrach and Connolly, *Saga of the Coeur d'Alenes*, 102.

34. Sergeant Kenny quoted in Scheuerman and Finley, *Finding Chief Kamiakin*, 78.

35. Joset manuscript.

36. I.G.T., "Indian Campaign in the North," 398. The author of the article is identified only as "I.G.T."; he was apparently a participant in both the Steptoe and Wright campaigns. His comments are similar to ones made by Joel Graham Trimble, who was on both expeditions and published similar accounts, with similar views of Wright and Steptoe. It is possible that the publisher mistook a *J* for an *I*.

37. Trafzer and Scheuerman, *Renegade Tribe*, 79.

38. The DeMoy quote is from Manring, *Conquest of the Coeur d'Alenes*, 103. The fight on May 17 started along Pine Creek, called Hngwsumm [Rope] Creek by the Coeur d'Alenes, since it was a place where Native people made ropes. The Steptoe battle is remembered by some Native people as the Hngwsumm Battle. Among the many accounts of the fight, two that offer detailed descriptions are Manring, *Conquest of the Coeur d'Alenes*; and Kriebel, "Battle of To-hots-nim-me."

39. Winder, "Account of a Battle," 57.

40. Capt. Oliver Hazard Perry Taylor was a West Point graduate, "exacting in discipline and rather hot-tempered, yet he was much loved and respected." Lieutenant Gaston was also a West Point graduate, a young man of twenty-four, who, Trimble claimed, had a cancerous growth on his neck that "troubled him so much that he feared death from the disease" (both quotes are from Trimble, "Soldier of the Oregon Frontier," 46). The information on casualties is from "Steptoe's Report," found in Manring, *Conquest of the Coeur D'Alenes*, 131–33.

41. Joset manuscript.

42. Oral history of Ignace Camille, ca. 1955, typescript from Lancaster Donation, Spokane Tribe of Indians archives, Nespelem, Wash.

43. Garrett Hunt, *Indian Wars of the Inland Empire,* 29.

44. Ibid.

45. Gregg to Manring, Feb. 3, 1909, private collection of Greg Partch Sr. Even amidst the chaos, there was an odd moment of normalcy. A messenger from Fort Walla Walla arrived and delivered mail, including a letter to Captain Winder from a friend. Winder wrote a reply: "About 7:00 PM an express reached us with our mail and t'was then your letter reached me. I soon read it and was glad to receive good accounts of all."

46. Kowrach and Connolly, *Saga of the Coeur d'Alenes,* 109, 110.

47. Joset manuscript.

48. Kowrach and Connolly, *Saga of the Coeur d'Alenes,* 110.

49. Gregg to Manring, Feb. 3, 1909, in the private collection of Greg Partch, Sr.

50. Winder, "Account of a Battle," 58.

51. Joset to Congiato, June 27, 1858, HED 2, 35th Cong., 2nd sess. (1858), 358, 359.

52. Joset manuscript.

53. Ibid.

54. Ibid.

55. *Harper's New Monthly* magazine, June–Nov. 1858, 403, 545.

56. *New York Times,* July 21, 1858.

57. Steptoe to Mackall, May 28, 1858, HED 2, 35th Cong., 2nd sess. (1858), 351–52.

58. Scott to Floyd, July 15, 1858, *Report of the Secretary of War,* HED 2, 35th Cong., 2nd sess. (1858), 348.

59. Clarke to Thomas, July 23, 1858, HED 2, 35th Cong., 2nd sess. (1858), 361.

60. Stevens's address, appendix to Cong. Globe, 35th Cong., 1st sess. (1858), 493.

61. "The Indian Victory in Washington Territory," *New York Times,* July 15, 1858. The column references Gen. Edward Braddock, who in 1755 led a poorly planned expedition against a combined force of French soldiers and Indian warriors. Braddock was killed in the fighting.

62. Stevens to Yantis, June 28, 1858, in Todd, "Letters of Governor Stevens," 444–45.

63. Stevens to Nesmith, July 18, 1858, ibid.

64. General Wool's reputation survived Stevens's broadsides, and in 1862 after successfully occupying Fort Monroe and Norfolk, Virginia, he was promoted to major general. The next year, he was appointed commander of the Department of the East. He was seventy-nine years old, the oldest general serving on either side during the Civil War.

65. Dr. John Randolph to Dr. Will Steptoe, Edward Steptoe's father, Apr. 8, 1861; Nannie Steptoe to Manring, May 2, 1911, both letters in the private collection of Greg Partch, Sr.

66. While a diagnosis today is impossible, the author asked several physicians to look at letters written by Dr. Randolph to Colonel Steptoe's father, who was a physician in Virginia. In addition, they reviewed a letter from Nannie Steptoe Eldridge, Colonel Steptoe's sister, in which she addresses the issue. Steptoe apparently took a medication known as "Blue Mass," which consisted of 33 percent mercury. It was used for a number of maladies, including syphilis.

67. Email and written correspondence between the author and Dr. Henry Mroch.

68. Wright to Mackall, May 26, 1858, HED 2, 35th Cong., 2nd sess. (1858), 350.

69. Steptoe to Nannie Steptoe, Oct. 27, 1856, in the private collection of Greg Parch, Sr.

70. Wright to Cooper, Sept. 15, 1860, and Wright to Hardie, Dec. 21, 1860, Letters Received, www.fold3/image/#294537825, and www.fold3/image/#294537536.

71. John Mullan, Topographical Memoir of Col. Wright's Campaign, SED 32, 35th Cong., 2nd sess. (1859), 59ff.

72. Manring, *Conquest of the Coeur d'Alenes*, 125.

73. Father Joset was convinced that there could not have been many Indian casualties, given the inexperience of the soldiers and the quality of their weapons. We know that three of the most popular Coeur d'Alenes were killed: James Nehlukteltshiye, Zachary Natatkem, and Chief Victor Smena.

74. Phelps, "Dedication of Steptoe Memorial Park," *Spokane Chronicle*, June 15, 1907.

75. As told by Lawrence Aripa, in Frey, *Landscape Traveled by Coyote and Crane*, 82–83.

76. Public Resource Org., United States Reports, 533 U.S. 262, June 18, 2001, https://law.resource.org/pub/us/case/reporter/US/533/533.US.262.00-189.html.

CHAPTER 9

Epigraph: Will J. Trimble, "Soldier of the Oregon Frontier," 47.

1. *Illustrated London News*, Oct. 2, 1858. The news of Wright's planned incursion reached London six weeks after his final preparations at Fort Walla Walla.

2. "Still Later, and Official," *Weekly Oregonian*, May 29, 1858.

3. Mackall to Wright, June 18, 1858, HED 2, 35th Cong., 2nd sess. (1858), 365.

4. Owen to Nesmith, July 16, 1858, and Aug. 2, 1858, SED 1, 35th Cong., 2nd sess. (1858), 618–23.

5. Birtle, *U.S. Army Counterinsurgency*, viii.

6. Gates, "Indians and Insurrectos," 59. Gates is quoting historian Robert Utley.

7. In September, while Colonel Wright was on his expedition, the army changed the command structure in the West. The Department of the Pacific was split into the Department of California, under General Clarke, and the Department of Oregon (including Washington Territory) under General Harney. Thus, William Harney in effect replaced George Wright.

8. Jefferson Davis, Report of the Secretary of War, appendix to Cong. Globe, 34th Cong., 3rd sess. (1857), 3.

9. Utley, *Frontiersmen in Blue*, 28.

10. Mackall to Wright, July 4, 1858, HED 2, 35th Cong., 2nd sess. (1858), 364. Some scholars, including Robert Burns, assert a connection between the conquering of the Pacific Northwest and the conquering of coastal Iberia in medieval times. In addition to *The Jesuits and the Indian Wars of the Northwest*, his other work includes *Medieval Colonialism: Post-Crusade Exploitation of Islamic Valencia* (Princeton, N.J.: Princeton University Press, 1975).

11. Mackall to Garnett, July 18, 1858, HED 2, 35th Cong., 2nd sess. (1858), 356–66.

12. Garnett's official report claims that fifty women and twenty-one men were taken prisoner and that three men were executed. The claim of four executions and one survivor is in Brown, *Indian Side of the Story*, 218–19.

13. Crook is quoted in Brown, *Indian Side of the Story*, 226–27. Crook would later gain fame during the Civil War, and after that conflict earned notoriety as an "Indian fighter."

14. Moses was chief of the Columbia Moses Interior Salish band, sometimes referred to as the Sinkiuse-Columbia or Isle-des-Pierres.

15. Burns, *Jesuits and the Indian Wars*, 208.

16. Morgan, "Recollections of the Spokane Expedition," 490.

17. Wright to Mackall, Aug. 14, 1858, found in Manring, *Conquest of the Coeur d'Alenes*, 180–81.

18. Kip, *Indian War*, 45.

19. Author interview with Dr. Robbie Paul, a descendant of Chief Utsinmalikan. Descendants of the various tribes involved in the Wright battles (Spokanes, Coeur d'Alenes, Nez Perces, Palouses, Yakamas, and others), still talk (and tease each other) about the complicated relationships between various tribal members and the army.

20. A company might consist of fifty to one hundred men, sometimes more. The number depended on strategic factors, as well as illness and desertion.

21. Morgan, "Recollections of the Spokane Expedition," 491; Brig. Gen. Michael Morgan served in Wright's 1858 command as a lieutenant.

22. Kip, *Indian War*, 42.

23. Joset manuscript.

24. Kip, *Indian War*, 43.

25. Ibid., 46. At the Cascades engagement, a bugler in Steptoe's force had alerted the warriors to the army's arrival. Wright knew his march was no secret

to the tribes, thus he was unconcerned about the presence of his buglers and drummers.

26. De Smet to Pleasanton, May 26, 1859, in De Smet, *Life, Letters, and Travels,* 3: 970.

27. The Rubicon is a river in Italy crossed by Julius Caesar in 49 BC, considered a "point of no return" because it was an important political boundary. Since Morgan's account was written later than Kip's well-known account, he may have borrowed the term from him.

28. Kip, *Indian War*, 48.

29. Ibid., 51.

30. Weather in the region in late August and early September is normally warm and dry, with cool nights. During Wright's expedition, the weather was hot and dry at first, although they did suffer through one severe thunderstorm. In late September, as the expedition was heading back south, the weather became cool and rainy.

31. "Hangman of Colonel Wright's Famous Expedition . . ." *Spokane Spokesman-Review*, Sept. 24, 1916. As one of the longest-surviving members of Wright's and Steptoe's expeditions, Beall gave several published interviews and wrote a number of letters detailing events. His accounts, some given in the early twentieth century, vary in minor detail, but in general they support, and are supported by, the accounts of others.

32. I.G.T., "Indian Campaign in the North," 399.

33. Morgan, "Recollections of the Spokane Expedition," 492. After the campaign, Capt. Edward Ord requested a brevet for Morgan, but it was rejected by army headquarters. Morgan, as well as other "Indian-fighters" believed many in the East "did not, at that time, appreciate what it was to be in an Indian Fight" (ibid.).

34. Keyes, *Fifty Years*, 285.

35. Kip, *Indian War*, 52. Kip was referring to *pedregal*, the Spanish term for rocky ground—specifically, a lava field. While Kip mentions only two men dying from eating roots, Louie Lee, a packer with the force, reported eight became ill (*Spokane Spokesman-Review*, May 8, 1892). The roots were most likely water hemlock.

36. Morgan, "Recollections of the Spokane Expedition," 492.

37. Two of the four lakes (Granite and Willow) lie along Interstate 90. Meadow Lake is less than a mile east of those two, and Silver Lake less than a mile west.

38. For additional details about the Indians' view of the war, see Brown, *Indian Side of the Story*.

39. Kip, *Indian War*, 53.

40. "Letter from the Seat of the Indian War," *Daily Alta California*, Sept. 26, 1858. The unidentified author was possibly Michael Ryan Morgan.

41. Kip, 55.

42. Ibid.

43. Keyes, *Fifty Years*, 277.

44. Kip was perhaps inspired by John Keats (1795–1821): from "Specimen of an Induction to a Poem": "Lo! I must tell of chivalry; / For large white plumes are dancing in mine eye."

45. The hill is today called Wright's Hill. Interstate 90 bisects the battlefield at the base of the hill.

46. "Fate of Schon-Shin," *Spokane Spokesman-Review*, Jan. 1, 1892.

47. "Locate Indian Battle Ground," *Spokane Daily Chronicle*, Feb. 1, 1917. The article refers to rifle pits at the top of the hill, which were still visible in 1917.

48. "Letter from the Seat of the Indian War."

49. Kip, *Indian War*, 57.

50. Keyes, *Fifty Years*, 269.

51. In 1855 the army ordered two hundred Sharps and gave most of them to the First Dragoons, who eventually made their way west and joined Colonel Wright's command: see Hornback, "Brief Introduction," 45–50.

52. Rosebush, *Frontier Steel*, 241–42. Nearly two years before George Wright's push into the upper Columbia Plateau, Secretary of War Jefferson Davis spoke of new weaponry. In his address to Congress of December 1856, Davis reported that small arms were undergoing a fundamental change, with rifles capable of firing Minie balls replacing the old flintlocks. The new arms used percussion self-priming locks, and the barrels were rifled for greater range and accuracy. Davis said, "With a population accustomed to the use of arms, familiar with, and competent to judge of their merits and defects, the moral effect of feeling themselves inferior and their armaments would be disastrous." The Springfield rifles were also called Harper's Ferry or Mississippi Jaeger rifles. One of Steptoe's companies carried the same type on his expedition.

53. Kip, *Indian War*, 59.

54. "Hangman of Wright's Expedition," 4. The village would have been at the north end of Meadow Lake, near the present-day town of Four Lakes.

55. "The New United States Arm," *Sacramento Daily Union*, Sept. 27, 1858.

56. The heroic battle image is from Kip, "Steptoe-Wright Campaign," 485.

57. "Indian Warfare around Spokane," *Spokane Spokesman-Review*, June 30, 1912.

58. Mullan to Mix, Sept. 5, 1858, Report of the Secretary of the Interior, HED 2, 35th Cong., 2nd sess. (1859), 632.

59. I.G.T., "Indian Campaign in the North," 401.

60. Dandy, "Reminiscences."

61. Ibid. The first shot was the canister leaving the barrel, the second the canister exploding and releasing a spray of deadly grapeshot.

62. Tyler's account was published in various newspapers, including the *New York Times*, Oct. 30, 1858. Accounts by Keyes, Wright, and Kip make no mention of the disposition of wounded Indians, which, given how detailed their accounts are, seems as if the omissions might be intentional.

63. Brown, *Indian Side of the Story*, 243.

64. "Letter from the Seat of the Indian War."

65. Reprinted in *New York Times*, Nov. 2, 1858. The estimates of Indian casualties varied considerably, depending on the source.

66. "Peace Memorial on Indian Battle Site Unveiled," *Spokane Spokesman-Review*, Oct. 21, 1935.

67. "Indian Battle Monolith Ready," *Spokane Spokesman-Review*, Oct. 16, 1935.

CHAPTER 10

1. Wright to Mackall, Sept. 6, 1858, SED 1, 35th Cong., 2nd sess. (1858), 392.

2. Brown, *Indian Side of the Story*, 229–50.

3. Joset manuscript.

4. Keyes, *Fifty Years*, 271–72.

5. Kip, *Indian War*, 66.

6. Northwest Power Conservation District report, www.nwcouncil.org/history/IndianFishing.asp. Today the Spokane River is home to trout, perch, bass, and scavenger fish. Fishermen are advised to limit fish consumption because of high levels of PCBs and other industrial chemicals that have accumulated over the years: see Washington State Department of Health, www.doh.wa.gov/Portals/1/Documents/Pubs/334–123.pdf.

7. Ruby and Brown, *Spokane Indians*, 99–100.

8. Wright to Mackall, Sept. 6, 1858, SED 1, 35th Cong., 2nd sess. (1858), 392.

9. Wright to Mackall, Sept. 15, 1858, ibid., 396.

10. Ruby and Brown, *Spokane Indians*, 135.

11. Brown, *Indian Side of the Story*, 259. The same issue is addressed in other accounts.

12. Manring, *Conquest of the Coeur d'Alenes*, 216.

13. Wright to Mackall, Sept. 6, 1858, SED 1, 35th Cong., 2nd sess. (1858), 392.

14. Keyes, *Fifty Years*, 272.

15. Ruby and Brown, *Spokane Indians*, 135–36.

16. William Ernoehazy, Jr., "Hanging Injuries and Strangulation," http://emedicine.medscape.com/article/826704-clinical. The "standard drop" came into common use in the mid-1860s. It required a drop of four to six feet, enough height to break the victim's neck and cause unconsciousness, then death. The "long drop," which kills much more quickly, began to be used in Great Britain in the 1850s: see "The History of Judicial Hanging in Britain 1735–1964," http://capitalpunishmentuk.org/hanging1.html.

17. Hanging emphasizes the power the judge has over the victim; in fact, the French word for gallows, *potence*, is derived from the Latin *potentia*, meaning "power."

18. Kip, *Indian War*, 70.

19. Smith, "Pioneer of the Spokane," 270.

20. I.G.T., "Indian Campaign in the North," 408.

21. Kowrach and Connolly, *Saga of the Coeur d'Alene Indians*, 131. The Cataldo Mission is in present-day northern Idaho, sixty miles east of Spokane. The mission's church still stands.

22. Manring, *Conquest of the Coeur d'Alenes*, 212.

23. Keyes, *Fifty Years*, 272.

24. Kip, *Indian War*, 71.

25. Dandy, "Reminiscences," 5.

26. I.G.T., "Indian Campaign in the North," 402. The account was published in 1884.

27. Tillie Nomee, Oral History No. 146, Eastern Washington State Historical Society Oral History Archives, Museum of Arts and Culture, Spokane.

28. Burns, *Jesuits and the Indian Wars*, 299.

29. Mullan, Sept. 11, 1858, *Journal of John Mullan during Wright Expedition of 1858*, copy of original from the National Archives courtesy of Richard Scheuerman.

30. Morgan, "Recollections of the Spokane Expedition," 493.

31. "Many Historic Places in Valley," *Spokane Spokesman-Review*, May 16, 1943.

32. Morgan, "Recollections of the Spokane Expedition," 493.

33. Keyes, *Fifty Years*, 273.

34. The rationalization for the slaughter is found in Schlicke, *General George Wright*; the Harney letter is in Reavis, *Life and Services of General Harney*, 280–81.

35. Mullan, "Topographical Memoir," 35.

36. Joset manuscript.

37. Wright to Mackall, Sept. 10, 1858, SED 1, 35th Cong., 2nd sess. (1859), 395.

38. Trafzer and Scheuerman, *Renegade Tribe*, 89.

39. Brown, *Indian Side of the Story*, 256.

40. Wright to Mackall, Sept. 10, 1858, SED 1, 35th Cong., 2nd sess. (1859), 395.

41. Waller, *Becoming Evil*, 247–51.

42. Wright to Mackall, Sept. 10, 1858, SED 1, 35th Cong., 2nd sess. (1859), 395.

43. Carl Schlicke, quoted in Beverly Vorpahl, "Three Relate Stories about Early Spokane," *Spokane Spokesman-Review*, May 13, 1989. In research conducted by Stanley Milgram at Stanford University, people who are at first horrified at the thought of harming someone will, if encouraged by an authority figure, inflict injury on an innocent victim. The research showed that some actually enjoyed inflicting pain, which is also not uncommon. Other research indicates that about five percent of a perpetrator group may exhibit sadistic tendencies. Mass killings can be undertaken at first for nonsadistic reasons, "but some learn to enjoy the activities and so may escalate them in an almost addiction-like quest for pleasure," Baumeister, quoted in Waller, *Becoming Evil*, 246. Those soldiers who were enjoying the horse slaughter were not psychotic—at least there is nothing to indicate they were—but they may have had sadistic tendencies that were brought out during the process of killing. One factor that allows those

tendencies to surface is repression of conscience, a common side-effect of dehumanization, in which, with a long enough desensitizing process, killers can adopt a callous attitude toward killing. Another factor in the desensitizing process is the diffusion of responsibility, as Wright did with his officers, and they, in turn, did with their subordinates—the men who had to fire the guns. In other words, the delegation and division of the authority to kill the horses softened the soldiers' consciences and made killing easier (Waller, 246). The men enjoying the horse slaughter were caught up in what sociologist Randall Collins calls "forward panic." According to Steven Pinker, "A forward panic is violence at its ugliest. It is the state of mind that causes genocides, massacres, deadly ethnic riots, and battles in which no prisoners are taken. . . . As the butchery gains momentum, rage may give way to ecstasy, and the rampagers may laugh and whoop in a carnival of barbarity" (Pinker, *Better Angels*, 487–88).

44. Chomsky, "United States–Dakota War Trials," 65.

45. Smith, "Pioneer of the Spokane Country," 271.

46. This quote and the extract above are from Wright to Joset, Sept. 10, 1858, Joseph Joset Papers, Gonzaga University Special Collections.

47. "Hangman of Wright's Expedition."

48. *Portland Oregonian* article reprinted as "Particulars of the Late Indian Battles, North," *Sacramento Daily Union*, Oct. 15, 1858.

49. Keyes, *Fifty Years*, 273.

50. Burns, *Jesuits and the Indian Wars*, 306–309.

51. "The End of the Indian War," letter from Lt. Robert O. Tyler, *New York Times*, Nov. 1, 1858.

52. *Harper's New Monthly* magazine, Dec. 1858.

53. *Puget Sound Herald*, Oct. 8, 1858.

54. Lee, *Barbarians and Brothers*, 222.

55. Kip, *Indian War*, 76.

56. Ibid., 77. Although Kip's accounts are usually concise, colorful, and accurate, sometimes he just quotes official reports, which are sometimes inaccurate or inflated.

57. Ibid.

58. Kowrach and Connolly, *Saga of the Coeur d'Alenes*, 17–30. In an endnote (268 n. 6) the editors point out that Circling Raven's prophecy "predates the coming of the Iroquois to the Pacific Northwest. The Coeur d'Alene Indians have long believed and transmitted this tradition from generation to generation."

59. Ibid., 37.

60. Kowrach and Connolly, *Saga of the Coeur d'Alene Indians*, 43–44.

61. Keyes, *Fifty Years*, 88.

62. Dandy, "Reminiscences," 6.

63. Wright to Mackall, Sept. 15 and 30, 1858, SED 1, 35th Cong., 2nd sess. (1859), 396, 403.

64. Kip, *Indian War*, 85.

65. Palmer, "Indian Pioneers," 22–47.

66. Tyler, "The End of the Indian War," reprinted in the *New York Times*, Nov. 1, 1858.

67. "Particulars of the Late Indian Battles."

68. Kip, *Indian War*, 85.

69. Tyler, "The End of the Indian War."

70. Trimble, "Soldier of the Oregon Frontier," 47.

71. Wright to Mackall, Sept. 21, 1858, SED 1, 35th Cong., 2nd sess. (1859), 000.

72. Kip, *Indian War*, 79.

73. Coburn, "George Wright, Peacemaker," 165.

74. John C. Tidball, "Report of a Journey made by General W. T. Sherman in the Northwest and Middle parts of the United States in 1883," *Spokane Spokesman-Review*, July 26, 1936.

75. Dandy, "Reminiscences," 5.

76. "Gonzaga History, 1887–1895," found at www.gonzaga.edu/Academics/Libraries/Foley-Library/Departments/Special-Collections/Exhibitions/Past_Exhibits/Gonzaga_History/GonzagaHistory1887.asp.

77. Alexi, *Reservation Blues*, 9–10.

78. Mullan, *Miners and Travelers' Guide*, 24.

79. "Monument Relocation Unearths Memories," *Spokane Spokesman-Review*, June 23, 2000.

CHAPTER 11

Epigraph: Item from the pro-Isaac Stevens newspaper, the *Olympia Pioneer and Democrat*, Sept. 24, 1858.

1. Kip, *Indian War*, 88. It was the second time Kip invoked James Fennimore Cooper's stereotype of Indians; he had also done so during the Walla Walla Treaty Council of 1855.

2. Croffut, *Fifty Years in Camp and Field*, 396.

3. *Olympia Pioneer and Democrat*, Oct. 22, 1858.

4. Wright to Mackall, Sept. 24, 1858, SED 32, 35th Cong., 2nd sess. (1859), 58.

5. Winthrop, *Canoe and Saddle*, 294–95. Loolowcan, son of Chief Owhi of the Yakamas, served as one of Winthrop's guides.

6. Wright to Mackall, June 11, 1856, SED 5, 34th Cong., 3rd sess. (1856), 161.

7. Beall to McWhorter, Jan. 6, 1917, L. V. McWhorter Papers, Manuscripts, Archives, and Special Collections, Washington State University, cage 55, box 45, folder 434 (hereafter McWhorter Papers).

8. Beall to McWhorter, Dec. 13, 1916, ibid. At the time of the letter, Beall was eighty-four years old. His version of events is roughly equivalent to those of others, with the greatest discrepancy being whether or not Qualchan's wife arrived at Wright's camp before, or at the same time as, Qualchan.

9. Kip, *Indian War*, 101.

10. Keyes, *Fifty Years*, 277.

11. Beall to McWhorter, Jan. 27, 1919, McWhorter Papers.

12. Keyes, *Fifty Years*, 278.

13. Beall to McWhorter, Dec. 13, 1916, McWhorter Papers.

14. Keyes, *Fifty Years*, 279.

15. Beall to McWhorter, Aug. 1, 1918, McWhorter Papers.

16. Wright to Mackall, Sept. 24, 1858, Letters Received, Office of Adjutant General, Main Series, 1822–1860, Wright, G. (P270), www.fold3.com/image/294360566.

17. Keyes, *Fifty Years*, 240.

18. Manring, *Conquest of the Coeur d'Alenes*, 235–36.

19. *Olympia Pioneer and Democrat*, Oct. 22, 1858. The soldier, who had been corresponding with the paper, is not named.

20. Kip, *Indian War*, 68.

21. "Hangman of Wright's Expedition." A note written by L. V. McWhorter suggests the act was "typical of the complete disarming and surrender of her husband. The spear represented the power of resistance, which was thus left with Col. Wright, and Qualchan was to come completely unarmed and defenseless." McWhorter Papers.

22. Beall to McWhorter, Jan. 6 and Aug. 1, 1918, McWhorter Papers. A granite monument sits at the place where some people believe the hanging tree once stood. However, some Native Americans claim it was actually at least one hundred yards away, across the creek from the monument. Walking the land, it is clear to the author that the location cited in Native histories is more likely. Taking Qualchan to the location marked by the monument would have meant traveling an unnecessarily long distance and crossing the creek.

23. "Yakima Indian History," narrated by Smith Luc-ie, Indian Police, Nov. 28, 1904, L. V. McWhorter Papers, 66, 1546.

24. Mary Owhi Moses interview by William Compton Brown, Nespelem, Wash., Aug. 1, 1918, William Compton Brown Papers, Manuscripts, Archives, and Special Collections, Washington State University, 196, 17, 190.

25. Dandy, "Reminiscences," 313.

26. Kip, *Indian War*, 116–17.

27. Wright to Mackall, Sept. 30, 1858, SED 1, 35th Cong., 2nd sess. (1858), 402

28. Ibid.

29. Kip, *Indian Wars*, 116–17.

30. Keyes, *Fifty Years*, 313.

31. Morgan, "Recollections of the Spokane Expedition," 496.

32. Beall to McWhorter, Feb. 13, 1916, McWhorter Papers.

33. "Concerning the Death of Chief Owhi," McWhorter Papers.

34. Skelton, *American Profession of Arms*, 322.

35. Kip, *Indian War*, 100.

36. I.G.T., "Indian Campaign in the North," 403.

37. Report of the Secretary of War, SED 1, 35th Cong., 2nd sess. (1858), 4. "Rapine" refers to plunder or thievery.

38. Keyes, *Fifty Years*, 288.

39. "News from the Indian War," *Olympia Pioneer and Democrat*, Oct. 29, 1858. A chaplet is "a wreath to be worn on the head" (*Merriam-Webster's Dictionary*).

40. De Smet, *Life, Letters, and Travels*, 2: 744–46.

41. Mix, Report of the Commissioner of Indian Affairs, Nov. 6, 1858, quoted in Prucha, *Documents of U.S. Indian Policy*, 93.

42. Burns, *Jesuits and the Indian Wars*, 297.

43. Skelton, *American Profession of Arms*, 319.

44. Chomsky, "U.S.-Dakota War Trials," 56–65.

45. Ibid., 74.

46. Email exchange between the author and Wayne E. Lee, Professor of History and Chair of the Curriculum in Peace, War, and Defense, University of North Carolina.

47. Mackall to Wright, June 25, 1858, SED 1, 35th Cong., 2nd sess. (1858), 364.

48. Lee, *Barbarians and Brothers*, 225.

49. Report of the Secretary of the Interior, Dec. 3, 1857, SED 11, 35th Cong., 1st sess. (1858), 65–66.

50. Ficken, "Three-Party Conflict," 70; Richard Kluger, *Seizing Destiny: The Relentless Expansion of American Territory* (New York: Vintage Books, 2007), 482–84.

51. Schlicke, *General George Wright*, 194.

52. "Local History Lecturer," *Spokane Spokesman-Review*, Mar. 31, 1970.

53. In *The Plains Across*, John Unruh addressed this issue in detail.

54. Skelton, *American Profession of Arms*, 322.

55. Stevens, *Life of Isaac Stevens*, 230–31. Peopeo-moxmox was the Walla Walla chief killed by the volunteer militia while trying to escape. In his biography of his father, Hazard Stevens twice referred to "Wool and his parasites" in his material about Wright's hangings.

56. Dandy, "Reminiscences," 9.

57. Frey, *Landscape Traveled by Coyote and Crane*, 86.

58. Delaware outlawed hanging in 1986. Anyone sentenced to death before 1986 may still choose hanging over lethal injection. In New Hampshire, hanging would be used only if for some reason lethal injection was not possible.

59. Baker, "American Indian Executions." David Baker compiled the *Registry of Known American Indian Executions, 1639–2006*, www.deathpenaltyinfo.org/documents/AmericanIndianRegistry.pdf. He identified 424 American Indians who were executed after going through "legal process." Leschi is included in his tally, but Wright's victims are not.

60. Bancroft, *History of Washington*, 173.

CHAPTER 12

1. *Olympia Pioneer and Democrat*, Oct. 1, 1858.

2. Ibid., Oct. 8, 1858.

3. *Portland Standard*, Oct. 6, 1858.

4. *San Francisco Daily Alta California*, Sept. 19, 1858.

5. Coleman, *Pig War*, 61–65.

6. Schlicke, *General George Wright*, chaps. 11 and 12.

7. Coleman, *Pig War*, 65.

8. Special Orders No. 18, July 11, 1861, *OR*, ser. 1, vol. 50, pt. 1, corresp.

9. Coleman, *Pig War*, 136.

10. Cullum, *Biographical Register*, 402. By the end of the Civil War, Keyes would attain the rank of major general of volunteers.

11. Johnston joined the Confederate Army and was killed April 6, 1862, at the Battle of Shiloh.

12. Keyes, *Fifty Years*, 420–21.

13. During the Mexican-American War and thereafter General Scott and General Worth engaged in a bitter feud. The claim regarding the impact of Wright's loyalty to Worth is in Schlicke, *General George Wright*, and a detailed account of Scott's attitudes toward officers is found in Keyes, *Fifty Years*.

14. Sumner was married to Hannah Wickersham Forster, Margaret's sister.

15. Wright to Cameron, May 16, 1861, in Schlicke, *General George Wright*, 219.

16. General Orders No. 1, Oct. 4, 1861, *OR*, ser. 1, vol. 50, pt. 1, corresp.

17. Wright to Nesmith, June 11, 1861, in Wright, Ingalls, and Himes, "Letters," 133–36. See this source for other examples of the tone of Wright's later letters.

18. Ibid. During the Civil War, Floyd was appointed to the rank of brigadier general in the Confederate Army.

19. Tate, *General Edwin Vose Sumner*, 123.

20. Wright to Townsend, Oct. 29, 1861, *OR*, ser. 1, vol. 50, pt. 1, corresp.

21. Wright to Sumner, Oct. 26, 1861, from original in Spokane Public Library Northwest Room.

22. A notable exception to the age ceiling was Wright's old commander Gen. John Wool, who at age seventy-seven assumed command of the Department of the East during the Civil War. For the conspiracy claim, see Schlicke, *General George Wright*, chapter 14.

23. Wright to Townsend, Oct. 28, 1861, *OR*, ser. 1, vol. 50, pt. 1, corresp.

24. An officer could hold two ranks: one in the regular army (colonel, Ninth Infantry), and another in the volunteers (brigadier general).

25. Robinson, "Ordeal of General Wright," 159.

26. McClellan to Wright, Nov. 2, 1861, *OR*, ser. 1, vol. 50, pt. 1, corresp.

27. The letters were dated Nov. 5 and 15 and Dec. 9, 10, and 20, *OR*, ser. 1, vol. 50, pt. 1, corresp.

28. Wright to Nye, Nov. 22, 1861, *OR*, ser. 1, vol. 50, pt. 1, corresp. In a subsequent letter, Wright states that the primary reason for providing food to the Indians is that it will reduce the chances of them attacking the train.

29. Wright to Thomas, Dec. 28, 1861, *OR*, ser. 1, vol. 50, pt. 1, corresp. In 1863, the Habeas Corpus Suspension Act was enacted, which allowed the suspension of writs while the Civil War was ongoing. Up to that point, the constitutional provision was inconsistently applied, primarily in regions directly affected by the Civil War.

30. Wright to Dole, Mar. 31, 1862, *OR*, ser. 1, vol. 50, pt. 1, corresp.

31. Wright to Thomas, Mar. 31, 1862, ibid.

32. Wright to Price, Apr. 25, 1862, ibid.

33. Wright to Murdoch, Apr. 19, 1862, ibid.

34. Ibid.

35. Wright to Thomas, Nov. 8, 1862, *OR*, ser. 1, vol. 50, pt. 2, corresp.

36. Wright to Lippitt, Apr. 7, 1862, *OR*, ser. 1, vol. 50, pt. 1, corresp.

37. Wright to Forman, May 2, 1862, ibid.

38. Wright to Hanson, May 24, 1862, ibid.

39. Wright to Thomas, Oct. 27, 1862, *OR*, ser. 1, vol. 50, pt. 2, corresp.

40. In the Union Army: George Dandy, Frederick Dent, Horatio Gates Gibson, David Gregg, William N. Grier, James Hardie, George Percy Ihrie, Erasmus Keyes, Ralph Wilson Kirkham, George B. McClellan, Michael Ryan Morgan, Edward Ord, Philip Sheridan, and Robert Ogden Tyler. In the Confederate Army: Henry B. Davidson, William Harney, Hylan Benton Lyon, William Pender, George Pickett, Gabriel Rains, and Charles Sidney Winder.

41. Wright to Thomas, Nov. 18, 1862, *OR*, ser. 1, vol. 50, pt. 2, corresp.

42. "Newly Uncovered Documents Claim Far Higher Number of Shoshone Killed in Bear River Massacre," *Salt Lake Tribune*, Feb. 17, 2008, www.sltrib.com/ci_8282225.

43. Drum to Wright, Feb. 1, 1863, *OR*, ser. 1, vol. 50, pt. 2, corresp.

44. General Orders No. 6, Feb. 19, 1863, ibid. Casualty counts for the volunteers at Bear River varied depending on the source.

45. Wright to Citizens of the Pacific Coast, Apr. 7, 1863, *OR*, ser. 1, vol. 50, pt. 2, corresp.

46. Wright to Halleck, July 7, 1863, ibid. For more information about the New Almaden mine issue, see Lenard Ascher, "Lincoln's Administration and the New Almaden Mine Scandal," *Pacific Historical Review* 5, no. 1 (Mar. 1936), 38–51. At the time, Leland Stanford was California's governor.

47. Lincoln to Swett and Low, July 9, 1863, *OR*, ser. 1, vol. 50, pt. 2, corresp.

48. Low to Lincoln, July 10, 1863, ibid.

49. Wright to Townsend, Sept. 28, 1863, ibid.

50. Schlicke, *General George Wright*, 290.

51. Ibid., 301–303.

52. Stanton to Grant, Aug. 18, 1864, *OR*, ser. 1, vol. 50, pt. 2, corresp.

53. Wright to "Loyal Citizens of the Pacific Coast," June 21, 1864, ibid.

54. Hunt, *Army of the Pacific,* 349.

55. "Speech of Brigadier General Wright," *Sacramento Daily Union,* Feb. 11, 1864.

56. Cullum, *Biographical Register,* 232.

57. Schlicke, *General George Wright,* 306.

58. *Condition of the Indian Tribes, Report of the Joint Special Committee, Appointed under Joint Resolution of March 3, 1865, with an Appendix* (Washington, D.C.: Government Printing Office, 1867) (hereafter Doolittle report). Wright's responses are found on pages 440–41, as well as in *OR,* ser. 1, vol. 50, pt. 2, corresp.

59. Doolittle report, 425–27.

60. Ibid., 440–41.

61. Carleton to Wallen, Mar. 9, 1864, ibid., 164.

62. Wright to Hopping, May 5, 1865, "Indian-White Relations in Northern California," Item # 3354, Cal State–Chico, Meriam Library Special Collections, www.csuchico.edu/lbib/spc/bleyhl/Bleyhl_all.pdf.

63. Alexie, *Reservation Blues,* 270.

CHAPTER 13

1. I.G.T., "Indian Campaign in the North," 397.

2. Lockley, "Reminiscences of Captain Gray," 328. Tribes in the area included Umatillas, Cayuses, Palouses, Yakamas, and possibly others. Chinook jargon was a trading language used by many tribes, traders, trappers, and settlers. It included components of various tribal languages, English, and French.

3. Data from City of Spokane website, www.spokanecity.org/services/about/spokane/history/population.

4. Comments about the challenges of assimilation are primarily derived from an interview with Spokane Tribal Preservation Officer Bill Matt, Dec. 18, 2013.

5. "The Life of Garry," *Spokane Spokesman-Review,* Jan. 17, 1892.

6. "Old Garry is Dead," *Spokane Spokesman-Review,* Jan. 13, 1892.

7. "Spokane History," *Spokane Spokesman-Review,* May 16, 1897.

8. *New York Times,* May 1, 1902. For killing at least twenty-five hundred civilians, General Smith was court-martialed and found guilty of "conduct to the prejudice of good order and military discipline." Smith's only punishment was a forced retirement from the army.

9. "By Red Men of Palouse," *Spokane Spokesman-Review,* Dec. 20, 2012. The "Improved Order of Red Men" was (and still is) a society dedicated to patriotic causes and charity work, particularly Alzheimer's disease. One of their ceremonies utilizes Native American regalia and other aspects of Native American culture. The national website for today's organization notes that one does not have

to be a Native American to join, but it is unclear if there are any Native Americans in the organization. One purpose of their organization is "perpetuating the beautiful legends and traditions of a once-vanishing race and the keeping alive some of the traditional customs, ceremonies, and philosophies": see www.redman.org.

10. Trafzer and Scheuerman, *Renegade Tribe,* 135.

11. Ibid., 129–130. Trafzer and Scheuerman explain the issues and individuals involved in Indian land rights.

12. Curtis, *North American Indian,* 7: 62. J. P. Morgan paid Curtis $75,000 to write and produce a twenty-volume set that ended up containing over 2,200 images. The volumes were produced on a subscription basis from 1907 to 1930. The original subscription price was $3,000, climbing to over $4,000 before the publication of the later volumes.

13. Dandy, "Reminiscences," 13.

14. W. D. Vincent, "Yesterdays in the Spokane Country," *Spokane Spokesman-Review* Sunday magazine, June 4, 1922. Chief Garry's Salish name was Slough-Keetcha, according to information uncovered in 2013 by Barry Moses and Brian Huseland (*Spokane Spokesman-Review,* Sept. 1, 2013), www.spokesman.com/stories/2013/sep/01/in-the-name-of-history.

15. Birtle, *U.S. Army Counterinsurgency,* 11.

16. Wheelan, *Terrible Swift Sword,* 256.

17. Report of Lieutenant General Sheridan, in Report of the Secretary of War, 44th Cong., 3rd sess. (1878), vol. 1.

18. "Lizzie Wright Owen," HED 1065, 50th Cong., 1st sess. (1888), 1–4. No action was taken on the pension request. It was resubmitted in 1890, but Lizzie Wright Owen died without any benefits having been paid.

19. For example, see Birtle, *U.S. Army Counterinsurgency*; author conversation with Lt. Col. Jason Pape, Oct. 16, 2013.

20. Wordnet: A Lexical Database for English, https://wordnet.princeton.edu.

21. *Oxford English Dictionary,* www.oxforddictionaries.com/us/definition/american_english.

22. For more on this issue, see Gates, "Indians and Insurrectos."

23. McLuhan, *Touch the Earth,* 10–11.

24. Statement on the Nez Perce War by Owhi, grandson of Chief Owhi, McWhorter Papers, subseries 2.1, box 7, folder 38; Curtis, *North American Indian,* 7: 32.

25. "The Last of the Redman's Freedom," *Salt Lake Herald,* Nov. 29, 1903.

26. Roberta Lynn (Tow-le-kit-we-son-my) Paul, *Historical Trauma and Its Effects,* 140.

27. Author conversation with Bill Matt, Dec. 18, 2013.

28. In the Spokane area, examples of place names include Fort George Wright, Fort Wright Boulevard, Hangman Valley Golf Course, Hangman Hills housing development, the Creek at Qualchan Golf Course, Hangman Creek, and the Qualchan Estates housing development.

29. Author conversation with Robert McDonald, communications director for the Confederated Salish and Kootenai Tribes and former reporter, *Spokane Spokesman-Review*, May 21, 2012. McDonald is of Salish/Nez Perce heritage.

30. Author interview with Charlene Teters (Spokane tribe), July 12, 2012. Ms. Teters is an artist and teacher and has been a prominent spokeswoman against the use of mascots based on Native American images and stereotypes. She is a founding member of the National Coalition on Racism in Sports and the Media.

31. Author interview with Michael Holloman, Feb. 22, 2012.

32. Author interview with Albert Andrews, June 28, 2012.

33. Frey, *Landscape Traveled by Coyote and Crane*, 81–82.

34. Ibid.

35. *Spokane Spokesman-Review*, letters to the editor, Feb. 7, 1994.

36. "George Wright Shamed His Name, Group Claims," *Spokane Spokesman-Review*, Feb. 3, 1994.

37. See Mukogawa Fort Wright Institute, www.mfwi.edu.

38. Advertisement in the *Spokane Daily Chronicle*, Nov. 15, 1933.

39. *Spokane Spokesman-Review*, Mar. 23, 1957. For a discussion of the use of western images and ideas in advertising, see West, "Selling the Myth."

40. "George Wright's Army Put Finish to Warfare," *Spokane Daily Chronicle*, Apr. 25, 1958.

41. Advertisement for First National Bank in the *Spokane Spokesman-Review*, Sept. 11, 1974.

42. "Ask 'Hangman' as Creek Name," *Spokane Daily Chronicle*, Oct. 13, 1934.

43. This sentiment was expressed in numerous interviews conducted by the author.

44. Feature Detail Report for Hangman Creek, http://geonames.usgs.gov/apex/f?p=136:3:0::NO:3:P3_FID,P3_TITLE:1505370,Hangman%20Creek. The U.S. Board of Geographical Names lists twenty-three historical variants of the creek's name, including "Lahtoo" and "Nedwhauld," both names that frequently appear in historical records.

45. Interview with Michael Finley, chairman of the Colville Confederated Tribes, Jan. 17, 2012.

46. Author interview with Charlene Teters.

47. Author interview with Albert Andrews.

48. "Golf panel likes Qualchan as name for new course," *Spokane Daily Chronicle*, Mar. 7, 1990.

49. "2013 Marks the 40th Anniversary of Decision to Eliminate Nickname," *Easterner* online, posted Mar. 7, 2013, http://easterneronline.com/2013/03/07/no-salvaging-savages.

50. Author conversation with Mark Stanger (Coeur d'Alene tribe), May 13, 2014.

51. Email exchange between author and Sen. Maria Cantwell. The resolution was in the 2010 Defense Appropriations Act, H.R. 3326. President Obama signed the resolution on Dec. 19, 2009.

52. Lise Balk King was a fellow at the Carr Center for Human Rights Policy, Harvard Kennedy School of Government. She is now active in various film and media projects for HBO, among other outlets: see http://indiancountry todaymedianetwork.com/2011/12/03/tree-fell-forest-us-apologized-native -americans-and-no-one-heard-sound.

53. "A Lost Heritage: Canada's Residential Schools," CBC Digital Archives, www.cbc.ca/archives/categories/society/education/a-lost-heritage-canadas -residential-schools/a-long-awaited-apology.html.

54. Both teams are owned by Brett Sports and Entertainment.

55. In the author's conversation with Charlene Teters, she noted that not all tribal members were comfortable with the Indian mascot.

56. "Mural drawn by public recalls 1858 slaughter of horses," *Spokane Spokesman Review*, June 27, 2015.

57. "Questions arise over Colonel George Wright's Legacy," *Spokane Spokesman Review*, May 17, 2015.

CONCLUSION

1. Mayo, "War Memorials as Political Memory," 75.

2. Schlicke, *General George Wright*, 193.

3. Gaddis, *Landscape of History*, 97.

4. Lee, author of *Barbarians and Brothers*, email exchange with the author, Sept. 30, 2013.

5. Gaddis, *Landscape of History*, 141.

6. Zinn, *People's History*, 10–11.

7. For background regarding the commission of violent or cruel actions of "normal" people, the author consulted with Cynthia Cutler, Professor of Honors and Integrative Studies at Eastern Washington University. The topic forms a substantial portion of Dr. Cutler's capstone courses in leadership.

8. Unitarian theologian Theodore Parker addressed issues of morality in *Ten Sermons of Religion* in 1852. Parker was an antislavery activist. Although he believed all people deserved equal justice, he viewed the white race as intellectually and culturally superior to others. Parker's concept of the arc of the moral universe has been used by various human rights activists over the years, including Martin Luther King.

Bibliography

ARCHIVAL RESOURCES

Dandy, George. "Reminiscences." William Compton Brown Papers, 1830–1963. Manuscripts, Archives, and Special Collections, Washington State University Libraries, Pullman. Cage 196.

Doty, James. *Digest of the Journal of James Doty*. Manuscripts, Archives, and Special Collections, Washington State University Libraries, Pullman. Manuscript collection 4718.

Joset, Joseph. Joset manuscript. Joseph Joset Personal Papers. Jesuit Oregon Province Archive, Gonzaga University Special Collections, Foley Center Library, Spokane, Wash. Box 2, file 2.

Lucullus Virgil McWhorter Papers, 1848–1945. Manuscripts, Archives, and Special Collections, Washington State University Libraries, Pullman. Cage 55.

National Archives. Commission Branch Files of the Adjutant General's Office. File number W1099-CB-1864.

OTHER ARCHIVES CONSULTED

California State Library, Sacramento

Eastern Washington Historical Society, Oral History and Photograph Archives, Museum of Arts and Culture, Spokane

Eastern Washington University Archives and Special Collections, Cheney

Northwest Room, Spokane Public Library

Oregon State Historical Society, Portland

Washington State Historical Society, Tacoma

Numerous other archival resources were consulted. Specific archives, including government and military records, are noted in endnotes or image credits.

BOOKS, DISSERTATIONS, AND THESES

Alexie, Sherman. *The Lone Ranger and Tonto Fistfight in Heaven*. New York: Grove Press, 2005.

———. *Reservation Blues*. New York: Grove Press, 1995.

Arendt, Hannah. *Eichmann in Jerusalem: A Report on the Banality of Evil*. New York: Penguin, 2006.

Arnold, Laurie. *Bartering with the Bones of Their Dead: The Colville Confederated Tribes and Termination*. Seattle: University of Washington Press, 2012.

Asher, Brad. *Beyond the Reservation: Indians, Settlers, and the Law in Washington Territory, 1853–1889*. Norman: University of Oklahoma Press, 1999.

Axtell, James, and William Sturtevant. "The Unkindest Cut, or Who Invented Scalping?: A Case Study." In *The European and the Indian: Essays in the Ethnohistory of Colonial North America*, by James Axtel, 16–37. New York: Oxford University Press, 1981.

Bagley, Will. *So Rugged and Mountainous: Blazing the Trails to Oregon and California, 1812–1848*. Norman: University of Oklahoma Press, 2010.

Ball, Durwood. *Army Regulars on the Western Frontier, 1848–1861*. Norman: University of Oklahoma Press, 2001.

Bancroft, Hubert Howe. *History of Washington, Idaho, and Montana*. Memphis: General Books, 2010. First published 1890.

Banner, Stuart. *How the Indians Lost Their Land: Law and Power on the Frontier*. Cambridge, Mass.: Harvard University Press, 2007.

Baumeister, Roy F. *Inside Human Cruelty and Violence*. New York: W. H. Freeman, 1997.

Beck, Paul N. *The First Sioux War: The Grattan Fight and Blue Water Creek, 1854–56*. Lanham, Md.: University Press of America, 2004.

Billings, John D. *Hardtack and Coffee; or, The Unwritten Story of Army Life*. Boston: George Smith, 1887.

Birtle, Andrew J. *U.S. Army Counterinsurgency and Contingency Operations Doctrine, 1860–1941*. Washington, D.C.: Center for Military History, 1998.

Boessenecker, John. *Lawman: The Life and Times of Harry Morse, 1835–1912*. Norman: University of Oklahoma Press, 1998.

Bogle, Lori. "Sylvanus Thayer and the Ethical Instruction of Nineteenth-Century Military Officers in the United States." In *Military Education: Past, Present, and Future*, edited by Gregory C. Kennedy and Keith Neilson, 63–81. Santa Barbara, Calif.: Praeger, 2002.

Bornstein, David. *How to Change the World: Social Entrepreneurs and the Power of New Ideas*. Oxford: Oxford University Press, 2007.

Bowers, Q. David. *The Treasure Ship S.S.* Brother Jonathan: *Her Life and Loss, 1850–1865*. Wolfeboro, N.H.: Bowers and Merena Galleries, 1999.

Boyd, Robert. *The Coming of the Spirit of Pestilence: Introduced Infectious Diseases and Population Decline among Northwest Indians, 1774–1874*. Seattle: University of Washington Press, 1999.

Boyden, T. G., *Warrior of the Mist: A Biography of Chief Qualchan, Chief Owhi's Son*. Fairfield, Wash.: Ye Galleon Press, 1996.

Brackett, Albert G. *History of the United States Cavalry*. New York: Harper and Bros., 1865.

Brown, William Compton. *The Indian Side of the Story.* Spokane, Wash.: C. W. Hill, 1961.

———. *Mary Moses' Statement.* Fairfield, Wash.: Ye Galleon Press, 1988.

Burns, Robert Ignatius. *The Jesuits and the Indian Wars of the Northwest.* Moscow: University of Idaho Press, 1966.

Cebula, Larry. *Plateau Indians and the Quest for Spiritual Power, 1700–1850.* Lincoln: University of Nebraska Press, 2003.

Churchill, Ward. *A Little Matter of Genocide: Holocaust and Denial in the Americas 1492 to the Present.* San Francisco: City Lights Books, 1997.

Clark, Ella E. *Indian Legends of the Pacific Northwest.* Berkeley: University of California Press, 1953.

Coffman, Edward M. *The Old Army: A Portrait of the American Army in Peacetime, 1784–1898.* New York: Oxford University Press, 1986.

Coleman, E. C. *The Pig War: The Most Perfect War in History.* Stroud, Gloucestershire: History Press, 2009.

Cox, Ross. *Adventures on the Columbia River.* Volume 1. London: Henry Colburn and Richard Bentley, 1831.

Cram, Capt. T. J. *Topographical Memoir of the Department of the Pacific.* Presented to Congress March 3, 1859. Washington, D.C.: n.p., 1859.

Crawford, Aaron L. "The People of Bear Hunter Speak: Oral Histories of the Cache Valley Shoshones Regarding the Bear River Massacre." MA thesis, Utah State University, 2007.

Croffut, W. A., ed. *Fifty Years in Camp and Field: Diary of Ethan Allen Hitchcock, U.S.A.* New York: Putnam, 1909.

Cullum, George W. *Biographical Register of the Officers and Graduates of the U.S. Military Academy at West Point, from 1802 to 1867.* Volume 1. New York: D. Van Norstrand, 1868.

Curtis, Edward. *The North American Indian.* Volume 7. Norwood, Mass.: The University Press, 1911.

Dart, Gregory. *Robespierre, Rousseau, and English Romanticism.* Cambridge: Cambridge University Press, 1999.

Deloria, Vine, Jr. *God Is Red: A Native View of Religion.* Thirtieth Anniversary Edition. Golden, Colo.: Fulcrum, 2003.

———. *Indians of the Pacific Northwest: From the Coming of the White Man to the Present Day.* Garden City, N.Y.: Doubleday, 1977.

Denzin, Norman K. *Custer on Canvas: Representing Indians, Memory, and Violence in the New West.* Walnut Creek, Calif.: Left Coast Press, 2011.

De Smet, Pierre-Jean. *Life, Letters, and Travels of Father Pierre-Jean De Smet, S.J., 1801–1873.* Edited by Hiram Chittenden and Alfred Richardson. 4 volumes. New York: Francis P. Harper, 1905.

———. *Oregon Missions and Travels over the Rocky Mountains, in 1845–46.* New York: Edward Dunigan, 1847.

Duran, Eduardo, and Bonnie Duran. *Native American Postcolonial Psychology.* Albany: State University of New York Press, 1995.

Durham, Nelson Wayne. *History of the City of Spokane and Spokane County Washington: From Its Earliest Settlement to the Present Time.* Volume 1. Spokane: Clarke Publishing, 1912.

Egle, William Henry. *Pennsylvania Genealogies.* Harrisburg, Pa.: Lane Hart, Printer, 1886.

Evans, Elwood. *History of the Pacific Northwest: Oregon and Washington.* Volume 1. Portland, Ore.: North Pacific History Co., 1889.

Fargo, Lucile F. *Spokane Story: A Colorful Early History of the Capital City of the Inland Empire.* Minneapolis: Northwestern Press, 1957.

Ficken, Robert. "The Three-Party Conflict: The Army and the Indian on the Pacific Northwest Frontier." In *Military Influences on Washington History: Proceedings of a Conference, March 29–31, 1984, Camp Murray, Tacoma,* edited by William Woodward and David Hansen, 59–78. Tacoma: Washington Army National Guard, 1984.

Foote, Kenneth E. *Shadowed Ground: America's Landscapes of Violence and Tragedy.* Austin: University of Texas Press, 2003.

Frey, Rodney, in collaboration with the the Schitsu'umsh (Coeur d'Alene Indians). *Landscape Traveled by Coyote and Crane: The World of the Schitsu'umsh.* Seattle: University of Washington Press, 2001.

Gaddis, John Lewis. *The Landscape of History: How Historians Map the Past.* Oxford: Oxford University Press, 2004.

Glisan, Rodney. *Journal of Army Life.* San Francisco: A. L. Bancroft, 1874.

Goodman, David Michael. *Western Panorama, 1849–1875: The Travels, Writing, and Influence of J. Ross Browne.* Glendale, Calif.: Arthur H. Clark, 1966.

Grant, Ulysses S. *Personal Memoirs of U.S. Grant.* New York: Charles Webster, 1894.

Grassley, Ray H. *Indian Wars of the Pacific Northwest.* Portland, Ore.: Binfords and Mort, 1972.

Green, Michael K., Laurie Winn Carlson, and Susan Allen Myers. *Washington in the Pacific Northwest.* Salt Lake City: Gibbs-Smith, 2005.

Halswelle, Keeley. *Poems by Thomas Moore,* Edinburgh: William P. Nimmo, 1863.

Harmon, Alexandra. *Indians in the Making: Ethnic Relations and Indian Identities around Puget Sound.* Berkeley: University of California Press, 1998.

———, ed. *The Power of Promises: Rethinking Indian Treaties in the Pacific Northwest.* Seattle: University of Washington Press, 2008.

Heitman, Francis B. *Historical Register and Dictionary of the U.S. Army, from Its Organization, Sept. 29, 1789, to March 2, 1903.* Volume 1. Washington, D.C.: Government Printing Office, 1903.

Hines, H. K. *An Illustrated History of the State of Washington.* Chicago: Lewis Publishing, 1894.

Hitchcock, Ethan Allen. *A Traveler in Indian Territory: The Journal of Ethan Allen Hitchcock.* Norman: University of Oklahoma Press, 1996.

Hoopes, Alban W. *Indian Affairs and Their Administration: With Special Reference to the Far West, 1849–1860.* Philadelphia: University of Pennsylvania Press, 1932.

Hope, Ian Clarence. "A Scientific Way of War: Antebellum Military Science, West Point, and the Origins of American Military Thought." PhD diss., Queen's University, Kingston, Ontario, Canada, 2011.

Horseman, Reginald. *Race and Manifest Destiny: The Origins of American Racial Anglo-Saxonism.* Cambridge, Mass.: Harvard University Press, 1981.

Howard, Oliver Otis. *Famous Indian Chiefs I Have Known.* New York: Century, 1908.

Hoxie, Frederick E., ed. *Encyclopedia of North American Indians.* New York: Houghton Mifflin, 1996.

Hunt, Aurora. *The Army of the Pacific, 1860–1866.* Mechanicsburg, Pa.: Stackpole Books, 2004.

Hunt, Garrett B. *Indian Wars of the Inland Empire.* Spokane, Wash.: Spokane Community College, 1900.

Irving, Washington. *A History of New York, by Diedrich Knickerbocker.* Philadelphia: M. Thomas, 1819.

Jackson, Helen Hunt. *A Century of Dishonor: A Sketch of the United States Government's Dealings with Some of the Indian Tribes.* Mineola, N.Y.: Dover, 2003. First published in 1881.

Jacoby, Karl. *Shadows at Dawn: A Borderlands Massacre and the Violence of History.* New York: Penguin, 2008.

Josephy, Alvin M., Jr. *The Nez Perce Indians and the Opening of the Northwest.* New York: Houghton Mifflin, 1997.

Kansas: A Guide to the Hawkeye State. Topeka: Writers Program at the WPA, Kansas Department of Education, Hastings House, 1949,

Karson, Jennifer, ed. *As Days Go By: Our History, Our Land, and Our People—The Cayuse, Umatilla, and Walla Walla.* Pendleton, Ore: Tamástslikt Cultural Institute and Portland Oregon Historical Society, 2006.

Keegan, John. *A History of Warfare.* New York: Random House, 1993.

Kelly, Plympton J. *We Were Not Summer Soldiers: The Indian War Diary of Plympton J. Kelly.* Tacoma: Washington State Historical Society, 1976.

Keyes, E. D., *Fifty Years' Observations of Men and Events: Civil and Military.* New York: Scribner's, 1885.

Kip, Lawrence. *The Indian Council in the Valley of the Walla Wallas, 1855.* Tarrytown, N.Y.: William Abbatt, 1915.

———. *Indian War in the Pacific Northwest: The Journal of Lieutenant Lawrence Kip.* Lincoln: University of Nebraska Press, 1999.

Kluger, Richard. *The Bitter Waters of Medicine Creek.* New York: Knopf, 2011.

Kowrach, Edward J., and Thomas E. Connolly, eds. *Saga of the Coeur d'Alene Indians: An Account of Chief Joseph Seltice.* Fairfield, Wash.: Ye Galleon Press, 1990.

Lancaster, Samuel G. *The Columbia: America's Great Highway*. Atglen, Pa.: Schiffer, 2004. First published in 1915.

Lang, H. O. *History of the Willamette Valley: Discovery of the Valley and Its Resources, with an Account of Its Discovery and Settlement by White Men, and Its Subsequent History*. Portland, Ore.: Geo. H. Himes, 1885.

Lee, Wayne E. *Barbarians and Brothers: Anglo-American Warfare, 1500–1865*. New York: Oxford University Press, 2011.

Leitz, Glenn, ed. *Long Ago in the Northern Palouse*. Spokane, Wash.: Marquette Books, 2005.

Lewis, Meriwether, William Clark, et al. *Travels to the Source of the Missouri River and across the American Continent to the Pacific Ocean: Performed by Order of the Government of the United States in the Years 1804, 1805, and 1806*. 3 volumes. London: Longman, Hurst, 1814.

Lyman, William Denison. *Lyman's History of Old Walla Walla County*. Volume 1. Chicago: S. J. Clarke, 1918.

———. *Recollections of the First White Boy in Walla Walla*. Chicago: S. J. Clarke, 1859.

Manring, Benjamin F. *The Conquest of the Coeur d'Alenes, Spokanes, and Palouses: The Expeditions of Colonels E. J. Steptoe and George Wright*. Spokane, Wash.: John Graham, 1912.

McLuhan, T. C. *Touch the Earth: A Self-Portrait of Indian Existence*. New York: Promontory Press, 1971.

McWhorter, Lucullus Virgil. *Hear Me My Chiefs! Nez Perce Legend and History*. Caldwell, Id.: Caxton Printers, 1952.

———. *Tragedy of the Wahk-Shum: The Death of Andrew J. Bolon, Yakima Indian Agent, in Mid-September 1855*. Fairfield, Wash.: Ye Galleon Press, 1968.

Meeker, Ezra. *Pioneer Reminiscences of Puget Sound: The Tragedy of Leschi*. Seattle: Ezra Meeker, 1905.

Meigs, William Montgomery. *The Life of Thomas Hart Benton*. Philadelphia: Lippincott, 1904.

Meinig, D. W. *The Great Columbia Plain: A Historical Geography, 1805–1910*. Seattle: University of Washington Press, 1995.

———. *Spokane and the Inland Empire: Historical Geographic Systems and a Sense of Place*. Pullman: Washington State University Press, 2005.

Meldahl, Keith Heyer. *Hard Road West: History and Geology along the Gold Rush Trail*. Chicago: University of Chicago Press, 2008.

Meyer, Bette E. *Fort George Wright: Not Only Where the Band Played, A Historical Geography*. Fairfield, Wash.: Ye Galleon Press, 1994.

Mielke, Laura L. *Moving Encounters: Sympathy and the Indian Question in Antebellum Literature*. Amherst: University of Massachusetts Press, 2008.

Miller, Christopher L. *Prophetic Worlds: Indians and Whites on the Columbia Plateau*. Seattle: University of Washington Press, 2003. First published in 1985.

Moore, MariJo, ed. *Genocide of the Mind: New Native American Writing*. New York: Nation Books, 2003.

Morrisey, Katherine G. *Mental Territories: Mapping the Inland Empire*. Ithaca, N.Y.: Cornell University Press, 1997.

Mullan, John. *Miners and Travelers' Guide to Oregon, Washington, Idaho, Montana, Wyoming, and Colorado via the Missouri and Columbia Rivers*. New York: Wm. M. Franklin, 1965. First published in 1865.

———. *Report on the Construction of a Military Road from Fort Walla Walla to Fort Benton*. Fairfield, Wash.: Ye Galleon Press, 1998. First published in 1863.

Nabokov, Peter. *Native American Testimony*. Revised edition. New York: Penguin, 1999.

Newcomb, Steven T. *Pagans in the Promised Land: Decoding the Doctrine of Christian Discovery*. Golden, Colo.: Fulcrum Publishing, 2008.

Northern Pacific Railroad Co. *The Pacific North-west: A Guide for Settlers and Travelers*. Portland, Ore.: n.p., 1882.

Paley, William. *The Principles of Political and Moral Philosophy*. Eighth American edition. Boston: West and Richardson, 1815.

Parker, Samuel. *Journal of an Exploring Tour beyond the Rocky Mountains*. Third edition. Ithaca, N.Y.: Mack, Andrus, and Woodruff, 1842.

Parker, Theodore. *Ten Sermons of Religion*. Boston: Crosby, Nichols, 1853.

Partridge, Henry Villiers. *A History of Norwich, Vermont*. Hanover, N.H.: Dartmouth Press, 1905.

Paul, Roberta Lynn (Tow-le-kit-we-son-my). *Historical Trauma and Its Effects on a NI Mii Puu Family: Finding Story—Healing Wounds*. PhD diss., Gonzaga University, 2007.

Peltier, Jerome. *Warbonnets and Epaulets*. Montreal: Payette Radio Limited, 1971.

Perry, Barbara. *Silent Victims: Hate Crimes against Native Americans*. Tucson: University of Arizona Press, 2008.

Pinker, Steven. *The Better Angels of Our Nature: Why Violence Has Declined*. New York: Viking, 2011.

Powers, Dennis M. *Treasure Ship: The Legend and Legacy of the S.S.* Brother Jonathan. New York: Citadel, 2006.

Prucha, Francis Paul, ed. *Documents of United States Indian Policy*. Third edition. Lincoln: University of Nebraska Press, 2000.

Ray, Verne F. *Cultural Relations in the Plateau of Northwestern America*. Publications of the Frederick Webb Hodge Anniversary Publications Fund. Los Angeles: Southwest Museum, 1939.

Reavis, L. U. *The Life and Services of General William Selby Harney*. St. Louis: Bryan, Brand, 1878.

Reid, John Phillip. *Forging a Fur Empire: Expeditions in the Snake River Country, 1809–1824*. Norman: Arthur H. Clark, 2011.

Reimers, Harry L. *Indian Country: Cultural Views of the Spokanes*. Minneapolis: T. S. Denison, 1973.

———. *Qualchan's Last Warpath.* Austin: Western Publications, 1970.

Richards, Kent D. *Isaac Stevens: Young Man in a Hurry.* Pullman: Washington State University Press, 1993.

Robinson, John W. "The Ordeal of General George Wright: A Study of Secessionist Sentiment in California, 1961–64." In *Brand Book 16, The Westerners, Los Angeles Corral,* edited by Raymund W. Wood. Glendale, Calif.: The Westerners, 1982.

Rosebush, Waldo. *Frontier Steel: The Men and Their Weapons.* Appleton, Wis.: C. C. Nelson, 1958.

Ross, John Alan. *The Spokan Indians.* Spokane, Wash.: Michael J. Ross, 2011.

Ruby, Robert H., and John A. Brown. *The Cayuse Indians: Imperial Tribesmen of Old Oregon.* Commemorative edition. Norman: University of Oklahoma Press, 2005.

———. *Indians of the Pacific Northwest: A History.* Norman: University of Oklahoma Press, 1981.

———. *The Spokane Indians: Children of the Sun.* Expanded edition. Norman: University of Oklahoma Press, 2006.

Ruby, Robert H., John A. Brown, and Cary C. Collins. *A Guide to the Indian Tribes of the Pacific Northwest.* Third edition. Norman: University of Oklahoma Press, 2010.

Scheuerman, Richard D., and Michael O. Finley. *Finding Chief Kamiakin: The Life and Legacy of a Northwest Patriot.* Pullman: Washington State University Press, 2008.

Schlicke, Carl P. *General George Wright: Guardian of the Pacific Northwest Coast.* Norman: University of Oklahoma Press, 1988.

Scott, Robert N. et al., eds. *War of the Rebellion: A Compilation of the Official Records of the Union and Confederate Armies.* Series 1, vol. 50, parts 1–2, correspondence. www.simmonsgames.com/research/authors/USWarDept/ORA/TOC .html.

Settle, Raymond W., ed. *The March of the Mounted Riflemen, From Fort Leavenworth to Fort Vancouver, May to October, 1849.* Glendale, Calif.: Arthur H. Clark, 1940.

Settler's Guide to Homes in the Northwest, Being a Handbook of Spokane Falls, W.T.; The Queen City of the Northwest, Its Matchless Water Power and Advantages as a Commercial Center. Spokane Falls, Wash.: Dallam, Ansell, and Edwards, 1885.

Sheridan, Philip H. *Personal Memoirs of P. H. Sheridan.* 2 volumes. New York: C. L. Webster, 1888.

Skelton, William B. *An American Profession of Arms: The Army Officer Corps, 1784–1861.* Lawrence: University of Kansas Press, 1992.

———. "The Army in the Age of the Common Man." In *Against All Enemies: Interpretations of American Military History from Colonial Times to the Present,* edited by Kenneth J. Hagan and William R. Roberts, 91–112. Westport, Conn.: Greenwood Press, 1986.

Smith, C. Coburn. "George Wright: Peacemaker in Eastern Washington's Clash of Cultures." In *West Pointers and Early Washington,* edited by John A. Hemphill and Robert C. Cumbow. Seattle: West Point Society of Puget Sound, 1992.

Smith, Sherry L. *The View from Officers' Row: Army Perceptions of Western Indians.* Tucson: University of Arizona Press, 1995.

Soennichsen, John. *Bretz's Flood: The Remarkable Story of a Rebel Geologist and the World's Greatest Flood.* Seattle: Sasquatch Books, 2008.

Stannard, David E. *American Holocaust: The Conquest of the New World.* New York: Oxford University Press, 1992.

Stevens, Hazard. *The Life of Isaac Ingalls Stevens.* 2 volumes. New York: Houghton Mifflin, 1900.

Stevens, Isaac. *Message of the Governor of Washington Territory.* Olympia, Wash.: Edward Furste, Public Printer, 1857.

Stewart, Richard W., ed. *American Military History.* Volume 1, *The United States Army and the Forging of a Nation, 1775–1917.* Washington, D.C.: Center of Military History, 2005.

Stratton, David H., ed. *Spokane and the Inland Empire: An Inland Northwest Anthology.* Pullman: Washington State University Press, 2005.

Swan, James G. *The Northwest Coast, or Three Years Residence in Washington Territory.* New York: Harper and Bros., 1857.

Swanton, John R. *The Indian Tribes of North America.* Washington, D.C.: Smithsonian Institution Press, 1984.

Tate, Thomas K. *General Edwin Vose Sumner, USA: A Civil War Biography.* Jefferson, N.C.: McFarland, 2013.

Trafzer, Clifford E. *The Chinook.* New York: Chelsea House, 1990.

———. "The Palouse Indians: Interpreting the Past of a Plateau Tribe." In *Spokane and the Inland Empire,* edited by David H. Stratton, 64–97. Pullman: Washington State University Press, 2005.

———, and Richard D. Scheuerman. *Renegade Tribe: The Palouse Indians and the Invasion of the Pacific Northwest.* Pullman: Washington State University Press, 1986.

Tsosie, Rebecca. "The BIA's Apology to Native Americans: An Essay on Collective Memory and Collective Conscience." In *Taking Wrongs Seriously: Apologies and Reconciliation,* edited by Elazar Barkan and Alexander Karn, 185–212. Palo Alto, Calif.: Stanford University Press, 2006.

Unruh, John D. *The Plains Across: The Overland Emigrants and the Trans-Mississippi West, 1840–60.* Urbana: University of Illinois Press, 1979.

Utley, Robert M. *Frontier Regulars: The United States Army and the Indian, 1866–1891.* Lincoln: University of Nebraska Press, 1973.

Vattel, Emerich de. *The Law of Nations, or, Principles of the Law of Nature Applied to the Conduct and Affairs of Nations and Sovereigns.* Translated from the French by Joseph Chitty. Philadelphia: T. and J. W. Johnson, 1883.

Victor, Francis Fuller. *The River of the West: Life and Adventure in the Rocky Mountains and Oregon.* Hartford, Conn.: Columbian Book Co., 1871.

Walker, Deward E., and William R. Sturtevant. *The Handbook of North American Indians.* Volume 12. Washington, D.C.: Smithsonian Institution, 1998.

Waller, James. *Becoming Evil: How Ordinary People Commit Genocide and Mass Killing.* New York: Oxford University Press, 2002.

Wells, Harry L. *A Popular History of Oregon from the Discovery of America to the Admission of the State to the Union.* Portland, Ore.: David Steel, 1889.

Wheelan, Joseph. *Terrible Swift Sword: The Life of General Phillip H. Sheridan,* Cambridge, Mass.: Da Capo, 2012.

Winthrop, Theodore. *The Canoe and Saddle: Adventures among the Northwestern Rivers and Forests.* New York: John D. Lovell, 1862.

Zimbardo, Philip. *The Lucifer Effect: Understand How Good People Turn Evil.* New York: Random House, 2007.

Zinn, Howard. *A People's History of the United States.* New York: Harper Perennial, 2010.

JOURNAL ARTICLES

Addis, Cameron. "The Whitman Massacre: Religion and Manifest Destiny on the Columbia Plateau, 1809–1858." *Journal of the Early Republic* 25, no. 2 (Summer 2005): 221–258.

"Army Officer's Report on Indian War and Treaties." *Washington Historical Quarterly* 19, no. 2 (April 1928): 134–41.

Baker, David V. "American Indian Executions in Historical Context." *Criminal Justice Studies* 20, no. 4 (2007): 315–73. doi:10.1080/14786010701758138.

Baker, Victor R. "The Channeled Scablands: A Retrospective." *Annual Review of Earth and Planetary Sciences* (December 30, 2008): 6.1–6.19. http://ice.tsu.ru/files/paul/Baker_-_Review.pdf.

Barnes, John. "The Struggle to Control the Past: Commemoration, Memory, and the Bear River Massacre of 1863." *Public Historian* 30, no. 1 (February 2008): 81–104.

Beall, Thomas B. "Pioneer Reminiscences." *Washington Historical Quarterly* 8, no. 2 (April 1917): 83–90.

Bischoff, William N., and Charles M. Gates. "The Jesuits and the Coeur d'Alene Treaty of 1858." *Pacific Northwest Quarterly* 34, no. 2 (April 1943): 169–81.

Bonura, Michael Andrew. "A French Inspired Way of War: French Influence on the U.S. Army from 1812 to the Mexican War." *Army History* 90 (Winter 2014): 7–22. www.history.army.mil/armyhistory/AH90(W).pdf.

Brown, Arthur J. "The Promotion of Emigration to Washington, 1854–1909." *Pacific Northwest Quarterly* 36, no. 1 (January 1945): 3–17.

Burns, Robert I. "The Missionary Syndrome: Crusader and Pacific Northwest Expansionism." *Comparative Studies in Society and History* 30, no. 2 (April 1988): 271–85.

Canis, George P. "Steptoe's Indian Battle in 1858." *Washington Historian* 1, no. 4 (July 1900), 162.

Card, Claudia. "Genocide and Social Death." *Hypatia* 18, no. 1 (Winter 2003): 63–79.

Carstensen, Vernon. "Pacific Northwest Letters of George Gibbs." *Oregon Historical Quarterly* 54, no. 3 (September 1953): 199–200. The letter from Gibbs to his mother is dated June 26, 1850.

Chomsky, Carol. "The United States–Dakota War Trials: A Study in Military Injustice." *Stanford Law Review* 43, no. 1 (November 1990): 13–98.

Clark, Ella E. "Thanksgiving in the Pacific Northwest." *Oregon Historical Quarterly* 61, no. 4 (December 1960): 437–56.

Clark, Robert Carleton. "Military History of Oregon." *Oregon Historical Quarterly* 36, no. 1 (March 1935): 14–59.

Coan, C. F. "The First Stage of the Federal Indian Policy in the Pacific Northwest, 1849–1852." *Quarterly of the Oregon Historical Society* 22, no. 1 (March 1921): 46–89.

Cohen, Daniel A. "In Defense of the Gallows: Justification of Capital Punishment in New England Execution Sermons, 1674–1825." *American Quarterly* 40, no. 2 (June 1988): 147–64.

Cook, Sherburne F. "The Little Napoleon: The Short and Turbulent Career of Isaac I. Stevens." *Columbia Magazine* (Winter 2001): 17–20.

Coone, Elizabeth Ann. "Reminiscences of a Pioneer Woman." *Washington Historical Quarterly* 8, no. 1 (January 1917), 14–21.

De Lorme, Roland L. "Crime and Punishment in the Pacific Northwest Territories: A Bibliographic Essay." *Pacific Northwest Quarterly* 76, no. 2 (April 1985): 42–51.

Denham, Aaron R. "Rethinking Historical Trauma: Narrative of Resilience." *Transcultural Psychiatry* (September 2008): 391–413.

Deutsch, Herman J. "Indian and White in the Inland Empire: The Conquest for the Land, 1880–1912." *Pacific Northwest Quarterly* 47, no. 2 (April 1956): 44–51.

Duffin, Andrew P. "Remaking the Palouse: Farming, Capitalism, and Environmental Change, 1825–1914." *Pacific Northwest Quarterly* 95, no. 4 (Fall 2004): 194–204.

Dwyer, Owen J., and Derek H. Alderman. "Memorial Landscapes: Analytical Questions and Metaphors." *GeoJournal* 73, no. 3 (2008): 165–78. doi:10.1007/s10708-008-9201-5.

Edwards, G. Thomas. "The Oregon Trail in the Columbia Gorge: 1843–1855, The Final Ordeal." *Oregon Historical Quarterly* 97, no. 2 (Summer 1996): 134–75.

Elliott, E. C. "The Dalles-Celilo Portage: Its History and Influence." *Quarterly of the Oregon Historical Society* 16, no. 2 (June 1915): 133–174.

Elliott, T. C. "Steptoe Butte and Steptoe Battlefield." *Washington Historical Quarterly* 18, no. 4 (October 1947): 285–314.

Fisher, Andrew H. "This I Know from the Old People: Yakima Indian Treaty Rights as Oral Tradition." *Montana: The Magazine of Western History* 49, no. 1 (Spring 1999): 2–17.

Fisher, Robin. "Indian Warfare and Two Frontiers: A Comparison of British Columbia and Washington Territory during the Early Years of Settlement." *Pacific Historical Review* 50, no. 1 (February 1981) 31–51.

Garth, Thomas R. "Early Nineteenth-Century Tribal Relations in the Columbia Plateau." *Southwestern Journal of Anthropology* 20, no. 1 (Spring 1964): 43–45.

Gates, John M. "Indians and Insurrectos: The U.S. Army's Experience with Insurgency." *Parameters* 13 (1983): 59–68. http://discover.wooster.edu/jgates/indians-and-insurrectos/#fn0.

Gough, Barry M. "The Indian Policies of Great Britain and the United States in the Pacific Northwest in the Mid-Nineteenth Century." *Canadian Journal of Native Studies* 2, no. 2 (1982): 321–37.

Graham, Joel. "A Massacre on the Frontier." *Washington Historical Quarterly* 2, no. 3 (April 1908): 233–36.

Hafen, P. Jane. "Rock and Roll, Redskins, and Blues in Sherman Alexie's Work." *Studies in American Indian Literatures* 9, no. 4 (Winter 1997): 71–78.

Hansen, Clark. "Oregon Voices: Indian Views of the Stevens-Palmer Treaties Today." *Oregon Historical Quarterly*, special issue, "The Isaac I. Stevens and Joel Palmer Treaties, 1855–2005" 106, no. 3 (Fall 2005): 475–89.

Harmon, Alexandra. "Indian Treaty History: A Subject for Agile Minds." *Oregon Historical Quarterly*, special issue, "The Isaac I. Stevens and Joel Palmer Treaties, 1855–2005" 106, no. 3 (Fall 2005): 358–73.

Hauck, Richard Boyd. Review of *An American Icon: Brother Jonathan and American Identity*, by Winifred Morgan. *American Literature* 60, no. 4 (December 1988): 659–660.

Hornback, Jack. "A Brief Historical Introduction to Oregon Firearms." *Oregon Historical Quarterly* 50, no. 1 (March 1949): 45–50.

Howard, Helen Addison. "The Steptoe Affair." *Montana: The Magazine of Western History* 19, no. 2 (Spring 1969): 28–36.

Hunn, Eugene. "Columbia Plateau Indian Place Names: What Can They Teach Us?" *Journal of Linguistic Anthropology* 6, no. 1 (1996): 3–26.

Hutton, Paul Andrew. "Phil Sheridan's Frontier." *Montana: The Magazine of Western History* 38, no. 1 (Winter 1988): 16–31.

I.G.T. "Indian Campaign in the North." *Overland Monthly* 4, no. 22 (Oct. 1884): 397–405.

Iman, Margaret Windsor. "My Arrival in Washington in 1852." *Washington Historical Quarterly* 18, no. 4 (October 1927): 254–260.

Jensen, Richard E. "The Wright-Beauchampe Investigation and the Pawnee Threat of 1829." *Nebraska History* 79 (1998): 133–43.

Kip, Lawrence. "The Steptoe-Wright Campaign against the Northern Indians in 1858." *Journal of the Military Service Institution of the United States* 42 (1908): 475–88.

Knuth, Priscilla. "Picturesque Frontier: The Army's Fort Dalles, Part Two." *Oregon Historical Quarterly* 68, no. 1 (March 1967): 4–52.

Kornweibel, Theodore, Jr. "The Occupation of Santa Catalina Island during the Civil War." *California Historical Society Quarterly* 46, no. 4 (December 1967): 345–57.

Levins, Turner F. "When Sheridan Was in Oregon." *Washington Historical Quarterly* 16, no. 3 (July 1925): 163–85.

Lockley, Fred. "Reminiscences of Captain William P. Gray." *Quarterly of the Oregon Historical Society* 14, no. 4 (December 1913): 321–354.

Mayo, James M. "War Memorials as Political Memory." *Geographical Review* 78, no. 1 (January 1988): 62–75.

McFarland, Ron. "Sherman Alexie's Polemical Stories." *Studies in American Indian Literature,* 2nd ser., 9, no. 4 (Winter 1997): 27–38.

McSloy, Steven Paul. "'Because the Bible Tells Me So': Manifest Destiny and American Indians." *St. Thomas Law Review* 9 (Fall 1996): 37–47.

Miles, Jo N. "The Life and Death of A. J. Bolon." *Pacific Northwest Quarterly* 97, no. 1 (Winter 2005–6): 31–38.

Morgan, Michael R. "Recollections of the Spokane Expedition." *Journal of the Military Service Institution of the United States* 42 (1908): 489–502.

Oliphant, J. Orin. "Journals of the Indian War of 1855–56." *Washington Historical Quarterly* 15, no. 1 (January 1924): 11–31.

Ott, Brian Richard. "Indian Fishing Rights in the Pacific Northwest: The Need for Federal Intervention." *Boston College Environmental Affairs Law Review* 14, no. 2 (December 1987): 313–43.

Palmer, Gary B. "Indian Pioneers: The Settlement of the Ni'lukhwalqu (Upper Hangman Creek, Idaho) by the Schitsu'umsh (Coeur d'Alene Indians)." *Oregon Historical Quarterly* 102, no. 1 (Spring 2001): 22–47.

Phelps, Netta W. "Dedication of Steptoe Memorial Park." *Washington Historical Quarterly* 2, no. 4 (July 1908): 344–51.

Prentiss, William C., et al. "The Archaeology of the Plateau of Northwestern America during the Late Prehistoric Period (3500–200 B.P.): Evolution of Hunting and Gathering Societies." *Journal of World Prehistory* 19, no. 1 (March 2005): 47–118.

Prosch, Thomas W. "The Evolution of Spokane and Stevens Counties." *Quarterly of the Oregon Historical Society* 5 (March–December 1904): 25–26.

———. "Notes from a Government Document on Oregon Conditions in the Fifties." *Quarterly of the Oregon Historical Society* 8, no. 2 (June 1907): 191–200.

Ray, Verne F. "Native Villages and Groupings of the Columbia Basin." *Pacific Northwest Quarterly* 27, no. 2 (April 1936): 99–152.

Richards, Kent. "Isaac Stevens and Federal Military Power in Washington Territory." *Pacific Northwest Quarterly* 63, no. 3 (July 1972): 81–86.

Schmitt, Martin. "The Execution of Chief Leschi and the 'Truth Teller.'" *Oregon Historical Quarterly* 50, no. 1 (March 1949): 30–39.

Sebring, F. M., "The Indian Raid on the Cascades in March 1856." *Washington Historical Quarterly* 19, no. 2 (April 1928): 99–107.

Skelton, William B. "Army Officers' Attitudes toward Indians." *Pacific Northwest Quarterly* 67, no. 3 (July 1976): 113–24.

Smith, John E. "A Pioneer of the Spokane Country." *Washington Historical Quarterly* 7, no. 4 (October 1916): 267–77.

Snipp, C. Matthew. "Perspectives on American Indians." *Annual Review of Sociology* 18 (1992): 351–71.

Todd, Ronald, et al. "Letters of Governor Isaac I. Stevens, 1857–1858." *Pacific Northwest Quarterly* 31, no. 4 (October 1940): 403–59.

Trafzer, Clifford E. "The Legacy of the Walla Wall Council." *Oregon Historical Quarterly*, special issue "The Isaac I. Stevens and Joel Palmer Treaties, 1855–2005" 106, no. 3 (Fall 2005): 398–411.

Trimble, Will. J. "American and British Treatment of the Indians in the Pacific Northwest." *Washington Historical Quarterly* 5, no. 1 (January 1914): 32–54.

———. "A Soldier of the Oregon Frontier." *Quarterly of the Oregon Historical Society* 8 (March 1907): 42–50.

Umatilla Cultural Resources Program and the Department of Natural Resources. *A Review of Oral History Information of the Confederated Tribes of the Umatilla Indian Reservation.* Attachment 2. www.friendsofpast.org/pdf/DOI/DOI07658.pdf.

Weidenbaum, Paul. "Necessity in International Law." *Transactions of the Grotius Society.* Vol. 24, *Problems of Peace and War, Papers Read before the Society in the Year 1938*, 105–132. Cambridge: Cambridge University Press, 1938. www.jstor.org/stable/742739.

West, Elliott. "Selling the Myth: Western Images in Advertising." *Montana: The Magazine of Western History* 46, no. 2 (Summer 1996): 36–49.

White, Lynn. "The Legacy of the Middle Ages in the American Wild West." *Speculum* 40, no. 2 (April 1965): 191–202.

Williams, Robert. "The Cascades Massacre." *Transactions of the 24th Reunion of the Oregon Pioneer Association*, 1896 (1897): 69–89.

Winder, Charles Sydney. "Captain C. S. Winder's Account of a Battle with the Indians." *Maryland Historical Magazine* 35, no. 1 (March 1940): 56–59.

Wood, C. E. S. "Famous Indians: Portraits of some Indian Chiefs." *Century Illustrated Monthly Magazine*, n.s., 24 (May 1893–October 1893): 436–45.

Woody, Frank H. "From Missoula to Walla Walla in 1857, on Horseback." *Washington Historical Quarterly* 3, no. 4 (October 1912): 277–86.

Wright, George, Rufus Ingalls, and George H. Himes, "Letters." *Quarterly of the Oregon Historical Society* 15, no. 2 (June 1914): 133–36.

NEWSPAPERS AND MAGAZINES

Cosmopolitan Magazine
Harpers New Monthly Magazine
Illustrated London News
Lewiston (Id.) Morning Tribune
Los Angeles Star
Olympia Courier-Herald (Washington Territory)
Olympia Pioneer and Democrat (Washington Territory)
Portland (Ore.) Standard
Portland Oregonian
Sacramento Daily Union
San Francisco Daily Alta California
Spokane Chronicle
Spokane Spokesman-Review
Steilacoom Truth Teller (Washington Territory)
The New York Times
Times (London)
Washington (D.C.) Union

Acknowledgments

During the five years I spent working on this project, I spoke with many generous and encouraging people. I apologize in advance if I have neglected to thank anyone; if I've done so, it's a reflection of a gap in my notes or memory, and not a reflection of the value of the help I received.

Among the many people with Native American ancestry who helped me, I am indebted to Laurie Arnold, chair of the Gonzaga University Native American Studies Department; Paul Wapato, former chairman of the Nez Perce Trail Foundation; Bill Matt, Spokane tribal environmental officer; Lynn Pankonin, Spokane tribal historian; Rob McDonald, communications director, Confederated Salish and Kootenai Tribes; Mark Stanger, Coeur d'Alene tribe; Michael Finley, former chairman of the Colville Business Council; Michael Holloman, chairman of the Plateau Center for Native American Studies; Dr. Roberta Paul; Les Doney; Guy Moura; and Albert Andrews. Charlene Teters, Spokane tribal member, educator, artist, and activist, provided invaluable insight.

Dr. Alexandra Harmon of the University of Washington was helpful with directing me to resources concerning historical memory and the Stevens treaties. Dr. Jean Lipman-Bluman of Claremont Graduate University was helpful with issues of toxic leadership and provided welcome support and encouragement. Jack Nisbet's wisdom about our place in the natural world was, as always, fascinating and helpful. Dr. Wayne E. Lee of the University of North Carolina was helpful with historical context. Dr. Sherry Smith of Southern Methodist University was generous with her time and helped guide me to helpful resources concerning military issues in the American West. She pointed out that my approach to this topic was likely to be seen as "revisionist," which to some observers makes me a "nefarious" historian. I have always admired her approach to western history and aspire to be as skilled and delightfully nefarious as she is.

Dr. Richard Scheuerman of Seattle Pacific University was particularly helpful and supportive. Dr. Scheuerman knows these events well and has worked closely with many tribal members to help educate the general public about issues facing Native Americans. Dr. Clifford Trafzer of the University of California–Riverside provided advice and encouragement. Dr. James Jewell of North Idaho College, a historian and educator, was generous with his time and information about the Steptoe events and related issues.

I am deeply grateful to the late Dr. Robert Ruby, who provided welcome encouragement early in the project. Dr. Ruby, along with the late John Brown, wrote some of the most comprehensive work about Plateau peoples.

Greg Partch, Sr., a longtime Whitman County resident, allowed me to sift through his treasure trove of original letters and photographs connected with the 1858 Steptoe and Wright expeditions. I am grateful for the advice and support of Dr. Ron McFarland and Dr. Rodney Frey, both of the University of Idaho. The late Jake Woodwell provided background for contemporary tribal issues. His strength and wisdom continue to inspire me.

Dr. Lawrence Briggs, dean of general studies at North Idaho College, is a longtime friend. He not only provided years of support and encouragement but read the manuscript and offered invaluable feedback.

Dr. Stan Gough, Director of Archeological and Historical Services at Eastern Washington University, and Steve Emerson, program director, provided information, insight, and encouragement. Eastern Washington University is fortunate to have faculty and staff with invaluable knowledge of regional history, including Dr. Dana Elder, Dr. Larry Cebula, Ruth Galm, and archivist Dr. Charles Mutschler. Friend and professional colleague

Dr. Lynn Briggs, professor of English, was always able to help me see alternative ways to express my views and provided welcome, energetic feedback. Dr. Larry Kiser and Gayle Kiser read manuscript drafts and asked the kind of questions that made me dig deeper. I am grateful to Rachel Toor and the rest of the faculty of the Eastern Washington University MFA program for their wisdom and support.

Archivists and research librarians were invaluable to me. Among them were Fred Poyner and Ashley Mead of the Washington State Historical Society; Daisy Njoku at the National Anthropological Archives; Chris Peterson, Oregon State University; Cheryl Gunselman, Washington State University; David Kingma, Gonzaga University; Katherine Purcell, Columbia Gorge Discovery Center; Jeff Creighton, Museum of Arts and Culture, Spokane; Riva Dean, Spokane Public Library Northwest Room; Jaime Bourassa, Missouri History Museum; John Deeben, National Archives Military Records; Jules Filipski, Oregon State Historical Society; Elena Smith, California State Library in Sacramento; and the staffs at Fort Dalles, Fort Vancouver, and Fort Walla Walla historical sites. Nona Hengen generously let me use three of her paintings depicting some of the 1858 events. Gerry Krieg created excellent maps for the book and did so without once complaining about the number of changes I asked for.

The staff at the University of Oklahoma Press were wonderful. Charles Rankin, the editor-in-chief, was patient with a first-time author and was always supportive and encouraging. Senior editor Steven Baker shepherded the project forward with admirable skill and diplomacy. A big thanks to Emmy Ezzell, Anna Maria Rodriguez, Amy Hernandez, and editorial assistants Bethany Mowry, Rowan Steineker, and Brittney Berling.

Leslie Tingle copyedited the manuscript and offered invaluable feedback. Her talent and patience are remarkable.

A special thanks to Mr. Daniel Pringle, whose review and feedback were critical to the book's completion.

As a professor of Integrated Studies at Eastern Washington University, my wife, Dr. Cynthia Maclyn Cutler, teaches senior capstone classes in leadership. She provided me with material regarding toxic leadership, which included the work of Phillip Zimbardo and Stanley Milgram. George Wright provides us an example of how a human being operating in an environment with few restrictions and consequences is enabled to commit cruelty.

When tackling a project like this it helps to have a rally squad. My children, all now adults, provided constant encouragement. They are all remarkable people, and a father could not love his children more. Thank you for your love and encouragement.

Index

References to illustrations appear in italic type.